FANCY PANTRY

ALSO BY HELEN WITTY

Mrs. Witty's Monster Cookies

Better Than Store-Bought
(with Elizabeth Schneider Colchie)

The Garden-to-Table Cookbook
(Compiler and Editor)

The Cook's Catalogue
(Editor)

FANCY PANTRY

By Helen Witty

Illustrated by Pierre Le-Tan

WORKMAN PUBLISHING
NEW YORK

For Richard, again;
and with more of the same.

Some of the recipes in *Fancy Pantry* have appeared, in somewhat different form, in periodicals that include *The Cook's Magazine, Cuisine, Family Circle, The Home Garden, Newsday,* and *Working Woman*.

Library of Congress Cataloging-in-Publication Data

Witty, Helen.
Fancy pantry.

Includes index.
1. Cookery. I. Title.
TX715.W845   1986   641.5   85-40897
ISBN 0-89480-094-9
ISBN 0-89480-037-X (pbk.)

Book design by Wendy Palitz
Cover photograph by Brian Hagiwara

Workman Publishing Company, Inc.
1 West 39 Street
New York, New York 10018
Manufactured in the United States of America

First printing April 1986
10 9 8 7 6 5 4 3 2 1

CONTENTS

A LITTLE OF WHAT YOU FANCY DOES YOU GOOD

APPETIZERS & OTHER WHETS

WITH GUSTO & RELISH

LITTLE PUT-UP JOBS

BREADS, BREADSTICKS, & CRACKERS

SEASONINGS & COVETED CONDIMENTS

DESSERTS & SWEET KICKSHAWS

SIPPIN' SUBSTANCES

MISCELLANY & MAVERICKS

A little of what you fancy does you good...
—Old English music-hall song

Time was when every house had an honest-to-goodness pantry, a room as large as many a modern kitchen, set aside for the keeping of fine foods and staples, plus the family turkey platter and the best china and crystal. Modern houses don't ramble the way houses once did, so it's now rare to find a new, true larder; but functioning pantry space is worth setting up (suggestions are in Pantry Ways & Means, below) *if* you care how interestingly you eat every day, how delightfully your guests are entertained, and how much money you'd rather not leave in the cash registers of luxury food shops.

WHO'S FOR PANTRYING?

I've noticed over years of writing and editing in the food field that there are lots of keen recreational cooks out there; lead them to an intriguing culinary enterprise, and they're off and running. *Fancy Pantry* is for them.

There are also now among us many more highly knowledgeable consumers (of food, of wine, of cookbooks) than ever before; they are interested in genuinely good, even luxurious food, and many are willing to turn their hand to creating it. Welcome to pantrying.

Fancy Pantry is also addressed to the many who are concerned that their food be reasonably free of the additives and preservatives that preserve mainly the profit margins of mass-marketers, not the quality of the food.

And this book is also for the value-conscious, those who want to live and entertain well without going in hock to the upscale groceries where the price of a specialty is several times what it would cost you to make it.

All such souls should have a pantry, however modest. *Fancy Pantry* shows how.

TECHNIQUES: IS IT ALL IN THE WRIST?

The techniques used in *Fancy Pantry* will be familiar to all but absolute tyros; but even for beginners, none of the operations are particularly difficult. For novices, or any other reader who'd like a brushup, the hows and whys of key techniques are discussed in Glossary, Ingredients, Equipment & Techniques, beginning on page 318. In those pages, too, you'll read about useful equipment, none of it esoteric, as well as how-to's; you don't even need a pressure cooker for putting things up in jars.

Putting up foods is, for most, the least familiar pantry-stocking operation in this book, although it involves perfectly ordinary routines of preparing, chopping, and cooking, plus a few easily understood procedures for sealing and storing. Before rolling up your sleeves to create a spectacular something, stored in jars or otherwise, check your chosen recipe as well as the glossary notes for the utensils and supplies you should have.

PANTRY KEYS.

There are two keys to wildly successful preserving, pickling, potting, jamming, and bottling: Use only first-rate raw materials, and take due care with (and use the right equipment for) each step.

Raw materials: To make your investment of time and effort worthwhile, use only high-quality ingredients, whether you're working with cheese, fresh herbs, meat, fish, flours, nuts, or liqueurs. Fruits and vegetables must be as freshly picked as possible, neither spectacularly under- or overripe, and free of damage that might foster "spoiler" bacteria. Don't even *consider* investing your skills and time in over-the-hill ingredients. In this respect the preserving pan is like a computer; for either one, it's "garbage in, garbage out." It's courting disappointment to hope to make metaphorical silk purses from piggy-ears.

Taking care... Impatient people shouldn't tackle preserving (or, come to think of it, most kinds of cooking); pantrying should be enjoyed in the doing as well as later, when you and your guests savor the good things you have shelved with pride. If working neatly and carefully toward a good result seems a burden, don't go in for preserving; there are better ways to spend your time. But for those who enjoy cooking as a relaxation or a challenge, few culinary activities offer more rewards.

Is It Time?

Time can be a problem; it's not always possible for the kitchen adventurer to spend as much time working (or playing) in the kitchen as people once did. However, when questing cooks do tie on an apron, they want to spend the available time *well* by enjoying both the immediate pleasure of creative work and the anticipation of later tastings and gift-giving.

If you find an irresistible buy in a good fresh something but can't use your produce at once to make a relish or a chutney or whatever, refrigerate it, properly protected, and get to the project as soon as you can, preferably within a day or, at most, two. Or freeze it (see below).

Freezing Time.

When you're out marketing and seasonal temptations set visions of sugarplums (or jelly, marmalade, or chutney) to dancing in your head even though there's no time for preserving right now, remember that you can freeze fruits, some vegetables (including tomatoes), berries, and many other good things and plan to put them up later. Consult a reliable reference on freezing, if you're not experienced. (Highly recommended: the latest edition of *Putting Food By,* by Ruth Hertzberg, Beatrice Vaughan, and Janet Greene.) With a frozen supply of makings, even in the depths of winter you

can indulge the mood for a jam session. (This is also a way to get around a lack of storage space for finished put-up jobs; fresh fruit, pulp, or juice in the freezer takes relatively little room, and the material will wait peaceably until you have time later on to tend your pots and space to store your jars.)

How's That Again About Healthful Food? This Recipe Looks *Rich*...

Fancy Pantry isn't about health food, except insofar as *all* good food is healthful, and food without additives is more wholesome than store-bought items loaded with chemicals meant to make them immortal. If you are limited, for reasons of health, in your consumption of salt, sweetening, butter, spices, or other normally alluring ingredients, you'll have to pick and choose here, as when using any other cookbook (or any menu). Not everything "fancy" is compounded of possible no-nos; elegant simplicities as well as elegant wickednesses are to be found here. There are even arrowroot biscuits.

Pantry Ways & Means: Finding House Room

A pantry, by architect's definition, is what nearly all houses used to have—a separate, cool room with shelves for storing food specialties and cherished tableware. Today most of us have to make do with much less space for the good things we "put by." Nevertheless, we needn't be discouraged; there are possibilities for finding space in almost any dwelling. Some are sketched below; others will come to mind if you really, truly want to find house room for your own keepables.

A Cool Cupboard Can Become a Pantry.

Look around for a cupboard or closet, not necessarily in the kitchen, that is reasonably cool—if possible, cooler than ordinary room temperature, which means that it shouldn't be near the kitchen stove, a heat register, or, in the basement, near the furnace. The prospective pantry should also be dry (or at least not damp) and dark (or at least dim); this means that open shelves near windows aren't desirable. (Light can bleach the color from foods stored in glass, and it also shortens their life expectancy.) In the basement there may be space to build a walk-in pantry, or at least to hang a cupboard or two, and a spare closet can easily be made to serve. A walk-in closet is ideal, especially if it is near the kitchen.

SHELVING.

In your cool pantry you'll want shelves for your jars of preserves, dessert compotes, special sauces and ketchups, relishes, pickles, and jellies and boxes and canisters of unsealed items. If shelving is lacking in a space that's otherwise suitable and you don't want to undertake carpentry, look into the inexpensive, free-standing metal storage units widely sold in hardware and houseware stores; they are easy to assemble and neat to behold, and they hold a lot in a small space. For a more modern high-tech look, heavy wire industrial shelving is dandy, too; it is widely available and easy to install.

Even the back of a door can be draped with wire hanging shelves.

NICHES.

Another possibility is to look for space in hallways, stairwells, or wherever there is an unused stretch of wall: you can install shelves directly on the wall, or convert the shallow space between studs into a shelved mini-pantry. This may involve removing wallboard to open up the space, but the job is a simple one. In most houses, the space between studs will be deep enough to shelve items the size of a coffee can or a quart canning jar, so a floor-to-ceiling panel will store quite a lot.

SHADES.

If you have open-fronted shelving in a brightly lighted area, some means of protecting the contents from light will be desirable; you can use something simple like a rolldown bamboo blind, or a colorful venetian blind; or you can install a door, sliding or hinged, if the space permits.

KITCHEN SPACES.

An ordinary kitchen cupboard is fine for such specialties as wine vinegar, fruit- or herb-flavored vinegars, seasoned oils, herbs, herb-spice mixtures, and other seasonings, so long as it is at room temperature or below. (Cupboards on outside walls of a room tend to be cooler, in winter, than those on internal walls.) Baked savory or sweet foods have varying storage needs, indicated alongside the recipes; many will be perfectly fine at room temperature if kept in an airtight canister.

CORNERING.

If you have a kitchen corner where two countertops or rows of cupboards come together, consider installing a lazy-susan arrangement in the unused corner space. (I have two such roundabout corners, and they hold an incredible amount.)

Other ideas for converting unused space can be found in kitchen-planning books and magazine articles.

The freezer is your final resource, especially for longer storage. Many *Fancy Pantry* foods that are keepable for a while in the refrigerator or the pantry can be frozen for longer preservation; recipes for such foods include the appropriate information.

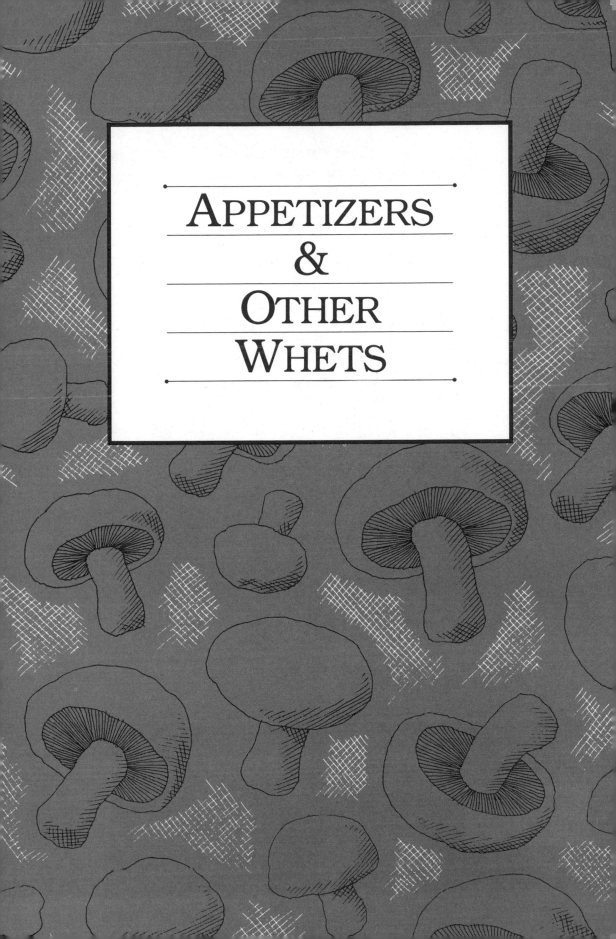

APPETIZERS
&
OTHER
WHETS

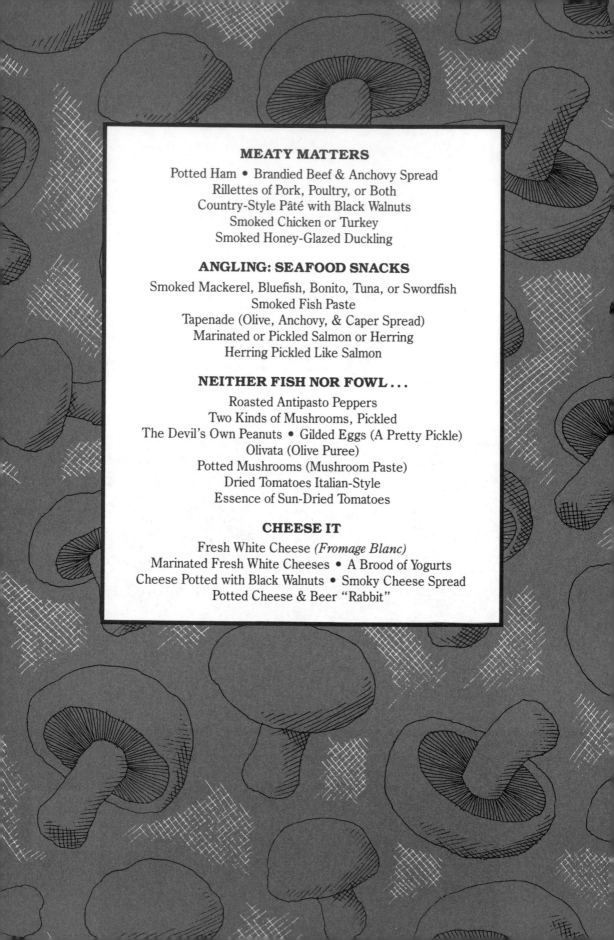

MEATY MATTERS

Potted Ham • Brandied Beef & Anchovy Spread
Rillettes of Pork, Poultry, or Both
Country-Style Pâté with Black Walnuts
Smoked Chicken or Turkey
Smoked Honey-Glazed Duckling

ANGLING: SEAFOOD SNACKS

Smoked Mackerel, Bluefish, Bonito, Tuna, or Swordfish
Smoked Fish Paste
Tapenade (Olive, Anchovy, & Caper Spread)
Marinated or Pickled Salmon or Herring
Herring Pickled Like Salmon

NEITHER FISH NOR FOWL ...

Roasted Antipasto Peppers
Two Kinds of Mushrooms, Pickled
The Devil's Own Peanuts • Gilded Eggs (A Pretty Pickle)
Olivata (Olive Puree)
Potted Mushrooms (Mushroom Paste)
Dried Tomatoes Italian-Style
Essence of Sun-Dried Tomatoes

CHEESE IT

Fresh White Cheese *(Fromage Blanc)*
Marinated Fresh White Cheeses • A Brood of Yogurts
Cheese Potted with Black Walnuts • Smoky Cheese Spread
Potted Cheese & Beer "Rabbit"

A "whet" may or may not be an appetizer, depending on when it's offered in the day's dietary. Before a meal, a whet is an appetizer; at other times, perhaps with drinks that don't immediately precede a repast, it can be appetizing but not an appetizer. All clear, I trust.

For whetting, this section includes several meaty things—potted ham or potted beef (the beef is compounded with brandy and anchovies), rillettes of pork or poultry, a country-style pâté enriched with black walnuts, and smoked poultry. There are a few seafood items, notably marinated salmon, pickled herring, home-smoked fish, and a rich fish paste. From the vegetable kingdom, sweet peppers, nuts, olives, mushrooms, and tomatoes, among other raw materials, are transformed into first-class first courses; and finally, the dairy division is represented by simple projects involving both homemade fresh cheese and store-bought Cheddar, the last made into either a smoky spread or a beer-based "rabbit" for serving on crackers (you'll find crackery breadstuffs farther along in the book).

One or two items, like basic yogurt and dried tomatoes, are included in this section because they're the foundation of final products that *are* appetizers—a variety of yogurt "cheeses" and an exceptional essence of dried tomatoes, in these instances.

Animal, vegetable, but not mineral, all these specialties are zesty bites designed to pique the palate, not sate the appetite. It's a collection, ranging from pâté and potted meats to smoked duckling to pickled mushrooms to rillettes to tapenade, meant to inspire the questing cook to put either plain or fancy first things, first.

MEATY MATTERS

Getting them potted isn't at all a bad move when you're thinking of good keep-able things to do with meats, cheeses, and seafood. Potting is an old-fashioned, highly satisfactory, and quite simple method of "putting by" savory preparations to serve as you will—as appetizers, as snacks, or even for breakfast in the old English fash-ion. Potted meats are here, among other meaty things; look a little farther along for other pottings based on seafood and dairy products.

In this section you'll also find rillettes of two kinds, an unusual pâté, and your choice of smoked whole chicken, whole turkey or turkey breast, or duckling.

 SEASON:
Any time

 YIELD:
About 3 cups

STORE:
Unsealed, for a week in the refrigerator; sealed with clarified butter, for 3 weeks in the refrigerator or for 2 months in the freezer

Potted Ham

Milder in its seasoning than deviled ham, this is an old-fashioned English delicacy of a kind that people used to make in this country, too, pounding the meat laboriously in a mortar. Modern machines make it amazingly simple to prepare. Make it from leftover ham, preferably home-cooked ham of pro-nounced flavor, not the bland delicatessen kind.

Serve your potted ham with crisp toast for Sunday break-fast or with salad for lunch, cutting wedges right down through the potful. Once the seal of clarified butter has been broken, use the remaining potted ham within a few days.

3 cups (about 1 pound) cubed cooked ham, mostly lean, all gristle and membranes removed

¾ cup Clarified Butter (page 315) at room temperature, plus ¼ to ⅓ cup more for sealing

½ teaspoon lemon juice

¼ teaspoon ground mace

⅛ teaspoon ground hot red (Cayenne) pepper

Small pinch of ground cloves

Small pinch of Powdered Bay Leaves (page 207), optional

1. Grind the ham very fine or, preferably, chop it fine in a food processor. (A blender can also be used, working in several batches.) Add the ¾ cup clarified butter, the lemon juice, mace, red pepper, cloves, and powdered bay leaves, if used, and blend very well, but avoid making a puree if you are using a food processor.

2. Taste the potted ham for seasoning and adjust it to taste, remembering that the flavor will develop further. Pack

the potted ham tightly into 4 small crocks, individual soufflé dishes, or pottery custard cups, being careful to leave no air spaces. Smooth the tops. Chill.

3. Melt enough additional clarified butter (about ⅓ cup) to seal each pot with a layer ¼ inch thick. Pour the butter over the potted ham, let it cool and begin to congeal, then cover and/or wrap the crocks for refrigerator or freezer (page 328); store. Frozen potted ham should be thawed unopened in the refrigerator. Serve the mixture at cool room temperature, for best flavor. After opening, use leftovers within a few days.

Brandied Beef & Anchovy Spread

Call it brandied or call it potted, by either name this meat mixture is a great thing to have on hand for sandwiches, canapés, or just a snack when you're suddenly hungry. It keeps for weeks in the refrigerator, and it freezes well.

The inspiration of this spread is James Beard's mother's enormous recipe for "Strathborough Paste," which Jim included in his memoirs some years ago. Intrigued by that delectable mixture, whose origins he said he had never learned, I did some delving into old British household books that Mrs. Beard could have known in her girlhood and found some very similar preparations, notably one called "Strasburg Potted Meat," whose name could well have been Anglicized at some point to "Strathborough." The recipe below is the end result of this recipe-sleuthing. I like it a lot.

Making potted meat is a good use for leftover well-done beef, either pot-roasted or boiled. The seasonings should be assertive, so taste the compound carefully before storing it.

1½ cups flavorful beef broth (not canned bouillon)

2 slices of a medium-size onion

1 small bay leaf

Pinch of dried thyme

2 cups, packed (about ¾ pound) cubed lean cooked beef, trimmed of all hard bits, gristle, or fat

1 can (2 ounces) fillets of anchovies in oil, drained

3 tablespoons brandy

1½ sticks (¾ cup) butter, sliced into chunks

1 teaspoon (or to taste) Spice and Herb Seasoning Mixture* or Quatre Epices* (page 210)

Salt, if desired

¼ to ⅓ cup Clarified Butter (page 315) for sealing

SEASON:
Any time

YIELD:
About 2½ cups

STORE:
Unsealed, for a week in the refrigerator; sealed with clarified butter, for 3 weeks in the refrigerator, or for 2 months in the freezer

*SPICE MIXTURES:

If you lack either of the spice mixtures listed, season the potted beef with freshly ground pepper, a pinch each of ground ginger and nutmeg, and a very tiny pinch of ground cloves. Optionally, add a generous pinch of crushed dried thyme, very tiny pinches of ground cinnamon and mace, and a small pinch of Powdered Bay Leaves (page 207). Taste and adjust seasonings.

1. Combine the beef broth, onion slices, bay leaf, and thyme in a saucepan. Heat the broth to boiling, lower the heat, and simmer, uncovered, until the liquid has reduced to ¾ cup. Strain into a cup or small bowl; discard the solids. Reserve the saucepan (no need to rinse it out).

2. Meanwhile, grind or chop fine the cubed beef together with the drained anchovies and the brandy; a food processor does this best, as you want a paste, not chunks. Scrape the beef and anchovy mixture into the saucepan. Add the reduced broth and heat the mixture over low heat, stirring it constantly, until it is boiling hot. Add the butter, stirring until it melts. Remove from heat. Stir in the seasoning mixture; taste and add a little salt if it is needed. Scoop out a sample of the paste and cool it for further tasting, and meanwhile stir the mixture over the heat until it is again boiling hot. Set it aside and taste the cooled sample for seasoning. Seasonings should be quite pronounced, so add more if they are needed.

3. A spoonful at a time (to prevent air pockets from forming), pack the potted beef, which will be a soft, moist mixture, into small crocks or straight-sided jars and smooth the tops. Let the mixture cool to room temperature, then melt enough clarified butter to cover the paste by about ¼ inch. Cover the beef with clarified butter, preferably making two thin layers, letting the first layer set before adding the second. (If you will be using the paste within a few days, the butter covering may be omitted.) Cover and/or wrap the crocks for refrigerator or freezer (page 328); store. Frozen potted beef should be thawed in its wrapper. Let either refrigerated or thawed paste stand at room temperature for a short time before serving it. Use leftovers within a few days.

Rillettes of Pork, Poultry, or Both

Meat potted in the French fashion—rillettes—is a rich and delicious pâté to serve as a first course; with it you need nothing more than crisp-crusted bread or toast and a cornichon or two alongside. (For Cold-Pickled Cornichons, see page 96.)

This rillettes recipe is flexible: The meat can be all pork, preferably the cut called "butt" or "Boston butt," which has a good balance of fat and lean; or combine the dark meat of turkey or chicken (drumsticks and/or thighs are fine) with lean pork; or transform a duck plus some pork into this delicacy. Additional pork fat is used in the cooking of all versions.

As is true of most classic dishes, there are many ways to prepare rillettes. I like to dry-marinate the meat overnight or

SEASON:
Any, but most
suitable for winter

YIELD:
5 to 6 cups

STORE:
Sealed with fat, for
at least 4 months
in the refrigerator;
or for up to a year
in the freezer

longer, but this isn't essential. The cooking should be done as gently as you can manage; an electric slow-cooker is ideal.

2 pounds boneless fresh pork butt, or 3 to 3½ pounds turkey or chicken drumsticks or thighs and drumsticks (enough to yield 2 pounds of meat after trimming), or a duckling weighing 4 to 4½ pounds (to yield 2 pounds of meat)

1 pound boneless fresh pork butt, regardless of meat chosen above

1½ tablespoons coarse (kosher) salt

½ teaspoon dried thyme leaves, crushed

¼ teaspoon Powdered Bay Leaves (page 207) or 3 large bay leaves, coarsely crumbled

About ⅛ teaspoon freshly ground white pepper

1 large clove garlic, peeled and minced very fine

2 pounds fresh pork fat, trimmed of all dried or discolored portions and ground coarsely or diced small

⅔ cup water or dry white wine, or half water, half wine

Quatre Epices or Spice and Herb Seasoning Mixture (page 210)

1. Prepare the 2-pound batch of meat: Skin and bone poultry (reserve the skin if you're using duck), then cut the meat or poultry into strips no more than ½ inch thick, removing the tendons from drumsticks. Place the strips in a bowl.

2. Cut the additional pound of pork butt into strips no more than ½ inch thick and whatever length is convenient. Combine the pork with the first batch of meat. Sprinkle the salt, thyme, bay leaves, white pepper, and garlic over the meats and mix in the seasonings thoroughly. Scrape the whole business into a sturdy plastic bag, close it tightly, and refrigerate overnight or for up to 2 days. (If this marinating is omitted, simply add the seasonings to the meat and fat in step 3.)

3. Place the pork fat in a large, heavy pot over low heat. If you are making rillettes from duck, add the duck skin, cut into 1-inch squares. Cook the panful, stirring it often, until a great deal of the fat has melted and the bits of crackling are turning golden. Add the marinated meats and the water or wine and bring the mixture to a simmer. Cook the meats very slowly: Cover the pot tightly (press foil over the pot before adding the cover, if the lid fits loosely) and use the lowest possible heat on top of the stove; or place the pot in a 275° oven; or transfer everything to an electric slow-cooker set at low heat. Cook the rillettes until the strips of meat are meltingly tender; this will take about 4 hours on the stovetop or in the oven, perhaps twice as long in a slow-cooker, depending on the appliance.

4. Pour the meat and fat into a colander set over a bowl

and drain off and reserve the liquid fat, pressing lightly on the meat to extract as much as possible. (Set the empty pot aside for the next step.) Pick out any bits of bay leaf, if you haven't used powdered bay.

5. For smooth rillettes (preferable for turkey, chicken, or duck), drop the meat in batches into the feed tube of a food processor with the motor running and process it to a slightly grainy paste, using on-off bursts of the motor; be careful not to overdo the processing. For a coarser texture, traditional for pork rillettes, pull the strips of meat into fibers with two forks, or mash them with a fork.

6. Taste the mixture and adjust the seasoning. Add, to your own taste, a little of either the Quatre Epices or seasoning mixture, starting with ½ teaspoon and adding more if you wish; you may also wish to add a little more garlic, minced to a paste, and more salt and pepper. Finally, stir in enough of the reserved liquid fat to make a creamy mixture; if any broth lies under the floating fat, avoid returning any of it.

7. Return the rillettes to the cooking pot (or to a saucepan, if you have used a slow-cooker) and stir the mixture gently over low heat until it is very hot, about 10 minutes.

8. Pack the rillettes into crocks or straight-sided canning jars, making sure there are no air spaces and leaving an inch of headspace. Let the rillettes cool, uncovered, to lukewarm.

9. Spoon off and remelt some of the leftover fat,* again avoiding any liquid in the bowl. Strain the fat over the rillettes to seal each jar with a ¼-inch layer. Let the seal cool, then cover and/or wrap the crocks for refrigerator or freezer (page 328); store. Allow rillettes to come to cool room temperature before unsealing. Scrape the fat layer aside to spoon out helpings; smooth the fat over leftovers, cover, and refrigerate.

*LAGNIAPPE:

The deliciously seasoned fat left over from making rillettes is great for cooking; strain it into a small jar, leaving behind any trace of liquid, and refrigerate it, covered.

 SEASON:
Any time

YIELD:
A loaf weighing about 2½ pounds

STORE:
For at least 10 days in the refrigerator

Country-Style Pâté with Black Walnuts

The most remarkable of all native American nuts are the secret ingredient of this pâté that tastes as if wild game had strayed into its compounding, although it is made of everyday meats and poultry. If you don't have access to black walnuts, which have a uniquely rich, deep, earthy savor, they can be omitted, but I do recommend that you include them if you can; they contribute much to this *pâté de campagne* American-style.

This recipe yields a good big loaf, enough for a dozen

servings or more. Let the pâté ripen in flavor for 2 or 3 days before slicing it, and let it come to room temperature before your guests dig in. To go with it as a first course or a luncheon main dish, your own Cold-Pickled Cornichons (page 96), Tarragon-Pickled Flame Grapes (page 85), or Tart Pickled Cherries in the French Style (page 88) would be a splendid foil. Other possibilities as accompaniments are Spiced Whole Blueberries in a Red-Wine Pickle (page 77), or a spoonful of Beach Plum or Wild Plum Sauce for Game & Meats (page 91).

The pâté *can* be frozen for storage, but I don't recommend it; sogginess might set in. If you'd like to double the recipe with future occasions in mind, a better strategy is to pack half of a double batch of the mixture into a second loaf pan lined with foil rather than pork fat. Cover this panful with foil, overwrap it, and freeze it until you foresee the need for another finished pâté in a few days. Thaw the unbaked loaf in the refrigerator and transfer it, sans foil, to a loaf pan lined with pork fat as in step 1, below. Top it with more fat and bake, weight, and chill it as described.

Final note: If you have prepared Quatre Epices (page 210), you can substitute 1½ teaspoons of that mixture for the pepper, allspice, cloves, ginger, and nutmeg listed as ingredients.

⅓ to ½ pound fresh pork fat, preferably fatback, cut into thin sheets*

½ pound lean pork, preferably from the shoulder, ground

½ pound lean veal, ground

½ pound skinned turkey breast, ground

¼ pound smoked ham, cooked or uncooked, ground

¼ pound additional fresh pork fat, diced into ¼-inch cubes or coarsely ground

¼ pound chicken livers, trimmed and diced into ¼-inch pieces

⅓ cup black walnuts, chopped medium-fine**

2 eggs

3 tablespoons flour

3 large cloves garlic, minced very fine

1 tablespoon finely minced mild onion

1 tablespoon salt

½ teaspoon (or more, to taste) freshly ground pepper

⅓ teaspoon ground allspice

½ teaspoon finely crumbled dried thyme

⅛ teaspoon Powdered Bay Leaves (page 207) or 2 or 3 whole bay leaves

Pinch *each* of ground cloves, ginger, and nutmeg

¼ cup Cognac or other good brandy, or use half Cognac and half Madeira

***PORK FAT:**

If you can't obtain sheets of pork fat (the firmest and best is from the back), salt pork or bacon can be used; bacon will alter the flavor of the loaf, however. If you opt for salt pork, rinse it well in warm water, then pat it dry, to remove some of the loose salt. Too-thick slices of fat can be pounded out between sheets of waxed paper, so don't despair if the meat man cuts it too thick, or if you have to slice it yourself.

****BLACK WALNUTS:**

These nuts are rich in oil, so they quickly lose flavor after they are shelled. Taste them before purchasing, and store them airtight in the refrigerator or freezer.

1. Line a 6-cup loaf pan with the thin sheets of pork fat, letting any loose ends hang over the sides of the pan; reserve part of the fat to cover the top of the pâté. Preheat the oven to 400°, with a shallow pan, larger than the loaf pan, set on a shelf in the center; pour about 1½ inches of water into the pan and let it heat.

2. Place the ground pork, veal, turkey, and ham, the diced or ground pork fat, the diced chicken livers, and the black walnuts in a large mixing bowl.

3. Beat the eggs and gradually stir in the flour. When the mixture is smooth, add the garlic, onion, salt, pepper, allspice, thyme, powdered bay (if you are using it; if you're using whole bay leaves, reserve them), cloves, ginger, and nutmeg. Stir the mixture into the meats for a few strokes, then add the Cognac and mix all the ingredients thoroughly. (A pair of well-washed hands will do the best job.) If you wish to check the seasonings, sauté a spoonful of the mixture in a small greased frying pan until it is well done, then taste; don't taste the raw mixture, or any other raw mixture containing pork.

4. Pack the pâté firmly into the lined loaf pan, being careful to eliminate any air pockets. If you are using whole bay leaves, lay them on top of the meat. Cover the loaf with the reserved sheets of pork fat (it isn't vital that the entire top be covered; if you have less than enough fat, lay the pieces down the center). Lay aluminum foil over the pan and press it tightly to the rim all around.

5. Set the loaf pan in the pan of hot water in the preheated oven and bake the pâté for 2 hours, adding boiling water to the outer pan as the level drops below the halfway mark. Remove the foil after 2 hours and check for doneness: if the juices run clear when the pâté is pricked and pressed with a spatula or spoon, it is done. If longer baking is needed—usually no more than 15 minutes or so—let the pâté bake uncovered until it tests done.

6. Remove the inner pan from the oven and set it on a platter or baking sheet to catch any fat that may spill over in the next step. Return the foil to the top (or add a fresh sheet) and set a suitable weight on it: a second loaf pan, plus about 3 pounds of weight (such as cans of food), is ideal. Lacking a second loaf pan, a wrapped brick will do, or a section of board, plus weights. Let the loaf cool with the weights, then unweight and refrigerate it, covered snugly, for at least 2 days before serving it; the resting period allows its flavor to develop.

7. To unmold the pâté, run a knife blade all around it, then dip the pan briefly into hot water. Either invert the loaf onto the platter or pry it out right side up by using a large rubber spatula. For neatness, scrape away any blobs of fat and/or meat juices. The sheets of fat can be removed or not, as you prefer, before the pâté is sliced, not too thickly, for serving.

Smoked Chicken Or Turkey

 SEASON:
Any time

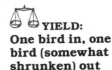 YIELD:
One bird in, one bird (somewhat shrunken) out

 STORE:
For up to 5 days in the refrigerator or for up to 3 months in the freezer

Smoked poultry used to be a rare delicacy produced in secret by elves who charged great sums for their product, which was sold only by mail order or in the most expensive of fancy-food shops. It turned out, though, that home-smoking a whole chicken or small turkey, or a whole turkey breast, was quite feasible for those who owned some kind of smoker. In an earlier book *(Better Than Store-Bought),* my co-author and I published a method that was then state-of-the-art; it employed a box smoker, which produces only moderate heat. (I still use the "box" for smoked fish, as indicated by the recipe on page 24.) Because a box smoker doesn't create enough heat to cook a large chunk of food thoroughly, the poultry, previously brined, was baked in an oven, then finished with a few hours' smoking. This method is still perfectly good, if a box smoker is what you have. And I still recommend a short curing in brine; the formula is below.

Today's smoke-cookers will produce enough heat for grilling as well as the more moderate heat needed for roasting or smoke-cooking big hunks of meat. For smoke-cooking, a temperature between 225° and 300° does the job beautifully; if your appliance lacks a thermometer, set an oven thermometer inside near the meat and check it occasionally. Regulate the heat as recommended by the manufacturer.

A covered barbecue grill can also be used for smoke-cooking: place the coals well away from the bird, either in a circle or in two bands, and roast it slowly, turning it occasionally; when it is about half done, begin adding a few soaked smoking chips to the coals from time to time. Continue the smoke-cooking until the poultry is done (see the recipe below) and as smoky as you like it. Again, keep the temperature low.

As all this indicates, with today's equipment smoke-cooking foods is no more complicated than grilling a few steaks, although it takes longer. There is a wide choice of smoke-producing chips and sawdust; experiment to find whether hickory, maple, cherry, or maple plus corncobs, or another kind of smoking chips such as mesquite, produces the flavor you like.

The instruction booklet provided by the manufacturer is the best guide to using either a smoke-cooker or covered barbecue, as there are many models. I recommend the brining formula below if you'd like to cure the poultry lightly before smoking it (this improves both texture and flavor); or, if you are eager to try your hand *today,* the bird can just be rubbed generously with salt and pepper (some like to add a little brown sugar), then with vegetable oil, and smoke-cooked at once.

A Curing Brine & General Smoking Method

Enough cold water to cover the poultry (see step 1)

FOR EACH QUART OF WATER:

¼ cup non-iodized fine salt, or ⅓ cup coarse (kosher) salt

3 tablespoons (packed) dark brown sugar, or 2 tablespoons (packed) brown sugar and 1 tablespoon honey

2 generous pinches freshly ground white pepper

Pinch of Powdered Bay Leaves (page 207) or ½ of a medium bay leaf, crumbled

1. Rinse a whole chicken or small turkey (or whole turkey breast), cleaning the cavity of a whole bird thoroughly; pull off all surplus fat. Drop the bird into a plastic bag, tie the neck of the bag, pressing out all possible air, and drop it into a bowl or crock that will hold it and leave room at the top. Run cold water into the bowl until the bag, held with the tied neck above the surface, is covered by at least an inch. Remove the bird and de-bag it.

2. Measure the water, return it to the bowl, and add the listed ingredients, multiplying them as necessary. Stir everything into the water until the sugar and salt have dissolved. Drop the bird into the brine. Cover it with a small plate to hold it under the surface and refrigerate it for a day or two.

3. When you are ready for smoke-cooking, remove the bird from the brine, rinse it briefly, and dry all surfaces thoroughly, giving particular attention to the cavity of a whole bird. Rub all surfaces lightly with vegetable oil and truss a whole bird as you would for roasting. (Skewer the neck skin over the opening. Fold wings behind the back; tie drumstick tips together, loop the string around the tail, and tie.)

4. Following the smoke-cooker or grill manufacturer's instructions, slow-cook the poultry for about an hour, then start adding a few soaked smoking chips to the coals from time to time and continue cooking the beast until a meat thermometer placed with its tip in the center of the thickest part of the thigh or breast registers 165° to 170°. If the skin appears dry at any point, brush it lightly with a little more oil. Exact timings are impossible to predict; the size of the bird, its temperature when cooking began, and the temperature inside the cooker all affect this; count on a minimum of 3 hours for a small bird. In general, slower rather than faster smoke-cooking results in a more succulent product.

5. Cool the smoked poultry to room temperature for immediate serving, or cool it completely and wrap it airtight in foil or plastic wrap for refrigerator or freezer storage.

6. To serve: For best flavor, serve smoked poultry at room temperature. If it has been frozen, thaw it in the refrigerator, then wrap it loosely in foil and freshen it in a low oven (325°) for about half an hour. Cool to room temperature before serving. Refrigerate leftovers promptly, and use them within a day or two.

Smoked Honey-Glazed Duckling

For this appetizing smoked bird, whose salty-sweet-smoky character is rather reminiscent of ham, try to obtain a fresh duckling—in some places easier said than done—weighing about 4½ pounds. If a fresh bird is not to be had, a frozen duckling will do; thaw it in its wrappings in the refrigerator before proceeding with the brining. Ducklings, like mature ducks, carry relatively little meat, so you may want to smoke two or more, depending on the capacity of your smoker, while you're about it.

The preceding directions for Smoked Chicken or Turkey apply here, but don't brush the bird with oil before smoking it; instead, use the honey-soy glaze below to create a mahogany gloss on the skin. Because ducklings tend to be exceedingly fat, you may want to cut open and flatten the bird(s) to facilitate removing all possible loose fat before the curing step. To do this, cut out and discard the backbone (or put it in the stock pot) and trim off the neck skin and the fat flaps from the base of the abdomen; press the duck with the hands to flatten it. I like to hang the duckling up for smoking, so I use a coarse needle to thread a stout string under the shoulder joints.

Brine the duck(s) for 2 days. When you proceed to the smoking, set a pan containing a little water under the duck to receive the abundant fat that will drip out. Add water as necessary as it evaporates. Smoking at a temperature between 225° and 300° will take 4 hours or longer, so plan accordingly.

To glaze the skin of the duck, brush it every hour or so during smoking with a mixture of ¼ cup honey and 2 tablespoons each light (or "thin") soy sauce and water.

To serve the duckling, let it return to room temperature if it has been chilled or frozen. Frozen smoked duck should be thawed in its wrappers in the refrigerator; the glaze will not survive, but the flavor will be there. Optionally, warm it (see the preceding recipe).

SEASON:
Any time

YIELD:
One raw bird yields one smoked bird; final weight will be about half the original weight

STORE:
For up to 5 days in the refrigerator or for up to 3 months in the freezer

SMOKED DUCKLING:

A few slices of smoked duck add elegance to a platter of potato, rice, mixed vegetable, or pasta salad or, in nippy weather, a hot vegetable or potato "ragout." For a first course or a light luncheon, arrange slivers of smoked duck on greens of an assertive kind—arugula, chicory, spinach, radicchio, and so on—and add to the plate peeled, seeded, chunked, and drained ripe tomatoes marinated in vinaigrette; or add a few strips of Roasted Antipasto Peppers (page 33), or Dried Tomatoes Italian-Style (page 41).

ANGLING: SEAFOOD SNACKS

Few whets are more appetizing than well-prepared things from the sea, as generations of delicatessen clients can testify.

To fix a few delicacies of your own, look here for the how-to's of smoking fish and making a savory paste of some of your product. You can also create a Provençal appetizer with anchovies, olives, and capers, or serve your own marinated salmon or herring.

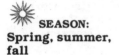
SEASON:
Spring, summer, fall

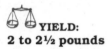
YIELD:
2 to 2½ pounds

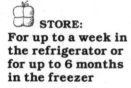
STORE:
For up to a week in the refrigerator or for up to 6 months in the freezer

Smoked Mackerel, Bluefish, Bonito, Tuna, or Swordfish

All of these fine rich fish are most appetizing when cured briefly in seasoned brine, then smoked at a temperature high enough to cook the flesh while the smoke flavors it.

Many home barbecues can serve as hot-smokers, as they easily produce sufficient heat. I have also used my box-type smoker, which is normally heated only moderately by its small electric element, as a hot-smoker with the help of a few separately ignited charcoal briquettes nested in the bottom, as described in the recipe.

Whatever smoking equipment you use, consult the manufacturer's recommendations.

3 to 3½ pounds fillets (with skin) or 1- to 1½-inch steaks of very fresh mackerel, bluefish, bonito, tuna, or swordfish

2 quarts water

⅔ cup coarse (kosher) salt

½ cup (packed) brown sugar

½ teaspoon Powdered Bay Leaves (page 207) or 6 bay leaves, crumbled

¼ teaspoon freshly ground white pepper

⅛ teaspoon ground allspice

Pinch of ground hot red (Cayenne) pepper, optional

Vegetable oil

1. Fish fillets should be cut from fish with the skin left on; first, of course, scales should be removed. Steaks should be at least 1 inch thick, better 1½ inches. Optionally, cut out with a

sharp knife the lengthwise strip of very dark and strongly flavored flesh in mackerel or bluefish fillets, and cut out the very dark roundish section of swordfish slices. Rinse the fish pieces quickly in cold salted water to remove any scales and blood.

2. Stir together the water, salt, brown sugar, bay leaves, pepper, allspice, and hot red pepper (if used) in a large stainless-steel or ceramic bowl until the salt and sugar have dissolved. Add the fish, placing fillets skin side up. Weight the fish with a small plate, cover the bowl, and set it aside for 3 hours, or refrigerate it for as long as 6 hours.

3. Rinse the pieces of fish briefly under running cold water and lay them on a rack (or hang each fillet up by means of a loop of butcher's string threaded through it with a needle) to dry until a slight membrane forms on the flesh and it does not feel sticky to a light touch; this takes about 2 hours, depending on the humidity of the air. (An electric fan speeds this stage along.)

4. Meanwhile, soak several handfuls of mild-flavored wood smoking chips in water—for fish, I like a mixture of corncobs and maple, but hickory chips are fine. Preheat your smoker according to the manufacturer's directions. When the temperature reaches the correct level for hot-smoking (at least 125°), sprinkle a small handful of drained chips onto the coals or the sawdust pan, as appropriate. (If you use a smoker that doesn't ordinarily produce the level of heat needed for hot-smoking, ignite a supply of charcoal briquettes separately and bed a half-dozen of them in improvised "pans" of foil in the bottom of the smoker. Keep a few extra briquettes burning separately, in readiness to replace the first batch.)

5. Brush the fish pieces lightly with vegetable oil and hang them in the smoker, or lay them on lightly oiled racks. Smoke the fish, maintaining the heat and the supply of soaked chips as necessary, until the pieces are golden and cooked through (test a thick portion with a skewer or the tip of a small sharp knife). The smoking temperature should be between 125° and a high of no more than 180°; try to keep it between 160° and 170°. During smoking, brush the fish once or twice with a little more oil. The time required for smoking will vary with the temperature and with the thickness of the pieces; from 2 to 3 hours is average for fish 1 to 1½ inches thick.

6. Cool the fish completely, then either serve it or wrap the pieces closely in aluminum foil, enclose them in plastic bags, and refrigerate or freeze them.

7. Frozen smoked fish should be thawed in its wrappers to prevent sogginess. Serve the fish at room temperature, cut slightly on the bias into thin slices. If you'd like to serve the smoked fish warm, steam the pieces briefly. Broken bits can be saved and made into Smoked Fish Paste (page 26); or you may want to dedicate a whole smoked fillet or steak to this purpose.

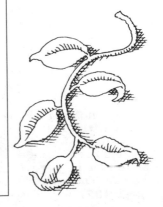

※ SEASON:
**Spring, summer,
fall**

🍵 YIELD:
About 1½ cups

🗄 STORE:
**Unsealed, for up to
a week in the
refrigerator;
sealed with
clarified butter,
for up to 2 weeks
in the refrigerator;
for 2 months in the
freezer**

Smoked Fish Paste

Any of the five fish for which smoking directions have been given (page 24) make a savory pâté for parties when blended with butter and a few seasonings. With such a use in mind, save bits and pieces when you serve slices of smoked fish, or dedicate a portion of your freshly smoked fish to this purpose.

Or, start with store-bought finnan haddie, kippers, smoked salmon, or smoked trout. Kippers can be a bit dry, depending on their cure; if so, cover the pieces with boiling water and let them soak 5 minutes before draining them and proceeding. If you want to use salmon, ask your delicatessen if trimmings are available—the price is much lower than that of whole slices. Pâté made with smoked trout is enhanced by a tiny bit of well-drained horseradish—a teaspoonful or so—blended with the other ingredients.

**½ pound (about 1½ average fillets) smoked
    mackerel, bluefish, bonito, tuna, or swordfish
    (page 24) or other smoked fish**
**¾ cup (1½ sticks) unsalted butter, softened at room
    temperature**
Few drops of fresh lemon juice
Freshly ground black pepper
Salt, if desired
Pinch of Powdered Bay Leaves (page 207), optional
**About ¼ cup Clarified Butter (page 315), if needed
    for step 4**

1. Flake the smoked fish, eliminating all bones, skin, and bits of hard or dark flesh; you should have about 1¼ cups.
2. Cream the butter in an electric mixer or food processor. Add the flaked fish and beat the mixture well. Taste, then beat in a few drops of lemon juice, freshly ground pepper to taste, a little salt if it is needed, and, if desired, a small pinch of powdered bay leaves.
3. Pack the fish paste firmly into small pots or custard cups that have been sterilized (by 10 minutes' boiling in water to cover) and cooled. In filling the pots, be careful to eliminate any air pockets and smooth the top of the paste.
4. Refrigerate the paste, covered airtight with plastic wrap or foil, if it will be consumed within a few days. If it is to be refrigerated or frozen for longer storage, melt enough clarified butter to cover the paste at least ¼ inch deep and pour it into the containers to form a seal. Cover and/or wrap the containers for the refrigerator or freezer (page 328) and store.

**Serve Smoked Fish
Paste with toasted
thin slices of
French bread, or
Melba Toast (page
162), or Oatcakes
(page 167).**

5. Frozen fish paste should be thawed in its wrappers. Once the butter seal has been opened, use the fish paste within a few days.

Tapenade (Olive, Anchovy, & Caper Spread)

 SEASON:
Any time

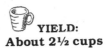 YIELD:
About 2½ cups

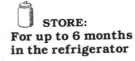 STORE:
For up to 6 months in the refrigerator

A gleaming bowlful of this Provençal specialty looks like nothing so much as caviar, but on the palate it's quite different though equally zesty. Tapenade is a decidedly olivaceous, anchovy-salty, and capery waker-upper of the taste buds that, Elizabeth David tells us, was probably the invention, perhaps based on a now-lost regional dish, of a chef in Marseilles. (When you try the originally Italian recipe for Olivata, page 38, you'll note its kinship with tapenade despite its lack of anchovies as an ingredient.)

However tapenade came to be devised, it has been widely adopted over southern France and beyond in the century or so it has existed; it is splendid as part of an hors d'oeuvre or as an accompaniment for a glass of wine or iced vodka, or any properly dry cocktail or aperitif. Spread it on rounds of crisptoasted French bread (or Semolina Loaves, page 156, or Whole-Oat Melba Toast, page 162) to enjoy it at its simple best.

Some formulas for tapenade contain such ingredients as tuna canned in oil—which is most harmonious—and mustard, which seems to my palate to be superfluous. Such dried herbs as thyme, powdered bay leaf, rosemary, or summer savory sometimes find their way into tapenade without harm, as do a few drops of brandy, but adding dried figs and even tea, which have been prescribed with a straight face by some writers, surely is going too far. The classic mixture seems quite perfect as it is.

Tapenade is slightly grainy when made as described here. The smoother, saucelike texture achieved by longer processing is good if you want a sauce upon which to bed halved hardcooked eggs for an hors d'oeuvre (Elizabeth David's recommendation) or to serve as a dip for raw vegetables or not-too-salty chips of some sort. In either form, tapenade is also an authentic Provençal seasoning for the mashed yolks of what would otherwise be deviled eggs (perfectly delicious) and for salads of cooked small potatoes and fresh tomatoes. I have also tossed it with freshly cooked thin pasta and a little extra oil for a quick hot meal. Recommended.

*UPPING THE
ANCHOVY:

For more anchovy
flavor, include the
oil from the can,
reducing the plain
olive oil accord-
ingly.

2 jars (6½ ounces each) black Mediterranean-style
    oil-cured olives (brined olives are not suitable),
    or about the same weight of bulk olives
2 tins (2 ounces each) flat fillets of anchovies,
    drained*
⅓ cup drained tiny (nonpareil) capers
⅓ to ½ cup high-quality olive oil, preferably oil with
    a pronounced character
2 large cloves garlic, peeled and minced
About 1 tablespoon strained fresh lemon juice, to
    taste
Freshly ground black pepper, to taste
Additional oil for storing the tapenade

1. Pit the olives (most easily done by squeezing each between fingers and thumb) and place them in the container of a food processor or a blender. (If you feel muscular and possess a large mortar and pestle, those implements are highly authentic.) Add the anchovy fillets, capers, ⅓ cup of the olive oil, and the garlic. Turn the machine rapidly on and off repeatedly to chop the ingredients to a grainy texture, or continue to process the mixture if you want a smooth sauce. Blend in 1 tablespoon of lemon juice and freshly ground pepper; taste the tapenade and add more seasoning if you wish (no salt will be needed because of the olives and anchovies). Stir in the remaining olive oil, or even more, if the mixture seems to need it (it should be unctuous).

2. Pack the tapenade into a crock or jar, pressing it down hard to eliminate air pockets. Smooth the top and pour on enough additional olive oil to cover it well. Cap the container and refrigerate it if the spread is not to be served immediately (it improves with mellowing).

3. Serve tapenade at room temperature. Refrigerate leftovers, covering the top with a little more oil to exclude air.

SEASON:
Spring through
fall, from scratch;
or at any season,
using salt fish

Marinated or Pickled Salmon Or Herring

Both of these sea-born preparations rate high among Scandinavian and European seafood delicacies in general and New York-style "appetizers" in particular. Marinated or Pickled Salmon, also called marinated or pickled lox around the Big Apple, is a rather rare specialty offered by a few fine purveyors, whereas pickled herring, a noble if commoner fish, is widely available. However, the herring is also worth preparing at home if you want custom quality, so directions follow the three steps for salmon (salt-curing the fish, pickling it in spiced vinegar with a tangle of sweet onions, and adding a sour-cream sauce).

You can skip the curing step if you wish to start with store-bought belly lox (the choicest cut) or other salted salmon, being sure you don't get by mistake the lightly smoked salmon that is sometimes loosely called "lox" in ill-informed shops.

Whether you start from scratch or from the second stage, the pickled salmon will be choice, and it keeps well enough to reward you for the considerable time (but little work) it requires. So although you must plan ahead, at each stage of the process the fish is keepable: salmon packed in salt keeps well for months, and in fact connoisseurs insist that it isn't at its best before three months' salting and it's even better after half a year. Marinated or Pickled Salmon, with or without the sour-cream sauce, also keeps well, so it's sensible to make a generous quantity while you're about it.

Salt-Cured Salmon

If you'd like to start from scratch and salt-cure your own supply of salmon to be pickled at a future date, you need an impeccably fresh fish or two, beheaded and split and with the backbone removed; or you can use only the narrow "fillet" sections of the fish (the area between the "steak" section and the tail), split and with the tail and backbone removed. (This portion is considered less choice.)

Salt-cured Pacific salmon was a staple food in Alaska and the Pacific Northwest from the mid-nineteenth century onward, and shipping the salt fish to the rest of the country, to Hawaii (where it was, and is, called *lomi-lomi*) and to Europe was an early and important industry. Northwesterners fixed their native salt salmon in various ways after freshening it in cold water; it could be steamed, then served with a sauce, perhaps melted butter and dill, or a cream sauce with chopped hard-cooked eggs folded in. The salmon was also poached, flaked, and creamed or scalloped, and it was made into hearty soups and chowders. Back East and in Europe, people didn't need to be told twice that they could pickle the Northwestern salt salmon in such good ways as the one detailed here.

**Pure non-iodized pickling or dairy salt, about 2
    pounds, or as needed**
4 quarts cold water
5 to 6 pounds split and boned fresh salmon

1. Stir 1 cup of the salt into the 4 quarts of water in a large bowl or crock until it has dissolved. Rinse the salmon pieces, add them to the brine, and soak them for 1 hour to free them of diffused blood and prepare them for the salt cure.

**SEASON:
Spring through fall**

**YIELD:
About 3 to 4
pounds**

**STORE:
For 6 months or
longer in the
refrigerator**

2. Rinse the pieces of fish agai and drain them well. Make a few shallow slashes about 2 inches apart in the flesh side of the thickest area of each fish piece.

3. Choose a flat-bottomed ceramic, enameled, plastic, or stainless-steel container that will hold the fillets in layers with depth to spare; if the fillets are too long for the container, cut them in halves or thirds. Spread a generous ¼ inch of salt in the dish. Make a layer of fillets on the salt, skin side down and slightly apart. Cover the fish pieces with a layer of salt, rubbing salt into the slashes, and fill the spaces between the pieces with salt. Make more layers of fish and salt, laying each succeeding layer at right angles to the preceding one, and with the final layer skin side up; finish with salt, being sure all spaces are filled. If you need more salt than the amount listed, don't hesitate to use it; the quantity needed depends on the shape of the container and the size of the fish pieces. Cover the dish loosely with plastic wrap, then add a light weight to press the fish down slightly (use a glass pie plate or baking dish or some other noncorrodible item). Slip the assemblage into a large plastic bag and close it, or overwrap it with plastic. Refrigerate the whole works for 2 weeks. Every few days, check to be sure the fish is covered with the brine formed by the salt. If necessary, rearrange the pieces to keep them submerged.

4. Drain off the brine, noting how much fresh solution you'll need to replace it, and repack the fish in the washed and dried container: make layers as before, but scatter additional pickling salt only lightly in the dish and between layers. Boil for 3 minutes a sufficient quantity of fresh brine, using ¼ cup salt to each quart of water. Cool the brine completely and pour it over the fish to submerge the pieces. Cover and refrigerate the fish as before. It will be ready to use after another 2 weeks, but it will be all the better if left longer. If you remove part of the fish, transfer the remaining pieces, with brine to cover, to a smaller container.

Marinated or Pickled Salmon

T his second-stage recipe gets down to the actual pickling (as opposed to salt-curing). The pickling solution is abundant enough to let 4 to 6 cups of fish pieces, plus 2 to 3 cups of onion rings, "swim" freely. A half-gallon glass jar makes a convenient container, or use two quart jars.

2 to 3 pounds (4 to 6 cups of pieces) of Salted Salmon, above, or salt-cured but unsmoked salmon ("lox" or "belly lox") from a delicatessen

1 quart distilled white vinegar

1 cup water

¾ cup sugar, or more, to taste

SEASON:
Any time

YIELD:
About 2 quarts

STORE:
For up to 3 weeks
in the refrigerator

**1 to 1½ tablespoons peppercorns, to taste; black
    and white mixed or all black or all white,
    slightly bruised in a mortar or with a rolling pin**

1 tablespoon mustard seed

**12 whole allspice, slightly cracked in a mortar or
    with a rolling pin**

8 whole cloves

4 bay leaves, crumbled

**⅛ teaspoon ground hot red (Cayenne) pepper, or 1 or
    2 small dried hot red peppers, optional**

**2 medium-size red onions or other mild onions,
    optional**

1. *If you use Salted Salmon:* Drain it and place it in a large ceramic, enameled, plastic, or stainless-steel bowl. Cover the fish with cold water, cover the container, and refrigerate it for 2 to 3 days to remove excess salt, changing the water at least twice a day. (To speed up the freshening, you can set the container under a barely running cold tap for part of the soaking period.) When the soaking water is no longer particularly salty, the fish has been freshened enough.

If you use commercially prepared lox: When buying, ask whether it has been freshened; if it has, omit the long soaking above. Instead, place it in a bowl under the cold tap and let the water run slowly over it for 15 minutes.

2. Combine the vinegar, water, sugar, peppercorns, mustard seed, allspice, cloves, bay leaves, and hot pepper in a saucepan, bring the mixture to a boil, cover, and simmer gently for 20 minutes. Let the mixture cool completely.

3. Drain the freshened fish and remove the skin: Lay the piece skin down on a cutting board. With a long, thin, very sharp knife, cut the flesh free of the skin, pressing the edge downward against the skin as you move the blade under the flesh from the tail end forward. Decide whether you want the marinated salmon in long strips, slices, or cubes. For 1-inch strips, cut lengthwise; for slices, cut crosswise, slightly on the bias, into slices at least ½ inch thick. Cubes should be a good inch square. As you cut, feel with the fingertips for any bones and remove them with tweezers.

4. Peel the onions, if you are including them, halve them from top to bottom, and slice crosswise about ⅛ inch thick.

5. Layer the fish and the sliced onions in a bowl, crock, or a wide-mouthed jar or jars. Pour the cooled spiced vinegar through a sieve over the fish and onions. If you wish, add a few pieces of bay leaf and some of the other spices to the contents of the jar.

6. Cover the pickled salmon and refrigerate it for 3 days or more before serving it. The salmon (and onions, if included) can be drained and served as is, but a sour-cream sauce (below) is a delicious enhancement; it should be added to the salmon at least a day before it is served.

SEASON:
Any time

YIELD:
About 4 cups

STORE:
For up to a week in the refrigerator

SEASON:
Any time

YIELD:
About 2 quarts

STORE:
In the refrigerator; in salt cure, will keep for at least 6 months; store pickled herring for up to 3 weeks, herring in cream sauce for up to a week

Marinated Salmon In Cream Sauce

Arrange drained pieces of Marinated or Pickled Salmon (recipe above), with their accompanying onions, in layers in a bowl, crock, or straight-sided glass jar. Make a sour-cream sauce by blending dairy sour cream (1 cup for about 3 cups of fish and onions) with 1 or 2 tablespoons, to taste, of the pickling liquid. Pour the sauce over the pieces, making sure it filters down among them. Cover the container closely and refrigerate it at least overnight before serving the salmon with bread and butter as a first course, or a light lunch, or (why not?) for breakfast, in the New York–nostalgia fashion.

Herring Pickled Like Salmon

"Where are you going, and what do you wish?"
The old Moon asked the three.
"We go to fish for the herring fish
That swim in the beautiful sea."
   —"Wynken, Blynken, and Nod," children's verse

Anyone who has made the acquaintance of classic New York pickled herring in cream will notice that the marinated salmon above resembles it stylistically. Recommendation enough, if you like creamed herring. If you have never fixed a batch of your own, try using these directions.

Salting your own: You can salt your own fresh herring. Before they are brined they should have been beheaded, split up the belly, and emptied. Open out the fish, leaving the sides attached by the back skin, and remove the backbones; rinse and drain. Salt the herring exactly as described for Salt-Cured Salmon (page 29). They will be ready to use after two weeks.

Starting with store-bought: Begin with the pickling step if you buy imported salt herring; beheaded but not emptied of innards, these come packed in small kegs at delicatessens.

Remove 2 to 3 pounds (ten to fifteen 3- or 4-ounce fish) from the brine. Use kitchen shears to slit the bellies and scoop out the skimpy innards. Soak the herring in abundant cold water in the refrigerator, changing it twice, for 12 to 24 hours. Drain the fish and cut off their fins and tails. Slit the herring fully open and, optionally, cut out the backbones with the scissor tips. Slice the herrring crosswise into 1-inch pieces.

Pickle and sauce the herring exactly like Marinated or Pickled Salmon, using the same ingredients.

NEITHER FISH NOR FOWL...

... Meaning that the delights that follow are mostly vegetable loves (except for the Gilded Eggs), savory trifles to make with mushrooms or sweet peppers or olives or peanuts or tomatoes. Have on hand such things as Roasted Antipasto Peppers, or Olivata, or Potted Mushrooms, or Dried Tomatoes Italian-Style (plus a relish or condiment made from part of the tomatoes) to serve as first courses, or to accompany drinks, or to graze on at any hungry moment. Whether you find yourself in a specific season or between seasons, there's something here you can put by for enjoyment at a future time when the pantry is your first and best fallback.

Roasted Antipasto Peppers

Roasted red-ripe sweet or "bell" peppers packed in olive oil are a delicious and faintly smoky appetizer to pull from the freezer when a hearty Italianate first course is wanted. After thawing, the peppers are showered with thinly sliced garlic (about a tablespoon to a cupful of pepper strips), tossed, and left to reach room temperature for an hour or two before they are served; you may also want to add minced parsley leaves and more vinegar, salt, and oil. Arrange them on a bed of greens on the antipasto platter or individual plates; top them, if you like, with criss-crossed anchovy fillets. The peppers are also a zesty addition to salads and cooked dishes.

Using both yellow and red sweet peppers makes an especially attractive mixture.

4 pounds (about 9) large, fully ripe sweet red peppers or a mixture of red and yellow sweet peppers

1 tablespoon salt

½ cup red wine vinegar

⅔ cup olive oil, preferably a full-flavored type

Sliced garlic (at serving time)

Minced parsley leaves, optional (at serving time)

1. *Roasting the peppers, stovetop method:* Rinse the peppers to remove any possible grittiness. Set a metal rack over a stove burner (I keep an inexpensive cake rack just for pepper roasting) and arrange several peppers on it, keeping them within the area of the gas flame (or heat, if your stove is

SEASON:
Late summer/early fall

YIELD:
About 4 cups

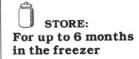

STORE:
For up to 6 months in the freezer

electric). Turn on the heat at the medium-high setting. Roast the peppers until they are well charred all over, turning them with tongs as often as necessary. As each pepper becomes well blackened, pop it into a pot and cover the pot with a lid. Continue until all the peppers are steaming in the pot. Let them cool until they can be handled comfortably.

Broiler method: Alternatively, the rinsed peppers may be broiled about an inch below a preheated broiler element; turn them frequently, using tongs, until they are blackened, then put them into the pot and cool them, covered, until they can be handled comfortably.

2. Using your fingers and a short sharp knife, remove the charred skin from the peppers (don't wash them at this stage) and cut out the stems and cores. Tear the peppers lengthwise into strips about an inch wide, dropping them into a bowl as you proceed. (For the moment, disregard any clinging seeds.)

3. Sprinkle the salt over the peppers and mix it in thoroughly (most easily done with your hands). Let them rest for 10 minutes.

4. Pour about a cupful of water into another bowl and rinse the pepper strips in it quickly, one or two at a time; as they are rinsed, drop them into a clean bowl. Add the vinegar and mix it well with the strips, then mix in the olive oil.

5. Spoon the peppers into freezer containers of convenient size and pack them firmly enough to eliminate air pockets; leave ½ inch of headspace in the containers. If the peppers are not covered with liquid, add more oil until they are covered. Seal the containers and freeze and store them at 0° or less.

6. Thaw the peppers slowly in the refrigerator to serve. Add the garlic and adjust the seasoning as described in the recipe headnote. Refrigerate any leftover peppers.

 SEASON:
Any time

 YIELD:
About 3 pints

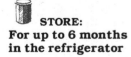 **STORE:**
For up to 6 months in the refrigerator

Two Kinds of Mushrooms, Pickled

Little button mushrooms make a pretty pickle, but their flavor is not in the same league with that of boletus mushrooms, dried specimens of which are used here to lend their fine, dark taste and deep, earthy color to a delicious preparation that's fit to grace any antipasto.

For the flavoring element, look for dried mushrooms labeled cèpes, porcini, boletus, boletes, and so on; sometimes they are to be found in bags marked "dried European mushrooms," and those imported from Chile can be quite good, too.

There is a bonus from this pickling job: the flavorful cooking liquid (and the pieces of dried mushroom, too, if you don't choose to pickle them) makes a fine base for a soup or a sauce.

2 pounds small, firm white button mushrooms

1 ounce (about ⅔ cup) dried porcini, cèpes, or other dried boletus mushrooms

4 cups water

3 teaspoons salt

1½ cups red wine vinegar

1½ cups distilled white vinegar

3 large cloves garlic, peeled and halved

2 dozen black or white peppercorns

6 medium bay leaves

9 whole cloves

3 large blades mace

1. Wipe the button mushrooms clean with a damp cloth and trim the bases of the stems; try to avoid washing them. If washing is necessary, do it quickly and roll the mushrooms in a towel to blot them. If the mushrooms aren't uniform in size, cut any overlarge specimens in halves or quarters.

2. Combine the mushrooms, the dried boletes, the water, and 1½ teaspoons of the salt in a large saucepan. Bring the liquid slowly to a boil and simmer the mushrooms, uncovered, until the buttons are tender, 10 to 15 minutes. Pour the whole business into a bowl, let the mushrooms cool, then cover them and refrigerate them overnight.

3. Drain the mushrooms in a colander set over a bowl (be sure to save the delicious liquid). Either remove the pieces of boletus and add them to the reserved liquid (puree this for a superb soup), or leave them mixed with the buttons; although not comely, the pieces are delicious.

4. Combine the remaining salt with the two vinegars, the garlic, peppercorns, bay leaves, cloves, and mace in a saucepan and bring the mixture to a boil. Cover the pan and simmer for 5 minutes.

5. Meanwhile, divide the drained mushrooms among heatproof storage jars that have snug lids. Divide the seasonings from the boiling-hot pickling liquid equally among the jars, then pour the spiced vinegar over the mushrooms. The liquid should cover them well; if not, add a little more vinegar (either kind) or water as required. Let the mushrooms cool, cover the jars, and refrigerate them to mellow for at least 3 days before serving them. At serving time, you may want to drain the mushrooms and toss them with a little good olive oil.

SEASON:
Any time

YIELD:
About 1 pound

STORE:
Airtight, for a few days at room temperature; for up to 2 weeks in the refrigerator; for 3 months in the freezer

The Devil's Own Peanuts

The firepower of these peanuts (or almonds, if you like) can be increased by stepping up the hot red pepper and/or by including the optional hot pepper sauce; but be warned—as written, the recipe supplies enough warmth for most palates.

2 tablespoons Worcestershire sauce

2 tablespoons soy sauce, preferably imported

2 cloves garlic, peeled and sliced

1 teaspoon salt, plus more for sprinkling if desired

⅜ teaspoon ground hot red (Cayenne) pepper, more if desired

¼ teaspoon ground cumin

Large pinch of freshly ground black pepper

2 dashes hot pepper sauce such as Tabasco, optional

2 egg whites

1 jar (16½ ounces, about 3 cups) dry-roasted unsalted peanuts (or substitute blanched almonds)

1. Combine the Worcestershire sauce, soy sauce, garlic, 1 teaspoon salt, ground red pepper, cumin, black pepper, and the hot pepper sauce, if it is used, in the container of an electric blender. Run the motor until the garlic has been completely pureed. Add the egg whites and run the motor just until the ingredients are blended.

2. Place the peanuts in a bowl and pour the pureed mixture over them. Let the peanuts stand for 30 minutes, stirring them several times.

3. Preheat the oven to 250° and oil two baking sheets.

4. Pour the nuts into a sieve set over a bowl and drain them for a moment or two; reserve the liquid. Spread the nuts on the prepared pans.

5. Bake the nuts on two shelves of the oven until they have dried slightly, about 10 minutes. Stir them and break apart any clumps, then drizzle the reserved liquid over them, mix them well, spread them out, and sprinkle them lightly with additional salt if desired. Return them to the oven, exchanging shelf positions, and bake them again until the glaze is dry, about 15 minutes. Turn off the oven and leave the nuts in it, with the door ajar, until they have cooled.

6. Store the completely cooled nuts in an airtight container in a cupboard, the refrigerator, or the freezer. If the nuts have been frozen, refresh them (no need to thaw them first) in a 200° oven for a few minutes; cool, and serve.

Gilded Eggs (A Pretty Pickle)

 SEASON:
Any time

YIELD:
2 dozen eggs (2 quarts)

STORE:
For at least 6 months in the refrigerator

Golden in color, spicy-tart in taste, these pickled eggs are perfect for picnics, as hors d'oeuvre (halve them, mash the yolks with mayonnaise, return the mixture to the halves), or—simply halved, quartered, or sliced—as an accompaniment for a salad, cold meats, or cheese. One or two gilded eggs, chopped, are a zesty addition to either mixed green salad or heartier salad mixtures involving potatoes, pasta, or tuna.

For those who like to know family relationships, gilded eggs are obvious relatives of all-American "red-beet eggs," which are flavored and colored by the spiced juice of pickled beets; to Chinese "tea eggs," prepared with brewed tea, orange peel, and star anise; and to the eggs pickled in strong malt vinegar that are a standard item in British pubs. But these are distinctive for their golden color (contributed by turmeric) and the selection of other spices with which they are packed. If you prefer palefaced eggs, omit the turmeric.

Pickled eggs are most attractive (and also ready to eat sooner) when very small eggs are used. If the smallest size of hens' eggs, usually called "pullet eggs," can't be had, use either U.S. "small" or "medium" eggs.

2 dozen *very* small, small, or medium eggs

3 cups distilled white vinegar

1 cup water

1 stick (2 to 3 inches) whole cinnamon, broken up

1 tablespoon sugar

1 tablespoon dried onion flakes, or 1 small onion or 2 or 3 shallots, peeled and sliced thin

2 teaspoons salt

2 teaspoons white peppercorns, slightly bruised

1½ teaspoons broken-up dried ginger

1 teaspoon whole allspice, slightly bruised

1 teaspoon turmeric

Pinch of ground hot red (Cayenne) pepper, optional

1. Place the eggs in a large saucepan and run in enough water to cover them by 1 inch. Bring the eggs gradually to the simmering point over low heat. Simmer them 10 minutes.

2. Meanwhile, combine all the remaining ingredients in a second saucepan. Heat this pickling mixture to simmering over medium heat and simmer, covered, for 15 minutes.

3. Set the pan of hard-cooked eggs under running cold water and cool them quickly. Shell the eggs and drop them into two scalded wide-mouthed quart jars.

4. Pour the boiling-hot pickling mixture over the eggs, dividing the spices equally between the containers. The pickling solution should cover the eggs well; if it does not, add more vinegar. Let the eggs cool uncovered, then seal the jars and store them in the refrigerator for at least a week or two before serving the eggs. The flavoring process continues for several weeks, so patience will be repaid.

SEASON:
Any time

YIELD:
About 2 cups

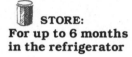

STORE:
For up to 6 months in the refrigerator

Olivata
(Olive Puree)

T his pungent Italian olive paste, redolent of Mediterranean herbs, is dandy as an appetizer; spread it on toasted French bread or melba toast. For a kissin' cousin that includes anchovies and capers, see Tapenade, page 27.

2 jars (6½ ounces each) oil-cured black olives, or equivalent in loose oil-cured olives, either with or without added herb and red pepper seasoning

¼ to ⅓ cup full-flavored olive oil

1 to 2 large cloves garlic, peeled and minced

Herbs to taste: ½ to 1 teaspoon crumbled dried oregano plus a pinch or two of crumbled dried rosemary (or twice as much minced fresh rosemary); or up to 2 tablespoons chopped fresh basil leaves; or a combination of ½ to 1 teaspoon crumbled dried thyme (or twice as much minced fresh thyme leaves), a pinch or two of dried rosemary (or twice as much chopped fresh rosemary), and a pinch of hot red pepper flakes

Freshly ground black pepper, to taste

A little strained fresh lemon juice, if needed

Additional oil for topping the olivata

1. Pit the olives (most easily done by squeezing each between fingers and thumb). Combine the olives, ¼ cup of the oil, the garlic, and your chosen herbs in the container of a food processor or blender (or use a large mortar and pestle and pound the ingredients if you feel like getting physical). Turn the machine rapidly on and off repeatedly to chop the ingredients to a grainy puree, or pound away if you are wielding a pestle; don't let it become too smooth. Taste the olivata and add more herbs, if needed, plus freshly ground pepper and a little lemon juice, if you think a touch of tartness is a good idea. (Bear in mind that the flavor of the mixture will develop further.) Add the remaining olive oil if the mixture needs it in order to be properly unctuous.

2. Pack the olivata firmly into a jar or crock and smooth the top. Cover the puree with a thin layer of olive oil, then cover the container closely and refrigerate it.

3. Let the olivata come to room temperature before serving it. Refrigerate leftovers, first adding a fresh topping of oil.

Potted Mushrooms (Mushroom Paste)

Use this buttery dark spread, pungent with the flavor of both dried and fresh mushrooms, on canapés or in thin-cut sandwiches, which are especially good when a few leaves of watercress are tucked in. It is also a fine snack on crackers. Use it, too, as the "butter" for substantial sandwiches of chicken or cheese, or swirl spoonfuls into hot noodles as sauce and seasoning, or spread a spoonful over a broiled steak.

To achieve the most intense mushroom flavor at the most reasonable cost, choose dried fungi labeled "European mushrooms" or, if you can find them, the otherwise anonymous dried mushrooms imported from Chile. You can also use dried mushrooms identified as boletes (boletus mushrooms), which have marvelous flavor but carry a high price tag. These will be found under such names as cèpes, porcini, funghi secchi porcini, and Steinpilze. Oriental dried mushrooms (shiitake and so on) are not suitable.

1 ounce (about ⅔ cup) imported dried mushrooms

⅔ cup warm water

2 tablespoons Madeira, plus more if needed

2 medium shallots, peeled and sliced

1 medium clove garlic, peeled and sliced

½ teaspoon salt, or to taste

¼ teaspoon ground mace

Large pinch (⅛ teaspoon) of dried thyme leaves

Scrap of bay leaf about ½ inch square, or large pinch of Powdered Bay Leaves (see page 207)

Tiny pinch of ground cloves

½ pound (weight after trimming) firm, fresh cultivated mushrooms, stems removed (about ¾ pound before trimming)

Freshly ground black pepper or ground hot red (Cayenne) pepper, to taste

½ to ¾ cup (1 to 1½ sticks) butter, sliced ¼ inch thick

About ½ cup Clarified Butter (page 315) for sealing

SEASON:
Mainly winter, but possible at any time

YIELD:
About 2½ cups

STORE:
Sealed with clarified butter for up to 3 weeks in the refrigerator; keeps for several days after seal is broken

1. Soak the dried mushrooms in the warm water, covered, for several hours or overnight, until the mushrooms are very soft.

2. Lift the mushrooms from their liquid with a slotted spoon and place them in the container of a food processor or a blender; let the soaking liquid settle for a moment, then pour it carefully into the food processor, leaving behind any sand that may be in the bottom. Add the Madeira, shallots, garlic, salt, mace, thyme, bay leaf, and cloves, and process the mixture to a puree. Scrape the puree into a bowl and reserve it.

3. Preheat the oven to 300°.

4. Working in batches, if necessary, chop the mushroom caps very fine in the processor or blender (no need to clean the container first). Add the puree and blend everything together well.

5. Scrape the mixture into a small baking dish (a 3-cup soufflé dish is just right) and set it into a slightly larger baking dish or pan. Cover the inner dish tightly with foil and add a metal lid or ovenproof plate to hold it in place. Pour enough boiling water into the outer dish to come within an inch below the rim of the inner dish.

6. Bake the mushroom mixture in the preheated oven, adding more hot water to the outer dish as necessary and stirring the mushrooms after 1½ hours. Check the mushrooms again after 2½ hours; the fragments should be tender, almost jellylike. When this point is reached, uncover the inner dish and let the mixture bake uncovered for an additional ½ hour. Remove the whole business from the oven and set the inner dish on a rack to cool to lukewarm.

7. Taste the potted mushrooms and add pepper to taste, plus a little more of any of the seasonings you think may be needed; the flavor should be pronounced. Using at least 1 stick of butter or as much as 1½ sticks, add the butter slices, about one-third at a time, whisking after each addition until the butter disappears. Taste the mixture again and make any final additions to the seasonings.

8. Pack the potted mushrooms into two or three attractive small crocks suitable for serving and smooth the tops. Chill the paste, uncovered, until it is firm; as it cools, it will begin to appear marbled.

9. Melt the clarified butter and pour a layer about ¼ inch thick over the paste, being sure that the butter layer is sealed to the sides of the containers. Cover the mushroom paste tightly and refrigerate it. Before serving, allow the potted mushrooms to soften slightly at room temperature. Leftovers should be used within a few days.

Dried Tomatoes Italian-Style

Among the good things that come in small jars at large prices are Italian sun-dried tomatoes packed in olive oil. Undeniably delicious but undeniably costly, they can be equaled by your own home-prepared supply.

The right kind of tomatoes are meaty, oblong "paste" or Italian-type tomatoes, also called "plum" and "pear" tomatoes; they are ready in late summer. The method used for drying them is less important than their subsequent handling; if you would like them to have authentic mellow-tart flavor, let them rest quietly in the jar for a while.

If you'd like to dry the tomatoes in the sun's heat, be aware that the process may take several days; the tomatoes are brought indoors at night or when the weather turns damp. For drying tomatoes indoors, a dehydrator is excellent, but it isn't essential; an ordinary oven or (even better) a convection oven does very well. (My convection oven has three extra stainless-steel mesh shelves designed for drying foods; these are worth having.)

When you're through with either outdoor or indoor drying, you'll have leathery, dark red strips with tangy, intensely tomatoey flavor; after they're packed in oil (and herbs, if you like), they will develop more flavor for weeks, so don't be in a hurry to serve them.

4 pounds ripe but not oversoft Italian-type tomatoes

Salt

Distilled white vinegar

Olive oil, preferably mild-flavored

Sprigs of fresh rosemary or a little dried rosemary, optional

1. Rinse the tomatoes and dry them. Cut out the stem scar and the hard portion of core lying under it. Halve the tomatoes if they are small, or quarter them if they are large. With the tip of a knife, scrape out most of the seeds without removing the pulpy core. (If you wish, the seeds may remain, but some prefer the texture of tomatoes dried without them.)

2. Arrange the tomatoes, cut surface up, on drying racks (cake racks with closely set wires are fine). Sprinkle them lightly with salt.

3. *Drying the tomatoes, using sunlight:* Set the racks in the sun and cover them with cheesecloth, propped up on jars or other objects to keep it from touching the tomatoes. Dry the tomatoes until they are leathery, which may take as long as 2 or 3 days; turn the pieces twice a day, and take the racks

 SEASON:
Late summer/early fall

 YIELD:
6 to 8 ounces (without oil), about 1 well-packed cup

STORE:
For up to a year in a cool cupboard; or refrigerate if desired

WAYS TO USE DRIED TOMATOES:

Although dried tomatoes have become fashionable adjuncts to salad plates, to my mind this isn't their best use; they are both too chewy and too dominant in flavor to be compatible with most salady things. (However, they are an intriguing relish when served on an antipasto plate.) Some other suggestions:

•Dried tomatoes are a wonderful intensifier for tomato flavor, especially in pizza or pasta sauces. Drain a handful of the strips (save the oil), snip them into bits, and simmer them in a little water or some of the sauce until they are soft; puree or not, as you wish.

•Add snipped-up dried tomatoes, either straight from the jar or

simmered as de-
scribed, to the top-
ping of a pizza;
drizzle some of the
tomato oil over the
topping before
baking the pizza.

•To make *essenza
di pomidori*, an-
other expensive
food-emporium
item, see Essence
of Sun-dried Toma-
toes, page 42.

•Don't fail to use
the delicious oil
from the tomato
jar in salads or in
sauces as well as
on pizzas.

indoors at night or when the weather turns damp. After they
have partially dried, flatten the pieces gently with a rubber
spatula. If the weather is uncooperative at any point, switch to
an oven (see below). Proceed with step 4 when the tomatoes
are dry.

Drying the tomatoes indoors: If you have a dehydrator,
follow the manufacturer's directions. Otherwise, place the
racks in an oven or convection oven. Turn the heat control to
200° and leave the tomatoes for 30 minutes. Reset the heat
control of a conventional oven to 140° and leave the oven door
ajar. Reset the control of a convection oven to the temperature
recommended by the manufacturer, or leave it at 200° (this
works very well with my particular oven) and leave the door
very slightly open unless the oven manufacturer directs otherwise. Dry the tomatoes until they are leathery, not hard,
switching the shelf positions of the racks occasionally. When
they are about half dry, flatten the pieces with a rubber spatula.
The time required will depend on your oven and the size of the
pieces, but as a rule the tomatoes should be ready in about 6 to
8 hours. (The drying can be done in more than one session, if
you like.)

4. Cool the tomatoes completely. Place them in a bowl
and sprinkle them quickly with the vinegar. Toss the pieces
rapidly (best done with the hands) to moisten them lightly.
Immediately empty the bowl onto a double layer of paper
towels and pat the tomatoes thoroughly dry with more towels.

5. Pack the tomatoes lightly into a clean pint jar, including
a sprig or two of fresh rosemary or a pinch or two of dried
rosemary if you wish. Pour in enough olive oil to cover the
tomatoes generously, being sure that no bits protrude. Cap the
jar tightly and shelve it at cool room temperature for at least a
month before serving the tomatoes. After removing tomatoes
from the jar, add more oil if necessary to keep the remaining
tomatoes covered.

 SEASON:
Any time

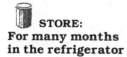 **YIELD:**
About 1 cup

STORE:
For many months
in the refrigerator

Essence of Sun-Dried Tomatoes

A relish or condiment? Sun-dried tomatoes are a recent
gastronomic gift to America from Italy, where they are nothing
new. Dispensed at high prices by food boutiques, they are a
delicacy worth its price to tomato fans, but you can make your
own—see Dried Tomatoes Italian-Style, page 41.

From either home-dried or purchased dried tomatoes,
you may want to make a batch of the Mediterranean mixture
described below, which is also available (also at towering

prices) in fine-food shops. Rich, dark and pungent, it is a decided pantry asset.

Serve *essenza di pomidori* as a relish; spread it on rounds of raw zucchini or slices of fennel as a snack; put some into a tomato-based pasta sauce for a deeper and darker flavor; adorn a pizza with it; make an instant *fake* pizza (spread the essence on split English muffins, top with cheese, broil); or let your imagination be your guide. Your imagination may lead you to eat it (as does one fancier I know) with a spoon.

1 cup (moderately packed) Dried Tomatoes Italian-Style (page 41), drained, or use purchased dried tomatoes, drained

2 medium cloves garlic, peeled

1 tablespoon drained capers

Scant 1 teaspoon crumbled dried basil, 1 tablespoon minced fresh basil, or frozen basil paste (see page 205), to taste

½ to 1 teaspoon salt, to taste

¼ teaspoon crumbled dried oregano

⅛ to ¼ teaspoon crumbled dried rosemary or ½ teaspoon finely chopped fresh rosemary leaves

3 to 5 tablespoons olive oil, preferably oil in which the dried tomatoes were packed

1 tablespoon red wine vinegar

1. Place the tomatoes in the container of a food processor and chop them to a coarse puree. Remove and reserve them.

2. With the motor of the processor running, drop in the garlic cloves and chop them fine, scraping down the bowl once or twice. Add the capers and process the mixture to a coarse puree. Turn off the machine.

3. Return the chopped tomatoes to the processor bowl. Add the basil, ½ teaspoon of the salt, the oregano, rosemary, 3 tablespoons of the olive oil, and the wine vinegar. Process the ingredients briefly, just long enough to mix them well; the texture should be slightly rough. Taste the mixture and add more seasonings and, if desired, more oil, stirring in the additions with a spatula to avoid overprocessing.

4. Scrape the tomato essence into a jar. Store it, covered, in the refrigerator; it will keep indefinitely. Let it come to room temperature before serving.

CHEESE IT

Given a whole second book's worth of space, we *could* go into the ways and means of making cured cheeses at home, something that's quite feasible now that specialized cheesemaking equipment and supplies are available to questing cooks. (See pages 330–331 for sources.)

Leaving ripened cheeses to the specialist for now, here we'll look into things to make with utensils and materials to be found in any kitchen: You can choose fine-quality fresh white cheeses, marinated and herbed white cheese, yogurt and a collection of yogurt spinoffs, a pair of choice potted cheeses, and a home-smoked Cheddar spread.

 SEASON:
Any time

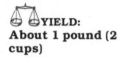YIELD:
About 1 pound (2 cups)

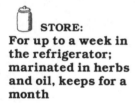 STORE:
For up to a week in the refrigerator; marinated in herbs and oil, keeps for a month

Fresh White Cheese *(Fromage Blanc)*

Deliciously fresh and sweet homemade white cheese, which has different names in various cuisines, is a versatile product of simple dairying. The formula for *fromage blanc* that follows is easy enough for absolute beginners; the main requirement is using the freshest available milk and buttermilk and paying close attention to thermometer readings.

Some ways to use the finished cheese:

•*To mold the cheese:* Line a 2-cup bowl with cheesecloth and pack the white cheese firmly into it. Fold the ends of the cloth over the top and invert the bowl onto a plate (some further draining will occur). Refrigerate the molded cheese for several hours or overnight. To serve the cheese, fold back the cloth, invert the cheese onto a dish, and peel off the cloth.

•*Pepper-Coated Cheese:* Sprinkle the molded cheese thickly with fresh, very coarsely ground black pepper; serve this with crackers as a snack with drinks.

•*Herbed Cheese:* Mix the freshly drained cheese with salt and pepper, plus a little mashed garlic and a good palmful of minced fresh herbs (a good combination is parsley, chives, and thyme and/or tarragon or basil). If it isn't possible to use fresh herbs, settle for fresh parsley, frozen chives, and dried thyme, tarragon, or basil in reduced amounts—about a third as much dried herb as fresh. Mold the cheese as described above and refrigerate it for several hours or overnight before serving.

•*Fresh White Cheeses Marinated in Oil with Herbs:* See the recipe that follows this one.

2 quarts whole milk, as fresh as possible (include ½ pint cream, if you want especially rich cheese)
2 cups very fresh cultured buttermilk
2 tablespoons strained fresh lemon juice
Salt, if desired (¼ to ½ teaspoon)
Cream, optional

1. Measure the milk into a heavy saucepan or pot, the heavier the better. Stir the buttermilk and lemon juice together thoroughly, then stir the mixture into the milk.

2. Set the pan over very low heat (it is desirable to use a heat-tamer mat even though the pot is thick) and begin to heat the milk. If you have a candy/jelly thermometer, attach it to the pan; otherwise, have at hand an instant-reading thermometer for frequent checks on the temperature. Heat the mixture slowly to a thermometer reading of 175°. Stir the milk very gently with a pancake turner or similar flat-ended implement once or twice after it begins to thicken, stirring only 2 or 3 strokes, and check the temperature often. Once a reading of 175° has been reached, turn off the heat and let the milk stand for 10 minutes undisturbed. There will be masses of white curd suspended in yellowish liquid (the whey).

3. Line a sieve or colander with 2 layers of dampened fine-textured cheesecloth or nylon net and set it over a large bowl. Ladle the curds and whey gently into it and let the curds drain until the drip of whey slows, a matter of a few minutes. Tie the corners of the cloth to make a loose bag and hang it from a cupboard handle or hook over the bowl (you can dispense with the sieve at this point) and let the cheese drain for up to an hour, or until it is the consistency you prefer, from creamy to quite firm. (The whey is excellent for use in breadbaking; it can be frozen for future use.)

4. For soft, light cheese to serve as is (perhaps with preserves for dessert), turn the drained cheese into a bowl and stir in a little salt and/or a little cream, if you wish. Cover the cheese and refrigerate it for use within a few days. If a smooth texture is wanted, beat the cheese briefly with an electric mixer.

Marinated Fresh White Cheeses

These little cheese balls keep for several weeks in their bath of olive oil and herbs, gradually becoming stronger in flavor. Well drained, they are a savory addition to a cheese tray, and they are especially good alongside a mixed green salad.

 SEASON:
Any time

YIELD:
About 1 pound

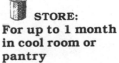 **STORE:**
For up to 1 month in cool room or pantry

Save the flavorful oil for making vinaigrette or other salad dressings when the cheese is all gone.

This marinade, by the way, is dandy for purchased small goat cheeses, which should be fresh, not aged. As the flavor of any goat cheese is more assertive than that of your own fresh milk cheese, you may want to increase the quantity of herbs by half.

Fresh White Cheese (page 44), drained as described in step 3 of that recipe

½ teaspoon salt, or to taste

2 medium cloves garlic, slightly flattened

4 teaspoons crumbled dried rosemary

4 teaspoons crumbled dried thyme

3 medium bay leaves, torn into quarters (or use ⅛ teaspoon Powdered Bay Leaves, page 207)

2 to 4 small dried hot red peppers, crumbled (or substitute ½ teaspoon, or to taste, dried hot red pepper flakes)

12 to 15 peppercorns, depending on size, slightly crushed

About 1½ cups olive oil

1 tablespoon white wine vinegar

1. After the cheese has been drained, mix it with about ½ teaspoon salt, then drain it again in the cloth bag until it is quite firm, perhaps 3 hours.

2. Form the cheese into a flat oblong about an inch thick, wrap it in the cheesecloth, set it on a plate, cover it with a flat dish or a pie plate, and weight it with a 1-pound can of food or another object of about the same weight. Let the cheese remain under the weight for an hour or two (or refrigerate it, weighted, for as long as overnight).

3. Unwrap the pressed cheese and cut it into 1-inch cubes; with your fingers, form them into balls (don't labor over making them absolutely spherical; a little roughness is more attractive). Place the little cheeses in a clean wide-mouthed quart jar as they are shaped, then drop in the garlic, rosemary, thyme, bay leaves, red peppers, and peppercorns. Pour in enough olive oil to cover the cheeses completely, then add the wine vinegar. Cover the jar with a tight lid and invert it gently two or three times to distribute the seasonings.

4. Marinate the cheeses at cool room temperature for at least 2 days before serving them; they will keep for at least a month. Shake the jar gently or invert it once or twice every few days. In very hot weather, you may wish to refrigerate the cheeses.

A Brood of Yogurts

T his is a three-way formula, with variations, for a food that has become as great a favorite in the United States as it is in Europe and the Middle East. Although this isn't a book of "health" food, except insofar as all *good* food is healthful, it is worth mentioning that this set of recipes tells how to make with skim milk a low-fat yogurt that's high in milk solids and low in cholesterol, a consideration that is important to some. Or the basic yogurt may be made with low-fat or whole milk; all three versions include added dry milk solids, and they can be drained for greater density. "Doubled" yogurt makes a good dessert with fruit or preserves, or it can be turned into any of the several kinds of "cheese" for which directions are given.

Basic Three-Way Yogurt

 YIELD:
About 6 cups

 STORE:
For at least 2 weeks in the refrigerator

6 cups skim milk, low-fat milk, or whole milk, as preferred
6 tablespoons nonfat dry milk powder
½ cup plain active-culture yogurt

1. Whisk together the milk and dry milk powder in a large saucepan or preserving pan and heat the mixture slowly to simmering, stirring it almost constantly. If you are using a thermometer (recommended), make sure the temperature reaches at least 180°. Set the milk mixture aside and let it cool to 110°, or until it feels only faintly warm when a few drops are tested on the inside of the wrist.

2. Whisk the yogurt smooth in a scalded bowl that is large enough to hold all the milk, then whisk in the lukewarm milk.

3. Cover the bowl and keep the contents warm: either wrap the bowl snugly in several layers of heavy towels; or set the bowl in an oven warmed only by a pilot light (the oven temperature should be around 100°); or set the bowl in a pan of warm (100°) water, overwrap the whole works to retain warmth, and replace the water as often as necessary to maintain its temperature; or decant the mixture into the scalded containers of a yogurt "machine" and follow the manufacturer's instructions for the incubation period.

4. The time required for the yogurt to reach a custardlike consistency may be as little as 4 hours, so check it often after that time has passed. For a flavor that is only mildly tart, be sure that the yogurt does not incubate past the point of soft coagulation; it will become more solid after it is refrigerated. Refrigerate the yogurt for several hours or as long as over-night, then go on to "double" it by draining, if you wish.

YIELD:
2½ to 3 cups

STORE:
For at least 2
weeks in the
refrigerator

Doubled (Drained) Yogurt

A batch of Basic Three-Way Yogurt, above
¼ to ½ teaspoon salt, optional

1. Line a colander or sieve with a double or triple layer of fine cheesecloth or close-woven nylon curtain material, with an ample overhang all around. Set the lined colander over a large bowl or pot. Stir the salt into the yogurt, if you are using it. Ladle the yogurt into the lined colander and drain it for an hour or two.

2. When the drip slows, tie the corners of the cloth together to make a bag. Hang the bag from a cupboard knob or a hook, with a bowl underneath to catch the drip; let the yogurt drain further, until it is as dense as you wish. This may take all day, or overnight. If the weather is warm, summon the inspiration of Rube Goldberg and devise a way to drain the yogurt in the refrigerator. One way is to run the handle of a long ladle or spoon (or a piece of dowel could be used, or a long, strong cooking chopstick) under the knots of the bag, then place the spoon across the top of a pot or bowl that will fit into the refrigerator; the bag should hang above the bottom of the pot. Empty the pot as necessary to keep the bag above the liquid.

3. When the yogurt is as firm as you wish, transfer it to a bowl and refrigerate it, covered. Serve the yogurt plain or with fruit or preserves. Or make it into a seasoned "cheese" spread or dip (below).

Fresh Yogurt Spreads & Dips

To make spreads, add to a cupful of firm drained yogurt your choice of the following sets of ingredients. For dips, soften the mixture with a little milk or cream, as appropriate. You can refrigerate these mixtures for up to 2 weeks.

•*Low-Cholesterol Caraway "Cheese" Spread:* Cream together a cupful of firm drained yogurt made with low-fat or skim milk, 4 tablespoons (½ stick) cholesterol-free margarine (corn oil margarine), a little salt to taste, freshly ground white pepper, and 2 teaspoons caraway seed.

•*Richer Caraway "Cheese" Spread:* Use a cupful of firm drained yogurt made with whole milk; beat in 4 tablespoons (½ stick) softened butter, salt, freshly ground white pepper, and 2 teaspoons caraway seed.

•*Herbed Yogurt "Cheese":* Add to firm drained yogurt (made with any kind of milk) 2 tablespoons softened butter (or margarine); a small clove garlic, finely minced; at least 3 tablespoons minced fresh herbs (combined parsley, thyme, chives, and tarragon; or parsley plus chives and oregano or basil; or any combination of your favorite fresh herbs); mix in salt and plenty of freshly ground white pepper. Taste; add drops of hot pepper sauce if you wish, or more of any of the seasonings, perhaps a few drops of lemon juice. Dried herbs (use about a third as much as fresh) can be substituted; their flavor will be livelier if they are soaked in a little white wine or dry vermouth for a few minutes before they are added.

•*Yogurt "Cheese" with Three Peppers:* Add to a cupful of firm drained yogurt 2 tablespoons of softened butter (or margarine), salt, a generous amount of imported paprika, and freshly ground white pepper to taste. Blend well, then stir in 2 or 3 tablespoons chopped, well-drained pimientos (for a mild spread) or chopped, well-drained pickled jalapeño peppers or some of your Pickled Hot, Hot Green Peppers (page 103).

•*Yogurt "Cheese" with Olives:* Add to each cupful of firm drained yogurt 2 tablespoons softened butter or 1 tablespoon full-flavored olive oil; chop enough oil-cured black olives and green olives to make 3 to 4 tablespoons and mix them in. You may want to include some fresh-ground pepper or a few chopped capers.

Cheese Potted With Black Walnuts

Potted cheese—which is the old and accurate name for a custom-made cheese spread, not "pot cheese"—is dandy to have on hand, especially if the mixture is one that becomes even better as it mellows. Here is one such; it includes black walnuts, whose deep, dark, almost gamy flavor makes them one of the best companions for certain cheeses.

The formula is flexible—the combination of Cheddar and a mild Monterey Jack is especially good, but all Cheddar or all Jack is fine, too, as is any other firm, fairly rich cheese such as Edam, Gouda, Colby, Jarlsberg, mild Munster, and so on. If black walnuts aren't available (mail-order sources can be found on pages 330–331), use any nut of assertive character; almonds are too mild, but English walnuts, hazelnuts, or pistachios are excellent.

Potted cheese will taste best if it is allowed to soften slightly at room temperature before it is served. Enjoy it on crackers or, even better, Oatcakes (page 167); shave curls onto

SEASON:
Any time

YIELD:
About 2½ cups

STORE:
Sealed with clarified butter, for several weeks, at least, in the refrigerator; for up to 2 months in the freezer

hot vegetables—broccoli or snap beans come to mind; and, for cheeseburger fans, top the cooked beef patties with a thin slice of potted cheese.

Smooth a piece of plastic wrap over the surface of leftover cheese before covering the container and refrigerating it again.

¼ pound sharp natural (not processed) Cheddar, shredded (about 1⅓ cups, lightly packed)

¼ pound mild young Monterey Jack cheese, shredded (about 1⅓ cups, lightly packed)

6 tablespoons (¾ stick) unsalted butter, slightly softened at room temperature

2 tablespoons dry vermouth, dry sherry, or dry white wine

Small pinch of ground mace

½ cup black walnut meats, chopped medium-fine (English walnuts or other nuts may be substituted)

Clarified Butter (page 315) for sealing

1. Beat the cheeses and softened butter together until the mixture is creamy and almost smooth (don't try to eliminate all texture), which is most expeditiously done in a food processor or in an electric mixer fitted with a paddle-type beater. Beat in the vermouth and mace, using a little more vermouth if necessary to make the mixture slightly soft. Stir in the black walnuts.

2. Pack the potted cheese tightly into small crocks or pottery custard cups. Smooth the tops and seal the cheese airtight with a ¼-inch layer of melted clarified butter. (The butter covering may be omitted if the cheese will be used within a couple of weeks.) Cover the containers and refrigerate the cheese. For longer storage, wrap for the freezer (page 328) and freeze.

**SEASON:
Any time**

**YIELD:
About 2 cups**

**STORE:
For 3 weeks or more in the refrigerator; freeze for longer storage**

Smoky Cheese Spread

Lightly smoked cheese is a toothsome bite, if it is really smoked—some commercial kinds, even expensive ones, have a smack of the chemical about them. Here is a cheese spread that gains its genuine hickory tang in either a box smoker or a smoke-cooker that doesn't create too much heat. (The temperature inside the smoker shouldn't go much above 100° to 120°.) Even at a low level of heat the smoking will soften the cheese considerably, but as the cheese is going to be mashed anyway, the melting is a help, not a hindrance.

This is a good "hitchhiking" recipe: the cheese can share the smoker when a larger smoking project is under way.

¾ pound firm natural Cheddar-type cheese

**½ cup (1 stick) unsalted or lightly salted butter,
slightly softened at room temperature**

Freshly ground white pepper

Ground hot red (Cayenne) pepper, optional

1. Preheat the smoker, then add soaked hickory chips or other suitable wood chips or sawdust and continue to heat the smoker until the flow of smoke is well started.

2. Meanwhile, cut the cheese into 1-inch cubes and arrange them on a cake rack set on a heat-resistant plate or flat pan that will fit into the available space in the smoker.

3. Set the plate in the smoker and leave it for 2 hours, renewing the supply of smoking chips as needed. Taste the now more or less melted cheese and decide whether you have a smoky flavor that suits you, keeping in mind that the flavor will be somewhat lightened when the butter is added. Continue to smoke the cheese as long as required; 3 hours in all seems about right for my box smoker.

4. Scrape the soft warm cheese into a mixing bowl or the workbowl of a food processor. Work the butter into the cheese to make a smooth spread; add white pepper and the optional ground hot red pepper to taste.

5. Pack the cheese into a crock or a bowl, cover it snugly with plastic or foil, and store it in the refrigerator. If it is to be frozen, wrap for the freezer (page 328) and freeze. Frozen cheese should be thawed in its unopened wrapping in the refrigerator. Let the spread come to room temperature before serving it.

Potted Cheese & Beer "Rabbit"

Thinis rabbit-by-courtesy reflects the flavoring of Welsh rabbit, but it's actually a kind of potted cheese, zestily flavored with beer and other oddments and readily kept on hand to serve with crisp toast or crackers. It is mellow but nippy, quite addictive with or without a cool glass of beer. It has been known to appear at breakfast at our house, as well as at cocktail time or with crackers whenever a nibble is needed.

 SEASON:
Any time

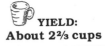 **YIELD:**
About 2⅔ cups

STORE:
Unsealed, for 2 weeks or more in the refrigerator; sealed with clarified butter, for up to 6 months in the refrigerator

¾ pound fine-quality natural Cheddar (choose mellow, sharp, or extra-sharp, or combine kinds to taste)

1 teaspoon dry mustard

⅔ cup excellent beer (it must be smooth and flavorful)

½ cup (1 stick) unsalted butter, slightly softened at room temperature

1 teaspoon Worcestershire sauce

Generous grinding of fresh white pepper

Pinch or two of ground hot red (Cayenne) pepper, or a few drops of hot pepper sauce

Salt, only if needed

¼ to ⅓ cup Clarified Butter (page 315) for sealing

1. Grate the cheese. Place it in a bowl and add the dry mustard and the beer. Stir the mixture, press the cheese down until it is covered by the beer, cover the bowl, and let it stand for a few hours to soften (it can rest as long as overnight, if that is most convenient).

2. Place the softened butter in the container of a food processor or a blender and beat it briefly until it is creamy. Add the beer-cheese mixture, the Worcestershire sauce, freshly ground white pepper, and ground hot red pepper or hot pepper sauce according to preference. Process the whole business until the mixture is smooth, scraping down the bowl once or twice. Taste the "rabbit" and add more seasonings if they are needed; some may want added salt, but this depends on the saltiness of the cheese. The mixture should be well seasoned.

3. Pack the "rabbit" firmly into one or more crocks or small bowls, smooth the tops, cover airtight with plastic wrap or foil, and refrigerate. It can be kept without further covering if it will be used up within 2 weeks or so. For longer storage, melt enough clarified butter to cover the potted cheese by ¼ inch; pour the melted butter over the chilled cheese, making sure it seals to the sides of the containers. Cover the containers airtight and refrigerate them again. Serve this at room temperature for best flavor and spreadability.

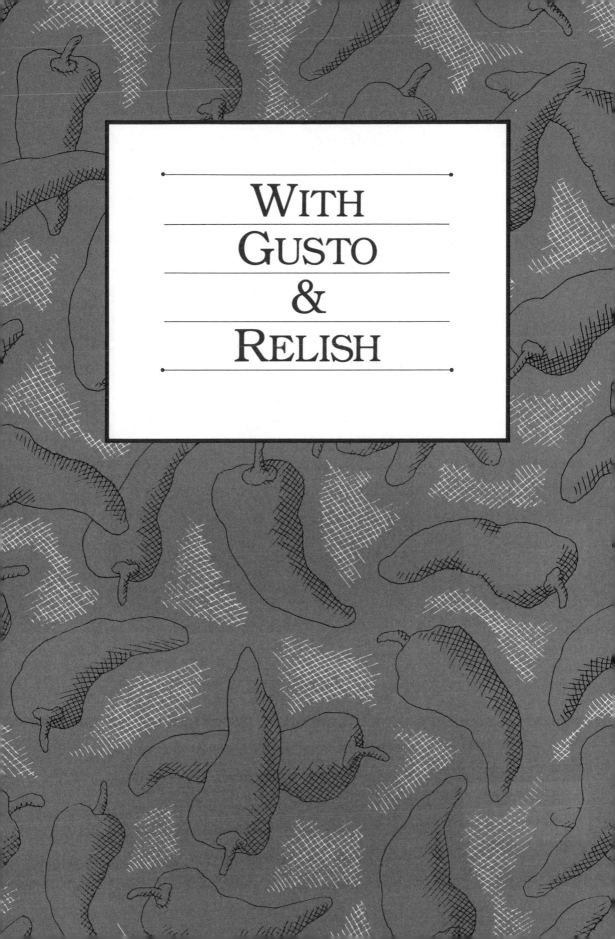

WITH
GUSTO
&
RELISH

A CLUTCH OF CHUTNEYS

Mango & Tamarind Chutney • Gingery Rhubarb Chutney
Four-Fruit Chutney • Green Tomato & Apple Chutney

A KINDNESS OF KETCHUPS

Mushroom Ketchup • Hot & Spicy Banana Ketchup
Concord Grape Ketchup • Cranberry Ketchup

RELISHES

Sweet & Hot Red Pepper & Onion Relish
Escoffier's Condiment of Sweet Peppers
Hot & Sweet Red Pepper Jam
Wimpy's Delight (A Hamburger Relish)
Corn Relish with Sweet Red & Green Peppers
Country-Style Chili Sauce with Hot Peppers
Blueberry Relish
Spiced Whole Blueberries in a Red-Wine Pickle
Fresh Herb Jellies (Basil, Tarragon, or Mint)
Purple Basil & Orange Jelly (A Relish)
Red Rosemary Jelly • Thyme-Plus-Three Herbal Jelly
Cranberry & Currant Relish

SWEET & SOUR FRUITY THINGS

Tarragon-Pickled Flame Grapes • Melon Moons
Tart Pickled Cherries in the French Style
Bing Cherries in a Sweet Nine-Day Pickle
Crab Apples in Cranberry Syrup
Beach Plum or Wild Plum Sauce for Game & Meats
Sweet & Tart Pickled Cranberries

PICKLE PICKS

Young Ginger Pickled in the Japanese Fashion
Cold-Pickled Cornichons • Grapeleaf Dills
Extra-Crisp Bread & Butter Pickle Slices
Quick Bread & Butter Onion Rings
Onion-Ring Pickles from Scratch
Pickled Hot, Hot Green Peppers
Sweet Pickled Green Tomato Slices
Red and/or Yellow Sweet Pepper Strips in Vinegar
Pub-Style Pickled Shallots or Small Onions

Delve into the five pigeonholes of this section for distinctive keepables that lend on-the-plate zest to both plain and fancy meals. When lunch is a simple sandwich, or supper is cold meat and salad, a tantalizing little something—chutney, a pickle, a fruity relish—will add allure. And when the menu is more elaborate, perhaps featuring game, or a fine roast or tender bird, an appropriately elegant complement, up to and including a sauce of the Cumberland type, can be found here.

These recipes in aid of "gusto and relish" (from the title of a quirky, likable old cookbook) start with a few choice chutneys; one is made with mangoes and dried tamarind, others with more common fruits or such garden stuff as rhubarb and green tomatoes.

The ketchup collection takes leave from the usual to demonstrate that there is life beyond the tomato: look here for ketchups based on cranberries, mushrooms, Concord grapes, or hotly spiced and rummy bananas.

The relishes include a sweet-pepper condiment for cold meats; Wimpy's Delight, born for hamburgers; and other appetizing trifles involving hot peppers, blueberries, or herbs (Purple Basil & Orange Jelly is one of several fresh herb jellies). When the mood of the meal is "down home," spoon out a bowlful of American corn relish made with two kinds of sweet peppers, or serve chunky Country-Style Chili Sauce, spiced with hot peppers, or Hot & Sweet Red Pepper Jam.

The pickles are both fruity and savory: there are French-style cherries tart-pickled with tarragon, and equally sophisticated pickled seedless red grapes. There are crisp globes of sweet-pickled cantaloupe and not-quite-classic crab apples put up in cranberry syrup, and whole cranberries preserved in a red-wine pickle. Piquant items are provided for the fire-resistant palate: notice Pickled Hot, Hot Green Peppers and Young Ginger Pickled in the Japanese Fashion. There are crackling-crisp things (bread and butter and green-tomato pickles, made by revived old-time methods), plus onion rings, classic dills, pickled shallots, and, as the ads say, "more." Among the "more" are my own favorites, cornichons.

A CLUTCH OF CHUTNEYS

Well, everyone knows that chutneys were born in India, and so far so good. But when it comes to making these distinctive relishes, we have to face the fact that most of our Western-style chutneys are hybrids, based only loosely on Indian originals. Before we set about rectifying this in the spirit of authenticity, we need to think about whether we want (and are up to producing) true Indian chutneys, regardless of how fond we may be of curries. Serving true Indian chutneys—which are traditionally freshly made and quite piquant (meaning hot)—involves toasting a rainbow of spices, grinding them with other ingre-dients, some of them not easy to find, and generally working quite hard before every principal meal.

No? I thought not. So we can relax into the Anglo-Indian notion of chutneys—spicy pantry-shelf relishes that are only mildly to rather hot, depending on taste, and are put up in jars in readiness for instant use. Here are some based on both common and exotic ingredients.

The following few recipes have been tempered to the heat tolerance of most of us in the matter of peppers, ginger, and other incendiaries, but the BTUs can be stepped up, if required.

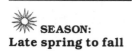
SEASON:
Late spring to fall

YIELD:
6 to 7 cups

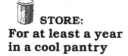
STORE:
For at least a year in a cool pantry

Mango & Tamarind Chutney

Mangoes mostly come to market from May until late fall, and they mostly arrive in a state of rock-hard unripeness that can be discouraging if you're looking for fragrant, melting fruit to eat out of hand. (They will ripen in time, if handled gently and left in an airy spot out of the sun.) Meanwhile, use the green fruit to make this luxurious chutney, which is given additional zing by tamarind, a seedy, stringy Indian fruit that is sold dried in compressed bricks by dealers in exotic foods. (Fresh lime juice can be substituted for tamarind, as described in step 1.) You can also make a chutney of softer texture by including part (or all) almost-ripe fruit.

If you like jammy chutney, cut the fruit into small bits; for a chunky product, use half-inch or larger cubes and stop cooking the mixture as soon as the fruit pieces are translucent.

The formula below yields a moderately hot and spicy relish. If you demand more fire, increase the ginger by as much as 2 tablespoons and increase the quantities of hot pepper. Plan to let the chutney rest in the jar for at least a month so that its many flavors can blend and balance.

½ cup (packed) dried tamarind pulp

2½ cups water

3 pounds unripe, half-ripe, or part unripe and part ripe mangoes

1 cup onions, in ¼-inch dice

1 cup golden raisins

1 cup dried currants

4 tablespoons minced fresh ginger, or more, to taste

3 large cloves garlic, minced fine

Grated zest (colored portion only) of 1 lemon

2 cups (packed) light brown sugar

¾ cup granulated sugar

2 tablespoons mustard seed

1 tablespoon salt

2 teaspoons crushed dried red pepper; or 2 dried hot peppers (2½ to 3 inches long), seeded, then crumbled; or 1 tablespoon finely minced fresh hot peppers, red or green (increase any of these if you are sure you want a hotter chutney)

2 teaspoons ground cinnamon

½ teaspoon turmeric

¼ teaspoon ground cloves

¼ teaspoon ground hot red (Cayenne) pepper, or more, to taste

1½ cups distilled white vinegar

    1. Crumble the tamarind into a small bowl and stir in 1½ cups of the water; let the tamarind soak for at least an hour, meanwhile preparing the remaining ingredients. (If tamarind isn't easily obtainable, substitute ½ cup strained fresh lime juice plus ½ cup water for the tamarind and its soaking water.)

    2. Peel and dice the mangoes, cutting them into small pieces for a jamlike chutney, into ½-inch or larger dice for a chunky mixture. Place the pieces in a preseving pan. Add the onions, raisins, currants, ginger, garlic, lemon zest, brown and granulated sugar, mustard seed, salt, crushed hot red pepper, cinnamon, turmeric, cloves, ground red pepper, white vinegar, and the remaining 1 cup water; stir the mixture and let it rest until the tamarind "juice" is ready, or for up to several hours, if that is convenient.

    3. When the tamarind pulp is very soft, strain the liquid through a sieve, pressing it to remove all possible liquid and any pulp that will pass through. Discard the pulp remaining in the sieve. Add the liquid to the chutney mixture.

    4. Set the pan over medium heat and bring the ingredients to a boil. Lower the heat so the mixture simmers and cook it, uncovered, stirring often, until the mango and onion pieces are translucent and the chutney has thickened to the consistency of preserves, 1 to 2 hours depending on the firmness of the

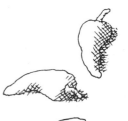

fruit. (The chutney will thicken further in the jar, so don't reduce it too much.) If the chutney threatens to stick before the mango pieces are translucent, add a little water.

5. Remove the chutney from the heat, cool a sample, and taste it for tartness, sweetness, and degree of hotness. (The overall flavor is elusive at this point, but these factors can be judged.) If you wish, add a little more vinegar, sugar, or ground hot red pepper.

6. Reheat the chutney to boiling and ladle it into hot, clean pint or half-pint canning jars, leaving ¼ inch of headspace. Seal the jars with new two-piece canning lids according to manufacturer's directions and process for 15 minutes (for either size jar) in a boiling-water bath (page 325). Cool, label, and store the jars for a few weeks before serving the chutney.

SEASON:
Spring into summer

YIELD:
About 7 cups

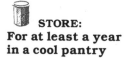

STORE:
For at least a year in a cool pantry

Gingery Rhubarb Chutney

Tender rhubarb from the garden patch (or a farm stand), plus fresh ginger, spices, and seasonings, makes a lively chutney to add zest to any curried main dish—or, for that matter, any kind of hot or cold roasted meat or poultry, not to mention a snack of cheese and crackers.

Don't hesitate to use green-stalked rhubarb instead of the pink kind, if that's what you have; peel off any tough skins and proceed as for tender pink stalks.

2 pounds trimmed red-skinned rhubarb, washed,
**   drained, and cut into ½-inch dice (6 to 7 cups)**
1½ cups coarsely chopped onions
1½ cups golden raisins
1½ cups sugar
4 cloves garlic, peeled and minced
2 tablespoons finely minced fresh ginger
1 tablespoon pickling or other fine non-iodized salt
2 teaspoons mustard seed
1 teaspoon ground allspice
1 teaspoon ground coriander
½ teaspoon dried red pepper flakes (or to taste)
¼ teaspoon ground cinnamon
¼ teaspoon ground cloves
2 cups cider vinegar
¼ cup light corn syrup

1. Combine all the ingredients except the vinegar and corn syrup in a preserving pan; mix well. Bring to boiling over medium heat, lower the heat, partially cover the pan, and simmer the mixture, stirring it occasionally, until the onion pieces are translucent, about 30 minutes.

2. Add the vinegar and corn syrup and cook uncovered over medium-high heat, stirring almost constantly, until the chutney is thick enough to mound up slightly in a spoon, 20 to 30 minutes.

3. Ladle the boiling-hot chutney into hot, clean half-pint or pint canning jars, leaving ¼ inch of headspace. Seal the jars according to lid manufacturer's directions and process for 10 minutes (for either size) in a boiling-water bath (page 325). Cool, label, and store the jars for 3 weeks before opening.

Four-Fruit Chutney

A little of this fruit and a little of that goes into this sweet and moderately hot fruit relish. It is a good accompaniment for roasted meats or for curries of lamb, seafood, or beef. Spread a little on the buttered bread for a chicken sandwich, or add it to the dressing for chicken, turkey, or fruit salad.

Adjust the texture to your taste: for chunky relish, cut the fruit more coarsely; for jamlike chutney, cut it finer.

2 pounds firm-ripe pears, any variety

1 pound firm-ripe freestone plums or prune plums

2 cups blueberries

4 cups cider vinegar

1½ cups water

1⅓ cups coarsely chopped onions

1½ cups coarsely chopped cored and seeded sweet red peppers

3 large cloves garlic, minced

2 tablespoons salt

2 tablespoons mustard seed

2 tablespoons ground ginger

2 tablespoons finely grated orange zest (outer skin only, no white pith)

1 teaspoon ground hot red (Cayenne) pepper

1 teaspoon ground cinnamon

2 cups (packed) light brown sugar

1 cup granulated sugar

1 cup golden raisins

 SEASON:
Late summer

 YIELD:
8 cups

 STORE:
For at least a year in a cool pantry

1. Peel, quarter, and core the pears, then slice the quarters crosswise about ¼ inch thick. Wash, pit, and quarter the plums. Sort, wash, and drain the blueberries. Reserve the fruits.

2. Combine the vinegar, water, onions, sweet red peppers, garlic, salt, mustard seed, ginger, orange zest, ground red pepper, and cinnamon in a preserving pan. Bring the mixture to a boil, adjust the heat, and simmer it, uncovered, 15 minutes, or until the onion pieces are translucent.

3. Add the brown sugar, granulated sugar, pears, and plums. Bring the chutney to a boil, lower the heat, and simmer it, uncovered, stirring carefully from time to time (try to prevent breaking the fruit pieces), for about 1 hour, until the chutney has thickened. Add the blueberries and raisins, stir them in gently, and cook the chutney 15 minutes longer, or until it is as thick as you'd like it. (It will thicken further as it cools.)

4. Ladle the boiling-hot chutney into hot, clean pint or half-pint canning jars, leaving ¼ inch of headspace. Seal the jars with new two-piece canning lids according to manufacturer's directions and process for 10 minutes (for either size jar) in a boiling-water bath (page 325). Cool, label, and store the jars. Let the chutney mellow for at least 3 weeks before serving it.

**SEASON:
Midsummer
through October**

**YIELD:
About 8 cups**

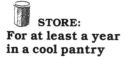

**STORE:
For at least a year
in a cool pantry**

Green Tomato & Apple Chutney

Pick or purchase totally green tomatoes for this spicy condiment; they should not be tinged with white, yellow, or pink. If they do show color other than jade-green, let them ripen peaceably for table use, choosing a ripening spot out of the sun; such tomatoes are past the correct stage for making chutney, but they'll become eligible for salad in time.

In early autumn, with frost in the offing, tomato vines are loaded with more green fruit than gardeners know what to do with. You can solve the problem by making, besides chutney, some Sweet Pickled Green Tomato Slices (page 104), which can be extra-crisp (the recipe tells how). More of the crop might be transformed into spicy, fruity Green Tomato, Apple, & Pear Mincemeat (page 304), a palate-teaser made without the meat or suet used in heavier versions.

3 pounds completely green tomatoes
2 pounds firm, tart apples
2 cups raisins, either dark or golden

1½ cups diced onions

2 teaspoons finely minced garlic

2 cups (packed) light brown sugar

1 cup granulated sugar

2 teaspoons pickling or other fine non-iodized salt

1½ cups cider vinegar, plus a little more if needed

3 to 4 tablespoons finely minced fresh ginger, to taste

1½ tablespoons mustard seed

2 teaspoons ground coriander

1 teaspoon ground cinnamon

1 teaspoon finely minced fresh hot red pepper, ½ teaspoon dried red pepper flakes, or ¼ teaspoon (or to taste) ground hot red (Cayenne) pepper

1. Rinse and drain the tomatoes. Cut out the stem scars and any blemishes and cut the tomatoes into ½-inch chunks. You should have about 8 cups. Place the tomatoes in a preserving pan.

2. Peel, core, and cut the apples into ½-inch chunks; add them to the tomatoes. Add the raisins, onion, garlic, brown and granulated sugar, salt, and vinegar. Mix the ingredients well and bring the mixture to a boil over medium-high heat. Reduce the heat and boil the mixture slowly, uncovered, stirring it often, for 30 minutes.

3. Add the ginger, mustard seed, coriander, cinnamon, and hot pepper. Return to a boil, adjust the heat, and continue to cook the chutney uncovered at a slow boil, stirring it often, until it holds a mounded shape when lifted in a spoon. Taste it carefully, remembering that the balance of flavors will improve as the chutney mellows in the jar; add, if needed, more vinegar, sugar, and/or salt. If more hotness is wanted— unlikely, as this is a peppy compound—add ground hot red (Cayenne) pepper judiciously.

4. Ladle the boiling-hot chutney into hot, clean pint or half-pint canning jars, leaving ¼ inch of headspace. Seal the jars with new two-piece canning lids according to manufacturer's directions and process for 10 minutes (for either size jar) in a boiling-water bath (page 325). Cool, label, and store the jars. Let the chutney mellow for a few weeks before serving it with a curry, cold meat, or any other dish needing an uplifting accompaniment.

A KINDNESS OF KETCHUPS

The "kindness" here, besides being a good name for a collection of unusual versions of a favorite condiment, lies in relieving creative cooks of the need to restrict ketchup making to the product of the delectable but ubiquitous tomato.

Ketchups, we learn from food history, probably began long ago with the fermented fish-based sauces of the Far East that are still going strong in many cuisines (think of *nuoc mam*). It was fairly late in the day that the ancient Romans developed the Mediterranean versions of such sauces, notably *garum,* a preparation that sounds odd, perhaps even disgusting; but it probably was no more icky than our modern anchovy sauces and pastes, which may (who knows?) sound a lot less than appetizing a few centuries down the culinary road.

Passing up a number of ketchups that can only be made from impossible-to-find ingredients like unripe walnuts, we proceed to four distinguished sauces with roots in the kingdoms of vegetables, fruits, and fungi.

 **SEASON:**
All year, but mushrooms are most abundant from late fall to spring

 YIELD:
4 cups

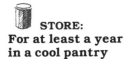 **STORE:**
For at least a year in a cool pantry

Mushroom Ketchup

Culinary history records many delectable-sounding condiments based on mushrooms. Some are liquid essences; others are similar in consistency to thick table sauces and are, like other preparations based on raw material ranging from tomatoes to oysters, called "ketchups" or "catsups." Here is one such, an asset to keep on hand.

Most of the old ketchup formulas were created for wild mushrooms, which are now mostly beyond reach, at least in the quantities required for a decent-sized batch of sauce. Therefore I worked out this recipe for cultivated mushrooms, whose flavor unfortunately doesn't come up to their looks, plus a flavorful "kick" supplied by dried boletus mushrooms. These peerless dried fungi, almost always imported, are stocked by specialty food stores; they may be labeled cèpes secs, funghi secchi porcini, boletus, boletes, Steinpilze, or sometimes, just "dried mushrooms." If the last is the only designation on the label, try to make sure you're getting boletus mushrooms (boletes)—lesser sorts are also sold in dried form. (The undersurface of boletus pieces show a layer of pores, not gills like those of the familiar cultivated mushrooms.)

Enjoy this condiment with steaks, lamb chops, the lowly hamburger, and seafood. It's also a good seasoning for gravies, savory sauces, and hearty salad dressings.

1½ pounds firm, fresh cultivated mushrooms, preferably with unopened caps

1½ tablespoons pickling or other fine non-iodized salt (increase by 1 teaspoon if coarse salt, such as kosher salt, is used)

1 ounce dried boletus mushrooms (cèpes, porcini, etc.)

3 cups hot tap water

2 cups white wine vinegar or distilled white vinegar

3 large shallots, peeled, or 1 small onion, peeled

1 clove garlic, peeled

10 whole allspice or ¼ teaspoon ground allspice

4 whole cloves

3 large blades mace

2 bay leaves

½ teaspoon ground ginger

½ teaspoon freshly ground pepper

¼ cup medium or dry sherry

1. Wipe the mushrooms clean with a damp cloth, or brush them clean. Avoid washing them if possible; if it is necessary, swish them rapidly through a bowl of water and lift and drain them promptly. Trim off any discolored stem ends or damaged portions. Slice the mushrooms thin (a food processor fitted with the thin-slicing disc makes short work of this task) and mix them thoroughly with the salt in a ceramic bowl. Cover the mushrooms with a cloth and let them stand 24 hours, stirring them occasionally. They will become very dark (the finished ketchup will be approximately the color of black bean soup).

2. At least an hour before the end of the salting period, combine the dried boletus mushrooms with the hot tap water; let them stand, covered, until completely soft.

3. Lift the soaked mushrooms from their liquid with a slotted spoon (this is to eliminate any grit that may be in the liquid) and place them in the container of a blender or food processor. Let the soaking liquid settle for a minute or two, then carefully pour it over the mushrooms, stopping before any grit is poured out. Puree the soaked mushrooms, then pour the puree into a preserving pan. Without rinsing the blender container, puree the salted mushrooms; add this puree to that in the pan.

4. Place about ½ cup of the vinegar in the blender and add the shallots and garlic; process them to a puree. Add this puree to the mixture in the pan, together with the rest of the vinegar, the allspice, cloves, mace, bay leaves, ginger, and pepper. Bring the mixture to boiling over medium-high heat, lower the heat, and simmer the ketchup, uncovered, stirring it often, for 1 to 1½ hours, or until the tiny fragments of mushroom are very soft, almost jellylike, and the ketchup is thick. To test for correct consistency, pour a spoonful onto a saucer and let it

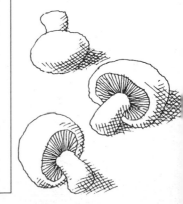

stand 10 minutes, with the pot off the heat; if very little or no liquid seeps from the solids, the ketchup has thickened enough. If it does not pass this test, resume the cooking for as long as necessary.

5. Press the ketchup through a sieve to remove the bay leaves and whole spices, then puree it again, in batches if necessary, in a blender or food processor, running the machine until the texture is velvety smooth.

6. Return the ketchup to the rinsed-out pan and bring it to a full boil again over medium-high heat, stirring it constantly. Stir in the sherry.

7. Ladle the boiling-hot ketchup into hot, clean half-pint or pint canning jars, leaving ¼ inch of headspace. Seal the jars with new two-piece canning lids according to manufacturer's directions and process for 15 minutes (for either size jar) in a boiling-water bath (page 325). Cool, label, and store the jars. Let the ketchup mellow for a few weeks before serving it.

 SEASON:
Any time

 YIELD:
About 7 cups

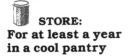 **STORE:**
For at least a year in a cool pantry

Hot & Spicy Banana Ketchup

Piquant, smooth, and red-brown, this Caribbean-spiced, rum-touched condiment has a fruit base that makes it highly compatible with roast pork or poultry, as well as hamburgers or cold meats or any other nibble that would benefit from a touch of the tropics.

For this ketchup, choose completely ripe but not mushy bananas, with well-freckled skins and decided fragrance. The spicing in the recipe produces moderately hot ketchup; for more zip, the ground hot red pepper can be increased. (However, I'd taste a cooled sample before adding more red pepper; a well-balanced flavor will let the fruitiness emerge.)

If fresh hot red peppers are available, they can be substituted for the ground hot red pepper. Use 3 or 4 peppers about 4 inches long, cored, seeded, and pureed with the other ingredients in step 1.

1 cup raisins, either dark or golden

¾ cup coarsely chopped onions

3 to 4 large cloves garlic, peeled

⅔ cup (6-ounce can) tomato paste

2⅔ cups distilled white vinegar or cider vinegar

3 pounds (about 8 large) very ripe, fragrant bananas

4 to 6 cups water

1 cup (packed) brown sugar

1 tablespoon salt

1 teaspoon ground hot red (Cayenne) pepper

½ cup light corn syrup

4 teaspoons ground allspice

1½ teaspoons ground cinnamon

1½ teaspoons freshly grated nutmeg

1 teaspoon freshly ground black pepper

½ teaspoon ground cloves

¼ to ⅓ cup dark rum, preferably Jamaican

1. Combine the raisins, onions, garlic, and tomato paste in the container of a blender (which does the best job of pureeing) or a food processor and puree them until smooth, adding some of the vinegar, as necessary, to help the job along. Scrape the puree into a preserving pan.

2. Peel the bananas, cut them into chunks, and puree them in turn, adding some vinegar to help. Add the puree to the mixture in the pan. Add the remaining vinegar, 4 cups of the water, the brown sugar, salt, and ground hot red pepper.

3. Bring the mixture to a boil over medium-high heat, stirring it frequently. Lower the heat to medium-low and cook the ketchup, uncovered, for 1¼ hours, stirring it often. If there is a threat of sticking at any point, add some of the remaining water as needed, up to 2 cups.

4. Add the corn syrup, allspice, cinnamon, nutmeg, black pepper, and cloves. Continue to cook the ketchup, stirring frequently, for 15 minutes longer, or until it is thick enough to coat a metal spoon. To test its consistency further, remove the pan from the heat, spoon a little ketchup onto a saucer, and let it cool; if very little or no liquid emerges around the dollop, the ketchup has thickened enough. If it does not pass this test, resume the cooking for as long as necessary. Let the potful of ketchup cool for a few minutes.

5. Puree the ketchup again in the blender or food processor until it is satin-smooth, or force it through a fine-meshed sieve. Rinse out the preserving pan and return the ketchup to it. Taste it for hotness and sharpness and add more red or black pepper, or more vinegar, or more sugar, if any or all seem to be needed. Be cautious about adding more of the aromatic spices because their flavors will become more pronounced later, and they shouldn't dominate the fruit.

6. Bring the ketchup to a boil again over medium heat, stirring constantly. Add the rum. Remove pan from heat.

7. Ladle the boiling-hot ketchup into hot, clean half-pint or pint canning jars, leaving ¼ inch of headspace. Seal the jars with new two-piece canning lids according to manufacturer's directions and process (15 minutes for half-pints, 20 minutes for pints) in a boiling-water bath (page 325). Cool, label, and store the jars. The ketchup will be ready to serve after 2 weeks, but it continues to improve in the jar for a month or so.

OTHER USES:

Beat a little banana ketchup into the butter for what would otherwise be a bland cheese or chicken sandwich, or stir a spoonful into mayonnaise to make a spicy but subtle dressing for cabbage slaw or fruit salad. The ketchup is also dandy in dressing for chicken salad.

SEASON:
October

YIELD:
About 5 cups

STORE:
For at least a year
in a cool pantry

Concord Grape Ketchup

Concord grapes, which are the descendants of a native grape discovered long ago in Massachusetts, have their brief season in October. Blue-black and dizzyingly fragrant, Concords are the starting point for many good things.

They are wonderful to eat as is, and they make fine pies. Jam, jelly, grape butter, and grape juice are preserve-shelf classics, but what we're thinking about here is a ketchup made of Concords. Lightly spiced and sweet-tart, it is a keen relish for turkey, goose, duck, chicken, ham, or pork chops.

You can use wild grapes instead of Concords for this ketchup if they are of good flavor; some are too bland to be of much interest, so taste before you go in for picking a quantity. Besides Concords, some other cultivated grapes that are also descended from native species have the distinctive "foxiness" or wild flavor; among them are Delawares and Catawbas, both good for this ketchup.

This recipe makes a small batch, in recognition of the reality that Concords are seldom available in great abundance. It can be doubled satisfactorily.

2½ pounds fully ripe Concord grapes, stemmed, rinsed, and drained

1 quart water

1½ cups (packed) dark brown sugar

1¾ cups granulated sugar

2½ cups cider vinegar

2½ teaspoons ground cinnamon

2 teaspoons salt

1½ teaspoons ground ginger

1 teaspoon ground allspice

½ teaspoon ground cloves

¼ teaspoon freshly ground black pepper

1. Combine the grapes and water in a large saucepan or preserving pan and bring them slowly to a boil over medium heat. Lower the heat and simmer the grapes, partly covered, until the skins are tender, about 15 minutes.

2. Press the mixture through a medium sieve or a food mill fitted with the medium disc; discard the seedy debris. Strain the pulp again, this time through a fine-meshed sieve. You should have about 6 cups.

3. Combine the pulp with the brown sugar, granulated sugar, vinegar, cinnamon, salt, ginger, allspice, cloves, and black pepper in a preserving pan. Bring the mixture to a boil,

KETCHUP CONSISTENCY:

Sometimes the ketchup may unexpectedly thicken too much, as the pectin content of grapes varies. If the ketchup jells on the saucer, thin the potful judiciously with up to ½ cup of water. Return the ketchup to boiling before ladling it into jars.

stirring, then reduce the heat and cook the ketchup uncovered, stirring it often, about 45 minutes, or until it has thickened. To test, remove the pan from the heat and chill a small amount of ketchup on a chilled saucer; it is thick enough if a track remains when a fingertip is drawn through the sample.

4. Reheat the ketchup to boiling and ladle into hot, clean half-pint or pint canning jars, leaving ¼ inch of headspace. Seal the jars with new two-piece canning lids according to manufacturer's directions and process for 15 minutes (for either size jar) in a boiling-water bath (page 325). Cool, label, and store the jars.

Cranberry Ketchup

This quickly made relish goes well with all the foods traditionally complemented by cranberries—a list not limited to poultry—and with others besides; because it is less sweet than conventional cranberry sauces, it is more versatile.

Try this in place of its ubiquitous tomato cousin with hamburgers or pork roast or chops, and serve it with baked beans. A little adds zest to the dressing for fruit salads, too. I serve it, in addition to the traditional sauce, at Thanksgiving.

1½ cups chopped mild onions

4 cups water

4 strips orange zest (outer peel only, no white pith), 1 inch wide, cut from top to bottom of orange

8 cups cranberries, fresh or frozen (thawed)

1 cup cider vinegar

1 cup (packed) light brown sugar, or more if needed

1 cup light corn syrup

1½ teaspoons salt

1½ teaspoons ground cinnamon

1½ teaspoons ground allspice

1 teaspoon ground ginger

¼ teaspoon ground cloves

1. Combine the onions with the water and orange zest in a preserving pan. Bring to a boil and simmer, covered, until the onion pieces are translucent, about 10 minutes.

2. Meanwhile, pick over and rinse the cranberries if fresh ones are used; frozen berries need only be thawed. Add the cranberries to the onions and orange zest. Return the pan to the heat and bring the mixture to a boil; partially cover the

SEASON:
October to late winter

YIELD:
About 6 cups

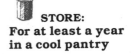
STORE:
For at least a year in a cool pantry

mixture and cook it, stirring it occasionally, until the berries have become quite soft, about 10 minutes. Empty into a bowl and cool slightly.

3. Scrape about half of the mixture into the bowl of a food processor or a smaller amount into the container of a blender and puree it to a moderately fine texture. Return the puree to the rinsed-out preserving pan. Puree the remaining mixture and add it to the puree in the pan. (A food mill fitted with a fine disc will also do this job.)

4. Add the vinegar, 1 cup of brown sugar, the corn syrup, salt, cinnamon, allspice, ginger, and cloves. Bring the ketchup to a boil over medium-high heat and boil it, stirring almost constantly, until it is thick, 3 to 5 minutes. It will usually be obvious when the mixture is thick enough (or even a bit inclined to become a jelly). However, if you are uncertain, test the consistency by removing the pan from the heat and spooning a little ketchup onto a chilled saucer. Set it in the freezer or refrigerator until it is cold. If a track remains when a fingertip is drawn through the sample, the ketchup is done.

5. If the ketchup is too thick—which can happen with some batches of cranberries—thin it with a little extra vinegar and water, half and half. Taste the ketchup and add more sugar and/or salt if desired. Press the ketchup through a fine-meshed sieve.

6. Reheat the ketchup to boiling and ladle it into hot, clean half-pint or pint canning jars, leaving ¼ inch of headspace. Seal the jars with new two-piece canning lids according to manufacturer's directions and process for 15 minutes (for either size jar) in a boiling-water bath (page 325). Cool, label, and store the jars. The ketchup will be ready to serve in a few days, but it continues to mellow for a few weeks.

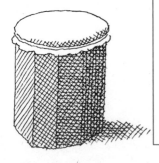

RELISHES

That zestful word says it all. This section is a big bag of goodies, ranging from the homey (Southern-style red-pepper "jam," or a crunchy corn relish) to the slightly highfalutin' (Purple Basil & Orange Jelly, Red Rosemary Jelly, Spiced Whole Blueberries in a Red-Wine Pickle). There is also a lot in between. The best idea is to leaf through the recipes for relishes made with your favorite fixings.

Sweet & Hot Red Pepper & Onion Relish

Like Hot & Sweet Red Pepper Jam (page 71), this chunky, glowing relish is made with both ripe sweet red peppers and equally ripe, though incendiary, hot red peppers. The proportions given below yield a mild result; feel free to tip the balance more toward the hot side if you are sure you have a sufficiently tolerant palate. Just make sure you are using 7½ to 8 cups of peppers in all.

This is great stuff with a hamburger, or with steak, or pot roast, or almost any bean dish.

7 cups chopped (medium-coarse) cored and seeded sweet red peppers

½ to 1 cup (to taste) finely chopped cored, deribbed, and seeded hot red peppers

2 tablespoons salt

2 cups finely diced onions

4 cups cider vinegar

3 cups sugar

2 cups light corn syrup

1. Combine the sweet and hot peppers and the salt in a pottery or stainless-steel bowl; mix them well and let them stand 3 hours.

2. Scrape the peppers and their liquid into a preserving pan. Add the onions, vinegar, sugar, and corn syrup. Bring the mixture to a boil over medium-high heat. Adjust the heat and cook the potful, uncovered, at a moderate boil, stirring it often, until the peppers and onions are translucent and the syrup is thick, about 45 minutes.

 SEASON:
Late summer and early fall

 YIELD:
7 cups

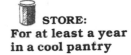 **STORE:**
For at least a year in a cool pantry

3. Ladle the hot relish into hot, clean half-pint canning jars, leaving ¼ inch of headspace. Seal the jars with new two-piece canning lids according to manufacturer's directions and process for 10 minutes in a boiling-water bath (page 325). Cool, label, and store the jars. Let the relish mellow for a few weeks, if possible, before serving it.

SEASON:
Late summer
through fall

YIELD:
3 to 4 cups

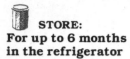

STORE:
For up to 6 months
in the refrigerator

Escoffier's Condiment of Sweet Peppers

Adapted from Escoffier's various formulas for a pepper relish, this recipe makes a commendable condiment that is absolutely delicious with cold meats—beef, pork, ham, lamb, or poultry.

The principal point of difference between this version and the several Escoffier sources is a reduction in the amounts of oil, sugar, and spices. Escoffier evidently made this, which he called a "pickle," whenever it was wanted; but I've found that it keeps for many months under refrigeration, becoming ever more suave.

½ cup fine-quality olive oil

1⅔ cups chopped onions

1½ to 1¾ pounds sweet red peppers

1½ cups red wine vinegar

1½ pounds ripe Italian-type (plum) tomatoes

1 to 1½ cups sugar, to taste

1 cup golden raisins

2 medium to large cloves garlic, minced

1 teaspoon finely minced fresh ginger or ¼ teaspoon
    ground ginger

½ teaspoon salt

⅛ teaspoon freshly ground pepper

¼ teaspoon ground allspice

2 small dried hot red peppers, optional

1. Measure the olive oil into a large heavy saucepan; add the onions and cook them over medium-low heat, stirring often, until the onion bits are golden, about 10 minutes.

2. Meanwhile, blanch the sweet red peppers in boiling water for 3 minutes, then plunge them into cold water to cool. Strip the skins from the peppers, quarter, core, and seed them, then slice the quarters crosswise into ¼-inch strips; you

should have about 2 cups, packed.

3. Add the pepper strips to the onions. Stir, cover, and cook the mixture over low heat for 10 minutes. Add the vinegar and boil the mixture, uncovered, until it has reduced by about half.

4. While the pepper mixture cooks, scald the tomatoes in boiling water for about 30 seconds, then plunge them into cold water. Strip off the skins, cut up the tomatoes, puree them in a food processor, then force the puree through a sieve or food mill. (Alternatively, chop the tomatoes, then force them through the food mill, which will take a little longer to do.) Measure 2 cups of the puree; reserve surplus for another use.

5. Add the tomatoes to the pepper mixture; add 1 cup of the sugar and the raisins, garlic, ginger, salt, pepper, allspice, and dried red peppers. Cover and cook over low heat until thick, about 1½ hours, stirring occasionally and uncovering toward the end. Taste; adjust the seasonings, adding more of the sugar if you like. Remove and discard the dried red peppers.

6. Ladle the condiment into hot, clean glass canning or storage jars. Let the relish cool, then cover tightly and store in the refrigerator.

Hot & Sweet Red Pepper Jam

Increase the fieriness of this piquant jellied relish by upping the proportion of hot peppers to suit yourself—just be sure to keep the total quantity of all peppers the same—or hot it up by adding drops of Tabasco or other bottled pepper sauce. Caution in changing pepper proportions is advised, however, if you're not sure just how incendiary your raw material may be; it's wisest to start out on the mild side if you're uncertain. That would mean using only 1 to 2 tablespoons of chopped hot stuff instead of the ¼ cup prescribed below. If you'd like a completely mild red pepper jam, omit the hot peppers and increase the sweet red peppers by ¼ cup.

People who are fond of red pepper jam (often called "jelly") don't need advice about how to serve it: it is something of a classic in the South, and it has clambered onto fancy-food shelves all over the country. For newcomers to its delights, the best advice is to serve it on the side with roast meats or poultry, or with crisp crackers spread with cream cheese, or in tiny cream-cheese pastry shells as an accompaniment for drinks.

 SEASON:
Late summer and early fall

 YIELD:
About 7 cups

 STORE:
For at least a year in a cool pantry

2 cups coarsely chopped seeded and deribbed sweet red peppers

¼ cup coarsely chopped seeded and deribbed fresh hot red peppers or chopped canned whole jalapeño peppers

1½ cups cider vinegar

1 teaspoon salt

6½ cups sugar

1 bottle (or 2 pouches) liquid pectin (6 ounces total)

Hot pepper sauce (Tabasco or other), optional

1. In two or more batches, chop the sweet and hot peppers to a fine texture (or a very coarse puree) in a blender or food processor, using some of the vinegar as liquid. Scrape the peppers into a preserving pan. Add the remaining vinegar and the salt.

2. Bring the mixture to a boil over medium heat; lower the heat and simmer it, uncovered, stirring occasionally, for 5 minutes. Remove from heat. Measure the mixture and return 3 cups to the pan. If you should have less than 3 cups, add water to make up the difference. Stir in the sugar.

3. Bring the mixture to a full rolling boil (a boil that cannot be stirred down) over high heat, stirring constantly, and boil it for 1 minute. Remove from heat.

4. Add the pectin, mixing well. Taste the jam mixture for hotness and add drops of hot pepper sauce, if desired. Skim off any foam. Cool the jam for 3 minutes, stirring it occasionally to prevent pepper bits from floating to the top.

5. Ladle the jam into hot, sterilized (page 327) half-pint canning jars, leaving ¼ inch of headspace. Seal the jars with sterilized new two-piece lids according to manufacturer's directions. Cool, label, and store the jars.

 SEASON:
Mid- to late summer

 YIELD:
About 7 cups

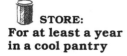 **STORE:**
For at least a year in a cool pantry

Wimpy's Delight (A Hamburger Relish)

Here's all the helper a hamburger sandwich needs, if it has been made with excellent meat and a bun of real substance and character.

Wimpy, for anyone who did not grow up with "Thimble Theatre," the comic strip starring the immortal Popeye, was the panhandling fellow with an inextinguishable passion for hamburgers.

1 quart cider vinegar

2 sticks (2 to 3 inches each) cinnamon, broken up

2 teaspoons whole cloves, slightly bruised

2 teaspoons whole allspice, bruised

4 cups coarsely chopped peeled and seeded tomatoes

2 cups sugar

4 teaspoons mustard seed

¼ teaspoon ground hot red (Cayenne) pepper

4 cups chopped unpeeled firm cucumbers (do not use waxed cucumbers)

1½ cups chopped cored and seeded sweet red peppers

1½ cups chopped cored and seeded sweet green peppers

1 cup chopped celery

1 cup chopped onions

1½ tablespoons turmeric

½ cup pickling or other fine non-iodized salt

2 quarts water

1. Combine the vinegar with the cinnamon, cloves, and allspice, all tied loosely in a square of cheesecloth, in a preserving pan. Bring the vinegar to boiling, adjust the heat, and simmer it, uncovered, 15 minutes. Add the tomatoes, bring the mixture to a boil, then adjust the heat and simmer the mixture, partly covered, until it resembles a puree, about 30 minutes. Add the sugar, mustard seed, and ground hot red pepper. Pour the mixture into a bowl, cool and cover it, and let it stand overnight at room temperature.

2. Meanwhile, combine the cucumbers, red and green peppers, celery, and onion in a ceramic or stainless-steel bowl. Sprinkle the turmeric and salt over the vegetables, then add the water. Stir the mixture, cover it, and let it stand overnight.

3. Drain the liquid from the salted vegetables and replace it with enough fresh cold water to cover them; let the vegetables soak 1 hour, then drain them in a colander, pressing lightly.

4. Return the vinegar and tomato mixture to the preserving pan and bring it to a boil over medium-high heat. Add the drained vegetables, then return the relish to a full boil, stirring frequently, and cook it, uncovered, over high heat, stirring occasionally, for 5 minutes. Remove the relish from the heat.

5. Remove the spice bag from the relish; squeeze all possible liquid from the bag into the pot, then discard the bag.

6. Ladle the boiling-hot relish into hot, clean half-pint or pint canning jars, leaving ¼ inch of headspace. Seal the jars with new two-piece canning lids according to manufacturer's directions and process for 10 minutes (for either size jar) in a boiling-water bath (page 325). Cool, label, and store the jars. Let the relish mellow and develop flavor for at least 3 weeks.

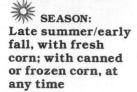

SEASON:
Late summer/early fall, with fresh corn; with canned or frozen corn, at any time

YIELD:
About 5 pints

STORE:
For at least a year in a cool pantry

Corn Relish with Sweet Red & Green Peppers

Fortunately this crunchy specialty, which has a way of being eaten up fast at our house, can be prepared from frozen corn or vacuum-packed whole-grain yellow corn quite as well as from fresh-picked ears. This makes it possible to resupply the shelf whenever sweet red and/or green peppers, the other chief ingredient, are available, which is most of the year.

This is a recipe that can be doubled without loss of quality.

6 cups cooked golden corn kernels*

2 cups diced onions

1 cup chopped cored and seeded sweet red peppers

1 cup chopped cored and seeded sweet green peppers (or use an additional cupful of sweet red peppers)

¾ cup chopped celery

1½ cups (packed) light brown sugar

2 tablespoons pickling salt or other fine non-iodized salt

2 tablespoons (lightly packed) dry mustard

2 teaspoons mustard seed

2 teaspons turmeric

1½ teaspoons celery seed

¼ teaspoon ground hot red (Cayenne) pepper

2½ cups cider vinegar

½ cup water

1. Combine all the ingredients in a preserving pan. Bring the mixture to a boil over medium-high heat, stirring occasionally. Lower the heat and simmer the mixture, partly covered, until it has thickened slightly, about 30 minutes; stir occasionally.

2. Ladle the boiling-hot relish into hot, clean pint canning jars, leaving ¼ inch of headspace. Seal the jars with new two-piece canning lids according to manufacturer's directions and process for 15 minutes in a boiling-water bath (page 325). Cool, label, and store the jars. Let the relish mellow for a few weeks before serving it.

*FRESH CORN:

For 6 cups of corn, cook 10 to 12 ears of fresh golden corn in boiling water for 5 minutes, cool them under the tap, and cut the kernels from the cobs. Leftover corn on the cob can be used in whole or in part.

Country-Style Chili Sauce with Hot Peppers

Adjust the seasoning of this hotted-up version of classic American chili sauce according to your taste. Use even more hot peppers if you'd like a condiment of real authority; or, for a mild sauce, omit the hot peppers, or add just a dash of ground hot red (Cayenne) pepper to the finished potful.

If you are using tomatoes of the slicing type, which have more seeds and juice than Italian or paste tomatoes, cut them crosswise after skinning and squeeze out most of the seeds and their surrounding watery pulp, then chop them. If sweet green (bell) peppers are what you have, they can replace the red ones; the sauce will not be the same vivid red, however, nor will the flavor be quite the same.

This recipe can be doubled, if you have a really large pot; the final cooking time will be slightly longer for a double batch.

2 quarts skinned, cored, and coarsely chopped ripe Italian-type (plum) tomatoes (about 4 pounds)

2 cups finely chopped seeded, cored and deribbed sweet red peppers

1½ cups finely chopped onions

1 large rib celery, finely chopped (about ½ cup)

1 fresh long hot red pepper* (about 5 inches), stemmed, seeded, deribbed, and very finely chopped, optional

1 large clove garlic, peeled and minced

1½ cups cider vinegar

2 tablespoons pickling salt or other fine non-iodized salt, or 2½ tablespoons coarse (kosher) salt

½ cup (packed) light brown or granulated sugar

¼ cup light corn syrup

¾ teaspoon ground cloves

¾ to 1 teaspoon ground cinnamon

1½ teaspoons mustard seed

Ground hot red (Cayenne) pepper or hot pepper sauce (such as Tabasco), optional

1. Combine the tomatoes, sweet peppers, onions, celery, hot pepper, garlic, vinegar, salt, sugar, and corn syrup in a preserving pan. Bring the mixture to a boil, stirring occasionally, then lower the heat and simmer it briskly, uncovered, for 1 hour. Stir it occasionally.

☀ **SEASON:**
Late summer into early fall

🥤 **YIELD:**
About 6 to 7 cups

🥫 **STORE:**
For at least a year in a cool pantry

*HOT PEPPERS:

For precautions when handling hot peppers see page 321.

2. Stir in the cloves, cinnamon, and mustard seed. Continue to cook the sauce, stirring occasionally, until it has thickened enough to release scarcely any thin liquid when a spoonful is placed on a plate and tilted; final cooking should take from 1 to 1½ hours. Taste the sauce and add, if desired, a little more vinegar or sweetening or salt; if you would like a hotter sauce, add a little ground hot red pepper or a few drops of Tabasco or other hot pepper sauce. If the chili sauce is too thin after the seasonings are adjusted, cook it a little longer.

3. Ladle the boiling-hot sauce into hot, clean pint or half-pint canning jars, leaving ¼ inch of headspace. Seal the jars with new two-piece canning lids according to manufacturer's directions and process for 15 minutes (for either size jar) in a boiling-water bath (page 325). Cool, label, and store the jars. Let the chili sauce mellow for about a month before serving it.

Blueberry Relish

Only lightly spiced and gently tart, this unusual whole-berry relish is a good plate mate for chicken, duck, turkey, ham, tongue, or roast pork. Serve it, too, with a snack of fresh, soft cheese and crisp crackers.

Because the berries are cooked only a short time, the relish has the consistency of a preserve, not a jam. I make this with cultivated blueberries; the delicate flavor of wild ones would be lost in the spicy relish, so I reserve them for Wild Blueberry Jam (page 123).

3 cups sugar

1½ cups water

3 pint baskets (about 9 cups) firm-ripe cultivated blueberries, picked over, rinsed, drained

1½ cups cider vinegar

Zest (outer peel only, no white pith) of 2 oranges, cut into ¾-inch-wide strips

3 sticks (2 inches each) cinnamon, coarsely broken

1½ teaspoons whole allspice

1 teaspoon whole coriander seed

½ teaspoon whole cloves

1. Combine the sugar and 1½ cups water in a preserving pan. Heat over medium heat to boiling; boil 1 minute. Add the blueberries and return the mixture to a boil. Reduce the heat to medium-low and cook the mixture, uncovered, at a hard simmer just until the berries are broken, about 5 minutes. Remove from the heat.

2. Pour the berries into a sieve set over a bowl and drain

❄ SEASON:
Mid- to late summer, but can be made at any season with frozen unsweetened blueberries

🥤 YIELD:
6 cups

🥫 STORE:
Sealed, for at least a year in a cool pantry; unsealed, for up to 3 months in the refrigerator

off the syrup. Set the berries aside; return the syrup to the preserving pan.

3. Add the vinegar, orange zest, cinnamon, allspice, coriander, and cloves to the syrup and heat it to boiling over medium-high heat. Boil the mixture, uncovered, stirring occasionally, until the syrup registers 220° on a candy-jelly thermometer or passes the jelly test (page 322); this will take 50 to 55 minutes, after which the syrup will be reduced by about half. Remove from heat.

4. Strain the spices from the syrup and discard them; return the syrup to the pan. Add the berries and any juices that have accumulated in the bowl and heat the mixture over medium-high heat to boiling. Reduce the heat to medium and boil the relish gently until the berries are boiling hot throughout and the syrup again registers 220° or passes the jelly test, 3 to 5 minutes.

5. Ladle the boiling-hot relish into hot, clean pint or half-pint canning jars, leaving ¼ inch of headspace. Seal with new two-piece canning lids according to manufacturer's directions and process for 15 minutes (for either size jar) in a boiling-water bath (page 325). Cool, label, and store the jars.

6. Alternatively, ladle all or part of the relish into suitable containers and store, covered, in the refrigerator for up to 3 months.

Spiced Whole Blueberries in a Red-Wine Pickle

The fragile texture of blueberries is preserved by the brief cooking of this relish. Spoon the sweet-tart berries alongside baked beans for a delicious change of plate partners; or offer them with roasted or broiled chicken, or with ham or smoked turkey, or with the hearty kind of salad plate that makes a meal. They are also good with bacon and eggs for brunch.

1½ cups red wine vinegar, cider vinegar, or distilled white vinegar

3 sticks (about 2½ inches each) whole cinnamon

1 teaspoon ground coriander

¼ teaspoon ground cloves

2½ pint baskets (about 8 cups) firm-ripe cultivated blueberries, picked over, rinsed, drained

2 cups sugar

SEASON:
Mid- to late summer

YIELD:
3 pint jars

STORE:
For up to a year in cool pantry

1. Combine the vinegar, cinnamon sticks, coriander, and cloves in a preserving pan. Heat the mixture to simmering over low heat, cover, and let it simmer 5 minutes. Add the blueberries and heat them slowly, shaking the pan (don't stir the berries) until they are steaming hot through, about 8 minutes; do not let them boil. Remove the pan from the heat and let the mixture cool for 10 minutes.

2. Pour the blueberries and juice into a large colander set over a bowl and drain off the liquid. Divide the berries equally among three hot, sterilized pint canning jars, placing one of the cinnamon sticks in each.

3. Return the juice to the pan and add the sugar. Bring the mixture to a boil, stirring it until the sugar has dissolved, and boil it briskly for 3 minutes. Fill the jars with the boiling-hot syrup, leaving ¼ inch of headspace. Remove any air bubbles (page 324). Seal the jars with sterilized new two-piece canning lids according to manufacturer's directions. Cool, label, and store the jars. The pickled blueberries should mellow in the jars for several weeks before they are served.

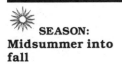 **SEASON:**
Midsummer into fall

 YIELD:
About 4 cups

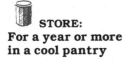 **STORE:**
For a year or more in a cool pantry

Fresh Herb Jellies (Basil, Tarragon, or Mint)

A little farther along there will be recipes for innovative jellies made with such herbal materials as coriander seed, fresh ginger, ornamental purple basil, fresh rosemary plus cranberries, and a combination of thyme, sweet marjoram, and a bay leaf. Here, for those who would like to try savory jellies made with commoner herbs, is a formula suitable for green-leaved (sweet) basil, tarragon, or mint. If you have a clump of sage (a kitchen-garden variety, not an ornamental) and want to try sage jelly with roast pork or chicken, this recipe will serve as a guide; but be warned that sage jelly is perhaps an acquired taste.

The color of these jellies will be pale yellow (basil) to yellow-green (mint), rather than a pretty (and improbable) green like that of commercial mint jelly; you may want to include a tiny drop or two of green food coloring—no more— but I don't mind the natural tints, and I'm generally in favor of avoiding colorings, however harmless they may be. (Green colorings, so far, have escaped censure as evil additives.)

Most herb jellies are at their best as a relish with meat, but basil and tarragon jellies, both delicate, almost honeyed, in flavor, are scrumptious spreads for toast or hot breads. Further, I think mint jelly is better on toast or a muffin, especially if the breadstuff has been spread with cream cheese, than it is alongside roast lamb, its hackneyed dinner-plate companion.

1¾ to 2 cups (packed) washed and drained leaves and tender stems of freshly picked green-leaved basil, tarragon, or mint (preferably peppermint, although spearmint is satisfactory)

2 cups water

3 tablespoons strained fresh lemon or lime juice or mild white vinegar, such as white wine vinegar or Oriental rice vinegar; or, with tarragon, use tarragon-flavored wine vinegar if you have it

3¾ cups sugar

1 pouch (3 ounces) or one-half 6-ounce bottle liquid pectin

A drop or two of green food coloring, optional

1. Place the herb you have chosen in a blender or food processor with the water. Run the machine to chop the herb briefly—be careful to avoid making a pulp, which can result in cloudy jelly. Scrape the mixture into a large saucepan (3 quarts or larger) and heat the mixture just to the boiling point over medium heat, stirring it once or twice. Remove the pan from the heat, cover it, and let the herb infuse for 15 minutes.

2. Pour the mixture into a very fine sieve set over a bowl (or use an ordinary sieve lined with one or two layers of dampened cheesecloth) and drain off the infusion, pressing on the herb pieces; discard the debris. Measure 1¾ cups of the herb infusion into the rinsed-out saucepan.

3. Stir in the lemon juice or vinegar and sugar and bring the mixture to a boil over high heat, stirring it often until the sugar has dissolved. When it reaches a full rolling boil (a boil that can't be stirred down), stir in the pectin. When boiling resumes, boil the mixture hard (a full rolling boil) for exactly 1 minute. Remove the pan from the heat.

4. Stir in the green coloring, if you are using it. Skim any foam from the jelly and pour it into hot, sterilized (page 327) jelly glasses or straight-sided half-pint canning jars, leaving ½ inch of headspace in glasses, ⅛ inch in jars. Seal the jelly in glasses with a thin layer of melted paraffin (page 326). Seal canning jars with sterilized new two-piece lids according to manufacturer's directions. Cool, label, and store the jelly. It will be ready to use almost immediately; however, like most other jellies, it will take a few days to reach maximum firmness.

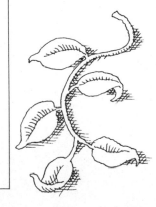

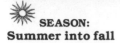 SEASON:
Summer into fall

YIELD:
About 4 cups

STORE:
**For a year or more
in a cool pantry**

Purple Basil & Orange Jelly (A Relish)

Going beyond the basics represented by Fresh Herb Jellies, above, this is a sumptuous, garnet-colored (not purple) sweet-tart jelly made with the choice herb called "purple-leaved basil," plus a touch of orange and clove. This basil, whose chief variety is named 'Dark Opal,' was once grown only by dedicated herb gardeners, but its merits—lovely looks plus especially rich, peppery basil flavor—made it appealing it to market growers, so it can often be found in summer at farm stands and specialty food shops. It is a beautiful plant, its royal-purple foliage crowned with pink blossoms; anyone who has a sunny patch can easily grow it, and its good looks recommend it for inclusion in flower plantings as well as the "eating" garden.

Serve this jelly with cold meats, or with crackers and cream cheese.

1½ cups (packed) washed and drained purple basil leaves, including tender stems and flower buds

Zest (outer peel only, no white pith) of a bright-skinned medium orange, cut off in 1-inch strips

6 whole cloves

1⅔ cups strained fresh orange juice

½ cup red wine vinegar

4 cups sugar

1 pouch (3 ounces) or one-half 6-ounce bottle liquid pectin

1. Chop the basil leaves, or crush them thoroughly in a large saucepan. Twist each strip of orange zest over the basil to extract the oil that will fly out in droplets, then drop each strip of zest into the pan. Add the cloves, orange juice, and red wine vinegar.

2. Set the pan over medium heat and heat the ingredients just to the boiling point, stirring the mixture once or twice. Remove the pan from the heat, cover it, and let it stand at least 15 minutes, better 30 minutes.

3. Pour the mixture into a fine sieve set over a bowl and press on the solids to extract as much flavor as possible. Measure 1¾ cups of the liquid into a preserving pan. Discard the solids.

4. Add the sugar to the liquid and heat the mixture to boiling over medium-high heat. As soon as it reaches a hard boil (a boil that can't be stirred down), stir in the liquid pectin.

When the jelly mixture again reaches a full, hard boil, led it boil, watching the clock, for 1 minute exactly. Remove the jelly from the heat.

5. Skim any foam from the jelly and pour it at once into hot, sterilized (page 327) jelly glasses or half-pint canning jars, leaving ½ inch of headspace in glasses, ⅛ inch in jars. Seal the glasses with melted paraffin (page 326); seal the jars with sterilized new two-piece canning lids according to manufacturer's directions. Cool, label, and store the jars.

Red Rosemary Jelly

Here for the herb gardener to make is a distinguished herbal relish, a jelly created by the abundant pectin in the oranges and cranberries and flavored by resinous, pungent rosemary leaves. The rosemary is not assertive here, but it makes the jelly especially compatible with venison, pork, game birds, or turkey.

If like most home herb growers you have a pot or two of rosemary, which is sensitive to cold weather and must be wintered indoors in most climates, it's worthwhile to postpone the autumn pruning of your plant or plants until fresh cranberries have come to market so you can use some of the fresh leaves to flavor this jelly. Dried rosemary could be substituted by those who don't possess living plants (use about one-half the quantity listed), and cranberries from the freezer will also work well, so there is some seasonal flexibility here.

2 medium oranges

3½ cups water

2 cups cranberries, fresh or frozen and thawed

¼ cup (lightly packed) fresh rosemary leaves (tender tips of the branches may be included)

4 whole cloves

Sugar

1. Wash the oranges and slice them very thin; quarter the slices. Combine the sliced oranges and water in a bowl, cover the bowl, and let it stand at least 8 hours or, if convenient, overnight.

2. Place the mixture of fruit and liquid in a saucepan, bring it to a boil, cover it, and simmer it 15 minutes. Mash the oranges slightly with a spoon or whisk, add the cranberries, rosemary, and cloves, re-cover the pan, and simmer the mélange until the oranges and cranberries are very soft, 15 to 20 minutes.

SEASON:
Fall

YIELD:
About 3 cups

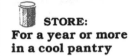
STORE:
For a year or more in a cool pantry

3. Ladle the mixture into a jelly bag (page 322) placed over a large bowl and allow the juice to drip until the pulp yields no more liquid, 2 or 3 hours. When the drip has slowed, it's permissible to press the sides of the bag slightly to encourage the last available drops, but don't squeeze the bag—that might force pulp into the juice and result in cloudy jelly.

4. Measure the juice—there should be 2½ to 3 cups. Place the juice in a preserving pan or large saucepan and heat it to boiling. Stir in 1 cup of sugar for each cup of juice and boil the mixture hard until it passes the jelly test (page 322). Remove the jelly from the heat, skim it if there is any foam or scum, and ladle it at once into hot, sterilized (page 327) jelly glasses or half-pint canning jars, leaving ½ inch of headspace in glasses, ⅛ inch in jars. Seal the glasses with melted paraffin wax (page 000); seal the jars with sterilized new two-piece canning lids according to manufacturer's directions. Cool, label, and store the jars.

**SEASON:
Midsummer into
fall**

**YIELD:
About 4 cups**

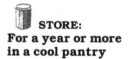

**STORE:
For a year or more
in a cool pantry**

Thyme-Plus-Three Herbal Jelly

This mostly-thyme jelly is a close cousin of the plain Fresh Herb Jellies (above), but its flavor involves, besides thyme, a little sweet marjoram, a bay leaf, and a measure of Tarragon Vinegar (page 197) or Tarragon Preserved in Vinegar (page 207). Its fragrant but delicate blend of herbal flavors makes it a subtle sweet-sour accompaniment for such straightforward meat preparations as roast pork, veal, or poultry. It's also dandy with charcuterie.

The color of the jelly will not be a vivid green if you leave matters to nature. If you want to modify the natural yellow-green tint, add a drop or two of green food coloring.

**1¾ to 2 cups (packed) washed and drained leaves
and tender tips of freshly picked garden thyme
(the so-called French thyme)**

A few sprigs of fresh sweet marjoram

2 cups water

1 large bay leaf

**3 tablespoons tarragon-flavored vinegar (or
substitute strained fresh lemon juice, white
wine vinegar, or Oriental rice vinegar)**

3¾ cups sugar

**1 pouch (3 ounces) or one-half 6-ounce bottle liquid
pectin**

A drop or two of green food coloring, optional

1. Place the thyme and the sweet marjoram, rinsed and drained, in the container of a blender or food processor and add the water. Run the machine to chop the herbs briefly—be careful to avoid making a pulp, which can result in cloudy jelly. Scrape the mixture into a large saucepan and add the bay leaf. Heat the mixture just to the boiling point over medium heat, stirring it once or twice. Remove the pan from the heat, cover it, and let the herbs infuse for 15 minutes.

2. Pour the mixture into a very fine sieve set over a bowl (or use an ordinary sieve lined with one or two layers of dampened cheesecloth) and drain off the infusion, pressing on the herbs; discard the debris. Measure 1¾ cups of the herb infusion into the rinsed-out saucepan.

3. Stir in the tarragon vinegar and the sugar and bring the mixture to a boil over high heat, stirring it often until the sugar has dissolved. When it reaches a full rolling boil (a boil that can't be stirred down), stir in the liquid pectin. When boiling resumes, boil the mixture hard (a full rolling boil) for exactly 1 minute. Remove the pan from the heat.

4. Stir in the green coloring, if you are using it (be stingy). Skim any foam from the jelly and pour it into hot, sterilized (page 327) jelly glasses or straight-sided half-pint canning jars, leaving ½ inch of headspace in glasses, ⅛ inch in jars. Seal the jelly in glasses with a thin layer of melted paraffin (page 326); seal canning jars with sterilized new two-piece lids according to manufacturer's directions. Cool, label, and store the jelly. It will be ready to use almost immediately; however, like most other jellies, it will take a few days to become fully firm.

Cranberry & Currant Relish

Cranberries have been around North America—and not just in New England—even longer than the native Americans, who introduced the Pilgrims to this scarlet autumn fruit. For most of the many generations since then, Americans and Canadians have been content with the standard cranberry sauce or jelly with Thanksgiving turkey, and that has been it, except for an occasional glass of cranberry juice or a pie.

For a delicious change, here is a stunning red relish that is crunchy in texture and sweet-tart in taste. It keeps well without fuss; after weeks in the refrigerator or months in the freezer, it emerges better than ever.

Offer the relish in place of the traditional chutney with a curry, and think of it when you are serving hot or cold ham, roast pork, or any poultry.

 SEASON:
From October through winter

 YIELD:
3 cups

 STORE:
For many weeks in the refrigerator; for 6 months or more in the freezer

A 12-ounce bag (about 3 cups) cranberries, fresh or frozen and thawed

3 tablespoons chopped red onion or other very mild onion, or substitute shallots

¾ cup golden raisins, soaked briefly in warm water if not quite soft, then drained

¾ cup red currant jelly

⅓ cup sugar

1½ teaspoons salt

Generous pinch of ground hot red (Cayenne) pepper

⅛ teaspoon ground ginger

3 tablespoons strained fresh lemon juice

1. Pick over the cranberries and rinse them. Chop them rather coarsely (this can be done in the food processor). Scrape the cranberries into a mixing bowl and add the onion.

2. Chop the raisins fairly coarsely and add them to the cranberry-onion mixture.

3. Combine the currant jelly, sugar, salt, ground hot red pepper, and ginger in a small saucepan. Heat the mixture, stirring, over medium heat until the sugar and salt have dissolved and it is smooth and quite hot; it need not boil.

4. Pour the hot jelly mixture over the cranberries, onion, and raisins. Add the lemon juice and stir the relish to mix it well.

5. Scrape the relish into a jar, cover it, and refrigerate it at least overnight before serving it.

Cranberry, Currant, & Horseradish Relish

To vary Cranberry and Currant Relish, above, add about 1 teaspoon well-drained bottled horseradish to a cupful. Taste and add more horseradish, if you like, but don't let the horseradish dominate. Especially good with cold meat—beef, pork, or veal.

SWEET & SOUR FRUITY THINGS

Call them sweet pickles (which sounds plebeian), call them kickshaws (which requires a trip to the dictionary), these are bits of fruit done up in sweet-and-tart ways that make them highly compatible with discriminating dining.

For example: Both cherries and 'Flame' grapes benefit by associating with white wine vinegar and tarragon so they may eventually accompany pâtés or other charcuterie; cantaloupe is marvelous when crisped with pickling lime and put up in a spiced sweet pickle; and plums, cranberries, and crab apples, preserved in several modes, round out the tally of fruits belonging to this section.

Tarragon-Pickled Flame Grapes

Seedless red grapes of the variety called 'Flame' are a welcome improvement on white seedless grapes; they are notable for their crisp sweetness. Delicious as they are to eat from the bunch, they are an unusual delicacy when pickled in mild vinegar with tarragon, salt, and a touch of sugar.

Serve these firm pickled grapes as you would cornichons—alongside pâtés or other charcuterie, with cold meats, ham or chicken sandwiches, and hearty salads—and nest them in clumps of watercress as a garnish for roast pork or poultry.

This recipe is fine for the green-white 'Thompson' seedless grapes, too. If you substitute, be sure the white grapes are ripe enough to be sweet—underripe ones can be puckery—but reject any that are ripe enough to be soft.

When the pickled grapes have been consumed, the pickling liquid is useful in place of tarragon vinegar; just remember to allow for its salt and sugar content when using it in salads.

3½ cups firm-ripe 'Flame' variety seedless red grapes or a similar variety, stemmed

8 sprigs (about 4 inches long) fresh tarragon (or substitute tarragon vinegar for the white wine vinegar listed below)

1½ cups white wine vinegar (substitute tarragon vinegar if you are not using the fresh tarragon)

3 tablespoons sugar

1½ teaspoons pickling salt or other fine non-iodized salt

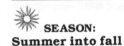 **SEASON:**
Summer into fall

 YIELD:
1 quart

 **STORE:**
For up to a year in a cool pantry or cupboard

1. Rinse the grapes and drain them well, then roll them in a towel until they are well dried.

2. Rinse the tarragon and pat the sprigs completely dry on a towel. Place the tarragon in a sterilized (page 327) quart jar. Add the grapes, which should come just to the shoulder of the jar, leaving the neck clear.

3. Stir together the vinegar, sugar, and salt until the sugar and salt have dissolved. Pour the solution over the grapes, which should be covered by at least 1 inch so they can "swim" freely. (If necessary, add a little more vinegar.) Remove any bubbles (page 324). Cap the jar with a sterilized new two-piece lid according to manufacturer's directions.

4. Store the grapes in a cool pantry or cool, dark cupboard for at least a month before serving them.

 SEASON:
Mid- to late summer

 YIELD:
5 to 6 cups

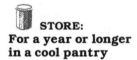 **STORE:**
For a year or longer in a cool pantry

Melon Moons

Sweet-pickled cantaloupe is a relish I hadn't tasted, much less fixed, for years until I was reminded of it as I browsed in my friend Jeanne Lesem's book *The Pleasures of Preserving and Pickling*. I'm indebted to her recipe for the use of pickling lime to add crispness to cantaloupe or muskmelon; back home in my California youth we weren't familiar with that wrinkle. The lime makes it possible to use fully ripe, therefore fragrant, melon and still get a firm result. Thought led to action in developing the version of pickled cantaloupe given below, with its light spicing of cloves and cinnamon.

These golden globes or cubes of melon are pretty enough for gift-giving, spooned into a fat-bellied jar and tied with a golden ribbon. Add a label or tag suggesting refrigerator storage and indicating compatible foods with which to offer the relish. Be sure to keep some pickled melon for yourself, to enjoy with roast duck, chicken, or turkey, or with an assortment of cold meats or a salad plate, or just with cottage cheese.

In this recipe, two commonly available forms of pickling lime were repeatedly tested against each other; they seem to give identical results, so use whichever is most convenient. The more highly refined drugstore form, formerly called "slaked lime," is labeled "calcium hydroxide U.S.P." and sold in small bottles (very expensive, but very available); the grocery-store version is labeled "pickling lime" and is usually packed in paper sacks holding a pound or so. If for any reason the use of calcium hydroxide isn't feasible, the melon can be prepared without it; directions follow the main recipe. The pieces will not be as firm, but the flavor is fine.

1 quart water

1½ teaspoons calcium hydroxide U.S.P. (available from druggists) or ¼ cup pickling lime

6 cups melon balls (or cubes) cut from 4 to 5 pounds firm-ripe, fragrant cantaloupe or muskmelon

2¼ cups cider vinegar

1½ cups water

3 cups sugar

2½ teaspoons whole cloves

1½ teaspoons broken whole cinnamon

1. Stir the water and calcium hydroxide together in a ceramic or stainless-steel bowl (do not use an aluminum container) and let the mixture stand for an hour. (The calcium hydroxide will not dissolve completely.)

2. Meanwhile, prepare the melon balls, scooping them with a ball-shaped cutter from melon from which the softest inner flesh, next to the cavity, has been scraped away together with the seeds. (Alternatively, cut the melon into 1-inch cubes.)

3. Add the melon balls to the lime mixture, stir it well, cover the bowl, and let the melon stand 4 to 5 hours. Drain off the solution, then rinse the melon balls well, stirring them gently, in three successive bowlfuls of fresh water; drain them again, then cover them with fresh cold water and let them stand for 2 to 3 hours. Drain the melon thoroughly.

4. Combine the vinegar, water, and sugar in a preserving pan. Tie the cloves and cinnamon loosely in a square of cheesecloth and drop the bundle into the pot. Bring the mixture to a boil over medium heat, cover it, reduce the heat, and simmer the syrup 5 minutes. Add the melon balls, bring the syrup again to a boil, cover the pot, and adjust the heat to maintain a simmer. Cook the melon until the pieces look somewhat translucent around the edges and feel tender-firm when probed with a skewer, 1 to 1½ hours, depending on the size and ripeness of the melon balls. Remove and discard the spice bag.

5. Spoon the melon balls into hot, clean pint or half-pint canning jars, leaving ½ to ¾ inch of headspace. Fill the jars with the hot syrup, leaving ¼ inch of headspace; remove any bubbles (page 324) and add more syrup, if necessary. Seal the jars with new two-piece canning lids according to manufacturer's directions and process for 15 minutes (for either size jar) in a boiling-water bath (page 325). Cool, label, and store the jars. The melon will be ready to serve in 2 weeks or so, but it continues to improve for some weeks. Chill the melon balls before serving.

Melon Moons
Pickled Without Lime

Melon balls prepared without lime will be softer in texture than those described above. To prevent a raggedy look and oversoftness, use melon on the firm side. It should not be too underripe, however—sniff the blossom end of each melon to make sure there is a detectable aroma.

Follow the preceding recipe, omitting the soak in lime water. In step 4, cook the melon balls briefly, just until they begin to look a little translucent here and there, 20 to 30 minutes. Let the melon cool in the syrup, overnight if possible.

Drain the syrup from the melon balls and return it, with the spice bag, to the preserving pan. Divide the melon pieces among hot, clean pint or half-pint canning jars, leaving ½ to ¾ inch of headspace. Boil the syrup until it has reduced by about a third. Remove the spice bag and ladle the boiling-hot syrup over the melon moons, leaving ¼ inch of headspace. Seal and process the jars as described in the basic recipe.

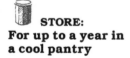 **SEASON:**
Midsummer

 YIELD:
1 quart

 STORE:
For up to a year in a cool pantry

Tart Pickled Cherries in the French Style

Generally Continental or perhaps specifically French in character, these cherries preserved in vinegar with tarragon have only a touch of added sugar and salt to enhance their tartness. (An early American version, prepared without tarragon, was called "cherry olives.")

Pickled cherries are a perfect accompaniment for charcuterie of almost any sort; they are especially appropriate with pâtés as a replacement for, or in addition to, cornichons.

If fresh tarragon is unavailable in cherry season, simply replace the white wine vinegar with tarragon vinegar. A caution, however: read the label of any commercial brand. Some bottles labeled "tarragon vinegar" contain tarragon-flavored distilled vinegar, which is sometimes quite harsh; look for a brand based on white wine vinegar.

Prudent people who have clumps of tarragon in the garden, or who can buy it locally, don't need to be told twice to prepare their own supply of tarragon vinegar—a project that takes only minutes (see page 196 or Tarragon Preserved in Vinegar, page 207).

1 pound ripe but firm Bing, Lambert, or other sweet cherries (sour cherries may be substituted)

5 or 6 sprigs (each at least 4 inches long) fresh tarragon

2 cups high-quality white wine vinegar

¼ cup sugar

2 teaspoons fine non-iodized salt

1. Sort the cherries, discarding any with soft spots or blemishes; rinse and drain them. Clip the stems to ½ inch; roll the cherries in a towel to remove all possible moisture.

2. Rinse the tarragon sprigs and pat them dry. Drop them into a dry, sterilized (page 327) 1-quart canning jar. Add the cherries, which should not quite fill the jar.

3. Stir together in a saucepan the vinegar, sugar, and salt. Heat over medium heat to simmering, stirring, until the sugar and salt have dissolved. Cool the liquid completely.

4. Pour the cooled liquid over the cherries, being sure to cover them completely; remove any bubbles (page 324), adding more liquid if necessary. Leave about ½ inch of headspace. Seal the jar with a sterilized new two-piece canning lid according to manufacturer's directions. Store the cherries for at least a month before serving them.

Bing Cherries in A Sweet Nine-Day Pickle

 SEASON:
June/July

 YIELD:
About 6 cups

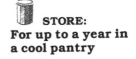 **STORE:**
For up to a year in a cool pantry

Two of my Great-Aunt Minnie's friends who were noted cooks shared with her their recipes for pickled cherries, handed down to me to become the basis of the formula below. There is a sturdy strain of Pennsylvania Dutch in the kitchens of northwestern New Jersey, as shown by this relish. The cherries are excellent with cold meats, or with smoked meat or poultry, or with any dish that is enhanced by a nibble of sweet/tart pickle.

The original recipes called for sour cherries, but the canning factories snaffle most of that fruit nowadays; if you can't get sour cherries, the recipe works well with Bing, Lambert, or other firm sweet cherries. Don't let the idea of 9 days' pickling give you pause—there is very little labor involved; time does most of the work.

The vinegar drained from the cherries in step 3 is far too good to pour away; I use it to make either Cherry Vinegar (page 193) or Four-Fruit Vinegar (page 190).

2 pounds ripe but firm sweet or sour cherries

**3 cups distilled white vinegar, or slightly more if
needed**

4 cups sugar

1. Rinse, stem, and pit the cherries; you should have about 7 cups. (For the uninitiated, an easy way to pit cherries is to hook out the pits with the head of a new hairpin; owners of antique or modern cherry pitters will prefer to use such a gadget.)

2. Combine the cherries with the vinegar in a half-gallon glass jar or a ceramic or stainless-steel bowl, being sure the fruit is covered with vinegar; if necessary, add more. Cover the container tightly and let it stand 3 days in a cool spot.

3. Drain off the vinegar and, if you like, reserve it for either Cherry Vinegar or Four-Fruit Vinegar, or add another batch of cherries to it for a second round of pickling.

4. Layer half of the cherries with half of the sugar in each of two sterilized (page 327) quart-size canning jars, finishing with sugar. Wipe the lips of the jars and cap them with sterilized new two-piece canning lids; do not screw the lids down tightly enough to seal them, as you want to remove them later. Set the jars in a cool spot where you'll remember to shake them gently every day or so, inverting them a few times as you shake. At the end of a few days (Aunt Minnie allowed 9 days) the sugar will have disappeared into the syrup.

5. Transfer enough cherries and syrup from one jar to fill the other almost to the rim, and transfer the remaining quantity to a sterilized (page 327) pint canning jar. Cap again, tightly this time, with sterilized new two-piece lids; label the jars and store them in a cool, dark spot. The cherries will look shriveled and the syrup will seem far too abundant at this point; just let everything rest for about a month, and the fruit will absorb most of the syrup and plump up considerably. Refrigerate the cherries after a jar is opened.

SEASON:
**Mid-August into
fall**

YIELD:
About 4 pints

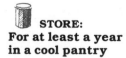
STORE:
**For at least a year
in a cool pantry**

Crab Apples in Cranberry Syrup

Sweet pickled crab apples are a most typically American relish, one that is highly compatible with fresh or cured pork, with poultry, especially smoked turkey or chicken (page 21) or crisp-roasted duck, and with platters of cold meats.

Most commercially pickled crab apples are tinted bright red with chemical dyes whose dubiousness is sufficient reason to put up your own. You can have undyed crab apples of good color if you start with red-skinned fruit, or if you add both color and flavor by including cranberry juice in the syrup for paler crab apples. Both ways are described below.

Crab apples are widely planted as ornamental trees, and several varieties bear picking-size fruit; so front and back yards are worth investigating as sources, if farm stands fail you. The fruit also makes brilliantly colored, fragrant jelly (page 132).

2½ quarts (about 2½ pounds) firm crab apples, about an inch in diameter

3 cups sugar

3 cups cider vinegar

2 cups cranberry juice,* bottled or homemade, or water

4 sticks (2 to 3 inches each) cinnamon, broken up

1 tablespoon whole cloves

1 tablespoon whole allspice

1. Sort the crab apples and discard any that are bruised or seriously blemished. Clean the blossom ends well (a small cotton swab does this handily) and trim the stems short. Rinse and drain the crab apples, then prick the skin of each all over with a coarse needle (this helps prevent bursting).

2. Combine the sugar, vinegar, and cranberry juice in a preserving pan. Tie the cinnamon, cloves, and allspice loosely in a square of close-woven cheesecloth or nylon net, then bash the bundle with a mallet or the handle of a knife a few times to bruise the spices. Add the spices to the mixture in the pot and boil it over medium-high heat, uncovered, 5 minutes.

3. To ensure unburst crab apples, cook them gently in small batches. Add just enough crab apples to the syrup to cover the surface without crowding. Over medium-low heat, simmer the crab apples very gently, uncovered—do not let the syrup bubble actively—until they are hot through but still somewhat firm at the heart, 10 minutes or more, depending on their size; test often with a wire cake tester or thin skewer. As the apples are done, transfer them carefully, using a slotted spoon, to a bowl. Continue cooking batches until all the fruit is done. Boil the syrup for 2 minutes, then pour it, with the bag of spices, over the fruit. Let the bowl stand, covered, at room temperature overnight or for up to 24 hours.

4. Pack the crab apples carefully in hot, clean wide-mouthed pint or quart canning jars, leaving ½ inch of head-space. Reheat the syrup and boil it 2 minutes. Discard the spice bag and pour the syrup over the fruit in the jars, leaving ¼ inch of headspace. Remove any bubbles (page 324), seal the new jars with new two-piece canning lids according to manufacturer's directions, and process for 15 minutes (for either size jar) in a boiling-water bath (page 325). Cool, label, and store the jars. Let the crab apples mellow for a few weeks before serving them.

*FRESH CRANBERRY JUICE:

To prepare cranberry juice from scratch, combine 2 cups (½ pound) fresh or frozen cranberries with 2½ cups water. Stew the cranberries until they are very soft, about 15 minutes. Drain off juice through a fine sieve.

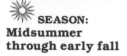

SEASON:
Midsummer
through early fall

YIELD:
About 3 cups

STORE:
Unsealed, for a few
months in the
refrigerator;
sealed, for a year
or more in a cool
pantry

*PLUM JAM:

To prepare plum
jam, simmer wild
plums or tart culti-
vated plums with a
very little water,
just enough to pre-
vent sticking, un-
til the fruit is soft,
15 to 30 minutes.
Press the plums
through a sieve or
a food mill; discard
the seeds. Measure
the pulp; add 1 cup
to 1¼ cups sugar
to each cup of
pulp. Boil the mix-
ture rapidly in a
preserving pan,
stirring often, un-
til it passes the
jelly test (page
322). If you will be
using the jam
within a few
weeks, ladle it into
sterilized jars
(page 327), cap
them, and store
them in the refrig-
erator. For pantry
storage, the jam
should be sealed
with canning lids
and processed 15
minutes (for pint
or half-pint jars) in
a boiling-water
bath (page 325).

Beach Plum or Wild Plum Sauce For Game & Meats

Although the title of this recipe does specify wild plums, this excellent sauce can be made satisfactorily with any plums that are truly *tart*. Where I live we pick beach plums every fall, and I use those; away from the East Coast there are places where other wild plums grow, and they, like beach plums, have a special tartness that makes them superb for the sauce.

This Cumberland-type sauce is based on the British original made with currant jelly. Serve the sauce with roast or broiled meat or poultry, and most especially with game.

2 tablespoons very finely diced shallots or mild onion

3 tablespoons very finely shredded orange zest (outer skin of orange only; no white pith)

1½ tablespoons very finely shredded lemon zest (outer skin of lemon only; no white pith)

2 cups pure plum jam, preferably made with beach plums or wild plums*

Strained juice of 2 medium oranges

Strained juice of 2 medium lemons

1 teaspoon dry mustard, preferably imported

¼ teaspoon ground mace

⅛ teaspoon ground ginger

2 big pinches (about ⅛ teaspoon) ground hot red (Cayenne) pepper

Few grains of salt, optional

½ cup red port wine

1. Place the diced shallots in a small pan, add boiling water to cover, and simmer 2 minutes. Drain and reserve.

2. Place the orange and lemon zest in the same pan and add boiling water to cover. Simmer the zest, covered, 5 minutes. Drain and reserve.

3. Combine in a large stainless-steel or enameled sauce-pan the plum jam, shallots, citrus zest, orange and lemon juice, mustard, mace, ginger, ground hot red pepper, and salt, if using. Heat the mixture to boiling, stirring, and boil it, stirring often, for 5 minutes. Add the port; remove from the heat.

4. Ladle the sauce into hot, clean half-pint canning jars, leaving ¼ inch of headspace. Cap the jars according to lid manufacturer's directions and process 15 minutes in a boiling-water bath (page 325). Cool, label, and store the jars.

Sweet & Tart Pickled Cranberries

Whole cranberries are "put up" in a tart-sweet syrup based on red wine vinegar to create this relish, which is very unlike traditional, heavily sweetened cranberry sauce.

Pickled cranberries are a versatile accompaniment for meats and a good garnish, too. Try them in place of the traditional cornichons (page 96) with pâtés and other charcuterie, or with a roasted bird of any kind, or with ham or pork, or with chicken or turkey salad.

2 12-ounce packages (about 7 cups) firm cranberries

3 cups red wine vinegar or cider vinegar

3½ cups sugar

1⅓ cups water

1 tablespoon coriander seed

1 teaspoon whole cloves

1 tablespoon coarsely broken whole cinnamon

1. Pick over and rinse the cranberries; let them drain in a colander.

2. Combine the vinegar, sugar, and water in a preserving pan. Tie the coriander, cloves, and cinnamon loosely in a square of cheesecloth; pound the bundle lightly to bruise the spices. Add the spice bag to the vinegar mixture.

3. Bring the mixture to a boil over medium heat, stirring until the sugar has dissolved. Simmer the syrup, partly covered, for 5 minutes.

4. Add the berries to the syrup and lower the heat. Cook them very slowly, uncovered, shaking the pan often, until they are thoroughly heated through and their skins have cracked, about 7 minutes.

5. Pour the berries, spice bag, and syrup into a bowl. Cool the mixture, then cover the bowl and leave it at room temperature for several hours or overnight.

6. Spoon the berries from the syrup into 3 hot, clean pint canning jars, dividing them equally. Reheat the syrup to boiling, discard the spice bag, and fill the jars with syrup, leaving ¼ inch of headspace. Remove any bubbles (page 324) and add more syrup, if necessary. Cover the jars with new two-piece canning lids according to manufacturer's directions and process for 15 minutes in a boiling-water bath (page 325). Cool, label, and store the jars. Let the cranberries mellow for at least 2 weeks before using them.

 SEASON:
October through winter

 YIELD:
About 3 pints

STORE:
For up to a year in a cool, dark place

PICKLE PICKS

Peter Piper's pecks of pickles, plus plenty of others from the more or less *haute* cuisine, are here.

Pickled peppers? Yes, succulent green ones. Cornichons of a classic type. Pickled ginger for sushi (or just ginger)

fans. Dills crisped by packing with grape leaves. Green tomatoes rescued from frost for a higher and crisper fate. Brilliant red and yellow peppers in vinegar, all-Amerian bread-and-butter slices, onions and shallots made immortal. Browse, and choose.

☀ **SEASON:**
Midsummer to fall, if you are using stem (young) ginger; otherwise, whenever fresh ginger is available

☕ **YIELD:**
About 1 quart, with liquid

🥫 **STORE:**
For a year or more in the refrigerator

Young Ginger Pickled in the Japanese Fashion

Those who especially enjoy the pungent ribbons of vinegar-pickled ginger that always accompany sushi in Japanese restaurants need not dine out to taste this relish, now that fresh ginger is stocked almost everywhere, by supermarkets as well as specialty greengrocers. Preparing your own supply of *sushoga* (or *gari,* in more informal Japanese) is remarkably simple.

Try to obtain the tender young ginger rhizomes (ginger "roots" are technically not roots) called "stem ginger," usually available for only a few weeks after midsummer in communities with sizable Oriental populations. Stem ginger has skin that is barely a skin at all—it is as baby-tender as that of a new potato; and the juicy rhizomes are further identifiable by the pink-tinted bases of the leaf sheaths showing where the stems have been trimmed away.

If stem ginger is not to be had, shop for very fresh ginger "hands" with smooth, silky skin and no sign of withering or mold. The fibrous cores of older ginger, left behind when you shave off the tender layer for pickling, can be used to make Fresh Ginger Jelly (page 130).

Pickled ginger goes well with all manner of foods: try a heap of the rosy-peach shavings as counterpoint to cold meats, alongside sandwiches or hearty salads (potato, pasta, or rice), and with seafood, either cooked or uncooked; try nibbling a bit of ginger after swallowing each icy-cold oyster or clam on the half-shell. Further, you may want to save the pickling liquid from the ginger to add zing to fruit salad dressings or other sauces that could use a little gingering-up.

The method of preparation in the following recipe is a hybrid: I am indebted to Shizuo Tsuji's fine book *Japanese Cooking: A Simple Art,* and to the directions for Chinese pickling in *A Popular Guide to Chinese Vegetables,* by Martha Dahlen and Karen Phillipps. The technique for dealing with elderly ginger is my own. Like Tsuji, I prefer to use Japanese rice vinegar for pickling ginger, but distilled white vinegar will serve.

1 pound tender young ginger (stem ginger), or at least twice as much mature ginger

1½ tablespoons pickling salt or other fine non-iodized salt

1½ cups Oriental rice vinegar or distilled white vinegar

⅜ cup water

⅜ cup sugar

1. To prepare stem ginger, break the rhizomes apart at the joints and trim off any bruised, withered, or callused portions. Scrape off the skin and papery bits of leaf sheath, using a small sharp knife. Rinse the pieces and pat them dry.

2. If the ginger is the fibrous mature kind, peel it, using a swivel-bladed peeler, or scrape off the skin. Shave its tender outer layer into thin lengthwise strips, using the swivel-bladed peeler; stop making strips and move to another area when the blade begins to encounter tough fiber. (Set the cores aside for another use.)

3. Combine the ginger sections or strips with the salt in a ceramic or stainless-steel bowl; turn the pieces to coat them with salt. Cover and set aside for 24 hours, turning the ginger in the salt a few times when you think of it.

4. Drain the ginger; discard the liquid. Dry the pieces or strips thoroughly with paper towels. Place the ginger in a clean, dry quart jar or two pint jars (it is not necessary to use canning jars).

5. Stir together the vinegar, water, and sugar until the sugar has dissolved. Pour the liquid over the ginger, covering the pieces by at least ½ inch. Cover with a lid, label, and refrigerate. The ginger strips will be ready to eat in 2 or 3 days; the knobs will require at least a week, depending on their size.

6. To serve the strips, simply drain them. To serve pickled ginger knobs, shave the thinnest possible lengthwise slices from them, using a swivel-bladed peeler. Serve the ginger in small heaps. If a fine white sediment appears in the liquid at any point, it is harmless starch from the rhizomes, not a sign of spoilage, and should be disregarded.

✳ SEASON:
July-August

☕ YIELD:
About 4 quarts

🥫 STORE:
In capped jars, for up to a year in a cool pantry

Cold-Pickled Cornichons

The French cucumber pickles called *cornichons* are a long-running favorite at our house; each summer is a time for experimentation with pickling formulas. I have prepared cornichons with lots of salt, with little salt; with hot vinegar, cold vinegar; with these spices and seasonings, or those. The recipe that follows is the current leader on points.

Obtaining cucumbers that are tiny enough can be a difficulty. The best solution is to grow your own, and this is easy if you have a sunny garden spot. You'll need either seeds of gherkins, a small, prickly sort (seed catalogues list them), or of another cucumber variety recommended for pickling. If you grow the pickling kind, gather the young fruits when they're gherkin-size, an inch or two long. If you rely on a farm stand for raw material, try asking in June about ordering a batch of their pickling cucumbers gathered when they are no more than 2 inches long. You might even find a farmer who will let you pick your own.

Pickle your cucumbers as soon as possible after they have been picked, preferably the same day.

When gift-giving time comes, a jar of cornichons will be welcomed by anyone who has ever tasted these little pickles, a traditional French accompaniment for pâtés and other charcuterie.

4 to 5 quarts (6 pounds) tiny freshly picked cucumbers, preferably no more than 1 inch long

1½ cups coarse (kosher) salt or 1¼ cups pickling salt (or other fine non-iodized salt)

¼ cup white wine vinegar or distilled white vinegar

18 to 24 sprigs (4 to 6 inches long) fresh tarragon

6 large or 10 medium shallots, peeled and sliced

1 tablespoon mustard seed

1 tablespoon peppercorns

1 teaspoon whole allspice, optional

¼ teaspoon whole cloves, optional

2 quarts white wine vinegar, more if needed

1. Cover the cucumbers with cold water and wash each with a soft cloth, being careful to remove any remnants of blossoms; do not scrub them. Rinse and drain them, then mix them gently with the salt in a stainless-steel or ceramic bowl. Cover the bowl with a cloth and let it stand for 24 hours, turning the cucumbers occasionally in the brine that forms.

2. Drain the cucumbers, then swish them through 3 quarts of cold water mixed with the ¼ cup white wine vinegar or distilled white vinegar. Drain them, then wipe each cucumber dry with a soft cloth.

3. Scald and drain two half-gallon or 2-liter jars or crocks. Dividing all the ingredients equally, layer the cucumbers and seasonings in the containers, starting with a few tarragon sprigs in the bottom of each. Pour in enough white wine vinegar to cover the cucumbers and seasonings by at least an inch, or better, by 2 inches; the amount of vinegar needed will depend on such variables as the shape of the container and the size of the cucumbers. Cover the containers with airtight lids or two layers of plastic wrap, held in place with rubber bands.

4. Leave the pickles in a cool, dark spot for a month, after which they will be ready to use. Once the pickling is complete, you may want to pack the cornichons in smaller jars; be sure to cover them well with the vinegar and cover the jars snugly; sealing isn't necessary.

Grapeleaf Dills

Seize the moment when fine, fresh pickling cucumbers and dill with young but fully formed seedheads are available and lay down a crockful of pickled bliss for eating straight from the crock or for putting up in jars for longer storage. Either way, this is a project worth tackling, especially as classic crock pickling involves little labor. Be aware, however, that the pickle crock must be skimmed daily for the 2 or 3 weeks fermentation will take, so don't plan to start dill-pickling just before you're due to go on vacation. The time required will depend on the ambient temperature—and, who knows, maybe the temperament of your cucumbers?

A word about ingredients: Only fresh, not too large pickling cucumbers should be used—don't use the kinds meant for salads—and they should not have spent more than a day or two off the vine when they go into the crock. Of course, cucumbers that have been waxed are out of the question.

Try to include the grape leaves (it doesn't matter whether they are from cultivated or wild vines); after shoulder-to-shoulder crock tests in several seasons, I'm satisfied that they do indeed increase the crispness of dill pickles.

If the dill you can get lacks seed heads, use it anyway and add a teaspoonful of dried dill seed from the spice shelf. When you find dill that's just right, you can freeze the stalks for later use, too. They keep well for several weeks.

SEASON:
Mid- to late summer

 YIELD:
About 5 quarts

STORE:
Unsealed, for a few months in the refrigerator; or heat-processed and sealed, for up to a year in a cool pantry

24 very fresh pickling cucumbers 4 to 6 inches long

8 large fresh grape leaves, optional

Large bunch of fresh dill with seed heads (use a bunch as large as one hand can encircle)

8 to 12 cloves garlic, to taste, unpeeled but slightly flattened

6 quarts water

1 cup less 2 tablespoons (⅞ cup) pickling salt or other fine non-iodized salt

3 tablespoons mixed pickling spice

1. Wash the cucumbers well and drain them thoroughly. Rinse and drain the grape leaves. Trim the roots and any wilted leaflets from the dill, rinse the sprigs well, and drain them on a towel.

2. Line the bottom of a 2-gallon crock or other deep, wide-mouthed glass or ceramic container with 3 of the grape leaves and some of the dill. Pack the cucumbers loosely in the crock, interspersing them with dill and grape leaves and sprinkling the garlic cloves here and there; save 2 grape leaves and a little dill for the top. Be sure to leave at least 3 inches of room at the top of the crock; if your cucumbers are strapping specimens and the crock is too full, transfer some of the contents to another container (2-quart canning or storage jars work well).

3. Combine the water, salt, and pickling spice in a large pot, bring it to a boil, and simmer it, covered, 5 minutes. Set the pot, uncovered, in a sink and cool the brine quickly by surrounding the pot with cold water. (Or let it cool naturally.)

4. Ladle the cooled brine over the contents of the crock, covering the cucumbers by at least 2 inches (more brine than that will be fine). Add the reserved grape leaves and dill. Set a plate on top to hold everything under the surface. Fill a pint jar with water and weight the plate with it; the brine should cover the plate. Cover the whole works loosely with a towel or a double layer of cheesecloth and leave it in a reasonably cool spot, one where the temperature won't go over about 70°.

5. Every day (or even twice a day if the scum forms rapidly), uncover the crock, remove the jar and the plate, and rinse them. Carefully skim all the whitish film from the brine (this skimming is essential to proper fermentation.) Wipe the inner rim of the crock; return the plate, jar, and cloth. Let fermentation continue until the pickles are uniformly olive green throughout; when you think they may be ready—in 2 weeks or so—halve one to check. After a few days' fermentation, you may want to taste the brine and add more pickling spice, being careful not to overwhelm the dill and garlic, which should predominate. If the brine depth should drop to less than 2 inches over the pickles, make more brine (¼ cup salt to each quart of water, boiled and cooled) and add it.

6. When they are pickled to suit, your cucumbers, now

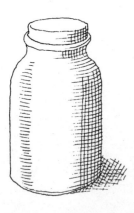

"full sours," may be devoured straight from the crock (continue to skim the brine whenever necessary), or they may be refrigerated or canned for longer storage:

Refrigerator storage: Drain the pickles, reserving the brine, and pack them into jars, adding 1 or 2 sprigs of fresh dill, 1 or 2 cloves of fresh garlic, and 1 or 2 tiny dried red peppers to each jar, if you wish. Strain the brine and fill the jars with it. (Disregard any whitish sediment; it is a harmless product of fermentation, and will settle to the bottom of the jars.) Cap the jars and refrigerate them; the pickles will keep for several months.

To process and seal the pickles for longer storage: Pack them into wide-mouthed quart canning jars, cutting some of them for a better fit, if you wish; leave at least ½ inch of headspace. If you wish, include 1 or 2 fresh cloves of garlic and 2 or 3 heads of fresh dill (or a good pinch of dill seed) to each jar. Strain the brine, bring it to a boil, simmer it 2 minutes, then fill the jars, leaving ¼ inch of headspace. Remove any bubbles (page 324). Cover with new two-piece canning lids according to manufacturer's directions and process for 15 minutes in a boiling-water bath (page 325). Cool, label, and store the jars.

Extra-Crisp Bread & Butter Pickle Slices

Of all the down-home pickles we know about, bread-and-butters are the one kind that's made at our house every summer. If we buy the cucumbers at a farm stand, we look for a pickling variety rather than one of the kinds meant for salad—the "picklers" tend to be firmer and less seedy—and we make sure they are freshly picked. Waxed cucumbers cannot be used. If salad cucumbers are what's available, we choose the smallest possible specimens.

This recipe produces spectacularly crunchy pickles, thanks to the use of old-fashioned pickling lime. This substance, also called "hydrated lime" or "slaked lime," has long been a standby, especially in the South, for making especially crisp pickle slices, green-tomato pickles, pickled watermelon rind, and a few other specialties. If you want to omit the lime, your pickles will taste just as good but they will not be as crisp.

Directions for making the pickles without lime and for making a variant that includes onions follow the main recipe. The oniony version, to many, is the authentic one, although it has been abandoned by commercial picklers.

 SEASON:
Mid- to late summer

 YIELD:
6 pints

STORE:
For at least a year in a cool pantry

12 firm, very fresh pickling cucumbers 5 to 6 inches
  long
4 quarts cool water
1 cup pickling lime (see page 324)
1½ quarts cider vinegar
5 to 6 cups sugar, to taste
1 tablespoon pickling salt or other fine non-iodized
  salt
1 tablespoon mustard seed
1½ teaspoons celery seed
1 teaspoon turmeric
1 teaspoon whole peppercorns
½ teaspoon whole cloves
¼ teaspoon ground ginger

1. Scrub the cucumbers. Cut off and discard both ends, then slice the cucumbers crosswise ¼ inch thick.

2. Measure the water into a ceramic or stainless-steel bowl (be careful not to use an aluminum container) and stir in the pickling lime very thoroughly (it will not dissolve completely). Add the sliced cucumbers, stir, cover, and set aside overnight, or for up to 24 hours. Stir them once or twice.

3. Drain the cucumbers in a colander; return them to the rinsed-out bowl and rinse them in three succeeding batches of cool water, stirring them well as you do so. Drain them again and add cool water to cover them by an inch or two. Set them aside for 3 hours.

4. Combine the vinegar, sugar, salt, mustard seed, celery seed, turmeric, peppercorns, cloves, and ground ginger in a stainless-steel or enameled saucepan. Heat the mixture to boiling, stirring until the sugar dissolves, then boil it, uncovered, for 5 minutes.

5. Meanwhile, drain the cucumbers well and return them to the bowl. When the syrup has boiled 5 minutes, pour it over the slices. Stir the slices gently, then push them under the surface, cover the bowl with a towel, and set it aside overnight.

6. Transfer the cucumbers and syrup to a preserving pan and cook the whole business, covered, over medium-high heat, stirring occasionally (be careful not to break the brittle slices), until the cucumbers are translucent, 30 to 40 minutes.

7. Using a funnel, a spoon, and a long fork, arrange the pickle slices in 6 hot, clean pint canning jars, leaving about ½ inch of headspace. Divide the spices from the syrup among the jars, then add boiling-hot syrup to reach ¼ inch from rims. Remove any bubbles (page 324) and add more syrup, if necessary. Seal the jars with new two-piece canning lids according to manufacturer's directions and process for 10 minutes in a boiling-water bath (page 325). Cool, label, and store the jars. Let the pickles mellow for a month, then chill them before serving.

Making Bread & Butter Pickles Without Lime

Follow the preceding recipe, but omit the soaking of the cucumber slices in the lime mixture. Instead, layer the sliced cucumbers in a bowl with ½ cup of coarse (kosher) salt and 2 trays of ice cubes, well crushed. Let the slices stand for 3 to 4 hours, then drain the cucumbers thoroughly, picking out any unmelted ice. Make the pickling solution as described in step 4, but omit the tablespoon of salt. Add the cucumbers to the pickling liquid, bring the mixture to a full boil (push the slices under and stir gently to heat them evenly), and boil them for 2 minutes, no longer. Ladle the pickles into jars and process as described.

Bread & Butter Pickles with Onions

Fans of bread-and-butter pickles often prefer an oniony version. If you are among them, add 1 quart of sliced small onions, cut ¼ inch thick, to the cucumbers just before adding the syrup to them in step 5 of the main recipe. Follow the remaining instructions for making either limed or unlimed pickles, but increase the vinegar to 2 quarts. The yield of this version will be about 8 pints.

Quick Bread & Butter Onion Rings

This is a use for the perfectly delicious syrup from Extra-Crisp Bread & Butter Pickle Slices, above. (For pickled onion rings "from scratch," see Onion-Ring Pickles from Scratch, page 102.)

Precise measurements aren't important; you can easily judge about how many sliced onions can be covered by the pickle juice on hand. My refrigerator is never without a jar of our own bread-and-butters, so I accumulate the syrup (there is no need to refrigerate it) until I have enough to fix a good-sized jar of these.

 SEASON:
Any time

STORE:
For months in the refrigerator

1. Peel small red (purple) onions or other mild onions and slice them about ¼ inch thick; separate them into rings. Sprinkle the onions with a little coarse (kosher) salt, mix them with ice cubes, and let them stand for about 3 hours.

2. Drain them well, rinse them briefly, and drain again.

3. Bring left over pickle syrup to a boil over high heat; add the onions, push them under the surface with a spoon, and let the liquid just return to a boil. Transfer the onions and syrup to a jar, let them cool uncovered, then cover and refrigerate the jar. The onions will be ready in 3 days or so, but their flavor continues to improve as they rest.

SEASON:
Any time

YIELD:
3 pints

STORE:
Unsealed, for many months in the refrigerator; sealed, for a year or more in a cool pantry

Onion-Ring Pickles From Scratch

Flavor, crunch, and color are what these onion rings have going for them: their oniony flavor is spiced up a bit, their crunch is preserved by minimal processing, and their bright gold color and a share of their flavor comes from turmeric.

•Serve pickled onion rings well chilled, with (or in) sandwiches, with cold cuts, pâté, or just cold meat loaf, or alongside hearty salads involving tuna, potatoes, rice, or pasta.

•When the rings have been consumed, save the pickling liquid. It adds pizzazz to dressing for potato or other cooked vegetable salads, and it makes a splendid glaze for freshly cooked corned beef (poached, not boiled): Place the hot corned beef in a baking dish with fat side up, drizzle it with the syrup from Onion-Ring Pickles, then sprinkle it generously with brown sugar. Bake the beef in a hot oven (425° to 450°), basting it occasionally with more of the pickle juice, until the coating has bubbled and is crusted, about 15 minutes. Let the meat rest for 20 minutes before slicing it. Good hot or cold.

1½ pounds small to medium crisp, mild onions
18 whole cloves
18 black peppercorns
3 teaspoons mustard seed
1½ teaspoons celery seed
2 cups distilled white vinegar or cider vinegar
½ cup water
1 cup sugar
2 teaspoons salt
1½ teaspoons turmeric
⅛ teaspoon ground cinnamon

1. Peel the onions and slice them ¼ inch thick; separate the slices into rings. Divide the onion rings among three pint canning jars.

2. To the onions in each jar add 6 whole cloves, 6 peppercorns, 1 teaspoon mustard seed, and ½ teaspoon celery seed.

3. Combine the vinegar, water, sugar, salt, turmeric, and cinnamon in a stainless-steel or enameled saucepan; heat to boiling, then simmer the mixture 2 minutes.

4. Fill the jars with the hot liquid, leaving ¼ inch of headspace. Remove any bubbles (page 324) and add more liquid, if necessary. If pickles are to be stored in the refrigerator, let them cool, then cover each jar with doubled plastic wrap and apply a cap; there is no need to seal the jars. If the pickles are to be pantry-stored, seal the jars with new two-piece canning lids following manufacturer's directions and process for 10 minutes in a boiling-water bath (page 325). Cool, label, and store the jars. Let the pickles mellow for at least a month before serving them.

Pickled Hot, Hot Green Peppers

The natural ferocity of crackling-hot green peppers is only slightly tamed by pickling, even with the further benison of olive oil, so... fair warning. These are *hot*. For those who can take it, they are fine companions for everything from a deli corned-beef sandwich to north-of-the-border Tex-Mex, Cal-Mex, or other incendiary menu items. They can also be used as an ingredient in recipes calling for pickled jalapeño peppers.

The ultimate hotness of pickled peppers will depend on the raw material you start with, but until you're sure what you're up against, please nibble gingerly both before and after pickling.

Let these little peppers mellow (if that's the word) in the jar for a month or more before sampling them.

**2 pounds small fresh hot green peppers 1 to 2
    inches long, preferably the oval kind**

4 cloves garlic, or more if you like, peeled

8 whole allspice

24 peppercorns

1 large bay leaf, torn into quarters

2 cups distilled white vinegar

2 cups water

2 teaspoons salt

4 tablespoons olive oil, or as needed

 **SEASON:
All year, but
especially early
summer through
fall**

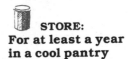 **YIELD:
4 pints**

**STORE:
For at least a year
in a cool pantry**

*HOT PEPPERS:

For precautions when handling hot peppers, see page 321.

1. Rinse and drain the peppers; trim stems to a stub.* Pack the peppers into 4 wide-mouthed pint canning jars, dividing them equally. As the peppers are packed, scatter among them a share of the seasonings: in each jar place 1 clove garlic, split; 2 whole allspice; 6 peppercorns; and a piece of bay leaf.

2. Combine the vinegar, water, and salt in a stainless-steel or enameled saucepan and heat the mixture to simmering. Pour the hot solution over the peppers, covering them completely and leaving 1 inch of headspace. Remove any bubbles (page 324) and add liquid if necessary to maintain headspace. (If there should be insufficient solution to cover the peppers, make more in the same proportions; no harm will be done if a few moments are required to do this.) Add enough olive oil to each jar to cover the surface of the liquid, about 1 tablespoon.

3. Seal the jars with new two-piece canning lids according to manufacturer's directions and process for 15 minutes in a boiling-water bath (page 325). Cool, label, and store the jars. The peppers are good to eat after 2 weeks, but they will be better after at least a month's rest in the jar.

 SEASON:
Fall

YIELD:
5 to 6 pints

STORE:
For at least a year in a cool pantry

Sweet Pickled Green Tomato Slices

Green tomatoes pickled American-style, in a spiced sweet-tart syrup, are a happy destiny for late tomatoes that must be salvaged from the garden before frost. (However, there's no reason why they can't be made whenever the raw material is available, even in midsummer). Use tomatoes that are completely green—they will be solid green all the way through—not yellowish or pink; if they have begun to color they will shed their seeds, or even disintegrate, during pickling. Set tomatoes that are changing color aside in a warm but not sunny spot to ripen for the table.

In this recipe, old-fashioned pickling lime is used to endow the slices with a great deal of crunch. If you prefer, omit the liming and prepare the pickles as described in the note following the recipe. Onions are optional, although I think they are a good addition. If you leave out the onions, add the same measure of additional tomatoes.

Count on these pickles to add zest to a baked-bean supper, once the snow flies. They're also good with any food that would be complemented by bread-and-butter pickles or other sweet-sour relishes.

4 pounds completely green tomatoes, preferably plum tomatoes (about 3 quarts, sliced)

4 quarts water

1 cup pickling lime (page 324)

1½ pounds small onions (about 5½ cups, sliced), optional (if omitted, increase sliced tomatoes by 5½ cups)

5 cups cider vinegar

5 cups sugar

¼ cup pickling or other fine non-iodized salt

3 tablespoons mustard seed

3 teaspoons celery seed

2 teaspoons whole peppercorns

2 teaspoons whole allspice

1 teaspoon turmeric

½ teaspoon ground cinnamon

¼ teaspoon ground cloves

1. Rinse and drain the tomatoes. Trim and discard a slice from the top and base of each and slice the tomatoes into rounds a generous ¼ inch thick. Leave the slices whole if the tomatoes are small; if they are large, halve or quarter the slices.

2. Measure the water into a ceramic or stainless-steel bowl (do not use aluminum) and stir in the pickling lime (it will not dissolve completely). Add the tomatoes, stir, cover, and set aside in a cool spot overnight or for as long as 24 hours.

3. Drain the tomato slices in a colander, then place them in the rinsed-out bowl and rinse them thoroughly in several changes of cool water, stirring them with care. Drain the tomatoes well.

4. Peel the onions and slice them into rounds a little thinner than the tomatoes. Reserve the onions.

5. Combine the vinegar, sugar, salt, mustard seed, celery seed, peppercorns, allspice, turmeric, cinnamon, and cloves in a preserving pan. Bring the mixture to a boil and boil, uncovered, 2 minutes. Add the tomatoes and onions, bring the potful to boiling again over medium-high heat, and boil the vegetables, pushing them under the surface from time to time, until the tomato slices begin to look translucent, about 15 minutes; be careful not to overcook them.

6. Ladle the hot pickles into hot, clean pint canning jars, leaving ¼ inch of headspace and dividing the spices equally among the jars. Remove any bubbles (page 324) and add more liquid, if necessary. Seal the jars with new two-piece canning lids according to manufacturer's directions and process for 10 minutes in a boiling-water bath (page 325). Cool, label, and store the jars. Let the pickles mellow for a month or so before using them.

Sweet Pickled Green Tomato Slices Without Lime

Follow the preceding recipe, but omit the soaking in the lime solution. Instead, combine the sliced tomatoes (and the sliced onions, if you are including them) with ½ cup of coarse salt, mix them well, and let them stand for 3 hours. Drain the vegetables rinse them, and drain them again. Follow the recipe, starting with step 5; omit the ¼ cup salt called for in the syrup. The pickles will require only about 12 minutes' cooking; the processing time for the jars is the same.

Unlimed pickles will taste much the same as a batch made with lime, but they will not be crisp.

SEASON:
Late summer
through fall

YIELD:
2 quarts

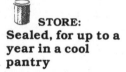

STORE:
Sealed, for up to a
year in a cool
pantry

Red and/or Yellow Sweet Pepper Strips in Vinegar

Bright as a banner, ripe scarlet and brilliant yellow peppers pickled together are a splendid accompaniment for sandwiches, salads, cold meats, or what have you. Or for an appetizer course, toss the drained strips with olive oil and finely minced garlic or parsley or both, bed them on curly chicory, and add, optionally, a few anchovy fillets.

2½ pounds (5 large) sweet red peppers and/or sweet yellow peppers

2 large cloves garlic, sliced

2 teaspoons fine non-iodized salt

3¾ cups distilled white vinegar

1¾ cups water

Olive oil, optional

1. Wash and dry the peppers. Cut out the stems and cores, remove the seeds, and cut the peppers into lengthwise strips from ½ to 1 inch wide.

2. Place 2 slices of garlic in each of 2 hot, clean quart canning jars, preferably with wide mouths (for ease in arranging the pepper strips). Arrange the strips attractively in the jars, making alternate stripes of color if you are pickling both yellow and red peppers. Pack the strips moderately firmly, scattering the remaining slices of garlic here and there among them. Sprinkle 1 teaspoon salt into each jar.

3. Combine the vinegar and water in a stainless-steel or enameled saucepan and heat the mixture to simmering. Pour the liquid into the jars, filling them to within 1 inch of the rim. Remove any bubbles (page 324). Add enough more of the vinegar mixture to bring the liquid to ¾ inch from the jar rims if you are using the olive oil, or ½ inch if you are not including the oil. If you opt for a topping of oil, pour in enough to cover the pickling liquid by ¼ inch.

4. Seal the jars with new two-piece canning lids according to manufacturer's directions and process for 15 minutes (for either size jar) in a boiling-water bath (page 325). Cool, label, and store the jars. Let the pickles mellow for a month or two before serving them, chilled.

Pub-Style Pickled Shallots or Small Onions

T he Britons' beloved pub-style pickled onions are traditionally put up in strong malt vinegar, either with or without spicing; but because malt vinegar seems too harsh, these directions use a combination of cider and white wine (or rice) vinegar. Pickled shallots are milder than most kinds of onions, but small onions are the usual raw material for this zesty pickle.

After mellowing in the jar, these are excellent with bread and cheese (this is the "ploughman's lunch" of traditional pubs), or with cold meats or any savory sandwich.

2 pounds firm juicy shallots, preferably of uniform size, or use small (up to 1 inch) white-skinned onions

Salt: 2 tablespoons pickling salt or other fine non-iodized salt for step 1, plus 1 to 2 teaspoons for pickling solution

3 bay leaves, coarsely crumbled

2 teaspoons whole black peppercorns

1½ teaspoons whole allspice

1 teaspoon mustard seed

½ teaspoon crushed hot red pepper, or 3 or 4 tiny dried hot peppers

3 cups cider vinegar

1½ cups white wine vinegar or Oriental rice wine vinegar

 SEASON: Late summer through fall

 YIELD: 3 pints

STORE: Sealed, for at least a year in a cool pantry; unsealed but refrigerated or kept cool, at least a year

1. Place the shallots in a bowl and pour enough boiling water over them to cover them well; let them stand for 2 to 3 minutes. Drain off the hot water and run cold water into the bowl to cool them quickly, then drain the shallots in a colander. Using a small sharp knife, trim away the base plate and slip off the papery skin and any dried or leathery inner layers of the shallots. Return them to the bowl and mix them well with the 2 tablespoons salt. Cover the shallots and let them stand overnight or for about 8 hours, stirring them once or twice if you think of it.

2. At the same time, combine 1 to 2 teaspoons additional salt with the bay leaves, peppercorns, allspice, mustard seed, hot red pepper, and the two vinegars in a stainless-steel or other non-reactive saucepan. Heat the pickling solution to simmering and simmer it for 2 minutes, then remove from heat and let it stand, covered, until you are ready to complete the pickles.

3. Strain the pickling solution into a preserving pot and set it over low heat. Meanwhile, rinse the shallots repeatedly with cold water, then roll them in a towel until they are well dried. When the pickling solution simmers, add the shallots and raise the heat until the mixture boils. Cover the pot, lower the heat, and simmer the shallots until they are about half-cooked (test them with a sharp fork), about 5 minutes.

4. Divide the shallots among 3 hot, clean pint canning jars and fill the jars with pickling solution, leaving ¼ inch of headspace. Cover with new two-piece canning lids according to manufacturer's directions and process for 10 minutes in a boiling-water bath (page 325). Cool, label, and store the jars. The shallots should be allowed to mellow for a few weeks before they are served.

Alternate method: After step 3, pack the shallots and pickling solution into sterilized jars and seal them with sterilized lids. Store the pickles in a cool pantry for at least 3 months before serving them.

LITTLE
PUT-UP
JOBS

HEAVEN'S PRESERVES

Strawberry Preserves • Apricot Preserves
Sour Cherry Preserves with Cherry Brandy or Amaretto
Sour Cherry & Walnut Conserve • Black Cherry Preserves
Blueberry & Orange Preserves • Huckleberry Spread
Seedless Blackberry Jam
Peach or Nectarine Jam with Brown Sugar & Rum
Tomato Jam with Ginger & Coriander • Wild Blueberry Jam
Peerless Red Raspberry Preserves
Purple Plum Jam with Orange Liqueur
Baked Cranberry Preserves with Orange & Cardamom
Dried Apricot & Amaretto Conserve

A QUIVER OF JELLIES

Naturally Sweet Apple Cider Syrup or Jelly
Fresh Ginger Jelly • Coriander & Honey Jelly
Crab Apple Jelly • Wine Jellies
Honey Jelly

FRUIT HONEYS

Pear Honey • Clear Quince Honey

MARMALADING

Melon Marmalade • A Marmalade of Apples & Apple Cider
Quince Marmalade • Temple Orange Marmalade
Ginger Marmalade

Because this chapter of preserves, conserves, jams, jellies, fruit-based honeys, and marmalades is mainly created from fruits, it is linked more closely to the summer than are most other *Fancy Pantry* sections. But if it shouldn't happen to be summer when you feel like putting up a few little jars, you'll also find here a number of delicacies to make from raw materials available in other seasons, or even the year around.

Suitable for making in any season are any of the plain or fancy Wine Jellies; Fresh Ginger Jelly and Ginger Marmalade; Dried Apricot & Amaretto Conserve; Coriander & Honey Jelly, which is flavored by a most delicate spice; or, if you'd like to try jellied honey "straight," there is Honey Jelly to make from your favorite kind, from mild and flowery to pungent and assertive.

Fall and winter possibilities that stretch the preserving season include Naturally Sweet Apple Cider Syrup or Jelly; Quince Marmalade; Clear Quince Honey; Pear Honey; Temple Orange Marmalade; and Baked Cranberry Preserves with Orange & Cardamom.

And, for those whose schedules don't permit following the seasons at all for putting fresh things by, first-rate preserves can start at any time of year with fruit from the deep-freeze, especially blueberries, cherries, strawberries, and raspberries. You may want to bear in mind that, besides those fruits, most of the fresh raw materials for preserves called for in this section—even tomatoes, for a scrumptious jam made with ginger and coriander—can be successfully frozen to await the day you feel like preserving them. Exceptions are fresh quinces, oranges, and ginger, which don't especially lend themselves to freezing; but of these, only quinces have a limited season.

HEAVEN'S PRESERVES

Preserves, here, include several kinds of delectable preparations. There are the classic fruit preserves, in which chunky fruit is suspended in syrup, sometimes with a liqueur added; conserves, which are preserves of two or more kinds of fruit, often enriched with nuts or liqueurs; jams, based on crushed fruit and cooked to a denser consistency than preserves; and fruit spreads, less dense and less sweet than jams.

The recipes that follow move with the seasons, from the first strawberries to cranberries and, finally, dried apricots, always available and always wonderful for making conserves and such.

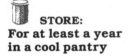
**SEASON:
Early summer**

**YIELD:
About 5 cups**

**STORE:
For at least a year
in a cool pantry**

Strawberry Preserves

The method described here for making classic pure strawberry preserves—whole berries suspended in a not-quite-jellied syrup made without added pectin—may require explanation for first-timer preservers.

Despite the several steps involved, the overall working time is not large. Don't be tempted to double the size of a batch being cooked, as the briefest possible cooking is essential; however, doubling or tripling the quantity of berries and sugar is feasible—just divide the macerated fruit and its syrup into halves or thirds and cook one batch at a time. All the jars can be processed at once; set the first batch(es) of filled and capped jars aside until the rest are ready, then place them all in the boiling-water bath and proceed with processing.

After the berries have been left to stand with the sugar (step 1), it will appear that all is lost—there is a frightful amount of syrup, and the berries appear shriveled, not to say puny. However, the remainder of the process plumps them up wonderfully, and by the time they are sealed in jars, they are perfect.

**2 quart baskets small firm-ripe strawberries, the
   finest-flavored you can find**

6 cups sugar

Strained juice of 1½ large lemons

1. Sort, hull, rinse, and drain the berries; use only those that are perfect, discarding any with either soft or unripened spots. Layer them with the sugar in a ceramic or stainless-steel bowl (do not use aluminum), then fold the fruit and sugar

gently together with a rubber spatula. Let the berries stand overnight, covered, stirring them gently a few times; the idea is to allow all the sugar to dissolve before proceeding.

2. Scrape the berries and syrup into a preserving pan or a very large (12-inch) sauté pan. Add the lemon juice. Bring the mixture to a boil, stirring it occasionally, and boil it briskly for 3 minutes, stirring from time to time.

3. Pour the mixture into a bowl and let it cool uncovered. Cover the bowl with a cloth and let it stand overnight or for at least 6 hours.

4. Drain all the syrup from the berries and return it to the preserving pan. Bring it to a boil over medium-high heat, then boil it hard until it passes the jelly test (page 322). Return the berries and any accumulated syrup to the pan and again bring the preserves to a boil, stirring gently with a spatula to prevent sticking; be careful not to break the fruit. Boil the preserves until the berries are translucent and the syrup again passes the jelly test; depending on the original juiciness of the strawberries, this will take from 2 to 4 minutes. Remove from heat.

5. Skim off any foam and stir the preserves from time to time for 5 minutes (this is to keep the fruit from floating).

6. Ladle the preserves into hot, clean half-pint or pint canning jars, leaving ¼ inch of headspace. Seal the jars with new two-piece canning lids according to manufacturer's directions and process for 15 minutes (for either size jar) in a boiling-water bath (page 325). Cool, label, and store the jars.

Preserves Made With Frozen Strawberries

 **SEASON:
Any time**

For preserving, you'll want strawberries that have been frozen loose, without sugar. If you do your own, spread them on baking sheets, freeze them, then roll them into freezer bags and seal them airtight. It will save time later if you weigh them and mark the bag with the weight and the date. Try to make the preserves before the berries have been held in the freezer too long; 6 months' storage is about the limit if you are aiming for the best flavor, although frozen berries will remain edible at least twice as long.

To make the preserves, follow the directions in the preceding recipe, using a pound (2 cups) of sugar for each pound (about 3 cups) of berries and adding lemon juice as described. There is no need to thaw the berries before stirring them with the sugar; dissolving the sugar will take longer, that's all.

SEASON:
Early summer

YIELD:
About 7 cups

STORE:
For at least a year in a cool pantry

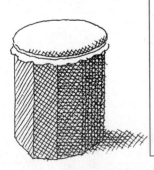

Apricot Preserves

When all's said and done, this may be the best fruit preserve of all, with the possible exception of . . . Well, let's not play favorites. Certainly ripe, fragrant apricots make a peerless preserve. Enjoy it with toast, or croissants, or any kind of muffins, or use it to glaze a fruit tart or to fill tartlets.

During their short season, buy only those apricots that look as if they might come to full ripeness—it is too much to hope, except perhaps in California, to find tree-ripened fruit. Very green or oversoft specimens will not give perfect results. If your apricots are a mixed bag, in order to have the whole batch at a decent stage of readiness at the same time, refrigerate the fruits as they become firm-ripe and let the rest catch up at room temperature.

3 pounds ripe apricots, preferably large ones
6 to 8 apricot kernels, optional (see steps 1 and 2)
⅓ cup strained fresh lemon juice
6 cups sugar

1. Scald the apricots in batches by placing them in a sieve and plunging them into boiling water for about 15 seconds; then drop them into a bowl of cold water and ice. Drain the apricots, strip off their skins, quarter them, and save the pits, if you wish to include a few of the kernels in the preserves— they contribute a delicate touch of almond-like flavor.

2. If you are using the kernels, crack the pits (a heavy-duty nutcracker, such as one designed for black walnuts, makes short work of this). Blanch them for a moment or two in a small saucepan of boiling water, drain them, and slip off the skins. Set aside 6 to 8 kernels; reserve the rest for another use.

3. Combine the apricots, the kernels, and the lemon juice in a ceramic or stainless-steel (not aluminum) bowl and mix them gently with a rubber spatula. Add the sugar and mix again. Set the mixture aside for a few hours (or for as long as overnight, in this case in the refrigerator), stirring it gently a few times.

4. When almost all of the sugar has dissolved, transfer the mixture to a preserving pan and set the pan over medium heat. Bring the mixture to a boil, then adjust the heat and simmer it, uncovered, for 10 minutes, stirring a few times with a straight-ended spatula. Skim off any foam, then cook the preserves for 20 minutes more, or until the fruit is translucent. (The actual time will depend on the variety and ripeness of the fruit.)

5. Pour the mixture into a bowl, let it cool, then cover it with a cloth and leave it at room temperature overnight or for at least 6 hours.

6. Lift the fruit with a slotted spoon into a sieve set over a bowl. Let the juice drain from the fruit for a few minutes. Return all the juice to the preserving pan and bring it to a boil over medium-high heat; boil it rapidly until it passes the jelly test (page 322). Return the fruit to the boiling syrup, together with any additional syrup it may have released, and bring everything to a boil; boil hard for 1 minute. Remove from the heat.

7. Cool the preserves for 5 minutes, stirring occasionally, then ladle into hot, clean half-pint canning jars, leaving ¼ inch of headspace. Seal the jars with new two-piece canning lids according to manufacturer's directions and process for 15 minutes in a boiling-water bath (page 325). Cool, label, and store the jars.

Sour Cherry Preserves with Cherry Brandy or Amaretto

One of the nicest things to do with sour cherries, which can be either fresh or frozen. The only sour cherries I can buy where I live are pitted and frozen, and they make fine preserves.

4 pounds fresh sour cherries (about 2⅓ quarts after pitting) or the same measure of frozen pitted sour cherries, thawed

½ cup water

¼ cup strained fresh lemon juice

5½ cups sugar

8 to 10 tablespoons Kirschwasser, other cherry brandy, or amaretto liqueur, optional

1. Rinse, stem, and pit fresh cherries, saving all the juice. Thaw frozen cherries. Combine the cherries, their juice, and the water in a preserving pan.

2. Cook the cherries over medium heat until they are tender, 15 to 20 minutes; stir the cherries or shake the pan occasionally.

3. Pour the cherries and juice into a colander set over a bowl. Drain off all possible juice and return it to the preserving pan (no need to rinse the pan between steps). Add the lemon juice and the sugar to the juice, stir it over medium heat until it

SEASON:
Summer; but can be made with frozen cherries at any time

YIELD:
About 6 cups

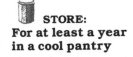
STORE:
For at least a year in a cool pantry

boils, and boil the syrup for 5 minutes. Add the cherries; remove from the heat.

4. Pour the cherries and syrup into a bowl and set the bowl aside, covered with a cloth, overnight or for as long as 24 hours.

5. Return the cherries and syrup to a preserving pan. Bring the mixture to a boil over medium-high heat, shaking the pan often or stirring the preserves gently with a straight-ended spatula. Boil the mixture, uncovered, 4 minutes, then set it aside for a day as described in step 4.

6. Repeat step 5, boiling the preserves only until the syrup has thickened slightly—it won't pass the jelly test—about 3 minutes. Remove from heat.

7. Skim off any foam from the preserves and add the cherry brandy or amaretto, if you are including it. Ladle the preserves into hot, clean half-pint or pint canning jars, leaving ¼ inch of headspace. Seal the jars with new two-piece canning lids according to manufacturer's directions and process for 15 minutes (for either size jar) in a boiling-water bath (page 325). Cool, label, and store the jars.

SEASON:
Summer, but can be made with frozen cherries at any time

YIELD:
About 5 cups

STORE:
For a year or more in a cool pantry

Sour Cherry & Walnut Conserve

A ruddy preserve, crunchy with nuts, this conserve is good fare for a leisurely breakfast; have it on toast spread with cream cheese, or with croissants. For dessert, spoon it into tiny pastry or cookie cups, or use it as a cake filling.

The conserve is doubly good when the optional liqueur is included. Kirschwasser, one of the best of cherry brandies, intensifies the basic flavor, and amaretto has an almond flavor that is highly compatible with both cherries and walnuts.

3 pounds fresh sour cherries (about 2 quarts after pitting) or the same measure of frozen pitted sour cherries, thawed

2 medium-large oranges, preferably seedless

2 lemons

½ cup water

1 cup walnut halves

5 cups sugar

¼ cup Kirschwasser or amaretto liqueur, optional

1. Stem, rinse, and pit the cherries, saving all the juice. Place the cherries and juice in a preserving pan.

2. Grate off the zest (outer skin only; no white pith) of the oranges and one of the lemons. Add the zest to the cherries.

Pare off all the white membrane from the oranges and lemons; cut out the pulp, leaving the tough dividing membranes behind. Chop the pulp and add it to the cherries, together with all the juice that can be squeezed from the membranes; discard the membranes. Add the water to the fruit.

3. Set the pan over medium heat and simmer the mixture, uncovered, stirring it occasionally, until the cherries are soft, 15 to 20 minutes.

4. Meanwhile, heat the oven to 350°. Spread the walnuts on a baking sheet and toast them until they are nuttily fragrant, about 10 minutes, stirring once or twice. Cool the nuts, then rub them in a cloth to remove loose skin and chop them coarsely. Reserve them.

5. When the cherries are soft, add the sugar, raise the heat to medium-high, and continue to cook the mixture, stirring often, until the syrup has thickened. (It may or may not pass the usual jelly tests at this point; for this mixture, it's most precise to drop a little syrup on a chilled saucer and set it in the freezer until it is cold, with the pot off the heat. If a finger leaves a clear path after being drawn through the sample, the conserve is thick enough.) Add the walnuts, return the mixture to boiling, and cook it 5 minutes longer. Remove from heat.

6. Stir the Kirschwasser or the amaretto into the conserve, if you are including it. Ladle the conserve into hot, clean half-pint canning jars, leaving ¼ inch of headspace. Seal the jars with new two-piece canning lids according to manufacturer's directions and process for 15 minutes in a boiling-water bath (page 325). Cool, label, and store the jars.

Black Cherry Preserves

Dark-red sweet cherry varieties (two of the best-known are named Bing and Lambert), traditionally called "black cherries," are the kind to use for this intensely dark preserve of whole fruit in rich syrup.

A word of advice about the fruit: If you'd like to make this preserve, possess your soul in patience through the season of the earliest cherries; the later crop that arrives in July, mostly from the Northwest, offers more substance and finer flavor.

2 pounds firm-ripe dark sweet cherries

½ cup water

4 cups sugar

¼ cup strained fresh lemon juice

About 4 drops almond extract, optional

SEASON:
Summer

YIELD:
About 5 cups

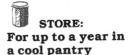
STORE:
For up to a year in a cool pantry

1. Stem, rinse, and drain the cherries. Remove the pits, saving any juice. Halve the cherries if they are exceptionally large.

2. Combine the cherries with the water in a preserving pan. Cook the cherries over low heat, covered, remembering to shake the pan occasionally, until the cherries have shriveled and given up a good deal of juice, 30 to 40 minutes. Pour the cherries and juice into a colander set over a bowl and drain off all possible juice; reserve the fruit.

3. Combine the juice with the sugar and lemon juice in the preserving pan (there is no need to rinse it between operations). Bring the mixture to a boil over medium-high heat, stirring until the sugar has dissolved. Boil the syrup hard for 2 minutes. Add the cherries, shake the pan to mingle them with the syrup, and remove it from the heat. Pour the cherries and juice into a bowl, cover it with a cloth, and set it aside overnight or for up to 24 hours.

4. Return the fruit and syrup to the preserving pan, set it over medium-high heat, and bring the mixture to a full boil, shaking the pan often or stirring the fruit gently with a straight-ended spatula. Boil the mixture hard until the syrup registers 220° on a jelly/candy thermometer, about 3 minutes; if the cherries are unusually juicy, the process may take a minute or two longer. Do not overcook the preserves—the cherries will reabsorb much of the syrup as they cool. Remove from heat; add the almond extract, if using.

5. Skim off any foam and stir the preserves gently from time to time for about 5 minutes to prevent floating fruit. Ladle the preserves into hot, clean half-pint or pint canning jars, leaving ¼ inch of headspace. Seal the jars with new two-piece canning lids according to manufacturer's directions and process for 15 minutes (for either size jar) in a boiling-water bath (page 325). Cool, label, and store the jars.

 SEASON:
Mid- to late
summer, for fresh
berries; any time
for frozen

YIELD:
About 8 cups

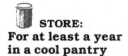 **STORE:**
For at least a year
in a cool pantry

Blueberry & Orange Preserves

A soft preserve of the classic type, this has chunky blueberries and tender shreds of orange zest suspended in rich syrup. For the proper delicate texture, be careful not to cook the preserves to the jam stage, which is considerably stiffer. If cultivated berries are what you have, though, their relative blandness is improved by a touch of spice.

The light spicing prescribed by the recipe is optional if you should be using wild blueberries, which are naturally more flavorful than the tame kind.

2 large, clear-skinned oranges, preferably seedless

1 cup water

3 pint baskets (about 9 cups) fresh blueberries, cultivated or wild

7 cups sugar

¾ cup strained fresh lemon juice

1 teaspoon ground coriander (or substitute cinnamon), optional

½ teaspoon ground allspice, optional

1. Remove the zest (outer skin only, no white pith) from the oranges with a coarse grater or a citrus zester and combine it with the water in a small heavy saucepan. Cook the shreds of zest, covered, over medium heat for 15 minutes; uncover the pan and continue to cook the zest until most of the liquid has evaporated. Reserve. Meanwhile, squeeze, strain, and re-serve the juice of the oranges.

2. Pick over the blueberries; rinse and drain them, then crush them slightly, a layer at a time, in a preserving pan. (Use a potato masher or the bottom of a heavy bottle.) Add the orange juice. Bring the mixture to a boil, cover the pan, and lower the heat; simmer the fruit 10 minutes, stirring it often.

3. Add the cooked orange zest and liquid, the sugar, the lemon juice, and the spices, if used. Stir the mixture and bring it to a boil over medium-high heat. Cook the preserves, stirring often, until the fruit pieces no longer float and the syrup passes the jelly test (page 322). Remove the pan from the heat and stir the preserves occasionally for 5 minutes.

4. Ladle the hot preserves into hot, clean pint or half-pint canning jars, leaving ¼ inch of headspace. Seal the jars with new two-piece canning lids according to manufacturer's direc-tions and process for 10 minutes (for either size jar) in a boiling-water bath (page 325). Cool, label, and store the jars.

Huckleberry Spread

Not everyone lives where the *real* huckleberries grow— I'm not talking about blueberries, often loosely called by the same name, but the genuine article, the fruit of shrubby wild bushes that come up to the knee; they are purple-black and have tiny hard seeds (blueberries are generally bigger and paler, and they have soft seeds). If you can pick wild huckleber-ries, by all means do so; they are delicious fresh with breakfast cereal, or baked into muffins, but we like them even better made into this midnight-dark spread for toast.

 SEASON:
July/August

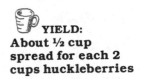 **YIELD:**
About ½ cup
spread for each 2
cups huckleberries

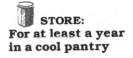 **STORE:**
For at least a year
in a cool pantry

The trick to making a suave spread is sorting out the rock-hard little seeds; for this you need a sieve with very fine mesh.

The rewards of huckleberrying can be variable, so this is a formula, not a recipe that assumes you'll be able to capture a given quantity of the raw material.

Freshly picked huckleberries

Water

Sugar

Cinnamon sticks

1. Pick over the huckleberries; rinse them and drain them well.

2. Combine the huckleberries in a preserving pan with enough water to cover them by ½ inch. Bring the water to a boil over medium-high heat, cover the pan, and simmer the berries until they are easily crushed with a spoon, ½ hour or longer, depending on the resistance of your particular batch.

3. Pour the huckleberries and their liquid into a very fine-meshed sieve set over a bowl. Using a large spoon or wooden implement made for the purpose (a *champignon*, in cookware shops), rub as much of the pulp through the sieve as possible. Discard the debris of seeds and intractable skins remaining in the sieve.

4. Measure the puree into the rinsed-out preserving pan. For each cupful add ½ cup of sugar and a ½-inch piece of stick cinnamon. Bring the mixture to a boil over medium-high heat, stirring constantly. Cook, stirring constantly with a straight-ended spatula, until the spread drops in a thick sheet from the edge of a metal spoon; how long this will take depends on the juiciness of the berries. Remove from the heat.

5. Ladle the huckleberry spread into hot, clean half-pint or pint canning jars, leaving the cinnamon stick behind; leave ¼ inch of headspace. Seal the jars with new two-piece canning lids according to manufacturer's directions and process for 15 minutes (for either size jar) in a boiling-water bath (page 325). Cool, label, and store the jars.

SEASON:
Mid- to late summer

YIELD:
6 cups

STORE:
For a year or more in a cool, dark cupboard

Seedless Blackberry Jam

Fully ripe blackberries are used instead of underripe ones for this jam, because the apples supply the pectin needed to make it jell, and lemon juice provides a little welcome tartness. The result is a preserve that captures the full flavor of one of the best of berries, too often neglected.

This makes a delicious filling for tiny tarts or a layer cake.

6 cups (about 4 half-pint baskets) ripe blackberries, picked over, rinsed, drained

2½ cups coarsely chopped tart cooking apples (2 or 3 medium-size apples), including skins and cores

1½ cups water, or more as needed

3 tablespoons strained fresh lemon juice, or to taste

Sugar

1. Place half of the blackberries in a preserving pan; crush them with a potato masher or a heavy bottle. Add the remaining berries and crush them. (Alternatively, chop the berries briefly in a food processor.)

2. Add the apples and 1½ cups water to the berries. Cook the mixture, uncovered, over medium-low heat, stirring often, until the fruit is very soft, 15 to 20 minutes. Add up to ½ cup more water if the fruit threatens to stick to the pan; if necessary, stir the fruit almost constantly.

3. Set a food mill with a fine disc (or use a medium-mesh sieve) over a bowl. Force the hot fruit through the sieve, using the back of a spoon or a rubber spatula; discard the seeds.

4. Measure the fruit pulp into the rinsed-out pan; you should have about 5 cups. Taste the pulp; add enough lemon juice to make the fruit pleasantly tart. Stir in 1 cup of sugar for each cup of pulp.

5. Heat the mixture over medium-high heat to boiling, stirring until the sugar dissolves. Cook the jam rapidly, stirring frequently, until it passes the jelly test (page 322).

6. Ladle the boiling-hot jam into hot, clean half-pint canning jars, leaving ¼ inch of headspace. Seal the jars with new two-piece canning lids according to manufacturer's directions and process for 10 minutes in a boiling-water bath (page 325). Cool, label, and store the jars.

Peach or Nectarine Jam with Brown Sugar & Rum

SEASON:
Late summer

YIELD:
About 6 cups

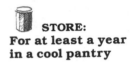
STORE:
For at least a year in a cool pantry

The blend of flavors here is like that of Fish House Punch, a notable American potable in which dark rum, peach brandy, and lemon juice all play a part. The jam isn't at all alcoholic; the alcohol evaporates during cooking.

Made as described below, the jam is a rich deep gold in color. If you'd like an even more pronounced brown-sugar flavor together with a darker color, substitute dark brown sugar for light brown. For more rumminess, the liquor might be increased by no more than 2 tablespoons.

Besides fulfilling its obvious destiny on buttered toast, this jam can be spooned into tiny dessert tart shells, or spread as an underlayer for the custard filling of a tart that is to be topped with sliced fresh fruit (peaches, nectarines, or pears).

**6 cups coarsely chopped peeled firm-ripe peaches or
  nectarines (about 4 pounds)
2 cups (packed) light brown sugar
6 tablespoons strained fresh lemon juice
¾ cup dark rum, preferably Jamaican
2 cups granulated sugar**

1. Combine the peaches with the brown sugar and lemon juice and about half of the rum in a large bowl and stir the mixture well. Cover it and let it stand overnight.

2. Pour the peach mixture into a preserving pan. Bring it to a boil over medium-high heat. Cover the pan, reduce the heat, and cook the mixture until the peach chunks are beginning to be translucent, 15 to 20 minutes; stir it several times. If the jam becomes too thick before the fruit clarifies, add 2 or 3 tablespoons of water. Add the granulated sugar and cook the jam rapidly, stirring almost constantly, until a spoonful placed on a chilled saucer and refrigerated for a few moments wrinkles instead of running when the saucer is tilted sharply. (Remove the pot from the heat while testing.) Stir in the remaining rum and cook the jam for 2 minutes, stirring.

3. Ladle the boiling-hot jam into hot, clean pint or half-pint canning jars, leaving ¼ inch of headspace. Seal the jars with clean two-part canning lids according to manufacturer's directions and process for 15 minutes (for either size jar) in a boiling-water bath (page 325). Cool, label, and store the jars. The jam is ready to use immediately.

**SEASON:
Midsummer
through fall**

**YIELD:
About 4 cups**

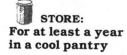
**STORE:
For at least a year
in a cool pantry**

Tomato Jam With Ginger & Coriander

A soft, fragrant jam with a delicate flavor and a rosy-apricot color, this preserve is one of the best of good things to make from "love apples." If you happen to have yellow tomatoes, they make a paler but very pretty jam.

Either jam is a special treat on crisp toast spread with cream cheese or your own Fresh White Cheese, page 44.

5 pounds firm but ripe fleshy tomatoes

2 large lemons

1 tablespoon very finely minced fresh ginger or 2 tablespoons chopped Crystallized Ginger (page 265) or Ginger Preserved in Syrup (page 267)

½ teaspoon salt

5 cups sugar

1 tablespoon ground coriander

1. Dip tomatoes a few at a time into boiling water for 10 seconds, then drop them into cold water. Skin the tomatoes, cut out the stem ends and hard cores, halve them crosswise, and squeeze the seeds into a sieve set over a bowl. Discard the seeds; reserve the juice. Chop the tomatoes coarsely and place them, with the juice, in a preserving pan.

2. Grate the zest (outer skin only, no white pith) from the lemons, and measure 2 packed teaspoons; add it to the tomatoes. Squeeze the lemons and add 6 tablespoons lemon juice to the tomatoes. Add the ginger and salt.

3. Bring the mixture to a boil, stirring occasionally, then lower the heat and simmer it uncovered, stirring occasionally, until the tomato pieces are soft, about 15 minutes. Stir in the sugar. Raise the heat to medium-high and cook the jam, stirring almost constantly, until a candy/jelly thermometer reads 219° (slightly under the usual "done" temperature for jam), or until a small amount of the jam placed on a chilled saucer congeals quickly when refrigerated and does not run when the saucer is tilted. (Take the pan from the fire meanwhile.) When the jam is done, stir in the coriander and remove the pot from the heat.

4. Ladle the boiling-hot jam into hot, clean half-pint canning jars, leaving ¼ inch of headspace. Cover with new two-piece canning lids according to manufacturer's directions and process for 15 minutes in a boiling-water bath (page 325). Cool, label, and store the jars.

Wild Blueberry Jam

Wild blueberries may be tiny, but oh, my—their spicy fragrance and flavor just can't be matched by the big cultivated berries, however beautiful and juicy the tame fruit may be. Wild blueberries don't need spice or other enhancement when they're made into preserves, but unless they are unusually tart, a little lemon juice is needed.

 SEASON:
Mid- to late summer, for fresh berries; any time, for frozen

 YIELD:
About 3 cups

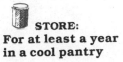 **STORE:**
For at least a year in a cool pantry

If wild blueberries are not a local asset, excellent jam can be made from frozen wild berries, which are widely available in one-pound bags.

2 pint baskets (about 6 cups) fresh wild blueberries, or two 1-pound bags frozen wild blueberries, thawed

2 to 4 tablespoons strained fresh lemon juice, as needed

3 cups sugar

1. Pick over the fresh blueberries, then rinse and drain them. If using packaged frozen berries, thaw them in their bags or wrappings; be careful to keep all the juice.

2. Crush the berries, in two batches, thoroughly with a potato masher or the bottom of a heavy bottle or chop them coarsely in batches in a food processor.

3. Scrape the berries into a preserving pan, including any juice from frozen berries. Taste them; they should be pleasantly tart. If they lack tartness, add 2 to 4 tablespoons lemon juice, to taste. Stir in the sugar. Set the pan over medium-high heat, bring the mixture to a boil, and boil the mixture rapidly, stirring constantly, until it passes the jelly test (page 322). The time required for reduction will depend on how juicy the berries are.

4. Ladle the boiling-hot jam into hot, clean half-pint canning jars, leaving ¼ inch of headspace. Seal the jars with new two-piece canning lids according to manufacturer's directions and process for 15 minutes in a boiling-water bath (page 325). Cool, label, and store the jars.

SEASON:
July through October; with frozen, any time

YIELD:
About 3 cups

STORE:
For at lest a year in a cool pantry

Peerless Red Raspberry Preserves

Not many classic preserves made the final cut for inclusion in this collection, but this soft raspberry delectability just can't be left out.

The secret of making brilliantly colored and fresh-tasting preserves from red raspberries is brief, fast cooking in small batches. Therefore you'll need a wide, shallow pan; a 12-inch (or larger) sauté pan or skillet is perfect. Don't try to cook a double batch; you'll slow down the process of evaporation too much and end up with a dark or gummy result.

Directions for a seedless jam follow the main recipe.

4 cups red raspberries, fresh or frozen unsweetened
3 cups sugar
¼ cup strained fresh lemon juice

1. Sort fresh raspberries, discarding any that are soft, moldy, or otherwise suspect. Rinse them and drain them well. Thaw frozen raspberries, saving all their juice.

2. Stir the raspberries (including the juice from thawed berries), the sugar, and lemon juice together in a bowl, using a rubber spatula; let the mixture stand, stirring gently once or twice, until the sugar has dissolved, about 2 hours.

3. Scrape the mixture into a large skillet or sauté pan. Bring it to a boil, stirring constantly with a straight-ended wooden or nylon spatula, and boil it rapidly, stirring often, until it passes the jelly test (page 322); this will take from 3 to 5 minutes, depending on the water content of the berries. Remove from heat.

4. Skim off any foam and ladle the boiling-hot preserves into hot, clean half-pint canning jars, leaving ¼ inch of headspace. Seal the jars with new two-piece canning lids according to manufacturer's directions and process for 10 minutes in a boiling-water bath (page 325). Cool, label, and store the jars.

Seedless Raspberry Jam

Use the preceding recipe, but begin with 5 to 6 cups of raspberries. Mash the berries thoroughly or puree them, then press them through a fine sieve to remove the seeds.* Combine the pulp (which will be very liquid), lemon juice, and sugar in a wide skillet or sauté pan and proceed to cook the jam at once, stirring it constantly until it passes the jelly test (page 322). Skim, seal, and process as described.

Purple Plum Jam with Orange Liqueur

This happy pairing of fruit and liqueur points up the fruit's distinctive flavor without calling undue attention to the spirits; a subtle added taste teases the palate—there's something more than just plain plum going on here, but what?

This is a soft jam, dark in color and rich in flavor; it's one of the best uses I know for the purple (or blue, or prune, or Italian) plums that round off the season of summer fruits.

* WASTE-NOT, WANT-NOT NOTE:

Much flavor remains in the seedy residue in the sieve. Stir it into a cupful of white wine vinegar or Oriental rice vinegar and let the mixture stand in a capped jar for a week or two; strain and scald the resulting raspberry-flavored vinegar and bottle it for future use.

SEASON:
Early fall

YIELD:
6 cups

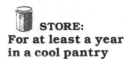
STORE:
For at least a year in a cool pantry

4 pounds firm-ripe purple (blue, Italian, or prune) plums

2 cups water

¼ cup strained fresh lemon juice

4 cups sugar

½ cup orange-flavored liqueur (Cointreau or other)

1. Rinse, drain, and pit the plums. Combine them with the water in a large saucepan, bring them to a boil, and simmer them, partly covered, until they are very soft and most of the liquid has evaporated, about 30 minutes.

2. Press the plums and their liquid through a food mill or a coarse sieve. Combine the plum pulp, lemon juice, and sugar in a preserving pan and stir the mixture over medium-high heat until the sugar has dissolved. Cook the jam at a brisk boil, stirring it often, until it passes the jelly test (page 322), about 10 minutes. Add the orange liqueur and cook the jam for another minute or so.

4. Ladle the hot jam into hot, clean pint or half-pint canning jars, leaving ¼ inch of headspace. Seal the jars with new two-part canning lids according to manufacturer's directions and process for 15 minutes (for either size jar) in a boiling-water bath (page 325). Cool, label, and store the jars.

SEASON:
From October to end of winter; or use frozen cranberries at any season

YIELD:
About 3 cups

STORE:
Sealed, for up to a year in a cool pantry; unsealed, for several months in the refrigerator

Baked Cranberry Preserves with Orange & Cardamom

Cardamom is a delightful spice with cranberries and orange, subtly underlining the flavors of both. If you have a spice mill, by all means grind the cardamom seeds yourself—the gain in flavor is worth the small effort. The cranberries in this preserve are translucent and almost whole, thanks to the cooking method, and there's a further bonus—while baking, the mixture requires little attention.

Besides being a turkey accompaniment that's different from most cranberry sauces in both flavor and texture, Baked Cranberry Preserves are a delicious topping for toast or hot muffins, so you may want to double the batch. If you do that, use a large shallow roasting pan for the baking. The timing is the same.

4 cups firm-fresh cranberries, picked over and rinsed (if they are frozen, it is not necessary to thaw them)

1 medium-size seedless orange

3 cups sugar

⅛ teaspoon ground cardamom, freshly ground if possible

¼ cup water

1. Spread the cranberries in an 8-inch square glass baking dish or other shallow non-aluminum pan of about the same overall area.

2. Remove the skin from the orange in strips and scrape the white pith from the inside; discard the pith. Chop the outer peel and the pulp of the orange very fine (a food processor will do this quickly).

3. Stir the chopped orange, sugar, and cardamom into the cranberries, mixing them thoroughly. Sprinkle the water over the mixture, then cover the dish tightly with aluminum foil.

4. Bake the mixture in the center of a preheated 350° oven for 30 minutes. Then lower the oven heat to 325°, uncover the dish, stir the fruit in the syrup that has formed, using a pancake turner or flat spatula, then continue to bake the preserves uncovered until the berries are translucent and the syrup has thickened, about 45 minutes; stir the mixture gently every 10 or 15 minutes.

5. Spoon the hot preserves into hot, clean half-pint or pint canning jars, leaving ¼ inch of headspace. Seal the jars with new two-part canning lids according to manufacturer's directions and process for 10 minutes (for either size jar) in a boiling-water bath (page 325). Cool, label, and store the jars.

6. Alternatively, refrigerate the preserves without processing or sealing the jar(s).

Dried Apricot & Amaretto Conserve

Not to worry if you'd like to give custom-made Christmas presents but your stock of choice preserves is running low—this golden, almond-studded conserve can be made at any season, because dried apricots are always to be had. Taste the fruit before buying; high-quality dried apricots positively shimmer with flavor, but lesser grades have mostly tartness to recommend them.

SEASON:
Any time

YIELD:
About 4 cups

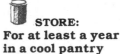
STORE:
For at least a year in a cool pantry

**½ pound high-quality dried apricot halves, about
1½ cups**

1 cup golden raisins

3 cups water, more if needed

**1½ teaspoons finely grated orange zest (outer skin
only, no white pith)**

1 cup strained fresh orange juice

2 tablespoons strained fresh lemon juice

2½ cups sugar

½ cup slivered blanched almonds

3 tablespoons amaretto liqueur

1. Snip the apricots into thin strips, using scissors. Combine them with the raisins in a bowl, add the water, and let the fruit soak until it is very soft, several hours (or overnight, refrigerated).

2. Tip the fruit and liquid into a heavy saucepan; if there is not enough liquid to come halfway to the top of the fruit, add up to another cup of water. Add the grated orange zest. Heat the mixture to simmering and cook it, stirring once or twice, until the fruit is very tender, about 15 minutes.

3. Stir in the orange and lemon juice and return the mixture to a boil. Add the sugar and cook the conserve over medium heat, stirring it almost constantly with a wooden spatula or other straight-ended implement, until it is thick, 20 to 30 minutes; to test, spoon a sample onto a chilled saucer and let it cool; when the saucer is held on edge, the surface should wrinkle. Add the almonds and cook, stirring, 5 minutes longer. Remove from heat.

4. Stir in the amaretto. Ladle the conserve into hot, clean half-pint canning jars, leaving ¼ inch of headspace. Seal the jars with new two-piece canning lids according to manufacturer's directions and process for 10 minutes in a boiling-water bath (page 325). Cool, label, and store the jars. The conserve is all the better for mellowing in the jars for a week or two before it is served.

A QUIVER OF JELLIES

Garden-variety isn't the right term for the jellies here, for not one of them is likely to be found on the shelf labeled "humdrum." If more basic fruit jellies are what you crave, the directions packed with either liquid or powdered commercial pectin give reliable results, even for neophytes. Advanced jelly-makers will be more interested in the possibilities of the delicate confections in this section. Novices shouldn't quail, though: there is enough information here for the beginner.

Naturally Sweet Apple Cider Syrup or Jelly

Old-fashioned "boiled cider," which is sweet cider boiled down to half-volume or less in order to increase its flavor and density, was a secret weapon of American cooks long before the recent rediscovery of good regional food. (Boiled cider is a traditional ingredient of the world's best apple butter.)

This recipe is for the ultimate boiled cider, which you can have either as a tart, fruity syrup, thick as honey, to pour over pancakes, waffles, or hot biscuits, or as a tart jelly that contains only the natural sugar of the apples. The small jar of intensely flavored sweet stuff you end up with is the concentrate of quarts of cider, so it's reasonable that the price tag for apple-cider jelly or syrup is high, if you can find a shop or a mail-order business offering either one.

In view of the tiny yield, you may want to double this recipe. If you do, use two pans; evaporation is too slow when a large amount of cider is put into a single pot. Try to use the juice of late-crop apples—the fruit is sweeter, and a good level of natural sugar is desirable here.

1. Measure 2 quarts of freshly pressed apple cider (sometimes labeled "apple juice"), which should have been made without preservatives, into a large, wide pot. Bring the cider to a boil over medium-high heat and boil it, skimming it often, until no more scum rises. Continue to boil the cider until it has reduced to a syrupy consistency, if you want apple syrup, or until it has reduced sufficiently to pass the jelly test (page 322), watching it closely toward the end of cooking to prevent scorching.*

2. Pour the syrup or hot jelly into a hot, dry scalded jar,

SEASON:
Autumn

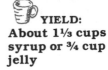
YIELD:
About 1⅓ cups syrup or ¾ cup jelly

STORE:
In a cool pantry (sealed) or refrigerator (unsealed); keeps indefinitely

*JELLY NOTE:

If the cider will not "sheet" from the spoon even though it has reached the jelly reading on your thermometer, it just won't jell, which happens occasionally. More cooking will just make it gummy, so stop at this point and call your product semi-jelly or thick syrup. It will taste wonderful even though it's less than perfect in texture.

cool and cap it, and store it in the refrigerator. To seal it for longer storage, seal the jar according to lid manufacturer's directions and process for 10 minutes in a boiling-water bath (page 325). Cool, label, and store.

⭐ SEASON:
At any time fresh ginger is obtainable

🍵 YIELD:
About 3 cups

📦 STORE:
For at least a year in a cool pantry

Fresh Ginger Jelly

Its tender peach-amber color belied by its take-charge flavor, sweet/hot Fresh Ginger Jelly can be made at almost any season because you don't need the very young, tender stem ginger that is in season for only a short time around midsummer. However, the ginger you use should not be withered and weary; choose "hands" that are plump and silky-skinned.

If, like me, you hate to waste bits and pieces of good stuff, you'll like to know that the jelly can be made with the fibrous cores of mature ginger you set aside when making Young Ginger Pickled in the Japanese Fashion (page 94) or Ginger Marmalade (page 145).

This jelly is absolutely the right spread for toast, muffins, or biscuits when ham, bacon, sausage, or other meaty doings are served for breakfast or brunch. Like Hot & Sweet Red Pepper Jam (page 71), which is much more pungent, it is a stimulating topping for crackers spread with cream cheese. It goes well with cold meats, too, especially cold chicken or cold roast pork, an unjustly neglected cold viand that makes fine eating on a hot day.

¼ pound fresh, juicy ginger (about 1 cup, sliced)
1 cup water
6 tablespoons strained fresh lemon juice
3½ cups sugar
1 pouch (3 ounces) or one-half 6-ounce bottle liquid pectin

1. Scrub the ginger; it is not necessary to peel it. Trim away any bruised, soft, or callused parts; slice roughly.

2. Combine the ginger pieces with the cup of water in the container of a food processor or blender and run the machine, preferably in on-off bursts, just until the ginger has been chopped—don't let it become a puree.

3. Pour the ginger mixture into a fine-meshed sieve set over a bowl and press as much liquid as possible out of the pulp. Discard the pulp. Let the liquid stand at least 1 hour to settle.

4. Carefully pour the ginger liquid off the starchy sediment into a 2-cup measure. You should have 1¼ cups; if not, add enough water to make that amount. Discard the sediment.

5. Combine the ginger liquid with the lemon juice in a

preserving pan. Heat to simmering over medium-high heat, then add the sugar and stir until the sugar has dissolved completely. When the mixture reaches a hard boil (a boil that can't be stirred down), stir in the pectin. When the mixture returns to a full rolling boil, start timing; boil for exactly 1 minute. Remove the pan from the heat.

6. Skim off any foam and pour the jelly at once into hot, sterilized (page 327) jelly glasses or straight-sided half-pint canning jars, leaving ⅛ inch of headspace in the jars or ½ inch in the glasses. Seal the jelly in glasses with melted paraffin (page 326); seal canning jars with new two-part lids according to manufacturer's directions. Cool, label, and store the jars.

Coriander & Honey Jelly

The subtle flavor compatibility of honey and coriander makes this jelly exceptional. The jelly is golden-amber in color and delicately spicy and only slightly tart in flavor. Serve it with buttered toast, English muffins, or tea biscuits, or all-American hot breads. A few spoonfuls, melted with a few drops of water, could be brushed over the fruit topping of a tart for a glistening and delicious glaze.

Coriander seeds, for any who may not know them, have a flavor and aroma, reminiscent of citrus, quite unlike the rather brash pungency of fresh coriander leaves. The leaves, which are much used in Oriental and Mexican cuisines, take some getting used to; but the fragrant seed is another matter entirely—delicate and delightful.

Coriander is remarkably easy to grow—you can simply sow some of your kitchen supply of seed in a sunny outdoor spot in spring, or buy a packet of seed from a garden center. To assure a seed crop, don't harvest the foliage too heavily; let the plants bloom undisturbed, then gather the seeds as soon as they are ready to drop to earth in late summer. Let them dry thoroughly, then store them in a stoppered bottle.

⅓ cup coriander seed

3 cups water

¼ cup strained fresh lemon juice

¼ cup mild-flavored honey

1 box (1¾ ounces) powdered regular pectin (do not use the kind meant for making low-sugar preserves)

3 cups sugar

 SEASON:
Any time

 YIELD:
About 4 cups

 STORE:
For up to a year in a cool pantry

1. Crush the coriander seeds in a mortar, or whirl them briefly in a blender, or spread them between sheets of plastic or waxed paper and crack them with a rolling pin.

2. Combine the seeds and the water in a saucepan. Heat the mixture just to boiling over low heat. Remove the pan from the heat, cover it, and let it stand for 3 to 6 hours.

3. Strain the liquid through a fine-meshed sieve lined with two layers of cheesecloth or a layer of very fine nylon net. Measure 2½ cups of the liquid into a preserving pan.

4. Add the lemon juice, honey, and pectin to the liquid and stir together thoroughly. Set the pan over medium-high heat and bring the mixture to a hard boil (a boil that can't be stirred down). Stir in the sugar and again bring the mixture to a boil; when it reaches a full rolling boil that can't be stirred down, begin timing; boil the mixture exactly 1 minute. Remove from heat.

5. Skim off any foam and pour the jelly at once into hot, sterilized (page 327) jelly glasses or straight-sided half-pint canning jars, leaving ½ inch of headspace in the glasses or ⅛ inch in the jars. Seal the jelly in glasses with melted paraffin (page 326); seal the canning jars with sterilized new two-piece lids according to manufacturer's directions. Cool, label, and store the jars.

Crab Apple Jelly

Few other preserves glow with the brilliant rose color of jelly made from red-skinned crab apples—it is as lovely to behold as the jelly is to taste. If merely pink-cheeked crab apples are what you can get, jelly made from them will nevertheless be pretty, although it will sport a more modest shade of pink; it will be equally fragrant to the nose and delicate on the tongue.

Like its apple and quince cousins, the crab apple is rich in pectin, so this is a "pure" jelly, made without added pectin. The fruit tends to be low in acid, however, so adding a little lemon juice is necessary.

Scale this recipe down if you have only a few crab apples; it can be made successfully with as little as a quart of fruit. Just use the same proportion of sugar to the juice you obtain.

2 rounded quart measures (about 2½ pounds) fresh crab apples, preferably a red-skinned variety

1½ to 2 quarts water, or enough to cover fruit in its cooking pan (step 1)

Strained fresh lemon juice (juice of 1 to 2 lemons)

Sugar

**SEASON:
Mid-August into fall**

**YIELD:
About 9 to 10 cups**

**STORE:
For at least a year in a cool pantry**

1. Stem and wash the crab apples and quarter them into a saucepan or preserving pan. If there are any bruised or otherwise dubious spots on the apples, cut them out as you go, but leave the cores. Add the water, using enough to just cover the fruit.

2. Bring the crab apples to a boil, then cover the pan and stew them over medium heat just until they are very soft, 45 to 60 minutes; stir and mash them occasionally.

3. Ladle the fruit and juice into a jelly bag (page 322) hanging from its rack or a hook over a large bowl and let the juice drip until the flow stops, a few hours (or leave the pulp as long as overnight). When the dripping has stopped it's okay to press a *little* on the outside of the bag to extract whatever liquid will emerge readily, but don't press hard or squeeze the bag or you'll end up with more or less cloudy jelly.

4. The jelly should be pleasantly on the tart side. Stir in the strained juice of one lemon and taste for tartness; if necessary, add more lemon juice, up to a total of 2 lemons' worth.

5. Measure the apple juice; you should have around 8 to 9 cups, but this will vary with the juiciness of the fruit and the length of its cooking. Place the juice in a large, wide preserving pan (or divide it into two batches for cooking in a wide sauté pan or saucepot). For each cup of juice in the pan stir in ¾ cup of sugar. Stir the mixture until the sugar has all dissolved, then set the pan over high heat.

6. Boil the jelly mixture rapidly (ideally with a candy/jelly thermometer clipped to the side of the pan) until it passes the jelly test (page 322). When the jelly tests "done," remove the pan from the heat.

7. Skim off any foam and ladle the jelly at once into hot, sterilized (page 327) half-pint or straight-sided pint canning jars, or jelly glasses of any size, leaving ⅛ inch of headspace in the jars or ½ inch in the glasses. Seal the canning jars with sterilized new two-piece lids according to manufacturer's directions; seal jelly in glasses with melted paraffin (page 326). Cool, label, and store the jars.

Wine Jellies

I've been asked surprisingly often how to make wine jellies—preserves, that is, not desserts—which are delicious (and expensive) specialty items. A little research located directions for basic wine jelly that have been published at one time or another by manufacturers of fruit pectin, but my inquirers plainly hadn't come across them. (The use of fruit pectin is necessary, as wine lacks this substance essential to

GLAZING A TART:

To glaze a 9- or 10-inch tart, melt a generous half-cup of wine jelly over low heat, stirring the mixture until smooth with a tablespoonful of water; brush the warm mixture over the cooked or uncooked fruit. When the glaze has set, the tart is ready to serve.

SEASON:
Any time

YIELD:
About 6 cups

STORE:
Sealed, for a year in a cool pantry; unsealed, for a few months in a refrigerator

jelling; wine *does* supply acid, which is, together with sugar, also essential.) For making wine jelly, I prefer powdered pectin to the liquid kind, as it can be used without boiling the wine (which would dissipate too much flavor).

Winy experiments demonstrated that jelly made with any decent table wine is good, but it pays in flavor to use a bottle of definite, even emphatic character. A red table wine for jelly-making should be full-bodied and fruity, a white should be fragrant and not too dry (most suitable whites are actually amber-tinged or golden), and a rosé should taste good, not just look pretty. Jellies made from premium-quality fortified wines—sherry, Marsala, Madeira, port, and so on—are even more delicious than table-wine jellies. Finally, for an exceptionally interesting relish to serve with meat or game, try Mulled Port Wine Jelly, flavored with spice and a roasted whole orange; it can also be made with a robust red table wine.

At our house we like *any* wine jelly with toast when breakfast includes ham or bacon or sausage. Wine jelly is delicious on crackers spread with cream cheese; and certain jellies, especially, make a beautiful glaze for fresh fruit tarts—you might use Sherry Jelly with peaches or apples, or a jelly made from a red wine, with a tart of uncooked blueberries.

Red, White, Pink, Golden, or Amber Wine Jelly

The intensity of flavor, as well as the color, of jelly made from table wine depends on using a wine with a lot of character. "Big" wines are better than delicate ones.

¾ cup water

¼ cup strained fresh lemon juice

1 box (1 ¾ ounces) powdered regular pectin (do not use the kind intended for low-sugar preserving)

3 cups full-flavored wine of your choice—red, white, amber, or rosé

4 ½ cups sugar

1. Measure the water and lemon juice into a preserving pan or large saucepan. Add the powdered pectin and stir the mixture until most if not all lumps have been eliminated. Set the pan over medium-high heat and stir the contents constantly until any remaining lumps are gone, then boil the mixture hard (at a boil that can't be stirred down) for exactly 1 minute.

2. At once add the wine and the sugar. Lower the heat and stir the jelly mixture just until the sugar has dissolved, which

will take 2 or 3 minutes; do not let it boil, or even approach a simmer. Remove from heat.

3. Skim off any foam and ladle the jelly at once into hot, sterilized (page 327) jelly glasses or straight-sided half-pint canning jars, leaving ½ inch of headspace in the glasses or ⅛ inch in the jars. Seal jelly in glasses with melted paraffin (page 326); seal jars with sterilized new two-piece canning lids according to manufacturer's directions. Cool, label, and store the jars.

4. If the jelly will be used fairly soon and you have refrigerator space, it can be refrigerated covered but unsealed.

Madeira, Marsala, Port, or Sherry Jelly

Jellies made from fortified wines are especially rich in flavor. Any type of Madeira, Marsala, port, or sherry can be used, but dry Marsala, red ports, and cream sherries are especially recommended.

¾ cup water

⅓ cup strained fresh lemon juice

1 box (1 ¾ ounces) powdered regular pectin (do not use the kind intended for low-sugar preserving)

2 ½ cups premium-quality Madeira, Marsala, port, or sherry

4 ½ cups sugar

1. Combine the water and lemon juice in a preserving pan. Stir in the powdered pectin, mixing it well to remove as many lumps as possible. Set the pan over medium-high heat and stir the mixture constantly until all lumps are gone. Boil the mixture hard (at a boil that can't be stirred down) for 1 minute.

2. At once add the wine and the sugar. Lower the heat and stir the jelly mixture just until the sugar has dissolved, a matter of 2 or 3 minutes at most; do not let it boil, or even approach a simmer. Remove from heat.

3. Skim off any foam and ladle the jelly at once into hot, sterilized (page 327) jelly glasses or straight-sided half-pint canning jars, leaving ½ inch of headspace in the glasses or ⅛ inch in the jars. Seal the jelly in glasses with melted paraffin (page 326); seal jars with sterilized new two-piece canning lids according to manufacturer's directions. Cool, label, and store the jars.

4. If the jelly will be used fairly soon, it can be refrigerated in covered containers without sealing.

SEASON:
Any time

YIELD:
About 6 cups

STORE:
Sealed, for a year in a cool pantry; unsealed, for a few months in the refrigerator

SEASON:
Any time

YIELD:
About 6 cups

STORE:
**Sealed, for a year
in a cool pantry;
unsealed, for a few
months in the
refrigerator**

Mulled Port Wine Jelly

Flavored with an orange that has been stuck with cloves and roasted, plus a touch of whole cinnamon and allspice, this is a rich, deep, dark-flavored wine jelly, superb as a relish with venison, other game, poultry, or cold meat.

For making this, a premium-quality California red port is fine; you do not need to invest in an imported bottle. Mulled-wine jelly is also very good when made with a full-bodied red wine—Rhone, Burgundy, Zinfandel, whatever you like most.

1 unblemished medium-size eating orange

8 whole cloves

1 stick (about 2 ½ inches) cinnamon, broken

6 whole allspice, slightly bruised

1 ½ cups boiling water

**1 box (1 ¾ ounces) powdered regular pectin (do not
   use the kind intended for low-sugar preserving)**

**2 ½ cups good-quality red port (or substitute
   Madeira, Marsala, or a full-flavored red table
   wine)**

4 ½ cups sugar

1. This is a two-stage recipe. One day (or at least several hours) before you'll make the jelly, rinse the orange and stick the cloves into it. Wrap the orange loosely in aluminum foil and bake it, set directly on the shelf, in a 350° oven for 1 hour. Open the wrapping and check the orange; if it is very soft and the juices have begun to caramelize inside the foil wrapping, it is ready; otherwise continue to bake it until it is soft and the juices in the wrapping are turning a rich brown.

2. Unwrap the orange and drop it into a deep bowl. Add the cinnamon and allspice and mash everything together. Pour in the boiling water, cover the bowl, and let it stand overnight.

3. Pour the mixture into a sieve set over a bowl and press the solids to strain off as much liquid as possible. Discard the pulp and strain the liquid again, this time lining the sieve with cheesecloth. Measure the liquid; if you don't have 1½ cups, add water.

4. Pour the liquid into a preserving pan. Add the pectin and stir to eliminate lumps. Set the pan over medium-high heat and bring the mixture to a boil, stirring constantly. Boil it hard (at a boil that can't be stirred down) for exactly 1 minute. At once add the wine and the sugar. Lower the heat and stir the mixture until the sugar has dissolved, 2 or 3 minutes; it should not simmer, much less boil. Remove from heat.

5. Skim off any foam and ladle the jelly into hot, sterilized (page 327) jelly glasses or straight-sided half-pint canning jars, leaving ½ inch of headspace in the glasses or ⅛ inch in the

jars. Seal the jelly in glasses with melted paraffin (page 326); seal canning jars with sterilized canning lids according to manufacturer's directions. Cool, label, and store the jars.

6. If the jelly will be used within a few months, it may be refrigerated unsealed but covered.

Honey Jelly

 SEASON:
Any time

 YIELD:
About 4 cups

STORE:
For at least a year
in a cool pantry

Unless you happen to be Winnie the Pooh or an equally accomplished bare-paws honey eater, there is always the little problem of keeping the honey on the toast and off the chin, fingers, and tablecloth. Well, Honey Jelly (or should it be Jellied Honey?) solves that problem; besides tasting good, Honey Jelly is certain to stay where you put it, even on hot biscuits (highly recommended).

If you should have on hand some honey that has crystallized in the jar, it can be used for making jelly so long as its flavor is intact; taste to be sure.

2 cups honey, preferably one of delicate flavor

1 cup light corn syrup (or substitute another cup of honey, if it is a mild one)

¾ cup water

3 tablespoons strained fresh lemon juice

1 pouch (3 ounces) or one-half 6-ounce bottle of liquid pectin

1. Stir the honey, corn syrup, water, and lemon juice together thoroughly in a preserving pan. Set it over medium-high heat and bring to a boil. As soon as there are vigorous bubbles all over the surface, stir in the pectin. Start timing when the mixture begins to boil hard (a boil that cannot be stirred down); boil the jelly for exactly 1 minute. Remove from heat.

2. Set the jelly aside for 1 minute, or just until the foam on top coalesces into a film. Quickly skim off the film and pour the hot jelly into hot, sterilized (page 327) jelly glasses, or straight-sided half-pint canning jars, leaving ⅛ inch of headspace in the jars or ½ inch in the glasses. Seal the jelly in glasses with melted paraffin (page 326); seal canning jars with sterilized new two-piece lids according to manufacturer's directions. Cool, label, and store the jars.

FRUIT HONEYS

Fruit honeys aren't necessarily clear, syrupy sweets like bees' honey (although they can be), but rather a cross between a full-bodied syrup and a fruit preserve.

Two examples of this genre of delicate preserves are included here: Pear Honey, to be made with the most flavorful, fragrant pears you can get your hands on, and Clear Quince Honey, which can be made with quince juice alone, or with both the juice and some of the shredded fruit.

These preserves are at their best with waffles, pancakes, or hot breads, or at least a slice of toast. Further, they are excellent dessert toppings. Our forebears served such preparations straight, with little spoons, on the fanciful dessert tables presented on special occasions: hence their old name, "spoon sweets," to distinguish them from sweets served with forks.

**SEASON:
Fall and winter**

**YIELD:
6 to 7 cups**

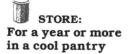
**STORE:
For a year or more
in a cool pantry**

Pear Honey

A delicate preserve of the type once called "spoon sweets," which were featured on elaborate nineteenth-century dessert tables, this is a delicacy to be made when the pears are ripe and honey-sweet. Wonderful on waffles, and not to be overlooked as a topping for a simple pudding or a scoop of vanilla or fruit ice cream.

4 pounds pears of a fragrant variety such as Bartlett, ripe but not soft

Water, as needed

3 tablespoons strained fresh lemon juice

Grated zest (outer skin only, no white pith) of 1 lemon

6 cups sugar

1. Pare, quarter, and core the pears, dropping them into a bowl of cold water as they are finished.

2. Combine 6 cups of fresh water with the lemon juice in a preserving pan. Shred or grate the pear sections medium-coarse; add the shreds to the acidified water.

3. Combine the grated lemon zest with about a quart of water in a saucepan and bring it to a boil; simmer 5 minutes; drain the zest and add it to the pear mixture.

4. Bring the pear mixture to a boil over medium-high heat. Gradually stir in the sugar; return the mixture to a boil. Adjust the heat and simmer the mixture, uncovered, stirring it from time to time, until the shreds of fruit are clear and the syrup has thickened, about 1 hour; toward the end of cooking, watch the mixture carefully and stir it often to prevent burning. The

pear honey is thick enough when a small spoonful placed on a chilled saucer thickens to the consistency of a soft preserve—not a stiff jam—when it is refrigerated for a few minutes; to prevent overcooking, set the pan off the heat while testing.

5. Ladle the hot pear honey into hot, clean pint or half-pint canning jars, leaving ¼ inch of headspace. Seal with new two-piece canning lids according to manufacturer's directions and process for 15 minutes (for either size jar) in a boiling-water bath (page 325). Cool, label, and store the jars.

Clear Quince Honey

For the pleasure of a pourable honey-like sweet with the flavor of quinces, try this on pancakes, waffles, scones, corn bread, muffins, or hot biscuits.

The honey can be a bonus from the making of Quince Paste or Quince Candy (page 263), but you can also start from scratch: just simmer 2 large or 3 medium-size cut-up quinces in 5 cups of water until the fruit is tender; drain the juice and make the honey as described.

If you like, include a little of the cooked quince, shredded, in the honey; a few tablespoonfuls will be enough. Combine the rest of the cooked fruit with apples for a heavenly "sauce" or compote, or make a quince and apple pie.

4 cups of quince juice from Quince Paste or Quince Candy (page 263) or juice prepared from scratch as described above

3 cups sugar

2 to 4 tablespoons strained fresh lemon juice, depending on tartness of the quinces

1. Strain the quince juice through a very fine sieve or a coarser sieve lined with dampened, closely woven cheesecloth.

2. Stir the quince juice, sugar, and lemon juice together in a preserving pan and bring the mixture to a boil over medium-high heat. Boil it rapidly to a candy/jelly thermometer reading of 216° to 218°, or until it is garnet-colored and as thick as warmed honey; if you lack a thermometer, remove the honey from the heat and spoon a little onto a chilled saucer. Cool the sample in the refrigerator and check the consistency.

3. Ladle the boiling-hot honey into hot, sterilized (page 327) half-pint canning jars, leaving ¼ inch of headspace. Seal the jars with sterilized new two-piece canning lids according to lid manufacturer's directions. Cool, label, and store the jars.

4. If you expect to keep the quince honey for a matter of weeks only, store it in any suitable container in the refrigerator.

SEASON:
Late fall

YIELD:
About 4 cups

STORE:
Sealed, for at least a year in a cool pantry; unsealed, for many weeks in the refrigerator

MARMALADING

There are a lot of silly culinary stories about how the name "marmalade" came to be, but for all practical purposes it's enough to know that marmalade designates certain fruit preserves with a jelly-like texture interrupted with shreds of fruit. Marmalades are often based on citrus fruit, but they can be confected from almost any fruit that can be named (although I have my doubts about some).

Thus there are infinite marmalades, including the uncommon kinds to be found here. If you want recipes for basic orange (or other citrus) marmalades, they can be found in good general cookbooks as well as specialized works on preserving.

 SEASON:
Mid- to late summer

 YIELD:
6 cups

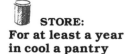 **STORE:**
For at least a year in cool a pantry

Melon Marmalade

Cantaloupes and muskmelons aren't the very first fruits you think of when marmalade-making seems a good idea, but they make a most pleasing spread. It has the lovely color of apricots and a teasing flavor that some find reminiscent of the same fruit. Choose flavorful melons; this silky substance cannot be made from fruit that is a metaphorical pig's ear.

Finely shredded or grated zest (outer skin only, no white pith) of 2 large lemons

1 cup water

½ cup strained fresh lemon juice

2 to 3 tablespoons, to taste, finely chopped Crystallized Ginger (page 265) or drained Ginger Preserved in Syrup (page 267)

8 cups chopped full-flavored ripe cantaloupe or muskmelon (allow about 6 pounds of melon)

1 box (1 ¾ ounces) powdered regular pectin

5 ½ cups sugar

1. Combine the lemon zest and water in a small saucepan. Bring it to a boil, cover it, and simmer it until the shreds are tender, about 10 minutes. Uncover the pan and continue to cook until almost all the moisture has evaporated.

2. Combine the lemon zest and any of its remaining liquid, the lemon juice, ginger, and melon in a preserving pan. Bring the mixture to a boil, cover it, and simmer it steadily for 10 minutes, stirring frequently; uncover the pan and continue to simmer the mixture, stirring it more often, for 5 minutes longer, or until the mixture has reduced by half. You should

have 4 cups, plus no more than a tablespoonful or two.

3. Stir the powdered pectin into the fruit mixture and bring it to a full boil over high heat, stirring constantly. At once add the sugar; continue to cook, stirring constantly, until the marmalade reaches a hard boil (a boil that can't be stirred down); boil the mixture, still stirring constantly, for 1 minute. Remove from heat.

4. Skim off any foam and ladle the marmalade into hot clean half-pint or pint canning jars, leaving ¼ inch of headspace. Seal the jars with new two-piece canning lids following manufacturer's directions and process for 15 minutes (for either size jar) in a boiling-water bath (page 325). Cool, label, and store the jars.

A Marmalade of Apples & Apple Cider

 SEASON:
Fall

 YIELD:
5 cups

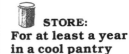 **STORE:**
For at least a year in a cool pantry

I f only for the fragrance of apples that fills the house when this marmalade is cooking, please make some when the first cider and the first really tart apples are in the market together in mid-autumn. To capture the finest flavor, don't wait until winter, when apples, however carefully stored, begin to turn mealy and lose their pristine flavor. The cider should be freshly pressed and without additives. In a pinch, condensed frozen apple juice, thawed and diluted about half as much as the label suggests, serves as a decent substitute.

Besides serving the marmalade as a spread, use it as a base for the sliced apples in a double-apple tart:

Spread a layer of the marmalade in a partially baked tart shell, cover it with neatly arranged paper-thin slices of peeled apple, sprinkle the apples lightly with sugar, and bake the tart in a 375° oven until the apples are tender. Serve while still faintly warm with some crème fraîche (page 316), sour cream, or lightly whipped sweet cream.

2 pounds firm, tart apples
2 cups water, or as needed
Juice of ½ lemon
3 cups freshly pressed sweet apple cider
3 cups sugar

1. Wash and drain the apples. Quarter them, then pare off the skins and remove the cores. Add the skins and cores to 2 cups water in a saucepan, dropping the apple quarters, as they

are pared, into a bowl of cold water acidified with the lemon juice. (This prevents darkening.)

2. Bring the apple trimmings to a boil; cover the pan and simmer the trimmings until the skins are very soft, about 25 minutes.

3. Empty the contents of the pan into a food mill or a sieve set over a bowl. Force as much of the pulp as possible through the food mill. Return the liquid and pulp to the pan; discard the skins and seeds.

4. Add the cider and sugar to the apple mixture and bring it to a boil over medium heat; boil for 3 minutes.

5. Meanwhile, slice the apple quarters paper-thin or grate them coarsely (a food processor is ideal for either job). Add the apples to the hot apple mixture and bring again to a boil, stirring vigorously. Cook the mixture over medium heat, uncovered, stirring often, until it has thickened and the apples are translucent, 30 to 40 minutes. (If the marmalade thickens too much while the apples are still opaque, add a little water, about ¼ cup, and continue cooking.) The marmalade is done when a spoonful placed on a chilled saucer and set in the refrigerator congeals within a few moments; to prevent overcooking, set the pan off the fire while testing.

6. Ladle the boiling-hot marmalade into hot, clean half-pint or pint canning jars, leaving ¼ inch of headspace. Seal the jars with new two-piece canning lids according to manufacturer's directions and process for 15 minutes (for either size jar) in a boiling-water bath (page 325). Cool, label, and store.

SEASON:
Late fall

YIELD:
About 8 cups

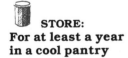

STORE:
For at least a year in a cool pantry

Quince Marmalade

There are other and perhaps equally good ways to make this delicate delight for spreading on breakfast toast (or filling tiny tart shells, come to think of it), but I like this one. (An alternative that eliminates the paring and coring of raw quinces—which are tough customers to handle—follows the main recipe.)

Quinces are admittedly sometimes hard to get (for retesting this favorite recipe, I had to arrange for a Care package from a child at a distant university), but the marmalade is worth the effort. If you should be blessed with an abundance of quinces, try, too, the recipes for Quince Paste or Quince Candy (page 263), and Clear Quince Honey (page 139).

When quinces are fully ripe and ready to use, they will be yellow or orange-yellow in color and very fragrant; unripe, they are tinged with green. Shopping tip: Farmers' markets and roadside stands are better bets than the supermarket.

2 pounds ripe quinces (4 or 5 medium to large)
8 cups sugar
2½ quarts water
Strained juice of 1 or 2 lemons, to taste

1. Pare, quarter, and core the quinces. Grate the quarters into fine shreds (a food processor does this most easily).

2. Combine the sugar and water in a preserving pan and bring the mixture to a boil. Boil the syrup 3 minutes, then add the lemon juice and the grated quinces.

3. Cook the marmalade, partly covered, over medium heat until the shreds of quince are very tender, stirring it often. Then uncover the pot, raise the heat, and cook the marmalade rapidly, stirring it almost constantly, until it has turned a deep rosy-garnet color and the syrup is as thick as warm honey, about 50 minutes in all. The consistency of the syrup should be like that of *cool* honey when the marmalade has cooled, so be careful not to overcook it.

4. Ladle the marmalade into hot, clean pint or half-pint canning jars, leaving ¼ inch of headspace. Seal the jars with new two-piece canning lids according to manufacturer's directions and process for 15 minutes (for either size jar) in a boiling-water bath (page 325). Cool, label, and store the jars.

Another Way to Make Quince Marmalade

2 pounds ripe quinces (4 or 5 medium to large)
2½ quarts water
Sugar
Strained juice of 1 or 2 lemons, to taste

1. Scrub the quinces and cut out the fuzzy business at the blossom end; remove any bruises or blemishes. Put the quinces and water in a pot (there should be enough water to cover the quinces) and bring the water to a boil. Set a thick plate on the quinces to keep them submerged and simmer them gently, partly covered, until they are tender when tested with a long fork, about 1½ hours.

2. Lift the quinces from the liquid (save it) and cool them. Using a swivel-bladed peeler and a paring knife, strip or pare off the skin and return it to the cooking liquid; quarter the quinces and cut out the cores and all the gritty portion around them; add the cores and trimmings to the liquid; set the quince sections aside. Bring this potful to a boil, regulate the heat to maintain a simmer, and cook the mixture, uncovered, until the liquid has reduced to about 4 cups, about 30 minutes.

SEASON:
Late fall

YIELD:
7 to 8 cups

STORE:
For at least a year in a cool pantry

3. Pour the trimmings and liquid into a fine sieve set over a bowl and press with a spoon to extract all possible liquid. Discard the pulp and measure the liquid into the rinsed-out pot or a preserving pan.

4. Grate the quince sections, measure the grated quince, and add it to the liquid. Add the lemon juice and heat the mixture to boiling. Stir in a cupful of sugar for each cupful of quince and liquid. Cook the mixture, stirring often at first and then almost constantly, until the marmalade is rosy-garnet in color and thick enough to jell quickly when a spoonful is placed on a chilled saucer and set in the refrigerator; to prevent overcooking, set the pot off the heat while testing. (This marmalade will be pulpier than the version above, so it requires a different method of judging doneness.) Be careful not to overcook it—it should not be stiff when cold.

5. Seal and process the marmalade as described in step 4 of the preceding recipe.

SEASON:
December through March

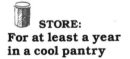

YIELD:
7 to 8 cups

STORE:
For at least a year in a cool pantry

Temple Orange Marmalade

A delicately bittersweet marmalade made with Temple oranges (which are named in honor of a person, not a place of worship), this celebrates one of the most delectable of the winter citrus fruits. Temples are closely related to tangerines, but they are larger and sweeter; they share with tangerines and mandarins the possession of "kid-glove" skins. They make an exceptional marmalade. Gild the lily, if you like, by adding a touch of orange-flavored liqueur or Scotch whisky.

6 medium-large Temple oranges, about 3 pounds

Water, as needed

4 medium-size lemons

8 cups sugar

3 tablespoons orange-flavored liqueur (Cointreau, Triple Sec, Curaçao, or other) or Scotch whisky, optional

1. Rinse and drain the oranges. Cut and discard a slice of skin from the stem and blossom ends and remove the peel in quarters. Reserve the orange flesh.

2. Place the peel in a saucepan with 2 quarts of water, bring it to a boil, and boil it 10 minutes. Drain the peel, add 2 quarts of fresh water, boil it again for 10 minutes, and drain it. Add the same amount of fresh water and bring to a boil for the third time; simmer the peel, partly covered, until it is very soft

and the liquid is reduced to 2 cups, about an hour. Reserve the peel and liquid, covered, at room temperature, until ready to add to the fruit pulp.

3. Chop the pulp of the oranges (this is quickly done in a food processor) and place it in a large ceramic or stainless-steel bowl (do not use aluminum).

4. Pare the peel and not quite all the white pith from the lemons and discard it. Chop the lemon pulp and add it to the orange pulp. Add 2 cups cold water; cover and let stand overnight.

5. Press the fruit pulp through the coarse mesh of a food mill, or use a coarse sieve; push through all possible pulp and juice. Discard the seeds and membrane left behind. Place the pulp in a preserving pan and add the liquid from the reserved peel.

6. Cut the reserved peel into exceedingly thin shreds, using kitchen shears or a sharp knife on a cutting board. Add the peel to the mixture in the pan.

7. Bring the mixture to a boil over medium-high heat and boil it, uncovered, 10 minutes. Gradually stir in the sugar and boil the marmalade, stirring often, over medium-high heat until it passes the jelly test (page 322), 20 to 30 minutes. Remove the pot from the heat and stir in the orange liqueur or the whisky, if you are including either. Cool the marmalade 5 minutes, stirring it several times.

8. Ladle the marmalade into hot, clean half-pint or pint canning jars, leaving ¼ inch of headspace. Seal the jars with new two-piece canning lids according to manufacturer's directions and process for 20 minutes (for either size jar) in a boiling-water bath (page 325). Cool, label, and store the jars. Like other fine marmalades, this improves with time.

Ginger Marmalade

One of the best of all possible marmalades is this tender jelly studded with tiny, crunchy shreds of ginger—a connoisseur's choice, when it can be found in shops.

Ginger marmalade is most readily made with stem ginger—young, juicy ginger—which is, alas, not available always, much less everywhere. However, wherever there is a Chinatown, it can be found in season, the few weeks from midsummer on. At other times and in other places, the tender layer of flesh just under the skin of regular (mature) ginger can be used; the modifications of method are noted below. Be careful to choose only unwithered "hands" if you are using mature ginger.

 SEASON:
Midsummer to fall, if stem ginger is used; at any time, if mature ginger is used

 YIELD:
About 5 cups

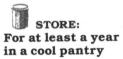 STORE:
For at least a year in a cool pantry

½ **pound unblemished stem ginger (young, pink-
tinged ginger) or 1 to 1¼ pounds mature ginger**

6 cups water

½ **cup strained fresh lemon juice**

4 cups sugar

Pinch of salt, optional

**1 pouch (3 ounces) liquid pectin, or one-half 6-ounce
bottle liquid pectin**

1. *Using stem ginger:* Scrape the skin of stem ginger
lightly with a small sharp knife, removing any blemishes as well
as the papery bits of leaf sheath that are attached here and
there. Trim away any dried ends. Rinse the pieces, pat them
dry, and break them apart at the joints. Using a citrus zester or
a grater with small sharp teeth, shred the ginger into threads,
working over a bowl in order to catch all the juice. You should
have 1⅓ to 1½ cups, lightly packed.

Using mature ginger: Pare or scrape off the skin and grate
the tender outer layer only (save the fibrous cores to make
Fresh Ginger Jelly, page 130); grate enough to obtain 1⅓ to
1½ cups, lightly packed. Combine the grated ginger with 1
quart of water, bring to a boil, and boil 5 minutes. Drain; add
fresh cold water and repeat the boiling and draining twice.

2. Combine the grated ginger, its juice (if you are using
stem ginger), and 6 cups of water in a preserving pan; bring
the mixture to a boil, cover, lower the heat, and simmer the
ginger gently until the shreds are very tender and almost
translucent, about 1¼ hours. Remove from the heat.

3. Measure the ginger and liquid. If you have more than 3
cups, spoon off the surplus liquid (save it—add sugar and mix
the resulting syrup with chilled club soda for a pleasant
refreshment while you make the marmalade).

4. Combine the measured ginger and liquid, the lemon
juice, sugar, and salt in the rinsed-out preserving pan. Bring
the mixture to a hard boil (a boil that cannot be stirred down)
over medium-high heat and boil it exactly 1 minute. Stir in the
liquid pectin and return to another full, rolling boil that cannot
be stirred down; boil exactly 1 minute. Remove from the heat.

5. Stir the marmalade for 5 minutes to cool it slightly, then
ladle it into hot, clean half-pint canning jars, leaving ¼ inch of
headspace. Seal the jars with new two-piece canning lids,
according to manufacturer's directions and process the jars for
15 minutes in a boiling-water bath (page 325). Cool, label, and
store the jars.

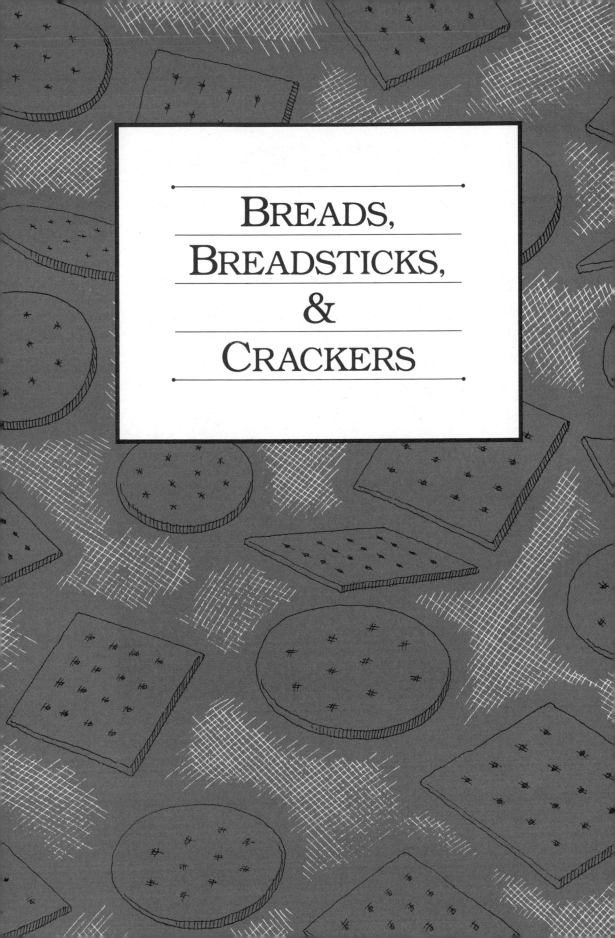

BREADS, BREADSTICKS, & CRACKERS

BREADS FOR SPREADS

Corn Meal & Buttermilk Slicing Loaves
Whole-Oat Long Loaves • Semolina Loaves
Sesame-Topped Bulgur Bread
Ultimately Cheesy Cheddar Bread
Whole-Oat & Other Melba Toasts & Croutons
Seeded Breadsticks

CRACKERS & OTHER CRISPS

Caraway Rusks • Ginger Crackers • Oatcakes
Cream Crackers to Go with Cheese
Beaten-Biscuit Crackers

T he not-so-basic yeast breads to be found in this chapter possess the kind of allure I hope you can't resist when you find a warm and fragrant loaf in a specialty shop. (Look in a general cookbook or one of many excellent books on baking for more fundamental types of loaves.)

The breads that made the cut for inclusion here begin with a yeast-leavened buttermilk corn bread that includes stone-ground meal to give its crumb a good character and its flavor a healthy boost. The Whole-Oat Long Loaves are crusty and slightly chewy, thanks to their content of whole oat grains. There are also formulas for richly flavorful Semolina Loaves and for a multigrain bread based either on bulgur—precooked cracked wheat—or regular cracked wheat; it is made even more interesting by measures of sesame seeds and whole-wheat flour. Finally, for cheese lovers, there is Ultimately Cheesy Cheddar Bread, a substantial, high-rising bread guaranteed to be irresistible either plain or toasted.

Any of these breads make good melba toast, for which directions are also included, as are the how-to's of preparing croutons from your own breads.

Seeded Breadsticks are made from a single yeast dough, with sizes, or seeded or salted variations, to taste.

The group of crackerstuffs that rounds off the chapter includes versatile rusks flavored with caraway, celery seed, and honey (make these more or less sweet, to your own taste), which are especially delicious with mild cheeses; Ginger Crackers, also highly compatible with cheese; Oatcakes, grainy and perfectly scrumptious with butter, pâté, or jam; a version of British Cream Crackers to go with cheese or a sweet spread; and Beaten-Biscuit Crackers in two guises, both patterned on classic Southern beaten biscuits. I like to keep on hand a stock of at least one or two of these crispy bites to accompany specialties of the house ranging from Rillettes to Potted Ham to Mulled Port Wine Jelly, all to be found elsewhere in *Fancy Pantry*.

First to be found below in this section, for breadmaking beginners or anyone who feels the need of a brushup, is "Breadmaking Basics," a review of what needs to be known before the recipes are tackled. Skip it if you're proficient.

BREADMAKING BASICS

The notion of baking with yeast has been known to terrify otherwise well-rounded and competent cooks who are perfectly willing to tackle complicated and unfamiliar recipes for anything but bread. This is too bad. Making a fine yeast-risen loaf is much simpler to do than to write about.

YEAST

For anyone who has been reluctant to plunge, the first thing to know is that yeast is not a mystifying substance that either grows (or doesn't) at will, like the Creature from the Black Lagoon. Yeast is simply an assemblage of tiny living organisms in hibernation; it comes, for home use, in the form of active dry yeast (by far the commonest) or a fresh yeast cake. When the yeast cells are physically liberated and supplied with moisture and food (starch and/or sugar in the dough), the dormant organisms revive and multiply rapidly, giving off carbon dioxide gas as they do so. That gas causes the dough to rise. Rising stops when the oven heat has expanded the gas bubbles to their utmost; the heat also kills the yeast as the dough enjoys this final burst of growth.

FLOURS

Recipes indicate the type of flour preferred for a particular bread. *All-purpose flour* is an in-between blend of hard (high-gluten) and soft (low-gluten) flours that can be used for such delicate things as cakes and for such substantial items as bread. It will make an acceptable loaf, but for a better "crumb," or structure, *bread flour* is preferable because of its high gluten content, which is exploited in kneading (see below). Happily, bread flour, milled from hard wheat, is now distributed to supermarkets by major millers; a few years ago, home bakers had to beg a pizzeria or bakery to sell a supply. If you can't lay hands on it, use all-purpose flour. *Semolina flour,* a golden, somewhat gritty flour milled from a certain portion of the grain of durum (extra-hard) wheat, is called for in one bread recipe here (and some pastas in the last chapter of the book). It is exceptionally rich in gluten. Look for a label reading "pasta flour" if you can't find flour marked "semolina." Mail-order suppliers of grain specialties are your best bet if a health-food or specialty store can't supply you.

KNEADING

Kneading is the word for manipulating dough vigorously, by machine or by hand (how-to's in a moment). Kneading causes the gluten in the flour to develop an internal structure strong enough to hold within the dough the tiny gas bubbles produced by the growing yeast. These bubbles expand further during baking—presto, a leavened loaf instead of a hard, inedible lump. Yeast doughs are not fragile; in fact, the more they are bashed about, in general, the better the texture of the breadstuff will be.

Kneading how-to's: Chances are that someone who has never heard a word on the subject could evolve a method of kneading bread that would work pretty well, once the operator understood that the dough should be pounded, thumped, pressed, knocked about, or otherwise manipulated so that all its cells feel the action.

For the non-experimental, here's one way to knead: Turn the dough out of its mixing bowl onto a dry, smooth work surface that has been dusted with flour; have a little heap of flour at one side, ready for further dusting of the surface and your hands. Flour your hands and pat the dough into a flattened ball. Then lean into the dough with the heels of one or both hands (styles vary), pushing it out and away from you. Fold the dough in half, turn it on the board so the crease is to one side, and repeat the pushing, folding, and turning as many times as necessary, dusting the board and your hands with more flour from time to time to keep the dough from sticking. Keep kneading until the dough is elastic and the surface is smooth, which will take several minutes at least; it's almost impossible to overdo this.

Various bread recipes specify the desirable consistency of the dough, from fairly soft to quite dense and firm, but any dough that has been kneaded enough will feel increasingly lively as you work. Achieving this liveliness is one of the nicest things about making bread; it tells you that this is no inert sludge you're working with, but a living substance.

Machines can help: If you have an electric mixer equipped with a dough hook, machine kneading is fine (follow the manufacturer's directions for timing); I like to finish machine-kneaded doughs with a few strokes on the board to be sure that the dough has the proper lively texture—something I don't trust the machine to tell me. Doughs can be mixed and kneaded satisfactorily in food processors, some of which have special dough-kneading blades that work very well.

The rising: Because yeast is temperature-sensitive, baking the dough puts an end to its rising, while freezing or refrigerating dough either halts the rising entirely or slows it substantially. However, yeast doughs will rise successfully within a surprisingly wide range of temperatures, from the chill of the refrigerator (when very slow rising is wanted) to the classic "draft-free spot," to an artificially warmed place such as an oven heated *slightly* by the viewing light. For most purposes a good place is the kitchen counter, or almost any other spot in the house that isn't positively chilly or superheated; around 70° is ideal. Cover the bowl snugly with plastic wrap. Wrap the covered bowl of dough in a towel if you think the spot too cool; the dough produces some warmth of its own, and the wrapping holds it in and speeds matters somewhat.

Warm can be too warm: If the dough is kept in too warm an environment—say where the temperature exceeds the mid-90's—rising may be fast enough to cause over-fermenting and collapse of the dough, so keep an eye on things. Relatively slower rising yields higher-quality breads.

Chilling news. Which brings up the matter of refrigerating yeast doughs. As indicated, yeast dough won't die when chilled (or even frozen), so the refrigerator can be a lifesaver when you're interrupted after a dough has been mixed. At any point either before or after the initial rising (or risings, if the recipe calls for them), dough can be refrigerated to slow the rate of rising until you can come back to the job, even several hours later. If the dough has partially risen when you are obliged to leave it, first punch it down (below). Cover the bowl of dough with plastic wrap or foil and stash it in the refrigerator. If it should be fully risen when you return to it, punch it down and resume where you left off. Otherwise allow the rising to continue out of the icebox. Chilled dough will take a little longer to complete its room-temperature rising, so be patient; it will warm up gradually.

How high? Always heed recipe directions as to how much a specific dough should rise at a given stage—to not quite double, or to double, or to triple its original volume, depending on the type of bread. Until you get used to gauging the rising by eye, consider marking the original level of the dough on the outside of the bowl with a wax pencil or crayon. Because the rate of rising can't be predicted by the clock, judge rising by dough volume and by the finger-touch test described in the recipes.

Punching down is the term for taking a few satisfying socks with your fist into the heart of the risen dough, with the object of driving out the gases that have fueled the first rising. Punch away until the dough is well deflated, then follow the recipe for the next stage.

Beyond these hints, follow any promising recipe.

And enjoy.

BREADS FOR SPREADS

This collection of choice breads has been shaped to provide for your enjoyment of any or all of the sweet or savory items in your pantry that call for a bread accompa-niment. Any of the breads can be converted into crisp melba toast, following the directions in Whole-Oat & Other Melba Toasts & Croutons.

 SEASON:
Any time

 YIELD:
2 loaves, 1½ pounds each

STORE:
Wrapped, for up to a week in a cool pantry or cupboard; freezer-wrapped and frozen, for up to 6 months

Corn Meal & Buttermilk Slicing Loaves

A yeast bread with a rich corn flavor, this makes especially good toast. It is also not to be overlooked for constructing a grilled cheese sandwich or for making exceptionally crunchy croutons or corn meal melba toast (page 162).

½ cup warm water (110° to 115°)

2 tablespoons sugar

1 envelope (1 scant tablespoon) active dry yeast

1¼ cups cultured buttermilk, at room temperature

1 egg, beaten

4 tablespoons (½ stick) unsalted butter, melted

2 teaspoons salt

2 cups stone-ground corn meal

3¾ to 4 cups bread flour (or substitute all-purpose flour), plus a little more if needed for kneading

Additional softened butter (2 teaspoons) for finished loaves

1. Pour the warm water into a large mixing bowl or the large bowl of an electric mixer and stir in a pinch of the sugar. Add the yeast, stir, and let stand until foamy, about 10 minutes.

2. Beat in the remaining sugar and the buttermilk, egg, melted butter, and salt, then beat in the corn meal and mix to a dough, either by hand or in the electric mixer. Gradually beat in the bread flour until the dough is too stiff to beat. Either turn it out onto a floured kneading surface and knead by hand, or change to the dough hook for machine kneading, and knead in the remaining bread flour; knead very thoroughly (about 5 minutes by machine) to make an elastic dough.

3. Form the dough into a ball and place it in a bowl (use the mixing bowl—no need to wash or butter it—unless you need it for something else). Cover the bowl with plastic wrap and set it in a warm spot to rise until the dough is not quite doubled in volume, about 45 minutes; it has risen enough when the pressure of a finger leaves a dent that fills slowly—the dough will still be somewhat elastic.

4. Punch the dough down with your fist, turn it over in the bowl, re-cover it, and let it rise again until almost doubled, about 30 minutes.

5. Turn the dough out onto a lightly floured work surface, knead it briefly, and divide it into 2 equal portions. Flatten each portion in turn into a rectangle about 10 x 7 inches and about an inch thick and roll it up from one short side, pinching the layers firmly together as you roll. Fit each roll, seam down, into a buttered 6-cup loaf pan (8½ x 4½ inches). Cover the pans lightly with a towel and let the loaves rise until fully doubled, 30 to 40 minutes. They are ready when the pressure of a finger at one side of the loaf leaves an imprint that doesn't fill up.

6. Preheat the oven to 375°, with a shelf in the center, a few minutes before the loaves will be ready to bake.

7. Bake the loaves in the center of the oven for 30 minutes, exchanging their shelf positions after 20 minutes. After 30 minutes, reduce the oven heat to 350°. Turn the loaves out of their pans and bake them directly on the oven shelf for a further 10 minutes, or until a loaf sounds hollow when its bottom is thumped.

8. Rub the top crust of the loaves with a little butter and cool the loaves on wire racks, lightly covered with a towel, for several hours before wrapping and storing them. This bread is all the better for resting overnight before it is served.

Whole-Oat Long Loaves

Make this good crusty bread studded with slightly chewy whole-oat grains either as long French-style loaves or as pan loaves, and reserve some to turn into melba toast (page 162). Besides being toothsome, the bread offers a good share of healthful fiber—in addition to whole oats, it contains oat or wheat bran and whole-wheat and all-purpose flour, the last supplying the needed gluten. Whole oats are most readily found in health-food stores.

This bread keeps exceptionally well, tasting even better than fresh-baked after a day or two and holding its quality for a week or more at room temperature.

SEASON:
Any time

YIELD:
4 long loaves, about 14 ounces each, or 3 pan loaves (8½ x 4½ inches), about 18 ounces each

STORE:
Loosely wrapped, for a week at room temperature; freezer-wrapped and frozen, for up to 6 months

4 cups water

1½ tablespoons salt

1 cup whole oats (oat grains, not rolled oats)

1¾ cups warm water (110° to 115°)

¼ cup honey

1½ tablespoons (slightly less than 2 envelopes)
    active dry yeast

½ cup oat bran (or substitute unprocessed wheat
    bran)

¼ cup corn oil or other bland vegetable oil

1½ cups whole-wheat flour

4 to 5 cups all-purpose flour (or substitute bread
    flour)

FOR PANS:

Vegetable oil or corn meal

GLAZE:

1 teaspoon cornstarch

⅔ cup water

1. Bring 4 cups of water to a boil in a heavy saucepan; add 1 teaspoon of the salt and the whole-oat grains. Simmer, covered, until the grains have burst but are still slightly chewy, about 40 minutes. Cool the oats, then drain off any surplus liquid in a sieve.

2. Combine ¾ cup of the warm water, a little of the honey, and the yeast in a mixing bowl or the large bowl of a heavy-duty mixer; stir the mixture and let it stand until foamy, about 10 minutes.

3. Stir in the remaining warm water, the remaining honey, the remaining salt, the oat bran, the oil, and the cooked oats. Beat in the whole-wheat flour thoroughly. Work in enough of the all-purpose flour to make a firm dough, either kneading by hand on a lightly floured work surface or by switching to the dough hook of the mixer; knead very thoroughly, about 5 minutes in a mixer or twice as long if kneading by hand. When ready, the dough will be elastic and no longer sticky.

4. Form the dough into a ball and return it to its bowl (no need to wash, dry, or grease the bowl); cover the bowl with plastic wrap and set it in a warm spot to rise until the dough has doubled in volume, about an hour; it has risen enough when the pressure of a finger leaves a deep print that doesn't disappear.

5. Punch the dough down with your fist, turn it over in the bowl, re-cover it, and let it rise again until doubled, about 45 minutes.

6. Turn the dough out onto a lightly floured kneading surface and knead it a few strokes to expel air, then form it into a ball. Divide the dough into 4 equal parts if you are making long loaves, or 3 parts for pan loaves.

For either kind of loaf: Flatten each portion in turn into an oval about an inch thick and roll it up, starting with one long side and pinching the layers firmly together as you roll.

To make long loaves: Roll each cylinder of dough under the palms, stretching it as you go until it is 11 inches long; pinch the ends to blunt points and lay the loaf, seam down, in a lightly oiled French-bread pan, or lay it on a baking sheet sprinkled with corn meal. Form the remaining long loaves and place them in pans or well apart on baking sheets, two to a sheet. Brush surplus corn meal from the pans.

To make pan loaves: Roll each portion of dough up as described, but don't stretch the rolls; lay each, seam down, in a greased 6-cup loaf pan (8½ x 4½ inches). Cover the formed loaves with a towel and let them rise until doubled, about 30 minutes. They are ready to bake when the pressure of a finger at one side of the risen loaf leaves an imprint that doesn't fill up.

7. Shortly before rising is complete, preheat the oven to 400°, with a shelf in the upper third and one in the lower third. Prepare the glaze: Combine the cornstarch and water in a small saucepan; stir the mixture over medium-low heat until it boils and becomes translucent, about 2 minutes. Let the glaze cool.

8. When the loaves have risen completely, brush the glaze over the tops of the loaves and slash them, using a very sharp knife or a razor blade held almost horizontally; make several short diagonal crosswise slashes down the length of the long loaves, and a single lengthwise slash in the top of each pan loaf.

9. *To bake long loaves:* Bake 20 minutes on two shelves of the preheated oven, then exchange shelf positions, brush the loaves again with the glaze, and bake the loaves 20 minutes longer, or until they are well browned and produce a hollow sound when thumped on the bottom.

To bake pan loaves: Bake 20 minutes at 400°, then brush them again with the glaze, switch the oven positions of the pans, reduce the oven temperature to 350°, and bake the loaves until they are well browned and sound hollow when one is turned out of the pan and its bottom is thumped, about 30 minutes longer.

10. Cool the loaves on racks, then store them in plastic bags at room temperature. For longer storage (up to 6 months), freezer-wrap the bread (page 328) and freeze it. To prevent sogginess, thaw it in its wrappers. Whether or not it has been frozen, the oat bread benefits from a few minutes' warming in a 350° oven before it is served.

FLOUR

Semolina Loaves

T he slightly coarse, almost gritty flour called semolina, which comes from the heart of durum wheat, is the essential ingredient of one of the most flavorful wheat breads it's possible to bake at home. The bread is creamy yellow in color, crusty outside, and considerably richer in flavor than other Italian long loaves. Only a few big-city bakeries seem to make a specialty of semolina bread; if you like it and there is no source nearby, it's worthwhile to seek out the flour, which also makes superb homemade pasta (there's a recipe on page 290). Look for semolina flour, often labeled "pasta flour," in health-food stores; mail-order purveyors of grain specialities are a good bet, too (some are listed on pages 330–331).

2½ cups warm water (110° to 115°)

¼ teaspoon sugar

4 teaspoons active dry yeast

1 tablespoon salt

¼ cup olive or vegetable oil

1 egg

4 cups semolina flour

**2½ to 3 cups bread flour (or substitute all-purpose
    flour)**

FOR PANS:

A little corn meal

GLAZE:

1 teaspoon cornstarch

⅔ cup cold water

1. Measure 1 cup of the warm water into a mixing bowl or the large bowl of an electric mixer and stir in the sugar, then the yeast. Let the mixture stand until it is foamy, about 10 minutes.

2. Add the remaining warm water, then stir in, in turn, the salt, olive oil, egg, and semolina flour. Beat by hand or with an electric mixer until a smooth dough is formed, then beat in about a cup of the bread flour and beat until the dough is smooth and elastic. If mixing by hand, turn the dough out onto a floured kneading surface, or switch to a dough hook if mixing by machine. Knead the dough vigorously, adding as much as necessary of the remaining flour to make an elastic and moderately stiff dough; knead the dough well, 7 minutes by machine or twice as long by hand.

3. Form the dough into a ball and return it to its mixing bowl (no need to wash, dry, or grease the bowl); cover it with plastic wrap and set it in a warm spot until it has tripled in

volume—the light print of a finger will remain when the top is pressed—about 1¼ hours.

4. Punch down the dough, turn it over in the bowl, recover it, and let it rise again until it has doubled, about 40 minutes.

5. Turn the dough out onto a lightly floured work surface and knead it a few strokes to expel the gas bubbles produced by the yeast; divide it into 4 equal parts. Let the dough rest, covered with plastic or a towel, for 5 minutes; meanwhile, sprinkle corn meal generously on two baking sheets.

6. One at a time, flatten each piece of dough into an oval about half an inch thick. Roll the dough up from one long side, pinching the layers firmly closed as you go; pinch the final seam firmly, then roll the dough under the palms into a tapering shape about 12 inches long, with smoothly rounded ends. Place the loaves, two to a pan, well apart on the baking sheets. Brush surplus corn meal from the baking sheets (if left, it will scorch).

7. Cover the loaves with towels and let them rise in a warm spot until they have doubled (the touch of a finger on the side of a loaf will leave an imprint that doesn't fill up), about 35 minutes.

8. Shortly before rising is complete, heat the oven to 425°, with a shelf in the upper third and one in the lower third. Prepare the glaze: Combine the cornstarch and water in a small saucepan; stir the mixture over medium-low heat until it boils and becomes translucent, about 2 minutes. Let the glaze cool.

9. When the loaves have risen completely, brush them with the glaze and slash each with several shallow diagonal cuts, using a very sharp knife or a razor blade held almost horizontally.

10. Bake the pans of bread on two shelves of the oven for 15 minutes, then reduce the oven setting to 375°, exchange shelf positions of the pans, and again brush the loaves with the glaze. Bake the loaves until they are golden brown and firm and sound hollow when thumped on the bottom, about 15 minutes longer.

11. Cool the loaves completely on wire racks, then wrap them in foil or plastic and store them at room temperature for up to a week; or wrap them for the freezer (page 328) and freeze for up to 6 months. To prevent sogginess, thaw frozen bread in its wrapping. Before serving, you may want to refresh the loaves, whether or not they have been frozen, in a preheated 325° oven for 10 minutes, or until they are warm and crisp-crusted.

SEASON:
Any time

YIELD:
4 long loaves,
about 1 pound
each

STORE:
Wrapped, at room
temperature for at
least a week;
freezer-wrapped
and frozen, up to 6
months

Sesame-Topped Bulgur Bread

B*ulgur* bread? Yes, by serendipity. When someone using an early version of this recipe mistakenly used bulgur instead of the cracked wheat I called for, this bread came into being. The bread's texture is less chewy than that of cracked-wheat bread because bulgur has been precooked. If regular cracked wheat is what you have or can get most readily, by all means use it; simply cook it for an additional 2 minutes in step 1.

Let bulgur bread rest in its wrappings for 24 hours before serving it; in that time the flavor "blooms" and the texture of the wheat grains mellows.

2 cups water
1 cup bulgur (or regular cracked wheat, if preferred)
1½ cups warm water (110° to 115°)
3 tablespoons honey or brown sugar
2 envelopes (scant 2 tablespoons) active dry yeast
½ cup yellow corn meal
⅓ cup hulled sesame seed
¼ cup corn oil or other vegetable oil
1 tablespoon salt
1½ cups whole-wheat flour
4½ to 5 cups all-purpose flour (or substitute bread flour)

FOR PANS:
A little corn meal
GLAZE AND TOPPING:
1 egg white
2 tablespoons water
Additional sesame seed, ¼ to ⅓ cup

1. Bring the 2 cups of water to a boil in a saucepan and stir in the bulgur. Lower the heat and simmer the bulgur, uncovered, for 7 minutes, stirring once or twice. Cool the bulgur mixture.

2. Combine ½ cup of the warm water, the honey, and the yeast in a mixing bowl or the large bowl of an electric mixer, stir the mixture, and let it stand until foamy, about 10 minutes.

3. Add the corn meal, ⅓ cup of sesame seed, oil, salt, the cooled bulgur mixture, and the remaining cup of warm water and beat until smooth. Beat in the whole-wheat flour, then beat in the all-purpose flour, 1 cup at a time, until the mixture is too stiff to stir. Either turn the dough out onto a floured kneading surface and knead it by hand, or change to the dough hook for

machine kneading and knead in as much of the remaining flour as needed to make an elastic dough that is no longer sticky. Knead the dough well, about 5 minutes by machine and twice as long by hand.

4. Form the dough into a ball and return it to its bowl (no need to wash, dry, or grease the bowl). Cover the bowl with plastic wrap and set it in a warm spot to rise until the dough has doubled (the pressure of a fingertip will leave an indentation that doesn't fill), about 1 hour.

5. Punch the dough down with your fist, turn it over in the bowl, re-cover it, and let it rise again until doubled, about 45 minutes.

6. Divide the dough into 4 pieces and knead each briefly to expel the gas bubbles produced by the yeast. Flatten each piece into an oval about 1 inch thick. Cover the dough with a towel and let it rest for 10 minutes.

7. Sprinkle 2 cookie sheets with corn meal. Brush surplus corn meal from sheets.

8. To shape the loaves, flatten each piece on a lightly floured surface into an oval about 12 inches long. Roll each up from one long side, pinching the layers firmly closed as you roll; pinch the ends closed and shape them to smooth ovals about 14 inches long. Place the loaves seam down on the corn meal–strewn pans, placing them well apart, two loaves to a pan. Cover the loaves with towels and let them rise until doubled, about 45 minutes.

9. Shortly before rising is complete, preheat the oven to 400°, with a shelf in the upper third and one in the lower third. Prepare the glaze: In a small bowl beat together the egg white and water.

10. Brush the loaves with the glaze and sprinkle them generously with sesame seed. Using a very sharp knife or a razor blade held almost horizontally, cut three slashes diagonally in the top of each.

11. Bake the loaves for 20 minutes on two shelves of the oven, then exchange the pan positions and lower the oven temperature to 350°. Bake the loaves 15 minutes longer, or until the loaves sound hollow when thumped on the bottom.

12. Remove the loaves to wire racks and cool them completely. Wrap the loaves in plastic wrap and store them at cool room temperature, or freezer-wrap them (page 328) and freeze them. To prevent sogginess, thaw frozen loaves in their wrappings.

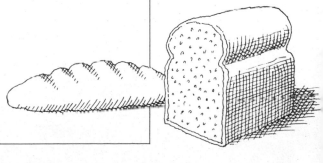

YIELD:
2 or 3 loaves, about
4½ pounds total
weight

STORE:
Wrapped, for at
least a week at
room temperature;
freezer-wrapped
and frozen, for up
to 6 months

Ultimately Cheesy Cheddar Bread

Thanks to Ella Elvin, one of New York's most knowledge-able food writers, for permission to use (and fiddle further with, if I wished) a bread recipe of hers. The considerable original cheesiness of the bread has been increased here by using extra-sharp Cheddar that has been dehydrated to con-centrate its flavor. If you want to skip the drying, just use the most flavorful natural Cheddar you can find.

This is a substantial bread; slice it thin. It is so good with butter alone that a loaf can vanish before there's a chance to toast any of it, but do try toasting, keeping it on the light side. Serve Cheddar toast for breakfast or with salads, or make ham or chicken sandwiches with it.

Cheddar-flavored melba toast is rewarding; see page 162. It keeps for many weeks in a covered canister.

2 cups milk
6 tablespoons (¾ stick) butter
2 teaspoons salt
½ cup warm water (110° to 115°)
½ teaspoon sugar
1 envelope (1 scant tablespoon) active dry yeast
1 egg, beaten
6 to 7 cups all-purpose flour
2½ cups Dried Cheddar Cheese, page 315, or finely
**   grated sharp natural Cheddar**
⅛ teaspoon ground hot red (Cayenne) pepper,
**   optional**
A little melted butter for brushing the finished
**   loaves**

1. Combine the milk, butter, and salt in a saucepan and heat the mixture, stirring, over low heat until the butter melts; set it aside to cool to warm (110° to 115°).

2. Meanwhile, measure the warm water into a mixing bowl or the large bowl of an electric mixer and stir in the sugar, then the yeast. Let the mixture stand until it is foamy, about 10 minutes.

3. Combine the milk mixture with the yeast mixture, add the egg, and beat to mix.

4. Stir 2 cups of the flour thoroughly together with the dried cheese and add the mixture gradually to the liquid mixture, beating by hand or with an electric mixer until well combined. Add the ground hot red pepper, if you are including it. Then gradually beat in more of the remaining flour, mixing

until the dough is too stiff to beat further.

5. Either turn the dough out onto a floured kneading surface and knead it by hand, or change to the dough hook for machine kneading; knead in enough of the remaining flour to make a satiny and elastic dough. Knead the dough very well, about 5 minutes by machine, twice as long by hand.

6. Form the dough into a ball and place it back in its bowl (no need to wash, dry, or grease the bowl). Cover the bowl with plastic wrap and set it in a warm spot until the dough has doubled in volume (the print of a finger will remain when the top is pressed), about 1 hour. Punch the dough with your fist, turn it over in the bowl, re-cover it, and let it rise again until doubled, about 45 minutes.

7. Turn the dough out onto a lightly floured work surface and knead it a few strokes to expel the gas bubbles produced by the yeast. Cut it into 2 or 3 equal portions. Pat each out into a rectangle measuring about 10 x 7 inches and roll up the dough from a short side, pinching the layers firmly closed as you roll. If you are making two loaves, fit each roll, seam down, into a buttered 8-cup loaf pan (9¼ x 5¼ inches); for three loaves, use 6-cup pans (8½ x 4½ inches). Cover the pans lightly with a towel and let the loaves rise in a warm spot until they are doubled (the pressure of a finger at the side of the risen loaf will leave an imprint that doesn't fill up), 45 minutes to 1 hour.

8. Preheat the oven to 375°, with a shelf in the center, a few minutes before the loaves should be ready.

9. Brush the tops of the loaves with melted butter and bake them for 15 minutes, then reset the temperature to 350° and continue to bake the loaves until they are golden brown and sound hollow when turned out of the pan and given a thump on the bottom; total baking time is 45 to 55 minutes for loaves of either size. Brush the tops with butter again and cool the loaves on wire racks, then wrap and store them in a cool spot. (The flavor improves after an overnight or 24-hour rest.) For freezer storage, freezer-wrap the loaves (page 328) and freeze them. To prevent sogginess, thaw the loaves before unwrapping them.

SEASON:
Any time

*CHEESE MELBA:

**If you are melba-
ing Cheddar Bread,
stop the toasting
as soon as the
pieces are crisp;
for the best flavor,
don't let them
brown at all.**

Whole-Oat &
Other Melba
Toasts
& Croutons

When Whole-Oat Long Loaves (or pan loaves), or any of the other breads in this section, have mellowed for at least a day—or at any subsequent point in the life of the loaf—slice the bread as thin as you can, no more than ¼ inch and preferably ⅛ inch.

Lay the slices directly on a shelf of the oven and bake them at 200°, turning them occasionally, until they are dry and pale golden, not actually brown.* Cool the slices, then store them airtight. The toast keeps for weeks.

Melba Toast
Bruschetta-Style

Rub slices of melba toast, either freshly made or taken from storage, lightly with garlic, brush one side lightly with good olive oil, and bake them for 5 minutes or so in an oven heated to 300°. Serve the slices warm.

Also good: Brush melba toast slices with olive oil and sprinkle them lightly with coarse salt; heat as described.

Croutons

For small crisp squares for soups and salads, cut half-inch slices of any of the breads in this section into half-inch cubes. (Trim off crusts first, if you wish.) Spread them on a baking sheet and bake them in a 200° oven until they are crisp and dry, turning them occasionally. Store the cooled croutons airtight at room temperature.

For herbed croutons: Drizzle the bread cubes with olive oil mixed with herbs of your choice (for 4 tablespoons of oil add ½ teaspoon each of crumbled dried thyme and dried tarragon or basil, a pinch of dried oregano, a tiny pinch of Powdered Bay Leaves, page 207, optional, a pinch of freshly ground pepper), plus a little salt. Use at least a tablespoonful of the seasoned oil to a cupful of bread cubes. Toss them well to mix, then bake the croutons as described. These will keep for a few days, stored in a closed jar in a cool cupboard or the refrigerator.

Seeded Breadsticks

T he versatile recipe below is one to be played with. Make long thin breadsticks, or shorter cigar-shapes. Coat them with sesame or poppy seed or a lighter coating of coarse salt, or leave them pristine.

The trick of turning the breadsticks over once during baking allows them to be coated all over with the seed or salt. Some breadstick fans like a sprinkling of caraway seed in place of sesame or poppy, and a mixture of cumin and caraway seed is good, too.

1½ cups warm water (110° to 115°)

½ teaspoon sugar

2 envelopes (scant 2 tablespoons) active dry yeast

¼ cup olive oil

2 teaspoons salt

4 cups all-purpose flour, or as needed

GLAZE AND TOPPING:

1 egg white, beaten

2 tablespoons water

**Sesame seed or poppy seed, about ¼ cup of either, or
   2 tablespoons of each; or use very coarse salt
   (such as sea salt), to taste**

1. Measure ½ cup of the warm water into a mixing bowl or the large bowl of an electric mixer. Stir in the sugar, then the yeast; let the mixture stand until it is foamy, about 10 minutes.

2. Beat in the remaining cup of warm water, the oil, salt, and 2 cups of the flour to make a smooth batter. Gradually beat in 1½ cups of the remaining flour, then turn the dough out onto a floured kneading surface, or change to the dough hook, if you are mixing by machine, and knead it until smooth and elastic, adding as much of the remaining ½ cup flour as necessary; knead well (3 or 4 minutes by machine, or 7 to 8 minutes for hand kneading).

3. Form the dough into a ball, return it to its bowl (no need to wash, dry or grease the bowl), cover the bowl with plastic wrap and set in a warm spot to rise until the dough is doubled in volume, about 1 hour; it has risen enough when the pressure of a finger leaves a print that doesn't disappear.

4. Without punching it down, remove the dough to a lightly floured work surface and divide it into 2 portions. Wrap and refrigerate one piece while you form the other piece of dough into a cylinder 18 inches long; cut the cylinder into 18 equal pieces. Cover the pieces and let them rest 5 minutes.

SEASON:
Any time

YIELD:
3 dozen long breadsticks, or twice as many shorties

STORE:
For 2 weeks or more in an airtight container at room temperature; or wrap and freeze for several months

Shape each piece into a rope 15 inches long, rolling the dough under the palms while stretching it. (If you would rather have short breadsticks, cut the ropes in half before placing them on the pans.) As they are shaped place the breadsticks on a greased baking sheet 1 inch apart (you'll need two pans for each half of the dough). Let the breadsticks rise, covered with a towel, until doubled, about 1 hour. Meanwhile, shape the second portion of breadsticks on greased sheets of foil (to be slipped later onto the cooled pans) and let them rise.

5. Preheat the oven to 300°, with a shelf in the lower third and another in the upper third, shortly before the first pans of breadsticks will be ready to bake. Prepare the glaze: In a small bowl beat together the egg white and water.

6. Brush the breadsticks with the glaze and sprinkle their top sides with seed (or salt, if you prefer); brush any excess seed or salt from the pans. Bake the breadsticks 10 minutes, then exchange pan positions and bake the breadsticks 10 minutes longer, until they are pale gold but still pliable. Remove the pans from the oven, turn the sticks over, brush them again with the glaze, and sprinkle the tops with more seed or salt. Bake them 10 to 15 minutes longer, until they are golden and feel firm when pinched. Remove the breadsticks to wire racks and cool them.

7. Bake the second batch of breadsticks, slipping the foil sheets onto the baking pans after they have cooled completely.

8. Reset the oven to 200° after removing the pans. Lay the cooled sticks directly on the oven shelves and turn the oven off. Leave the breadsticks in the oven for 15 minutes, then remove and cool them again.

9. Store the breadsticks in an airtight container, or bag or wrap them for freezer storage (page 328). At serving time, refresh the breadsticks in a 300° oven, especially if they have been frozen; there is no need to thaw them first.

CRACKERS & OTHER CRISPS

From Caraway Rusks to Oatcakes to Cream Crackers to updated cracker-like beaten biscuits of two kinds, this is a rundown of keepable breadstuffs that go with cheeses, potted meats, fish paste, or any of the sweet preserves your pantry can offer. The Ginger Crackers are especially versatile—they're a delicious base for either savory or sweet spreads, from potted meat to marmalade.

Caraway Rusks

Especially good with cheese, these crisp, twice-baked toasts lightly flavored with spices and honey are also welcome with wine, coffee, or tea. They are not especially sweet; if you'd like them to be more like cookies, double the sugar.

For rusks with good caraway flavor but no whole seeds, omit the celery seed and grind the caraway seed in a spice mill.

3½ cups all-purpose flour

2 tablespoons sugar (double the amount for sweeter rusks)

4 teaspoons baking powder

¾ teaspoon salt

2 teaspoons caraway seed, slightly bruised

1 teaspoon celery seed

½ teaspoon ground nutmeg or mace

2 eggs

2 tablespoons milk

⅓ cup honey

½ cup melted unsalted butter

1. Preheat the oven to 325°, with a shelf in the center. Cover a baking sheet with aluminum foil.

2. Sift together the flour, sugar, baking powder, and salt. Stir in the caraway seed, celery seed, and nutmeg.

3. Beat the eggs and milk together in a mixing bowl to blend them, then beat in the honey until it disappears. Stir in the melted butter, then the dry ingredients. Mix the dough well with a spoon, then knead it a few strokes by hand, working in the bowl; it should be quite compact.

4. Divide the dough into 2 parts. Form each into a firm, flat-topped loaf on the baking sheet; make the loaves 12 inches long and 2½ inches wide and place them well apart.

SEASON:
Any time

YIELD:
3½ dozen

STORE:
In a closed canister, for several weeks at room temperature

5. Bake the loaves until they are firm to the touch and light gold in color, about 20 minutes. Remove them from the oven and reset the oven control to 275°.

6. Cool the loaves on the pan for 5 minutes, then remove them from the foil to a wire rack and let them cool 15 minutes longer. Using a very sharp serrated knife, cut the loaves crosswise at a slight diagonal into ½-inch slices. Lay the slices flat and close together on the baking sheet.

7. Re-bake the rusks for 10 minutes, then turn them over and bake them 10 minutes more, until they are crisp and golden. Turn the oven off and let the rusks cool in it with the door open.

8. Store the cooled rusks in an airtight canister.

 SEASON:
Any time

YIELD:
About 3½ dozen

STORE:
Airtight, for up to 2 weeks at room temperature, or for several weeks longer in the refrigerator; or freeze for several months

Ginger Crackers

Cookies? Crackers? Or biscuits, which is what the British would call them? Whichever, these unsweet crackers are good with cream cheese or with thin slices of Cheddar, or Monterey Jack, Edam, Gouda, or other firm cheese. Preserves, too, are enhanced by their light gingeriness.

⅓ cup milk, plus a little more if needed

3 tablespoons butter

1 tablespoon vegetable oil

1¼ cups whole-wheat pastry flour

¾ cup all-purpose flour

2 tablespoons cornstarch

2 teaspoons sugar

2 teaspoons ground ginger

¾ teaspoon salt

¼ teaspoon baking powder

1. Preheat the oven to 325°, with a shelf in the lower third and one in the upper third. Butter two baking sheets lightly.

2. Heat the milk and butter together in a saucepan over low heat just until the butter has melted. Remove the mixture from the heat and add the oil. Set aside to cool slightly.

3. Sift the pastry flour, all-purpose flour, cornstarch, sugar, ginger, salt, and baking powder together into a bowl. Make a well in the center. Pour the warm milk mixture into the well, then stir the liquid into the drys from the center, mixing gradually and thoroughly to make a crumbly dough that just holds together when squeezed; if the dough is too crumbly (this will depend on the moisture content of the flour), gradually add up to a tablespoonful more of milk and blend it in thoroughly. Form the dough into a ball.

4. Divide the dough into 2 parts. One portion at a time, roll the dough out ⅛ inch thick between sheets of plastic wrap. Cut the dough into rounds with a 2½-inch fluted biscuit cutter; transfer the rounds to the prepared pans, placing them half an inch apart. Gather the scraps, reroll them, and cut more crackers until the portion of dough has been used. Repeat with the second half of the dough. Brush the crackers with a little additional milk, then prick them all over with a sharp fork.

5. Bake the ginger crackers on 2 shelves of the oven for 10 minutes, then exchange shelf positions of the pans and continue to bake the crackers until they are firm and very light golden brown, 6 to 8 minutes longer. Be careful not to overbake the crackers.

6. Cool the crackers on wire racks, then store them airtight; or freezer-wrap them (page 328) and freeze. Frozen crackers should be thawed in their wrappings. Before serving, stored crackers benefit from a brief refreshing in a 300° oven.

Oatcakes

Not exactly crackers and certainly not "cakes" in the American sense, these grainy biscuits, native to Scotland, are just the thing to have with good butter alone, or with cheese, or preserves. They are crammed with oaty flavor and, further, they contain a measure of bran that contributes to both texture and flavor and adds healthful fiber.

Serve oatcakes straight from the canister, or warm them for a few minutes in a moderate oven.

3½ cups old-fashioned rolled oats

½ cup oat bran or unprocessed wheat bran

1½ teaspoons salt

1½ tablespoons butter

1 tablespoon vegetable shortening

½ cup warm water (110° to 115°)

1. Preheat the oven to 350°, with one shelf in the lower third and one in the upper third.

2. Grind the oats to a coarse meal—there should be small flakes as well as fine grains—using a food processor, a blender (work in batches), or a coffee or spice mill (work in even smaller batches). Measure 2 cups of the meal into the container of a food processor or a mixing bowl and reserve the remainder for rolling out the oatcakes.

3. Add to the meal the oat bran and salt and mix them thoroughly. Cut in the butter and shortening, using the processor or, if working by hand, a pastry blender or two knives; the

SEASON:
Any time

YIELD:
About 5 dozen

STORE:
Airtight, at room temperature for 2 weeks; or freezer-wrap and freeze for longer storage

bits of fat should disappear into the mixture. Add the warm water and mix the dough, by machine or by hand, until it will form a coherent ball. Depending on the degree of moisture in the oats, the dough may seem wet at first, but it soon becomes firm.

4. Divide the dough into 2 portions. Spread a thin layer of the remaining ground oatmeal over a work surface and flatten half the dough on it. Sprinkle the top with a little more meal and roll the dough out ⅛ inch thick, lifting it from the board and sprinkling more oatmeal under it if necessary to prevent sticking. If the dough should crack during rolling, dip a fingertip into water and paint the cracked areas, then press them together and complete rolling. Cut the dough into rounds with a 2-inch cutter. Lay the rounds on ungreased cookie sheets, leaving an inch of space between them. Gather the scraps and re-roll and cut them, if necessary working in a few drops of water if the dough is too dry because of the oat flour it has gathered from the board. In the same fashion, make oatcakes from the second half of the dough. (If you have only two baking sheets, lay the rest of the oatcakes on a sheet of foil the size of one of the pans, to be slipped onto a cooled pan for baking after the first two pansful are done.)

5. Run the rolling pin back and forth over the oatcakes on the pan, shaping them into ovals. Prick each oatcake several times with a fork.

6. Bake 2 pansful of oatcakes 10 minutes on two shelves of the oven, then exchange shelf positions of the pans and bake them until they have turned pale gold around the edges, 7 to 8 minutes longer; watch them carefully during this time—they should not actually brown.

7. Remove the oatcakes to wire racks and let them cool; meanwhile, bake and cool the third panful.

8. Store the oatcakes in an airtight canister at room temperature or, for longer storage, double-bag them and freeze (page 328). Refresh stored or frozen oatcakes by warming them for a few minutes in a 325° oven.

 SEASON:
Any time

YIELD:
3 to 4 dozen

STORE:
Airtight, for 2 to 3 weeks at room temperature; freeze for longer storage

Cream Crackers to Go with Cheese

These are crisp bites to go with cheese and a glass of wine for dessert or a snack, and they are also very good by themselves or with a sweet spread, especially the Wine Jellies beginning on page 134. Closely related to several kinds of venerable British crackers of the type called "water biscuits" (even when they are made with cream or milk, as here), these are considerably more flavorful than most commercial versions. Sprinkling a few grains of salt on top is optional; mostly I omit the added salt, as most cheeses taste better with a breadstuff that doesn't compete in saltiness.

The crackers may be made thick or thin, as you prefer. The yield will depend on that.

2 cups all-purpose flour

1 teaspoon baking powder

½ teaspoon salt

¼ cup Clarified Butter (page 315), chilled (unsalted butter that has not been clarified may be substituted)

¼ cup chilled heavy cream

2 to 4 tablespoons cold water, as needed

TOPPING (OPTIONAL):

A little coarse salt

1. Sift or whisk together thoroughly the flour, baking powder, and salt. Work in the butter as if you were making pie crust, using the fingers, a pastry blender, two knives, or a food processor (the fastest way); don't make the mixture too fine— it should be mealy. Mix in the cream and 2 tablespoons of the cold water; if necessary, add enough more water to make a medium-soft dough (the amount of liquid will depend on the moisture content of the flour). Mix the dough very thoroughly—if you are using a food processor, run the motor until the dough forms a ball atop the blade; if you mix it by hand, finish by kneading a few strokes in the bowl. Wrap the dough in plastic wrap and let it rest at room temperature for 20 to 30 minutes.

2. Preheat the oven to 400°, with a shelf in the center. Grease and flour 2 or more cookie sheets, preferably using clarified butter as the fat.

3. Divide the dough into quarters or thirds and roll out one piece at a time between two sheets of plastic wrap until it is ⅛ inch thick (for thin crackers) or about ¼ inch thick for puffier ones. As you roll, the plastic will cling to the dough and both plastic and dough will wrinkle; as this happens, lift the top sheet, smooth it, turn the whole business over, and repeat the smoothing of the plastic; then continue rolling.

4. When rolling is complete, lift the top plastic and cut out rounds, using a 2½- or 3-inch biscuit cutter, plain or with a fluted edge. Lift the rounds onto a prepared baking sheet, stretching them en route into ovals with your fingers; place them about ½ inch apart on the sheet. When the sheet is filled, prick the crackers closely all over with a table fork. If you wish, sprinkle a very few grains of coarse salt on each cracker (don't overdo the salt). Repeat the rolling and shaping with the remaining portions of dough.

5. Bake one sheet of crackers at a time in the preheated

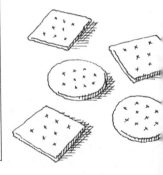

oven until they are firm and pale gold, 8 to 10 minutes for thin crackers, 10 minutes or more for thicker ones. Watch the crackers after 8 minutes' baking; as they reach the right shade of light gold, remove individual crackers from the sheet to a wire rack. Cool the crackers.

6. Store the crackers in an airtight container at room temperature, or double-bag them and freeze them for longer storage (page 328). Let the package come to room temperature before opening the freezer wrapping.

7. However they have been stored, the crackers benefit from a brief freshening in a warm oven before they are served. Spread them on a baking sheet and warm them at around 250° for 3 to 5 minutes, then cool them again.

Beaten-Biscuit Crackers

A shameless borrowing from Southern beaten biscuits, these crackers are pale, rather dense but crisp, very good indeed with a sliver of fine country ham, cheese of any kind, or any savory spread you can think of (see the index for candidates).

The thoroughly modern method of making these, replacing the traditional lengthy thumping of the dough with a club or another weapon, is using a food processor or a heavy-duty mixer. Either machine "beats" the dough to the requisite state of exhaustion while the cook enjoys a cup of coffee or a cold drink. If you use your mixer, or if you have a large-capacity food processor, this recipe can be doubled.

1 cup all-purpose flour

1 cup cake flour

¾ teaspoon salt

½ teaspoon baking powder

2 tablespoons unsalted butter

2 tablespoons high-quality lard, preferably homemade*

About ½ cup ice water

1. Preheat the oven to 350°, with a shelf in the center.

2. *Using a food processor to make the dough:* Combine the two flours, the salt, and the baking powder in the bowl of a food processor fitted with the steel blade. Turn the motor rapidly on and off two or three times to mix them. Add the butter and the lard and run the machine in short bursts until the fats are incorporated; the mixture should be mealy. With the motor

SEASON:
Any time

YIELD:
2 to 3 dozen crackers

STORE
Airtight for a week or more at room temperature; refrigerate or freeze for longer storage, up to 3 months

***LARD:**

For high-quality lard (the commercial kind is usually sorry stuff), you can prepare your own, using fresh, sweet pork fat; most butchers can supply the fat, given a little advance notice. Grind or chop the fat and place it in a heavy saucepan with 3 or 4 tablespoons of water per pound of fat.

running, pour most of the ice water (reserve 2 tablespoons)
through the feed tube. If a dough mass doesn't form atop the
blade within a few seconds, add as much more of the water,
with the motor running, as necessary.

3. When the dough ball has formed, process ("beat") it
for 2 to 3 minutes longer in short sessions (no more than half a
minute each), letting the dough cool each time before resuming. (Cooling is desirable because considerable heat develops
in the dough as it wallops around the bowl.) As the dough
cools, break up and redistribute it around the bowl with your
fingers. When the dough has been "beaten" sufficiently it will
be quite relaxed, not elastic. You can hardly overbeat it.

4. *Alternatively, use an electric mixer:* To mix the dough in
an electric mixer equipped with a flat paddle beater, follow the
preceding steps; the paddle will cut in the fat and form a dough
when the liquid is added. Then beat the dough for 15 minutes
at moderately low speed. Again, the finished dough will be
velvety and relaxed.

5. To shape the crackers, roll the dough out ⅛ inch thick
on a lightly floured surface. Either cut out 2-inch crackers with
a fluted round cutter and arrange them slightly apart on
ungreased cookie sheets, or trim the dough to a rectangle that
will fit on a reversed jelly-roll pan or cookie sheet. Cut the
sheet into oblong crackers, using a plain or fluted pastry
wheel. Prick each cracker two or three times with a table fork.

6. Bake the crackers in the center of the oven until they
are very pale buff-gold, about 20 minutes. Cool the crackers on
a rack, then serve or store them. (For extra crispness, return
the cooled crackers to a 200° oven for 8 to 10 minutes, cool
them again, and store.)

7. Frozen crackers should be thawed in their wrappings.
However stored, the crackers will gain taste and crackle from a
freshening session, about 5 minutes in a 250° oven. Watch to
prevent overbrowning, and cool the crackers or not, as you
prefer, before serving them.

Cheese-Flavored Beaten-Biscuit Crackers

Make the crackers as described in the preceding recipe,
adding ⅓ cup finely grated Parmesan cheese or Dried Cheddar
Cheese (page 315) to the dry ingredients before incorporating
the lard and butter. "Beat" or knead the dough and shape the
crackers as described. Bake them at a reduced temperature—
300°—just until they are very pale gold in color, about 20
minutes; don't let them deepen too much in color, as overbaking cheese crackers will spoil the flavor. After they have
cooled, if you'd like more crispness, return them to a 200°
oven for a few minutes, watching them carefully.

**Simmer the mixture over low heat
(you don't want either the solid or
liquid fat to brown)
until all possible
liquid lard has
been obtained.
Spoon the clear liquid from the top of
the panful frequently and strain
it into a storage
jar. Cool the lard,
cover it, and refrigerate it indefinitely. If you have
an electric slow-
cooker, it's dandy
for this job.**

SEASONINGS
&
COVETED
CONDIMENTS

HOT CONDIMENTS

Green-Fire Pepper Sauce • Dr. Kitchener's Hot Stuff
Hot Red Pepper Oil

MAKING YOUR OWN MUSTARDS

Green Peppercorn Mustard • Horseradish Mustard
Mixed Herb Mustard • Shallot Mustard • Chive Mustard
Lime or Lemon Mustard with Coriander
Coarse-Ground Mustard with Honey & Tarragon
Many-Fruited Mustard • Balsamic Mustard
Creamy Mustard Sauce

WINE VINEGAR REVISITED

Red Wine Vinegar • White Wine Vinegar • Sherry Vinegar

FRUIT-FLAVORED VINEGARS

Four-Fruit Vinegar • Strawberry Vinegar • Cherry Vinegar
Blueberry Vinegar • Blackberry Vinegar
Red Raspberry Vinegar

HERB-FLAVORED VINEGARS

Chervil Vinegar • Chinese Chive Vinegar
Herbal Vinegar for Marinades • Juniper Vinegar

SEASONED OILS

Olive Oil Flavored with Fresh Herbs
Three-Flavor Oil for Chinese Stir-Frying

HERBS: STRETCHING THE SUMMER

Drying Fresh Herbs • Freezing Fresh Herbs
Tarragon Preserved in Vinegar • Powdered Bay Leaves
Encouraging the Bouquet Garni

HERB & SPICE BLENDS

Spice Blends for Savory Dishes • Quatre Epices
Spice & Herb Seasoning Mixture

OTHER SEASONINGS: A MIXED BAG

Mushroom Essence • A Stash of Shallots
Vintage Tangerine or Orange Peel
Strategy for the Bitter Orange

Customizing your cupboard is never more enjoyable than when you prepare your own choice condiments and seasonings. A glance down the contents of this chapter will show a range of possibilities from the positively demure (dried tangerine or orange peel) to incendiary—the hot condiments, like Dr. Kitchiner's Hot Stuff, grouped under "Fire When Ready." Somewhere in between are such things as seasoned oils, herb blends, and other preparations of herbs and spices. There is also a set of suggestions for drying, freezing, and otherwise preserving fresh herbs to stretch the summer.

The sterling collection of vinegars in this section includes the basic information—see "Wine Vinegar Revisited"—that equips you to brew your own choice bottlesful from domestic or imported wines. You can also go beyond the detailed formulas for flavoring either store-bought or homemade vinegars to create a your own fruit- or herb-flavored condiments.

Similarly, you can build on the basic information on mustard making, in "Starting with Store-Bought Mustard," plus the information in the detailed mustard recipes, to develop your own favorites. Or, short of branching out, you can choose to make your own mustards according to the recipes ranging from Green Peppercorn through Lime or Lemon, Chive, Honey & Tarragon, Horseradish, Shallot, Mixed Herb, Many-Fruited, and Balsamic—taken together, enough interesting mustards to keep charcuterie, or plain old cold cuts, superbly matched for a long time.

Miscellany include Mushroom Essence, which I like to use with (tasteless) cultivated mushrooms to add real flavor.

FIRE WHEN READY: HOT CONDIMENTS

Here's a small handful of condiments—Dr. Kitchener's Hot Stuff, Green-Fire Hot Pepper Sauce, and Hot Red Pepper Oil—for real fire-eaters, who will find additional piquant edibles elsewhere in these pages:

Look in With Gusto & Relish for several mildly hot chutneys, Hot & Spicy Banana Ketchup, Hot & Sweet Red Pepper "Jam," and Pickled Hot, Hot Green Peppers. In Sippin' Substances there's a Fire-and-Ice Cocktail compounded of vodka and several kinds of peppers, and in Miscellany & Mavericks you'll find noodles that can be made with hot as well as sweet red peppers, with piquancy according to the taste of the noodlemaker and diners.

SEASON:
Whenever fresh hot peppers are available, generally in late summer but often the year around

YIELD:
About 3 cups

STORE:
At room temperature; keeps indefinitely

Green-Fire Pepper Sauce (Hot Pepper Vinegar)

For an exquisitely hot condiment to sprinkle on cooked greens—a noble old Southern custom—or for seasoning any dish that needs a touch of torchiness, try this simply made vinegar sauce.

As written, the recipe produces a moderately hot vinegar; add more peppers if you're sure that your palate would be grateful.

9 to 12 small fresh hot green peppers, any shape
3 cups distilled white vinegar
Small dried hot red peppers, optional

1. Rinse and dry the peppers. Protecting your hands with rubber gloves (page 321), stem the peppers and chop them, veins, seeds and all, into medium-coarse pieces. Place the peppers in a clean, dry heatproof quart-size jar with a snug lid.

2. Heat the vinegar to simmering in a saucepan and pour it over the peppers. Cool the peppers and vinegar, uncovered, then cap the jar with an enamel-lined canning lid, or use a recycled lid (from mayonnaise, etc.) over 2 layers of plastic wrap.

3. Let the mixture stand for at least 2 weeks or for as long as 3 months, shaking the jar occasionally.

4. When you think it might be ready, taste the liquid cautiously—it's a good idea to sample it on a bit of bland food,

rather than directly. If it is fiery enough to suit, strain it through a very fine-meshed sieve, pressing lightly on the debris of the peppers to extract all possible flavor.

5. Bottle the sauce in clean, dry bottles or jars and cap it airtight. Optionally, place a single whole dried hot pepper in each bottle; or tie one or two hot peppers to the neck to indicate the heat quotient of the contents. It's wise to label the container(s) explicitly, especially if the sauce is to be a gift.

Dr. Kitchener's Hot Stuff

Simple to prepare, this quite piquant (well, very *hot*) sauce provides an excuse for buying beautiful little hot bird peppers (the round ones), small pointed Cayenne or Tabasco peppers, or the somewhat less fiery long, thin red peppers of various varieties when any of these appear in early fall.

Let this seasoning sit in peace to develop for a few weeks before it is served. To acquaint yourself with its degree of heat, sample a drop or two on a bland food; made with full-firepower peppers, it would satisfy even Texans.

The title of the recipe commemorates Dr. William Kitchener, the author of *The Cook's Oracle*, one of the most delightful of nineteenth-century cookbooks; he is said to have first published a formula for a Caribbean condiment along these lines. On its home grounds, the sauce was known in many versions; sometimes quinine was added and the liquid was drawn off to be used as bitters in drink mixing. Made as described here, it is a table or kitchen sauce of real authority.

¼ to ⅓ pound small fresh hot red peppers of any kind available

½ cup dry sherry

½ cup brandy of good quality

½ cup strained fresh lime juice

½ teaspoon salt

¼ teaspon ground hot red (Cayenne) pepper, optional

1. Taking due precautions (page 321), rinse and drain the peppers. Cut out and discard the stems, being careful to retain the cores and seeds. Slice the peppers roughly into the container of a blender or food processor.

2. Cover the machine and chop the peppers; gradually add the sherry and the brandy, continuing to run the machine until a rough puree is made. Add the lime juice and salt; add the ground hot red pepper if mild peppers have been used.

SEASON:
Early fall

YIELD:
About 1 cup

STORE:
In the refrigerator or a cool cupboard; keeps indefinitely

3. Scrape the mixture into a clean, dry pint-size jar. Cover the top with a square of nylon net or 2 layers of cheesecloth, held in place with the band portion of a canning lid. Set the jar in a warm spot in the kitchen and allow the mixture to ripen and swap around its flavors for at least 2 weeks, better 3, giving it a gentle shake now and then.

4. Taste the sauce and add more ground hot red pepper if you think it is needed. Pour the sauce into the container of a blender and puree it again, this time making it as smooth as possible; some fragments of skin and some seeds will refuse to be pulverized, however. Press the sauce through a very fine-meshed sieve, then funnel it into a bottle suitable for table use. Cap the sauce tightly and store it in the refrigerator (to keep hotness longer) or the cupboard. It separates a bit as it stands, so it needs to be shaken before use.

Hot Red Pepper Oil

A little bottle of flame-red hot oil, purchased from an Oriental food store, is indispensable for those who like a few drops of unctuous heat as a condiment with foods of both the Orient and the Occident; hot pepper oil is marvelous on plain buttered pasta, for instance. And try a few drops in salads, or on spinach or other hot, cooked greens.

It's the work of minutes to brew your own hot oil. Use the freshest possible dried hot red peppers, preferably the very small (and very hot) kind; they should be red and firm, not yellowed or crumbly. I like the added touch of paprika flavor, which isn't traditional; consider it optional.

1¼ cups peanut or corn oil

⅓ cup crushed tiny dried hot red peppers, or more if desired

1 tablespoon medium or hot imported Hungarian paprika, optional

1. Place the oil and dried hot peppers in a heavy saucepan and heat them slowly over low heat until fizzing stops and the oil is very hot (but don't let it smoke). Remove from heat.

2. Let the oil and peppers cool for 5 minutes, then stir in the paprika, if you are using it. Let the mixture stand until it is completely cool (it can stand as long as overnight), then strain off the oil through a fine sieve lined with fine-meshed nylon net; press on the debris to obtain as much oil as possible.

3. Funnel the oil into a clean, dry bottle and cap it closely. Store the oil in a cool spot, or refrigerate it; cloudiness of refrigerated oil is harmless, as is any sediment (bits of hot pepper) that may appear.

SEASON:
Any time

YIELD:
About 1 cup

STORE:
For at least 6 months in a cool cupboard

MAKING YOUR OWN MUSTARDS

Goodness knows that there are some "boutique" mustards in the shops that are less than appealing, not to say far out, but the world's mustard makers have been commendably interested in offering more than the bare-bones basics recently.

The good news for pantry fanciers is that it's not only feasible but fun to whip up your own epicurean mustards. Your choice might be as uncomplicated as customizing purchased mustard (see page 180), but do try some of the others, too.

SHOPPING

When it comes to raw materials, it's useful to know that dark mustard seed (black or brown—few dealers distinguish) is more pungent than the more readily available light (white or yellow) seed, a supermarket staple; however, the difference isn't great enough to justify a safari in search of the dark kind. Either light or dark mustard seed may be used in the recipes. Mail-ordering dark seed from a spice dealer is usually the best bet, if you want to try it.

POWDER POWER

Dry mustards are not all alike. Some domestic brands, unfortunately, are virtually without flavor, having only hotness to offer. Imported mustard powder is recommended, and here a brand must be mentioned: Colman's dry mustards, from England, are hard to beat. They are all *hot;* Colman's Special Mild Blend, for example, is mild only in comparison to their other blends, which are Genuine Double Superfine (hottest) and Double Superfine (quite hot). The ferocity of Colman's mustards sold in Britain is toned down by adding wheat flour; for the United States the mustards are packed at full strength.

TAMING THE FIRE

Experimenting with a variety of mustards over the years has led to the key to full-flavored and sufficiently "hot" mustard without bitterness: Combining the powdered mustard and/or cracked or ground mustard seeds with water and letting the mixture stand and "breathe" for an hour or more allows the volatile bitter components to depart in peace. I prefer to "soak" the mustard for at least 3 hours, and I have left it overnight when that has been most convenient.

LESS WORK FOR MOTHER

As will be noted from the recipes, it isn't necessary to cook the ingredients of table mustards, which will thicken very nicely if drys and wets are correctly proportioned.

FEELING FREE

The mustard recipes offered below are guides, not blueprints. So long as the basic proportions of mustard and moisture are more or less maintained, the rest is negotiable. Increase the herbs, spices, salt, acid, or sweetening, but do taste carefully first.

THE POT THICKENS

Prepared mustard thickens somewhat upon standing; this is mentioned because the moisture content of mustard seed and powder can vary, and a finished mixture can be a little thin if you haven't kept your powder dry, so to speak. If it is clear that time alone won't correct the consistency, a quick fix is to add another tablespoonful of mustard seeds and process the mixture briefly again in a blender (it isn't necessary to soak such a small addition of seeds.)

STORAGE

Room-temperature storage is fine for homemade mustards (and store-bought too, for that matter), but they do lose pungency in time. Whether or not this pleases you is an individual matter; to maintain the original hotness, refrigerate.

SEASON:
Any time

Starting with Store-Bought Mustard

It's a simple matter to flavor purchased mustard to taste, letting your palate be your guide. Some suggested additions for smooth Dijon-style mustard follow.

Green Peppercorn Mustard

To 1 cup of smooth Dijon-style mustard add 1 tablespoon (or more) green peppercorns, crushed; drain them well before crushing if they were packed in brine. Stir in a pinch of ground allspice, a pinch of cinnamon, and about ¼ teaspoon of well-crumbled dried tarragon. Mix, taste, and add more spice or herbs, plus a little salt, if it seems a good idea.

Horseradish Mustard

Add 1 tablespoon or more of drained bottled horseradish from a fresh bottle to 1 cup of smooth Dijon-style mustard. Stir in a small clove of garlic, peeled and minced to a paste, a pinch of ground allspice, a pinch of sugar, and perhaps a little salt.

Mixed Herb Mustard

To 1 cup of smooth Dijon-style mustard, add 1½ teaspoons (total) of crumbled dried tarragon, thyme, sweet marjoram (or basil) and a very little oregano; add a small clove of garlic, peeled and minced to a paste (or ½ teaspoon of very finely snipped chives or Chinese [garlic] chives), and 1 teaspoon of very finely chopped parsley, a little lemon juice, salt if it is needed, and a twist or two of freshly ground pepper. Refrigerate this mustard.

Shallot Mustard

Peel shallots and mince enough to make a tablespoonful. Place the shallots in a cup and cover them with boiling water; blanch the shallots 1 minute, drain them thoroughly, and fold them into 1 cup of smooth Dijon-style mustard. Add freshly ground pepper and a bit of salt, if desired. Store this mustard in the refrigerator.

Chive Mustard

Ⅰf you have steeped a batch of Chinese Chive Vinegar (page 198) or flavored some vinegar with ordinary garden chives as described in that recipe, by all means use some of it to mix this mustard. If unflavored vinegar is used, the amount of snipped chives listed below should be increased.

¼ cup light mustard seed

1 tablespoon (lightly packed) dry mustard powder, preferably imported

⅓ cup water

⅓ cup Chinese Chive Vinegar (page 198), plain chive vinegar, white wine vinegar, or Oriental rice vinegar

1 tablespoon light or dark corn syrup

1 teaspoon sugar, or more to taste

1 teaspoon salt

Large pinch of ground cloves

2 to 4 tablespoons finely snipped fresh or frozen chives

1. Grind the mustard seed to the texture of fine meal in an electric spice mill, or grind the seed in a blender, adding the mustard powder to the seed to increase the volume enough to permit the blender to do the job.

2. Stir the ground mustard seed, mustard powder, and water together in a bowl, mixing them thoroughly. Leave the mixture, uncovered, at room temperature for at least an hour or for as long as 4 hours; when you think of it, stir it a few strokes.

3. Combine the mustard mixture with the vinegar, corn syrup, sugar, salt, and cloves in the container of a blender and process them to as smooth a texture as you like, scraping down the sides of the container now and again.

4. Place the chives in a bowl and pour 2 cups of boiling water over them. Blanch the chives for half a minute, then drain them thoroughly in a sieve. Add the chives to the mustard, beginning with 2 tablespoons if you have used chive vinegar, and run the blender for a moment. Taste the mustard, which will be quite assertive because it hasn't yet mellowed, and add more chives to taste. You may also want to add more salt or sweetening.

5. Scrape the mustard into a clean, dry jar, cap it, and store it at room temperature or in the refrigerator. It will be ready to serve after 2 or 3 days.

 SEASON: Any time, if frozen chives are used; otherwise, spring and summer

 YIELD: About 1 cup

 STORE: At room temperature, or in the refrigerator; keeps indefinitely

SEASON:
Any time

YIELD:
About 2 cups

STORE:
**In the refrigerator
or a cool cupboard;
keeps indefinitely**

Lime or Lemon Mustard with Coriander

W hen fresh limes are at their best—from midsummer to early fall—I prefer them to lemons as flavoring for this balanced, mild, rather dark mustard, which has a citrus undertone from the coriander seed as well as the fruit. Make sure that the limes you use are strongly aromatic—scratch the skin of one and sniff. (It's also a good idea to check lemons this way if you're making Lemon Mustard; they, too, can vary in fragrance.)

Like all freshly made mustards, this should be stored in the refrigerator if you wish to preserve its (mild) hotness. If you prefer a mustard that will gradually become even milder, store it at room temperature. In either case, it is virtually immortal if it is not allowed to dry out.

½ cup mustard seed, preferably light

2 tablespoons (lightly packed) dry mustard powder, preferably imported

½ cup water

¾ cup berry- or fruit-flavored vinegar, white wine vinegar, or Oriental rice vinegar

3 tablespoons light corn syrup or mild honey

2 tablespoons sugar (increase to 3 tablespoons if wine or rice vinegar is used)

2 teaspoons salt

2 teaspoons ground coriander seed, preferably freshly ground

2 teaspoons (packed) very finely chopped fresh lime or lemon zest (outer skin only, no white pith)

About 2 tablespoons strained fresh lime or lemon juice

1. Grind the mustard seed to the consistency of fine meal in a spice grinder or a blender; if using the blender, add the mustard powder to the seed to add volume. Combine the ground mustard seed, dry mustard, and water in a bowl and mix them to a smooth paste. Let the mixture stand, uncovered, at room temperature for at least an hour, better 3 or 4 hours. If you think of it, stir it a few times.

2. Scrape the mixture into the container of a blender or food processor and add all the other ingredients except the lime juice (for lime mustard) or lemon juice (for lemon mustard). Process the mustard until it is smooth as possible,

scraping down the sides of the container as necessary. Taste the mustard (the flavors won't be completely pulled together yet) and add more salt and/or sweetening if needed. Add lime or lemon juice, as appropriate, to taste; blend it in.

3. Scrape the mustard into a clean, completely dry glass jar or jars, cap it tightly, and store it at room temperature or in the refrigerator. It can be used at once, but it is better after a few days' rest, during which its flavors can get well acquainted.

Coarse-Ground Mustard with Honey & Tarragon

L ike the other mustard recipes, this one is a guide, not a blueprint. After the mustard has rested for a day or two, taste it and decide whether to add more tarragon, or honey, or vinegar.

This aromatic condiment is especially good with the picnicky foods of summer and when made with summer's fragrant fresh tarragon.

½ cup mustard seed, light or dark

3 tablespoons (lightly packed) dry mustard powder, preferably imported

⅔ cup water

¾ cup white wine vinegar or Oriental rice vinegar

3 tablespoons mild-flavored honey, or 2 tablespoons white corn syrup plus 1 tablespoon strongly flavored honey

2 teaspoons salt

2 tablespoons chopped fresh tarragon leaves, or more to taste (2 teaspoons crumbled dried tarragon, or to taste, may be substituted)

1. *If you possess a spice mill:* Grind the mustard seed in it to the texture of coarse meal. Stir the ground seed with the mustard powder and water and set it aside, uncovered, for at least 2 hours or as long as overnight, giving it a stir when you think of it.

If you use a blender or food processor to do the grinding: Combine the seed, mustard powder, and water in the container and process everything to a coarse puree. Set the mixture aside as described.

2. Combine the mustard mixture with the vinegar, honey,

 SEASON:
Any time

 YIELD:
About 2 cups

 STORE:
At room temperature or in the refrigerator; keeps indefinitely

salt, and tarragon. Process the mixture in a blender or food processor to the texture that suits you, from slightly coarse to creamy.

3. Store the mustard in a clean, dry jar, tightly capped, at room temperature if you would like it to mellow gradually, or refrigerate it at once to retain maximum hotness. It can be used at once, but a few days' rest in the jar will allow the flavor to develop.

⭐ SEASON:
Any time

☕ YIELD:
About 1½ cups

🥫 STORE:
In the refrigerator; keeps indefinitely

MARMALADE MUSTARD

**This is delicious with cold ham, smoked poultry, or any other cold meat that is enhanced by an accompaniment with a touch of pungent sweetness.
Mix Many-Fruited Mustard half-and-half with Temple Orange Marmalade (page 144) that has been chopped up slightly. Lacking the marmalade made with Temple oranges, use any good bitter-orange marmalade.**

Many-Fruited Mustard

Inspired by *mostarda,* the Italian specialty of mixed fruits pickled in a sweet mustard syrup, this mélange is studded with bits of dried and glazed fruits and zipped up with orange or tangerine zest. Other fruits may be added or substituted for those listed, depending on what you have; glazed pineapple is good, as are dried pears, candied citrus peel, and a few of the Candied Cranberries on page 259; if you use the cranberries, you may wish to rinse off their sugar coating first. The precise combination of fruits isn't vital, so long as the total amount is around 10 tablespoons and the fruits are balanced for sharpness and sweetness.

½ cup (lightly packed) dry mustard powder

¾ cup cold water

1½ tablespoons (packed) coarsely shredded orange or tangerine zest (outer skin only, no white pith)

2 tablespoons (packed) diced dried apricots

2 tablespoons (packed) diced dried peaches

2 tablespoons (packed) diced dried figs, preferably white figs

2 tablespoons (packed) diced candied cherries

2 tablespoons (packed) golden raisins

½ cup white wine vinegar, Oriental rice vinegar, or cider vinegar

½ cup sugar

1 teaspoon salt

2 to 4 tablespoons strained fresh lemon juice

1. Stir the mustard and cold water together in a bowl, mixing until all lumps vanish. Let the mixture stand at least an hour, better 3 or 4 hours.

2. Simmer the orange zest in about a cupful of water for 5 minutes. Drain the shreds, then chop them very fine; reserve the zest.

3. If the dried fruit is not tender, cover the pieces with boiling water and let them stand 5 minutes, then drain them well.

4. Combine the drained orange zest, the vinegar, and the sugar in a medium-sized saucepan and boil the mixture, uncovered, over medium heat for 5 minutes, until the syrup has thickened somewhat. Stir in the salt, then add the fruit and the mustard mixture. Stir the mixture over medium-high heat until it comes to a boil and thickens smoothly. Remove from the heat.

5. When the mustard has cooled, taste it and add lemon juice to taste. Scrape the mustard into a clean, dry jar and store it, covered, in the refrigerator. If it should thicken too much upon standing, thin it with more lemon juice or with water.

Balsamic Mustard

A slightly coarse-grained dark mustard that will be even darker if made with black or brown mustard seed, this one is especially mellow because the key ingredient is once-rare Italian balsamic vinegar. Now that this smooth, rather sweet, and dark vinegar has found its culinary niche in the United States, it is available in fine supermarkets as well as specialty food shops.

Feel free to adjust this recipe to your own taste. There are those who would double the garlic, for a more authoritative pungency; others might substitute shallot for garlic, or make the blend sweeter or saltier or more tart. In adjusting the flavorings, taste first and remember that the flavor will develop for a few days after the mustard is made.

½ cup light or dark mustard seed

2 tablespoons (lightly packed) dry mustard powder

½ cup water

⅓ cup Italian balsamic vinegar

3 to 4 tablespoons white wine vinegar or Oriental rice vinegar (or a homemade fruit- or berry-flavored vinegar could be used)

2 tablespoons sugar

2 teaspoons salt

1 large clove garlic, sliced

1. If you possess a spice mill, use it to grind the mustard seed to the texture of fine meal. If not, use a blender, adding the mustard powder to the seed to increase the volume enough to permit the blender to function well.

 SEASON:
Any time

 YIELD:
About 1½ cups

STORE:
At room temperature or in the refrigerator; keeps indefinitely

2. Combine the ground mustard seed, dry mustard, and water in a bowl, mixing them thoroughly. Let the mixture stand, uncovered, for at least an hour or for up to 4 hours; when you think of it, give it a stir (it will become quite stiff).

3. Scrape the mustard mixture into the container of a blender or a food processor and add the balsamic vinegar, 3 tablespoons of the white wine vinegar, and the sugar, salt, and garlic. Cover the container and process the mustard until the garlic has been completely incorporated and the mustard is fairly smooth; scrape down the sides of the container now and again. Taste the mustard, remembering that it will mellow, and add the remaining tablespoon of wine vinegar, if it is needed (balsamic vinegars vary in acidity) and any other additions to the seasoning.

4. Store the mustard in a clean, dry jar, tightly capped, in a cupboard or refrigerator. It will be ready to use in a few days.

SEASON:
Any time

YIELD:
1¾ cups

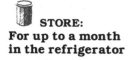

STORE:
For up to a month in the refrigerator

Creamy Mustard Sauce

Although it is quite piquant, this sauce is milder than straight mustards and also more versatile. By itself it has sufficient body to serve as a spread for the bread when you're making meat or cheese sandwiches or canapés, and it's a good condiment to serve with such meats as ham, tongue, or corned beef. Other possible uses for creamy mustard sauce:

• Use the sauce as the base for a creamy vinaigrette for green salads: To each spoonful of sauce add two of oil and one of vinegar. Add salt, pepper, or other seasonings to taste; if you have them, add minced fresh herbs—tarragon, dill, parsley, chives, or a mixture. Whisk vigorously.

• Add Creamy Mustard Sauce to basic mayonnaise for potato, pasta, meat, or fish salads. Dress finely sliced celery with Creamy Mustard Sauce and let this celery "slaw" stand and mellow for a few hours before serving.

• Stir an equal amount of heated heavy cream into Creamy Mustard Sauce and serve the mixture warm with hot green beans; steamed scallions or leeks; or hot Brussels sprouts, cauliflower, or any other member of the cabbage tribe.

• For caper sauce to accompany "boiled" (poached) beef or dill sauce for poached lamb, reduce some of the degreased poaching stock to half its volume. Cool the broth slightly, then whisk Creamy Mustard Sauce into a cupful of the broth until the flavor is to your taste; add drained capers for beef, minced fresh dill or dried dillweed for lamb, and serve the sauce warm.

⅓ cup water

1 medium clove garlic, sliced

⅓ cup (lightly packed) dry mustard powder,
    preferably imported

⅔ cup cider vinegar

⅓ cup sugar

3 tablespoons corn oil or other bland vegetable oil

1 tablespoon cornstarch

2½ teaspoons salt

⅛ teaspoon freshly ground white pepper

⅛ teaspoon ground cinnamon

⅛ teaspoon ground allspice

1 egg

Hot pepper sauce (Tabasco or other), optional

1. In the bowl of a food processor or the container of a blender, combine the water and the garlic and run the machine until the garlic has been completely pureed.

2. Add the dry mustard, vinegar, sugar, oil, cornstarch, salt, pepper, cinnamon, and allspice. Process the mixture until it is smooth. Add the egg and process again briefly.

3. Pour the mixture into a heavy saucepan and cook it over medium-low heat, stirring constantly with a whisk or a straight-ended spatula, until the sauce has thickened smoothly almost to mayonnaise consistency; do not let it boil. Remove the pan from the heat.

4. Scrape the sauce immediately into a clean, completely dry jar, first straining it through a fine-meshed sieve if you suspect any lumps. Let the sauce cool, then taste it for seasoning and add salt, a pinch more sugar, a drop of vinegar, a bit more spice; a few drops of hot pepper sauce are an addition I like. Cover the sauce and store it in the refrigerator.

WINE VINEGAR REVISITED

Down cellar at our house there's a tidy little two-gallon barrel that we used to use for making red wine vinegar. The barrel worked very well, but it took a lot of wine to get it up to speed, and evaporation from the wide surface of wine exposed to the air reduced the yield of vinegar.

Our wine vinegar "factory" is now a couple of half-gallon jugs kept right in the kitchen. This note, and the following recipes, tells how they are used.

For any wine vinegar, it's essential to start with wine that hasn't been pasteurized; further, the fewer chemicals that have been used in its making, the better. Wine of decent quality will produce better-tasting vinegar than nondescript "plonk," of course. Don't let your wine become sour (or even stale) before using it; although some stored-up leftover wine can be used as part of the total, rely mainly on lively, freshly opened wine.

 SEASON:
Any time

STORE:
Cupboard or
pantry,
indefinitely

Red Wine Vinegar

For making vinegar from red wine, you need some good finished vinegar, preferably from France, to use as a starter. Or, if it is available, use instead a handful or so of "mother," the gelatinous (not to say slimy) matter that grows in wine vinegars as well as other vinegars; this substance contains the yeast cells and bacteria that convert wine, apple juice, or certain other liquids into vinegar. If you can't get some mother from a friend who makes vinegar, check for its presence in a bottle of vinegar that has been open for a while; to obtain it, simply strain it out with a fine-meshed sieve.

Combine the wine with the mother, or with about one-fourth of its volume of "starter" wine vinegar, in a half-gallon or gallon jug; don't fill the jug above its widest point, as you want an ample surface exposed to air. Tie a double layer of cheesecloth over the top of the jug and set it in a moderately warm spot where you will remember to look at it once in a while. Leave the jug in peace for several weeks, or until a sniff and a taste indicate that you have created vinegar.

Strain the vinegar into a clean, dry bottle and cap or cork (use a clean cork only). Return the "mother" which will have developed by this time, even if you started with none, to the jug. If you don't want to make more vinegar just yet, add enough wine (or use some of the vinegar you have just made) to keep the mother well covered. Cap the jug until you're ready to make another batch of vinegar.

Pasteurizing the vinegar is optional, but pasteurized vinegar keeps better, without overproduction of "mother," which you no longer want, than vinegar that hasn't been heated. Simply heat the vinegar to the simmering point in a stainless-steel or enameled saucepan and simmer it (don't let it boil), uncovered, for 5 minutes. Cool the vinegar, then bottle and cap or cork it as described.

White Wine Vinegar

Before you tackle this, read the information in the preceding general discussion of wine vinegar as well as that included with the directions for Red Wine Vinegar.

For reasons related to the high acidity of white wines, this is trickier to produce than red wine vinegar. Dilute freshly opened white wine half-and-half with water; then add mother, as for red wine vinegar, and allow plenty of time for the vinegar to develop; it can take months.

Strain, bottle, and pasteurize (optional) the vinegar as described in the preceding recipe.

Sherry Vinegar

First, see the information in the preceding recipes and the introduction to wine vinegar making.

The white-wine vinegar method applied to a medium-dry sherry will produce, very slowly, an exceptionally mellow vinegar. It's worth waiting for, though, if you'd like to try your hand.

Once you have achieved sherry vinegar, strain, bottle, and store it as described for the other wine vinegars. Pasteurize it or not, as you prefer; I think it's a good idea, as this vinegar is most prolific of "mother."

FRUIT-FLAVORED VINEGARS

Vinegars richly flavored with berries or other fruit are among the nicer things to become better known during the current culinary excitement about "new" cooking. However, such vinegars are revivals, not innovations, in the United States. (For example, early settlers in New England found wild raspberries in abundance, and it wasn't too long before shrub—sweetened raspberry vinegar—began to be stirred into cold spring water as a refreshing drink in hot weather.)

Nowadays we tend to sweeten fruit vinegars very little if at all, as they are most used in cooking and in dressing salads, but the basic method of making them hasn't changed much.

THE VINEGARS TO FLAVOR

A mild white vinegar made from white wine or rice is my first choice for flavoring with berries or fruit, but distilled white vinegar (which is higher in acid) can also be used. If you wish to reduce the acidity of distilled vinegar slightly, replace 1 or 2 tablespoons of each cup with water.

OTHER RAW MATERIAL

The detailed recipes for fruit vinegars in this section do not exhaust the possibilities. Peaches, nectarines, tart plums, and currants, for example, are all fine makings. Here is a general rule for trying any fruit that suits your fancy:

Use about a cupful of vinegar to a pound of fruit, stoned if necessary, that has been crushed or chopped. Leave the fruit and vinegar in a clean, dry container, tightly closed, in a cool spot for a minimum of 2 weeks, better 3 or 4. After straining, the now flavored liquid should be simmered gently (in a stainless-steel or enameled saucepan) with a little sugar—use 1 to 1½ tablespoons per cup of vinegar—for 3 minutes. Cool it, then filter or strain it into sterilized (page 327), dry bottles. Store it, tightly capped or corked (use new corks only), in a cool, preferably dark cupboard or pantry.

Fruit vinegar can also be unsweetened, as are some of the best imported brands; see the recipe for Red Raspberry Vinegar.

☀ **SEASON:**
Summer

YIELD:
About 3 cups

STORE:
For at least a year in a cool cupboard or pantry

Four-Fruit Vinegar

Built on the tutti-frutti system of macerating one fruit at a time, this rich vinegar begins with cherries early in summer and winds up with blueberries a few weeks later.

You can start it, if you like to avoid wicked waste, with the vinegar drained from one or two batches of cherries being prepared as Bing Cherries in a Sweet Nine-Day Pickle (page 89). If pickling a batch of cherries isn't in your plans, begin with plain vinegar and crushed cherries, as outlined below, or omit the cherries entirely and begin with the strawberries, in which case you'll be making Three-Fruit Vinegar.

2 cups white wine vinegar or Oriental rice vinegar, or use distilled white vinegar drained from cherries while making Bing Cherries in a Sweet Nine-Day Pickle (page 89)

2 cups stemmed, rinsed, and crushed sweet cherries, if you are starting with plain vinegar

To Be Added at Intervals:

1 cup hulled, rinsed, and crushed strawberries

1 cup rinsed and crushed raspberries

1 cup rinsed and crushed blueberries

For Final Step:

5 tablespoons sugar, or more to taste

1. If beginning with plain vinegar, add the crushed cherries to the vinegar in a sterilized (page 327), dry quart or 1½-liter jar; cover the jar and let it stand for 1 to 2 weeks.

2. If you are using vinegar drained from cherries being pickled, add the strawberries to that vinegar and let the mixture stand for 1 or 2 weeks.

3. Using a fine-meshed sieve or a sieve lined with very fine nylon net or 2 layers of dampened cheesecloth, strain the vinegar from step 1 or 2; press lightly on the pulp to extract as much flavor as possible. Discard the pulp.

4. Prepare and macerate in turn the remaining fruits listed, letting each remain in the vinegar for at least a week or for as long as 2 weeks. After each steeping, drain the vinegar as described.

5. After the final draining, place the vinegar and sugar in a stainless-steel or enameled saucepan and heat it just to simmering; simmer the vinegar, uncovered, for 3 minutes. Cool completely.

6. Skim off any foam and strain the vinegar into a sterilized, dry bottle. For greatest clarity, you may want to filter it before bottling, passing it through a coffeemaker cone or funnel lined with dampened filter paper. Cap or cork the vinegar (use a new cork only) and store it, preferably in a spot out of the light. If sediment should form in it, it is harmless; simply filter the vinegar again, or decant it carefully, or disregard the deposit.

SWEET & SOUR NOTES: FLAVORED VINEGARS

One of the greatest pleasures of pantry-keeping is building, season by season, a small stock of delightfully flavored vinegars. Whether based on berries or cherries or tarragon or more unusual fruits and herbs, the special vinegars you flavor for yourself (or buy at pricey shops) are useful far beyond their roles in sauces and salads; try them as innovative flavorings wherever a touch of tartness plus fruitiness or a delicate herbal character is an improvement in a dish. For example: Add a little fruit vinegar to sugared fresh berries for a subliminal lift, particularly if the berries are on the bland side. Or pour in a little fruit vinegar to add delicate tartness when you're making fruit preserves or stewing fruit that needs a touch of acid for a well-rounded flavor.

🌿 SEASON:
**Late spring/early
summer**

☕ YIELD:
About 4 cups

🍾 STORE:
**For a year or more
in a cool cupboard
or pantry**

Strawberry Vinegar

Besides using Strawberry Vinegar in sauces and fruit salad dressings, try sprinkling a little over lightly sweetened strawberries sliced for dessert; it intensifies their flavor remarkably.

Strawberry Vinegar can also be used to add delicate acidity to fruit preserves in place of lemon juice; add it toward the end of cooking to preserve its fragile flavor.

This vinegar may be prepared without sweetening if you prefer; in that case, simmer it without the sugar. Unsweetened fruit vinegars are more versatile than sweetened versions; it's simple enough to add a little sugar to any dish that requires it.

1½ quart baskets ripe strawberries
3 cups white wine vinegar or Oriental rice vinegar
6 tablespoons sugar, or to taste

1. Sort the berries and discard any overripe specimens; rinse them and drain them very well, then remove their hulls. Crush or chop the berries (a food processor, run briefly, does this fast) and combine them with the vinegar in a sterilized (page 327), dry 2-quart jar or crock. Cover the container closely and let the mixture stand for a month, shaking or stirring it occasionally, even daily if you think of it.

2. Empty the mixture into a fine-meshed sieve lined with fine nylon net or 2 layers of dampened cheesecloth and set over a bowl. Let the vinegar drain, finally pressing lightly on the debris to obtain the last of the juice. Discard the pulp.

3. Combine the vinegar and sugar in a stainless-steel or enameled saucepan and heat it just to simmering, then simmer it, uncovered, for 3 minutes. Let it cool completely.

4. Skim off any foam and strain the vinegar into one or more sterilized, dry bottles. Cap or cork the bottles (use new corks only), and store in a cool spot out of the light. If sediment should appear in time, do one of three things: ignore it, decant the vinegar carefully, or filter it through dampened filter paper placed in a coffeemaker cone or a funnel.

Cherry Vinegar

 SEASON:
Midsummer

YIELD:
About 4 cups

 **STORE:**
In a cool cupboard
or pantry; keeps
indefinitely

While we're on the subject of fruit vinegars, cherry vinegar should not be overlooked. It is less strongly fruity than berry vinegars, but it is a pleasant member of the family; use it as you would any other in this group.

If like me you at least occasionally heed the precept "Waste not, want not," you may want to prepare this vinegar in conjunction with Bing Cherries in a Sweet Nine-Day Pickle (page 89). Directions for this double play are included below.

2 pounds firm-ripe sweet or sour cherries

3 cups white wine vinegar, Oriental rice vinegar, or distilled white vinegar

6 tablespoons sugar

1. If you are making Bing Cherries in a Sweet Nine-Day Pickle, rinse, stem, and pit the cherries for that recipe and follow it through step 3.

2. If you are intent on cherry vinegar only, rinse, stem, and crush the cherries listed above. Combine them with the vinegar in a sterilized (page 327), dry 2-quart jar or crock, being sure they are well covered; if not, add a little more vinegar. Cover the crock and leave the cherries to steep for a week to 10 days.

3. Drain the vinegar from either batch of fruit. If you're making pickled cherries, proceed with step 4 of that recipe. (Optionally, instead of proceeding directly to the next step below, you may want to add to the strained-off vinegar a second batch of fruit and steep it for 3 days, then drain off the vinegar to use here and proceed with the pickle recipe plus step 4 below.) If you're making vinegar alone, proceed with step 4 below.

4. Strain the vinegar through a fine sieve (no need to line it) into a stainless-steel or enameled saucepan, pressing on the pulp to obtain all the liquid. Discard the debris in the strainer. Add the sugar to the vinegar and heat the mixture just to simmering over medium heat; simmer it, uncovered, for 3 minutes. Cool the vinegar.

5. Skim off any foam and strain the vinegar into one or more sterilized (page 327), completely dry bottles. For ultra-clear vinegar, before bottling you may want to filter it through dampened filter paper fitted into a coffeemaker cone or a funnel. Cap or cork the bottles (use new corks only) and store in a cool spot out of the light. If sediment should form, it is harmless; it can be removed by filtering the vinegar again, or by decanting it.

☀ **SEASON:**
**Mid- to late
summer**

🥤 **YIELD:**
About 4 to 5 cups

🍾 **STORE:**
**In a cool cupboard
or pantry; keeps
indefinitely**

Blueberry Vinegar

Blueberry-flavored vinegar is a good addition to hot sauces that need a touch of fruity tartness—try a little when deglazing the pan after sautéing chicken breasts, for instance—and it's also great for salad dressings—combine it with honey for salads of mixed fruit, or use it with a delicate salad oil in a vinaigrette for mixed greens.

To use the vinegar as a drink base or "shrub," pour 2 or 3 tablespoons into a glass, add sweetening to taste and a few ice cubes, and finish with chilled club soda; or fill the glass with sparkling white wine for an unusual spritzer.

Note that the vinegar recipe calls for only moderate sweetening; there's just enough sugar to smooth the edge of acidity without distorting the character of what is, after all, a vinegar. Add more sugar if you're sure you want it.

Use wild blueberries, if you can get them (the frozen ones are fine), for exceptional flavor.

**2 pint baskets (about 6 cups) ripe blueberries, wild
or cultivated, or two 1-pound bags frozen wild
blueberries**

3 cups white wine vinegar or Oriental rice vinegar

5 tablespoons sugar

1. If you're using fresh blueberries, sort, rinse, and drain them, then freeze half of them in a suitable container (you'll use them later); if frozen berries are what you have, thaw half of them and reserve the rest in the freezer.

2. Crush the berries thoroughly, or chop them (don't puree them) in a food processor. Combine the crushed blueberries and the vinegar in a sterilized (page 327), dry 2-quart jar or crock and stir the mixture well. Cover the container closely (put layers of plastic wrap over a crock before setting the lid in place, if the lid does not fit snugly). Set the container aside for 2 to 3 weeks; stir the mixture often, even daily.

3. At the end of the steeping period, thaw the frozen berries and crush them. Strain the vinegar off the first batch of berries through a fine-meshed sieve or a medium sieve lined with fine nylon net or a double layer of dampened cheesecloth; press on the residue to extract all juice. Discard the debris.

4. Return the juice to the jar and add the fresh batch of berries. Repeat the steeping and stirring, letting the mixture stand for another 2 or 3 weeks; exact timing isn't crucial.

5. Strain the vinegar off the berries as before.

6. Stir the vinegar with the sugar in a stainless-steel or enameled saucepan. Heat the mixture just to simmering over medium heat and simmer it, uncovered, for 3 minutes. Cool the vinegar.

7. Skim off any foam and strain the vinegar through a very fine sieve or a medium sieve lined with nylon net or dampened cheesecloth. Funnel it into one or more sterilized (page 327), dry storage bottles. Optionally, add a few firm, fresh blueberries, rinsed and dried, to each bottle as a garnish. Cap or cork the bottles (use new corks only), and store in a cool spot out of the light. If sediment should develop in time, either ignore it or decant the vinegar from the harmless substance or filter the vinegar through dampened filter paper placed in a coffeemaker cone or a funnel.

Blackberry Vinegar

This can be used exactly like other berry and fruit vinegars—in fruit salad dressings, vinaigrette dressings for green salads, and in sauces—and it can also be enjoyed as a beverage base, the old-fashioned "shrub": stir blackberry vinegar to taste into chilled club soda and add sugar.

4 cups (3 half-pint baskets) fully ripe blackberries

3 cups white wine vinegar, Oriental rice vinegar, or distilled white vinegar

6 tablespoons sugar, or more to taste

1. Sort, rinse, and drain the blackberries. Crush them with the back of a spoon, or whirl them briefly (do not puree them) in a food processor. Combine the crushed blackberries and the vinegar in a sterilized (page 327), dry 2-quart jar or crock. Cover the container closely and let the mixture stand at room temperature for from 2 weeks to a month, stirring the contents occasionally.

2. Set a sieve lined with fine nylon net or a double layer of dampened cheescloth over a bowl and strain off the liquid. When all possible liquid seems to have dripped through, press the blackberry pulp lightly to extract the last few drops. Discard the pulp.

3. Pour the liquid into a stainless-steel or enameled saucepan and add the sugar. Heat the vinegar to simmering over medium heat and simmer, uncovered, for 3 minutes. Cool the vinegar completely.

4. Skim any foam from the surface and funnel the vinegar into sterilized (page 327), dry bottles. Cap or cork (use new corks only) and store in a cool, dark spot. If sediment should appear, it is harmless; to remove it, decant the vinegar into another bottle, or filter it through dampened coffee filter paper fitted into a funnel.

SEASON:
Mid- to late summer

YIELD:
About 4 cups

STORE:
In a cool cupboard or pantry; keeps indefinitely

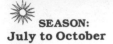

SEASON:
July to October

YIELD:
About 5 cups

STORE:
In a cool cupboard
or pantry; keeps
indefinitely

**USING
RASPBERRY
VINEGAR:**

•Use raspberry
vinegar with a del-
icate salad oil in
vinaigrette dress-
ing for mild-
flavored greens.

•As the acid ele-
ment in dressing
for fruit salads,
use raspberry vin-
egar to replace
lemon juice.

•Take a hint from
Italy and add a
spoonful of rasp-
berry (or straw-
berry) vinegar to
sliced and sugared
strawberries for
added aroma and a
welcome tartness.

•Stir raspberry
vinegar into
lightly salted sour
cream as a dress-
ing for very finely
shredded young
cabbage and let
the salad marinate
for several hours
or overnight.

•Use a few drops
in the pan sauce in
place of lemon
juice when prepar-
ing a sauté of veal
scallops, calf's
liver, or chicken
breasts.

Red Raspberry Vinegar

Raspberry vinegars command high prices in food boutiques, but if you can pick (or buy) fresh red raspberries in
season, making your own is inexpensive and simple. The
vinegar you make, because it's unsweetened, will be highly
suitable for use in sauces and salads.

You should choose to follow the method described in the
Strawberry Vinegar recipe (page 192) if you prefer a sweetened vinegar.

**6 half-pint baskets (8 to 9 cups) raspberries, picked
over**

**3 cups white wine vinegar, Oriental rice vinegar, or
distilled white vinegar**

1. The vinegar will be flavored in two steps, each requiring about 4 cups of raspberries. Seal half of the berries in a
freezer container and freeze them until they are needed, or
plan to obtain fresh berries when the time for the second
steeping arrives. Rinse the remaining berries and drain them
well.

2. Crush the rinsed raspberries and place them in a
sterilized (page 327), well-drained heatproof 2-quart jar. Add
the vinegar and cover the jar. Set it in a deep saucepan and fill
the pan with water to come halfway up the jar. Set over medium
heat and bring the water to a boil; reduce the heat and keep the
water simmering for 20 minutes. Remove the jar and set it
aside, uncovered, to cool the contents.

3. Add a lid to the jar of berries and vinegar and set it
where you will notice it; give it a shake every day for 2 weeks.

4. Thaw the reserved berries (or use rinsed and drained
fresh berries), crush them, and strain the vinegar onto them
through a fine sieve, pressing the old batch of berries lightly to
extract the juice; discard the pulp in the sieve. Return the
vinegar, with the new raspberries, to the jar and repeat the
scalding operation described in step 2. Let the vinegar stand
with the second batch of berries for 2 weeks, as before.

5. Strain the vinegar off the berries through a sieve lined
with fine-meshed nylon net or 2 layers of dampened cheesecloth, pressing the berries lightly to extract juice. Discard the
pulp. Line a funnel with filter paper, dampen the paper, set the
funnel over a sterilized, dry jar or bottle, and filter the vinegar
through it. Cap or cork the container (use a new cork only) and
store the vinegar in a cool, dark cupboard or pantry. The
vinegar may develop sediment as it stands. This is harmless,
but if you prefer a sparkling-clear bottleful, filter the vinegar
again as described above.

HERB-FLAVORED VINEGARS

Red wine vinegar is the best base for flavored vinegars to be used in marinades, and it's also the best match with garlic or shallots. For steeping with delicate herbs, a white vinegar made from wine or rice, or distilled white vinegar, is preferable. Cider vinegar is well suited for flavoring with mint, basil (green or purple), or dill.

The detailed recipes that follow include specific directions for using chervil, Chinese chives (or ordinary chives), juniper berries, and a collection of dried herbs and spices. Also worth trying are several combinations of fresh herbs:

TO FLAVOR VINEGAR WITH FRESH HERBS

Place about a lightly packed cupful of rinsed and dried fresh herbs in a sterilized (page 327), dry heatproof jar. Heat 2 cups of the chosen vinegar to simmering and pour it over the herbs, which should be completely immersed (if not, heat more vinegar and add it). Cap the jar and let the herbs steep for at least 10 days, shaking the jar occasionally. Decant the vinegar, filter or strain it if desired, and bottle it in a sterilized (page 327), completely dry bottle. Store it, capped, in a cool, dark spot.

HERBS TO USE SINGLY

Mint
Basil
Tarragon
Dill (either foliage alone, plus any young seed heads; or dried seed, at the rate of 3 tablespoons to a pint of vinegar)
Chives: Make like Chinese Chive Vinegar (page 198)

SOME HERBAL COMBINATIONS

Tarragon & rosemary
Basil & chervil
Thyme & sweet marjoram
Oregano & sweet marjoram
Savory & thyme (more savory than thyme)
Thyme & chives or shallots, & tarragon & a little rosemary
Sliced or flattened garlic or shallot cloves may be added to any of the combinations above, 1 clove to a pint.

TO MAKE STRAIGHT GARLIC OR SHALLOT VINEGAR

Steep a palmful of peeled and slightly flattened cloves of garlic or shallots in a bottle containing 3 cups of white or red wine vinegar. When the flavor is strong enough, pour off and bottle the vinegar.

Chervil Vinegar

Here is a recipe for the use of gardeners who are growing a little patch of chervil—a ferny-leaved, delicately anise-flavored annual herb best known as one of the *fines herbes* of French cooking. It's for herb gardeners because no one else is likely to be in a position to make this vinegar, as fresh chervil is a rarity in even the most *haute* food markets. Its season is short, it wilts rapidly after being gathered, and the fresh leaves do not retain their flavor through drying or freezing, so it is feast or famine for even the home gardener.

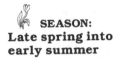 **SEASON:**
Late spring into early summer

 YIELD:
2 cups

STORE:
For at least a year in a cool cupboard or cool pantry

If you have sown chervil or plan to sow some, plan, too, to flavor a bottleful of vinegar with it as a way to stretch the season. This is a pale straw-yellow vinegar, mild in both acid and flavor, but delightful in dressings for delicate green salads.

A big handful—all that can be clutched around the stems—of fresh chervil, including any flower heads or young green seeds

2 cups white wine vinegar or Oriental rice vinegar

1. Rinse the chervil and pat it thoroughly dry with paper towels. Pack it loosely into a sterilized (page 327), dry heat-proof quart jar.

2. Heat the vinegar to simmering in a stainless-steel or enameled pan. Pour it over the chervil; push any wayward stems or leaves under the surface. Let the vinegar cool, then cap the jar and leave it at room temperature (or in a sunny window, if handy) for 2 weeks, shaking the jar occasionally.

3. Strain the vinegar off the debris and bottle it in a sterilized, dry bottle. Cap or cork it tightly (use a new cork) and store in a cool spot or a cupboard.

4. If you still have chervil available and would like a more pronounced flavor, replace the original chervil with a fresh batch after the steeping period; let the second batch steep for 2 weeks. If you like, drop an attractive sprig of the herb into the bottle when the finished vinegar has been funneled in.

SEASON:
Late August into early September

YIELD:
3 cups

STORE:
For up to a year in a cool cupboard or pantry

Chinese Chive Vinegar

C hinese chives, also called garlic chives, are a rewarding (and very easy) herb to grow; they can also be bought fresh, though only in Chinatowns. Although an excellent vinegar for salads can be made with other chives, the Chinese kind, both oniony and garlicky in flavor, makes an especially good condiment.

Chinese chives have straplike (not tubelike) leaves, and toward the end of summer they bear lacy white flower heads that—surprise—are sweetly fragrant. (Florists use them in bouquets.) If you grow culinary herbs, you may want to add *Allium tuberosum* to your plantings.

Big handful (all you can grasp) of freshly cut Chinese (garlic) chives, with a few unopened flower heads, if possible

3 cups Oriental rice vinegar or white wine vinegar

1. Sort and rinse the chives and pat them dry on paper towels. If there are flower buds, cut the stems of a few back to a few inches and fold the flowers gently into a small jar; fill the jar with a little extra vinegar, cap it, and set it aside until the rest of the vinegar has steeped. (Do not use open flowers, which have too much sweet fragrance to suit the pungency of the vinegar you're making.)

2. Snip the chives into 1- to 2-inch lengths and place them in a sterilized (page 327), dry heatproof jar. Heat the vinegar to simmering in a stainless-steel or enameled pan and pour it over the chives. Let the vinegar cool, then cap the jar. Set it where you'll remember to shake it once a day or so.

3. After 10 days, sniff and taste; if the flavor suits, strain the vinegar through a fine sieve and store it in a sterilized, dry bottle that has a snug cover (if you cork it, use a new cork only). Add the flower buds and their vinegar as a garnish.

4. If you'd like vinegar with a more intense flavor, either steep it longer (for up to a month) or strain out the first batch of chives and pour the vinegar, without heating it, over a fresh batch and let it steep again.

USING ORDINARY GARDEN CHIVES:

Use garden chives early in summer, when the growth is at its juiciest; if you'd like to use garlic as a flavor supplement, peel and flatten a clove and steep it along with the chives. If the garden chives are in bloom when the vinegar is being bottled, add a blossom or two as garnish in the container; there is no problem of fragrance with these.

Herbal Vinegar for Marinades

This pungent blend of vinegar, herbs, spices, and red wine is a fine starting point for marinating game, or for giving a gamy tang to beef, pork, or domestic rabbit. It's also good, added sparingly at the finish, as a seasoning for gravies and sauces.

To use the vinegar, substitute it for any other acid called for in your marinade recipe; or combine 2 or 3 tablespoons of the vinegar with 3 tablespoons of olive oil, ⅔ cup of dry red wine, and such fresh seasonings as onions, celery tops, and sliced carrots (no salt). Turn the meat in the mixture at intervals for several hours or (refrigerated) for up to 2 days before draining and cooking it. Use some of the drained-off marinade as part of the cooking liquid or in making the sauce.

2¼ cups distilled white vinegar

1 cup full-bodied dry red wine

4 cloves garlic, peeled and flattened

4 bay leaves, crumbled

4 tablespoons dried or fully ripe fresh juniper berries (see page 208), bruised

3 teaspoon peppercorns, bruised

1 teaspoon dried thyme

 SEASON:
Any time

 YIELD:
About 3 cups

STORE:
In a cool cupboard or pantry; keeps indefinitely

RECYCLING NOTE:

After straining the vinegar from the seasonings, they may be recycled for a smaller second batch. Replace the garlic with fresh cloves and add about half as much heated vinegar and red wine as you did the first time around.

1. Combine the vinegar and red wine in a stainless-steel or enameled saucepan and heat the mixture to a bare simmer.

2. Meanwhile, place the garlic, bay leaves, juniper berries, peppercorns, and thyme in a clean, dry heatproof quart jar. Pour the hot mixture over the seasonings. Let the vinegar cool, then cap the jar and let it stand at room temperature for at least 2 weeks; leave it longer for a stronger flavor.

3. Strain the vinegar off the seasonings when the flavor suits you and funnel it into a sterilized (page 327), dry bottle. If you'd like to garnish a bottle of vinegar to be given as a gift, drop in a small bay leaf, two or three juniper berries, and a few peppercorns.

Juniper Vinegar

If you have access to juniper trees or shrubs that bear well-flavored berries, this is a condiment that can be made at little cost. If you pick your own juniper berries, be sure they are fully ripe—they will be almost black—and rich in flavor; taste one to learn where gin gets its aroma. Fall is the best time to gather the berries. If there are no junipers in your yard, scout the neighbors' places, and don't overlook wild plants. If the outdoor search fails, the vinegar can always be made with dried juniper berries from the spice shelf.

Juniper vinegar is a valuable addition to marinades for red meat and, especially, game; it is also good in sauces and gravies—add a few drops to the gravy of a pot roast, for example. As the flavor is strong, don't rely on juniper vinegar to supply all the acidity required in a marinade unless you want a lot of juniper taste as well; use a little of this for flavor, and add plain wine vinegar or red wine if more acidity is required. For a basic marinade formula, see the note preceding Herbal Vinegar for Marinades (page 199).

2¼ cups red wine vinegar or cider vinegar

¼ cup fully ripe fresh juniper berries or purchased dried berries

1. Heat the vinegar to a bare simmer in a stainless-steel or enameled saucepan.

2. Meanwhile, bruise the juniper berries slightly (a mortar and pestle will do this best) and place them in a sterilized (page 327), dry jar. Pour the hot vinegar over the berries. Let the vinegar cool, then cap the jar and let it stand at room temperature for at least 2 weeks and as long as 4 weeks.

3. Strain the berries from the vinegar and bottle the liquid in a sterilized, dry bottle; cap or cork (with a new cork only). If you like, drop a few juniper berries into the bottle as a garnish.

SEASON:
Any time, using purchased berries; fall, if you pick your own

YIELD:
About 2 cups

STORE:
In a cupboard or cool pantry; keeps indefinitely

SEASONED OILS

Besides trying the recipes in this section, you may want to flavor your favorite kind of salad or cooking oil with your own herbal combinations: just add the fresh or dried herbs of your choice to oil in the manner outlined in Olive Oil Flavored with Fresh Herbs. Until you hit on what you like best, it would be wise to experiment with small amounts of oil, perhaps a cup or so. Allow enough time for the flavor to develop; a month is a reasonable minimum.

Try rosemary or basil alone; or pair either with a bay leaf or two and a few sprigs of thyme or oregano. Rosemary and garlic together season an oil that's especially compatible with lamb and beef.

Straight garlic oil is the work of minutes to assemble. Peel several cloves of garlic per cup of oil, flatten them slightly (just press each under the flat of a knife blade), and drop them into a bottle containing the oil.

Once you have on hand a supply of Three-Flavor Oil for Chinese Stir-Frying (page 203), you'll find yourself ready to make fresh, fast stir-frys often, either for a complete light meal or as a vegetable accompaniment for meat or fish. For good basic directions (and ideas) if you're not experienced with Oriental cooking, you can't do better than to look into Grace Zia Chu's classic *The Pleasures of Chinese Cooking* (widely available), which blazed the way for the Oriental cookbooks with which we are now blessed.

Try, too, Hot Red Pepper Oil, which is placed with the other hot condiments, on page 178.

Olive Oil Flavored with Fresh Herbs

Flavors redolent of . . . Provence? . . . . make this oil a luxurious standby, to be used whenever you would use fine, plain olive oil plus one or more of the herbal flavorings listed in the recipe.

Once the oil has attained full flavor, experiment to find favorite uses. Try it as dressing, with lemon juice, for a salad of sliced oranges, Mediterranean-style olives, and rings of sweet purple onion. Or use it, with the addition of finely minced garlic according to conscience, as a quick sauce for freshly boiled pasta. Rub it into a beef or lamb steak, boneless duck breasts, or halved chickens before broiling, and brush on more oil as a baste.

Bottle your herbed oil in a pressed-glass bottle for a gift, but don't fail to save some for yourself.

 **SEASON:**
Summer into fall

 YIELD:
About 4 cups

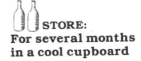 **STORE:**
For several months in a cool cupboard

A big, bushy 6-inch branch of fresh rosemary that
   can be fitted into a decorative quart bottle (or
   use a recycled wine bottle)

A handful of sprigs of fresh or dried thyme, the most
   flavorful available

A 4-inch sprig of fresh basil, either green, violet, or
   purple

3 large bay leaves

2 cloves garlic, peeled and split

1 teaspoon freeze-dried green peppercorns (or use
   white or black peppercorns)

Piece (about 1 inch square) of dried orange or
   tangerine peel, or about 2 square inches of fresh
   orange zest (outer skin only, no white pith)

OPTIONAL: Two or three sprigs of dried oregano; a
   dried seed head of lavender; a small sprig or two
   of fresh or dried sweet marjoram; any or all

Olive oil, preferably a full-flavored kind

1. Rinse the fresh herbs well and shake off all possible
moisture, then roll them in a towel to remove as much dampness as you can.

2. Push the fresh and dried herbs, beginning with the
biggest branches, into a completely dry and squeaky-clean
quart bottle. Drop the garlic, peppercorns, dried citrus peel,
and any of the optional additions into the bottle, arranging them
with the help of a thin chopstick if you are interested in good
looks. Funnel in enough olive oil to fill the bottle almost to the
brim. Cork the oil tightly (with a new cork only) and store it for
a month in a cool spot to allow flavor to develop.

3. If you are in a hurry to sample the herbed oil, set the
corked bottle in the sun for a day or two to "cook" slightly,
which will speed up the extraction of flavors. The sun bath will
cause the oil to become cloudy, but don't be concerned; the
murkiness will clear up quickly.

4. As the oil is used, add more to keep the herbs covered.
When the herbal flavor begins to wane, stop adding oil;
instead, strain the remaining oil into a smaller bottle or jar that
it will fill to the top and cap it. Olive oil isn't immortal,
especially if it is exposed to air as the level in the bottle drops,
so plan to use the herbed oil within half a year or so. It may be
refrigerated if that's the only way to keep it cool; chilling (like
the sun) will make it cloudy, but that doesn't affect its quality;
it clears upon return to room temperature.

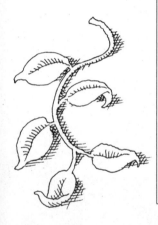

Three-Flavor Oil for Chinese Stir-frying

 SEASON:
Any time

YIELD:
2 cups

STORE:
In the refrigerator, indefinitely; or for a month or two in a cool cupboard

For *au courant* cooks who fix fast stir-frys of vegetables (or meat, or tofu, or seafood plus vegetables) in the Chinese fashion fairly often, a bottleful of preseasoned peanut oil is a great time-saver. Without it, the razor-edged cleaver must move to the cutting board, garlic must be minced, fresh scallions must be dug from the refrigerator and trimmed and sliced, fresh ginger must be peeled and minced, all for the seasoning of a dish that will otherwise take only a few minutes to prepare for the wok. With Three-Flavor Oil on hand, you set the wok over the heat, add your oil, and proceed to cook any Chinese dish that calls for oil plus aromatics (garlic, ginger, and sometimes scallions) to be heated together before the cooking of the "eating materials" begins.

2 cups peanut oil (preferable) or corn oil

8 quarter-size slices of fresh ginger root, ⅛ inch thick (no need to peel it)

6 medium or large scallions

4 large cloves garlic

1. Measure the oil into a heavy saucepan.

2. Smash the slices of ginger slightly on a cutting board, using the flat side of a large knife or cleaver. Drop the slices into the oil. Trim the scallions of their roots, loose skin, and all but an inch or so of their green tops. If you rinse them, pat them dry. Slice them crosswise into thin rounds and add them to the oil. Flatten the unpeeled garlic cloves by laying the flat of your knife or cleaver on each in turn, then hitting the metal a sharp blow with your fist. Drop the garlic into the oil.

3. Set the pan over low heat and warm the contents gradually; a gentle sizzling will begin as the moisture begins to emerge from the seasonings. Keep the heat low and cook the oil slowly for 10 minutes, or until the pieces of scallion appear translucent and the mixture smells delicious. Do not let the flavorings brown at all. Remove from the heat.

4. Let the mixture cool completely, then strain it through a fine sieve into a clean, dry bottle. Discard the seasonings. Store the oil, capped, in the refrigerator or in a cool spot. If it is refrigerated it may become (harmlessly) cloudy; the cloudiness clears when it returns to room temperature.

HERBS: STRETCHING THE SUMMER

Perhaps because its' unimaginable to exist without living herbs around (outdoors in summer, in pots indoors in winter), I feel the flavor of one's own harvest, put away carefully for off-season use, can't be matched by supermarket supplies. For those who feel the same and have a garden patch and/or access to locally grown herbs, here are some tips on extending the season by drying, freezing, and otherwise processing the various leaves, stems, seeds, and roots. (See the index for herb-flavored vinegars, jellies, and mustards, too.)

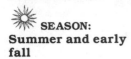 **SEASON:**
Summer and early fall

STORE:
Dark cupboard or pantry, for up to a year

Drying Fresh Herbs

Good herbs for drying include those listed below. Some, you'll notice, are also suitable for freezing.

Basil (but freezing preserves truer flavor).

Bay leaves (true bay, *Laurus nobilis*). Can be ground after drying (see the directions a little farther along).

Fennel leaves

Horseradish root (scrape and slice thin; dry in low oven).

Marjoram (sweet marjoram)

Mint

Oregano

Rosemary

Sage

Sweet woodruff. This pretty ground-cover plant is the soul of May wine and similar punches.

Thyme

Preliminary drying techniques: If the herb in question is a flowering one, cut the branches or sprigs before the flowers open. Harvest any herb before the heat of the day comes on. Only if the plants are dusty should the herbs be rinsed; after rinsing them, shake off all possible moisture, then roll them in a terry towel to blot them further.

Drying in bunches: This is suitable for tall branches (oregano, mint, sage, sassafras, prunings of bay trees, etc.). Gather a few branches together, tie the stems loosely, and place them, head down, in a large paper bag. Tie the neck of the bag around the stems; hang the bag upside down in a warm, dry, airy spot—an attic, a shed, or a shady spot outdoors, which is fine when the weather is hot and dry (take the herb bags indoors before nightfall, return them to the outdoors for as many days as needed). When the herbs are brittle-dry, strip the leaves from the stems and pack them into screw-top jars. Store the jars out of the light and away from too much warmth. Crumble or crush the herb when you're about to use it.

Oven drying: Divide herbs into small sprigs or strip large, thick leaves (as of bay trees) from their branches—this makes for uniform drying. Arrange herbs on wire cake racks or mesh drying shelves (these are available for convection ovens). Dry them at a low temperature (around 100° is ideal, but up to 140° is acceptable) with the oven door propped slightly open. If wet weather interferes with outdoor drying, switch to this method. When the herbs are crisp-dry (watch them carefully—drying may take only a couple of hours), cool them and pack them as described above.

Herbs and How-To's For Freezing

T he flavor of some favorite garden herbs can be preserved better by freezing than drying. Here are some of which this is particularly true, with directions for handling them. There are also a few notes on other ways of preserving certain herbs.

Basil. Blanch sprigs a few seconds in boiling water, then chill them well in ice water. Pat the sprigs dry, then pack them flat in small plastic bags, removing all air, and seal and freeze them.

Alternatively, place unblanched basil leaves in a clean, dry jar, cover them with olive oil, and cover and refrigerate the jar.

Or make a paste of unblanched basil leaves plus olive oil (¼ cup to each packed cup of leaves), using a blender or food processor; pack the puree in a clean container with an airtight lid, leaving ½ inch of headspace; freeze. Or make and freeze Pesto (page 313).

Chives and Chinese (garlic) chives. Bunch the spears, then slice them fine with a very sharp knife. Freeze the bits loose on a baking sheet. When they are frozen hard, pack them tightly into a clean, dry screw-top jar, cover the jar, and place it at once in the freezer. To use, scoop out what you need without allowing the chives to thaw and return the jar to the freezer immediately.

Coriander. Pick the leaves from the stems, then puree

SEASON:
Summer and early fall

STORE:
Freezer, for up to 9 months

them in a blender with a very little water. Freeze the puree in an ice-cube tray. Unmold the cubes, pack them in a freezer-weight plastic bag, press out all possible air, seal the bag, and store it in the freezer. Remove as many cubes as needed for use; most cubes are equivalent to about 2 tablespoonfuls.

Dill. Mince the leaves fine, freeze them loose on a baking pan, pack quickly into a clean, dry screw-top jar, and pop the jar into the freezer at once. To use, scoop out the amount wanted and replace the jar in the freezer before its contents can soften.

Fennel leaves. Same as dill.

Horseradish. Scrape fresh roots clean; wrap them airtight in plastic or foil freezer wrap and freeze them. Grate a portion off the unthawed root as needed.

Sweet marjoram. Blanch, chill, and pack small sprigs in the same way as blanched basil.

Mint. As for blanched basil.

Parsley. As for dill.

Sage. As for blanched basil.

Summer savory. As for blanched basil.

Tarragon. As for blanched basil; or strip the leaves from the stems, freeze them loose on a baking pan, pack them firmly into a clean, dry screw-top glass jar, and store it in the freezer. Or prepare Tarragon Preserved in Vinegar (page 207).

SEASON:
Mid- to late
summer

STORE:
Dark, cool
cupboard, for a
year or so

The Seed-Herb Story

Seed-bearers in your herb garden—anise, caraway, coriander, cumin, dill, and fennel—should be watched like a hawk after the seeds have formed. Let the seed heads dry on the plants, but don't leave them so long that the seeds drop and scatter; check daily to see which heads are ready to harvest.

When the heads are ripe, clip them into a paper bag. Spread them on a tray and let them dry thoroughly in a warm airy spot out of the sun, or in an oven set very low, about 100°.

When the material is thoroughly dry, fan away any loose bits of stem or leaf, then pack the seeds in clean, dry jars with airtight lids. If any sign of dampness appears on the inside of the jars after a day or two, remove the seeds and dry them further in the oven (120° or under). Store the seeds away from heat and light. They will keep longer than dried leafy herbs, although they will be at their best for only about a year.

Seeds will yield more flavor if they are bruised or slightly crushed (use a mortar) just before use. For baking, grind coriander just before use; a spice mill does this fast.

Tarragon Preserved In Vinegar

This formula provides both tarragon leaves to use in cooking and a small supply of flavorful vinegar for salads and such. Top up the jar with additional vinegar (no need to scald it) whenever the level of liquid drops enough to uncover the tips of the tarragon.

How-to's: Rinse freshly cut sprigs or branches of tarragon only if they are dusty; roll them in a terry towel to blot them dry. Pack the tarragon upright into a sterilized (page 327), dry heatproof jar, filling the jar only moderately snugly. Cover the herb well—at least half an inch over the tips—with scalding-hot mild white vinegar (Oriental rice vinegar and white wine vinegar are both good). Let the jarful cool uncovered, then cover it closely and store it. The tarragon can be used at any time; if you wish to use some of the vinegar, wait for at least a week.

Powdered Bay Leaves

Spice packers used to offer jars of ground bay leaves, but no more, alas. So I grind my own, a simple matter for anyone who possesses a little electric spice mill, or even a coffee mill that has a horizontal, or "windmill," grinding apparatus.

Tips: Remove any bits of stem (these are hard to grind) and crumble the leaves coarsely before starting to grind them. Grind enough bay leaves for a tiny jarful at a time, as whole leaves retain their flavor longer than the powder does. Pack the powder firmly into its jar and store it away from heat and light.

Encouraging the Bouquet Garni

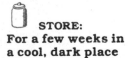
This isn't a recipe, but rather an encouragement to assemble your own ready-to-go bundles—bouquets—of the herbs you use most often in stews, soups, stocks, or sauces.

WILD STUFF FOR THE HERB SHELF

Juniper berries. **Well worth collecting. In autumn check in your garden or along sunny roadsides for heavily berried bushes. Pick only fat, dark-blue berries (the others are immature—juniper berries take three years to reach full flavor). Spread them on a screen or a pan in a shady spot to dry for a few days, until they seem leathery (they will not dry completely). Store them in a capped jar.**

Sassafras leaves. **Gather young leaves from a wild tree in early summer. (Popular guides to tree identification will help you recognize the plants, if you're not familiar with them.) Dry the leaves as described for other herbs. Grind them in a spice or coffee mill to make filé powder, the indispensable seasoning for authentic gumbos.**

Stored in a jar, these are more convenient to reach for than containers of individual seasonings. And if you have a garden of herbs, drying some of them (see page 204) and filling a few apothecary jars with bouquets is a good preparation for gift-giving season. Purchased herbs can also be used; be sure they are fresh. You'll notice that parsley isn't included in bouquets here, although it is one of the three classic elements, together with thyme and bay leaf. That's because dried parsley is sadly lacking in flavor; it's much better to add fresh sprigs, preferably of flat-leaved or Italian parsley, when the bouquet goes into the pot. Either tie the parsley to your basic bouquet (or "faggot"), or leave it loose, to be fished out at the end.

Bundling the bouquets. Tie firmly together, using soft string, a generous sprig of dried thyme and a bay leaf (or two, if they're small). If you leave generous ends of string, you can secure two or three sprigs of fresh parsley to the bouquet when you use it. Another way to bundle is to tie coarsely crumbled dried herbs loosely into small squares of cheesecloth, optionally leaving ends long enough to tie around fresh parsley. Dandy alternatives to cheesecloth squares are the small filter-paper bags, designed to be filled with your own teas, available in kitchen shops. These come with plastic ties that are doubtfully desirable during lengthy cooking, so it's better to tie the bags with string. The "tea" bags won't let the tiniest scrap of herb emerge through the tough paper, a good point when you're hoping to keep a stock especially clear.

Some herb combinations. Each bouquet below starts with bay leaf and dried thyme. Fresh parsley is to be added at the time of use. Garlic, too, is to be added at cooking time, if you want to use it; for easy retrieval, impale the garlic on a toothpick.

• *For Beef:* Add a sprig or two of dried celery leaves (just leave celery tops in an oven at keep-warm temperature until they're crisp), a sprig of dried sweet marjoram and/or a sprig of dried summer or winter savory, and a *tiny* bit of rosemary if you like it. A scrap of dried orange or tangerine peel (page 213) is an addition beloved in Provence.

• *For Fish Stock or Soup:* Add a dried fennel branch or a little fennel seed, and dried celery leaves.

• *For Poultry:* Add dried sprigs or leaves of tarragon. If you grow special thymes in your garden, add a *small* bit of lemon thyme to the basic garden thyme.

• *For Pork:* Add sage or fennel; sweet marjoram is also delightful, as is rosemary.

• *For Tomato Sauces:* Basil and/or oregano, added to a bouquet made without bay leaf. Another good addition is dried celery leaves.

• *Other Possibilities:* Such enhancements as peppercorns, dried onion, a clove or two, or other spices are easily included in bagged bouquets.

HERB & SPICE BLENDS

The formulas that follow indicate the possibilities of creating your own custom seasonings, which is far more fun (and more satisfactory, in terms of quality) than shelling out for a costly little jar in a specialty shop. You'll find that there is an enormous difference between tired factory mixtures (and not just the cheap ones) and what you can blend to your taste.

Experimenting. Try making little mixtures of the herbs and/or spices you like with fish, or in vinaigrettes, or on broiled meat. Add salt and pepper to your seasonings, or not, as pleases you. Store the mixtures as directed in the recipes below.

Raw materials. Do look for the best and freshest possible spices and dried herbs; some mail-order sources are listed in the back of this book, and you'll find the advertisements of other reputable spice merchants in culinary publications.

Equipment. It is easiest to prepare your own seasonings if you possess a little electric spice mill; some of them are identical to small coffee mills, and may be marketed as such. Mine is always within reach near the herb cupboard, for pulverizing whole herbs or spices and for making blends.

It's also feasible to use a blender for grinding all herbs and most spices *if* it will deal with a fairly small quantity of material. If your blender spins its wheels fruitlessly when put to work on the quantity of ingredients listed for Quatre Epices, say, it will function properly if you double the recipe. Doubling shouldn't be a problem, as these mixtures keep well, and an attractive little jar of any of them, labeled with suggested uses, would be a welcome gift.

Spice Blends for Savory Dishes

 **SEASON:
Any time**

Blends such as the two below, often called *quatre épices* regardless of how many components they include, are endlessly useful for seasoning meat-based preparations, most especially pâtés, meat loaves, sausage mixtures, sauces, and ragouts. Once you have made a supply of either, you'll reach for it often.

The first formula below has many versions, some including many more than four spices. The second formula represents the school that adds dried herbs. It is more complex than Quatre Epices, and perhaps even more versatile. If you'd like to compare the two compounds, prepare a batch of Quatre Epices; to half of it, add half the quantity of each additional ingredient listed for the second blend and grind them together. This way, you'll have a half-batch of each mixture.

Quatre Epices

⅓ cup peppercorns (all white, or half white, half black)
4 teaspoons ground ginger
4 teaspoons freshly grated nutmeg
1 teaspoon whole cloves

Place the spices in an electric spice mill and grind them to a fine powder. Sift the mixture through a fine sieve and pack it tightly into a small jar. Cork it, or cover it with a screw top, and store it away from heat and light.

Spice & Herb Seasoning Mixture

The ingredients for Quatre Epices (above), plus:
2 average-size sticks of whole cinnamon, broken up
4 medium-large bay leaves, crumbled
1½ tablespoons dried thyme leaves
1 teaspoon blades whole mace, crumbled before measuring
½ teaspoon whole allspice

Combine all the ingredients and grind them in an electric spice mill, working in batches if necessary, or use a blender. Sift the mixture through a fine sicve and pack it tightly into a jar or jars. Cork or cover the container(s) closely and store the mixture away from heat and light.

OTHER SEASONINGS: A MIXED BAG

Whatever doesn't fit in somewhere else in this chapter will be found here. If you are bored by bland cultivated mushrooms, see Mushroom Essence for a way to rescue them.

If it's feast or famine as far as shallots are concerned, learn here how to keep a supply on hand for many months.

You can also put away for future use an essence of bitter oranges, or a jarful of dried tangerine peel that only gets better as time goes by. The dried peel is also the prime ingredient in a delicious liqueur (page 284).

Mushroom Essence

Designed for the freezer, this preparation came about as first aid for the terminal blandness of cultivated mushrooms; it is also a good addition to any dish or sauce requiring a touch of authentic wild mushroom flavor. (Toss a cube or two into the liquid in which pot roast is braising; the gravy will be exceptional.)

To impart flavor to tame mushrooms, add a cube of the essence to half a pound of mushrooms as they sauté; cover the pan and let the whole business simmer a few minutes, then either uncover the pan and cook the mixture longer to evaporate the liquid, or use the liquid together with the mushrooms as your recipe requires.

1 ounce (⅔ cup) high-quality dried boletus
    mushrooms (cèpes, porcini, Steinpilze, etc.; or
    boletes marketed as "Chilean dried
    mushrooms")
6 cups very warm water
2 medium shallots, peeled and chopped
6 peppercorns
1 blade whole mace or pinch of ground mace
½ small bay leaf

1. Combine the mushrooms in a bowl with 4 cups very warm water. Push them under the surface, weight them with a saucer, and let them soak overnight or for at least 6 hours, until they are very soft. Stir them occasionally.

2. Lift the mushrooms from the liquid with a slotted spoon (save the liquid) and chop them fine, saving as much juice as

 SEASON:
Any time

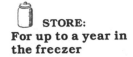 **YIELD:**
16 cubes, about 2
tablespoons each

STORE:
For up to a year in
the freezer

possible. Combine them with the remaining 2 cups water in a saucepan, bring them to a simmer, and simmer them, covered, for 20 minutes.

3. Meanwhile, to clear the soaking liquid of grit, pour it carefully into a bowl, leaving behind the sediment—this is certain to be sandy. Let the liquid settle again and again pour it off; repeat, if necessary, to be sure any grit has been left behind.

4. Pour the simmered mushrooms and their liquid into a sieve set over a bowl and lined with fine nylon net or 2 layers of dampened cheesecloth. Press hard on the mushrooms to extract all possible liquid; discard the debris. Let this second batch of liquid settle, then decant it as described for the soaking liquid; repeat if necessary.

5. Combine the two batches of liquid with the shallots, peppercorns, mace, and bay leaf in a saucepan. Bring the liquid to a boil over medium-high heat and simmer it briskly, uncovered, until it has reduced to 2 cups.

6. Strain out the solids and let the concentrated liquid settle for one last time—we're still on the track of any sand that may remain. Decant the cooled essence, then freeze it in an ice-cube tray. Remove the cubes from the tray and store them in an airtight freezer container.

**SEASON:
Late summer
through fall**

**STORE:
For up to a year in
the freezer**

A Stash of Shallots

F resh shallots, firm yet bursting with juice, are pearls beyond price to the discerning cook. But they are often hard to find even in their harvest season, and they usually enjoy only a short life in most kitchens, which are too warm for them. They keep longer, but not as long as one could wish, when they are refrigerated.

Faced with these facts, I've experimented with extending the life expectancy of shallots, which are often available on farm stands near my home in late summer and early fall.

What works best for me is to peel them immediately and freeze them promptly. Freeze them at 0° or less in a clean, dry screw-top jar, filling the jar as snugly as possible without pressing down on the bulbs. (The jar has the advantage of protecting other items in the freezer from any possible aroma of the shallots, and it is also easy to open and re-close.)

When shallots are needed for a recipe, you'll find your frozen stock to be quite pristine. Remove what you want and return the jar at once to the freezer so the remaining shallots don't thaw even slightly. Shallots are easy to chop while they are still frozen or semi-frozen.

Vintage Tangerine Or Orange Peel

Not for Chinese cooking only, this jarful of fragrant, burnt-orange-colored shards of dried peel; and not for immediate use only—dried tangerine or orange peel improves with age. I keep two or three small jars in the pantry, using peel from the oldest vintage and adding to the youngest jar during tangerine season. The imported dried peel can be bought in Chinatown, but it's fun, and the job of a few minutes, to prepare your own.

Unless you find some oranges (such as clementines and mandarins, which closely resemble tangerines) with richly flavorful skin, tangerines are your best bet as a dried seasoning. Unlike most other citrus, they have peel whose flavor is recognizably like that of the fruit. Tangerine varieties do differ in intensity of flavor, though, so dry only peel that seems especially fragrant and fresh; don't bother with it if it has a dull or dry surface. When in doubt, scratch the skin—tiny droplets of oil should spring up—and sniff.

How-to's: Remove the peel from the fruit either by pulling it off in chunks or by scoring it into neat segments, then prying it off the fruit. Lay each piece in turn on a work surface, skin side down, and scrape off as much as possible of the white pith; a grapefruit spoon, with its finely serrated edge, does this fast. You have scraped enough when the pore pattern of the skin can be seen from the wrong side. Dry the peel on a wire cake rack in a warm, dry spot until the pieces are dry and curled but still slightly pliable, 1 to 3 days, depending on the humidity. Store the peel in a capped jar at room temperature.

SEASON:
Winter

USES FOR THE PEEL:

•Use the dried peel in Oriental recipes for beef, chicken, or lamb stir-frys, or for smoking and deep-frying a duck Chinese-style—for specifics, see Barbara Tropp's *The Modern Art of Chinese Cooking,* or Nina Simonds' *Classic Chinese Cuisine,* or Irene Kuo's *The Key to Chinese Cooking.* Or use the peel in what Irene calls "flavor-potting"— braising meat or poultry in a sauce that is saved, supplemented, and re-used time after time, even for years.

•In Western-style cookery, add a strip or two to the seasonings for pot roast, beef stew, or a more elaborate daube of beef.

Strategy for the Bitter Orange

The bitter orange (or Seville orange, or bigarade orange), botanically *Citrus aurantium,* was one of the first citrus species to arrive in Europe, at an unknown date and probably from the Orient. It was widely planted in warm regions and came to be much used in cookery and was exported on a large scale to British marmalade factories. In Seville today, the wistful traveling cook who can't find bitter oranges at home for love or money sees laden trees lining the streets; in the

 SEASON:
Late winter

 **STORE:**
"See the text."

Caribbean the trees are common in many landscapes, their fruit often neglected.

Of all the world's citrus fruits, the bitter orange is the most difficult to get your hands on in the U.S. unless you live in a Southern region where occasional trees can be found. The fruit seems to be stocked in its brief winter season only by big-city greengrocers catering to connoisseur-cooks or to a Latin American or Caribbean clientele. Other stores just don't offer these unprepossessing, often rusty-looking, and very seedy oranges, useless for eating fresh.

The marmalade question. When I can get a good supply of bitter oranges—which isn't every winter—I make them into marmalade (my way is described in an earlier book, *Better Than Store-Bought*). In other years I make Temple Orange Marmalade (page 144) from a more widely available fruit in season at the same time as bitter oranges; and I have sometimes used for marmalade a quite satisfactory canned base—cooked bitter oranges, their peel, and water, nothing else. It's imported from Great Britain.

Bitter-orange zest and juice for use in cooking. This is to have on hand for preparing duckling à l'orange or other dishes dependent on a touch of the right citrus. Here's how:

Scrub bitter oranges well and pare off any badly damaged or hardened areas of skin. Grate off the zest (the colored outer layer). Halve the oranges, squeeze and strain the juice, and mix it with the grated zest. Freeze the mixture in ice-cube trays. Bag the cubes airtight and return them to the freezer, where they will remain usable for a year.

Last-ditch substitution. All is not lost if your sauce needs bitter orange and you have none. Substitute orange juice into which grated grapefruit zest (avoid all underlying white pith) has been stirred.

DESSERTS
&
SWEET
KICKSHAWS

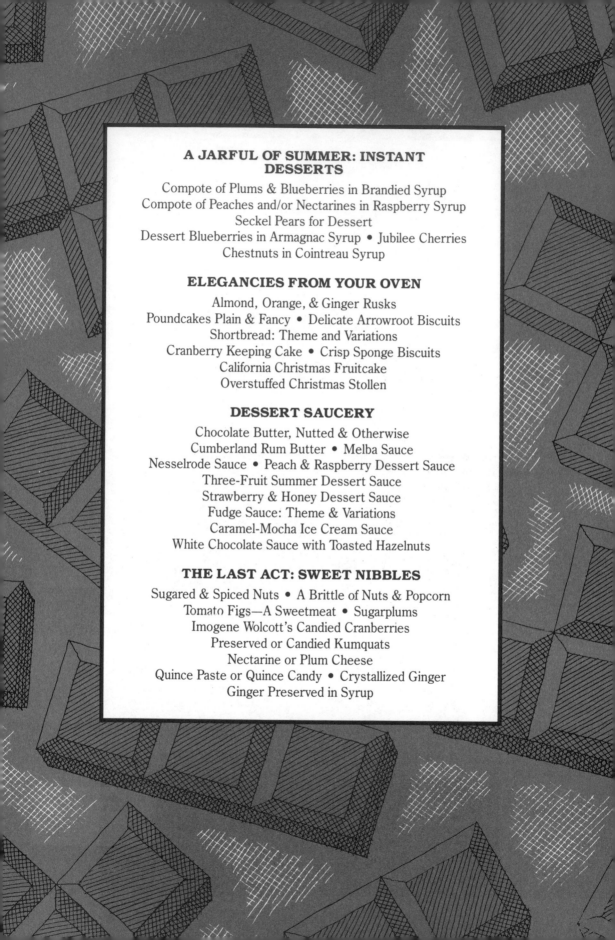

A JARFUL OF SUMMER: INSTANT DESSERTS

Compote of Plums & Blueberries in Brandied Syrup
Compote of Peaches and/or Nectarines in Raspberry Syrup
Seckel Pears for Dessert
Dessert Blueberries in Armagnac Syrup • Jubilee Cherries
Chestnuts in Cointreau Syrup

ELEGANCIES FROM YOUR OVEN

Almond, Orange, & Ginger Rusks
Poundcakes Plain & Fancy • Delicate Arrowroot Biscuits
Shortbread: Theme and Variations
Cranberry Keeping Cake • Crisp Sponge Biscuits
California Christmas Fruitcake
Overstuffed Christmas Stollen

DESSERT SAUCERY

Chocolate Butter, Nutted & Otherwise
Cumberland Rum Butter • Melba Sauce
Nesselrode Sauce • Peach & Raspberry Dessert Sauce
Three-Fruit Summer Dessert Sauce
Strawberry & Honey Dessert Sauce
Fudge Sauce: Theme & Variations
Caramel-Mocha Ice Cream Sauce
White Chocolate Sauce with Toasted Hazelnuts

THE LAST ACT: SWEET NIBBLES

Sugared & Spiced Nuts • A Brittle of Nuts & Popcorn
Tomato Figs—A Sweetmeat • Sugarplums
Imogene Wolcott's Candied Cranberries
Preserved or Candied Kumquats
Nectarine or Plum Cheese
Quince Paste or Quince Candy • Crystallized Ginger
Ginger Preserved in Syrup

Kickshaws," whose sound if not its sense is derived from the French *quelque chose,* can mean what you will: here kickshaws are sweet amusements for the mouth, whether served as dessert or otherwise. A lot of room here for kicking up the heels.

Looking through this chapter in search of sweet conclusions that are ready when you want them, we find fruits in spirited compotes—instant desserts—and other fruit concoctions to be offered in luxurious combinations with ice cream, such as Jubilee Cherries.

Superb baked things-that-keep range from a repertoire of fine poundcakes through a shoal of unusual shortbreads to a "keeping cake" based on cranberries, a richly fruited stollen, and another big cake, especially for Christmas, packed with California fruits. There are also rusks, twice-baked by definition, and other small sweet biscuits.

Sauces: how shall we count them? There is Cumberland Rum Butter, the best (and perhaps original) version of hard sauce; quick-change Chocolate Butter, with or without nuts or liqueur, to use in five or six ways; classic fruit sauces, including a marvelous Nesselrode, rich with chestnuts; a number of fresh fruit combinations to preserve in summer; and a whole raft of other ice-cream toppings, including a white chocolate sauce that's sheer heaven over dark, dark chocolate ice cream.

The grand finale is a splash of small nibbles—nuts, confections, and fruits and ginger preserved in sugar, to be enjoyed with or after the after-dinner coffee.

In a later section of miscellany (page 287) you'll find some dessert makings (praline powder, lemon or lime curd, vanilla flavorings, candied fruits, and so on) that don't qualify as desserts in themselves.

A JARFUL OF SUMMER: INSTANT DESSERTS

Open one of the compotes or single put-up fruits in this section and you'll have dessert ready in no more time than it takes to spoon the fruit into pretty dishes. Add a crisp biscuit—Delicate Arrowroot Biscuits or perhaps Almond, Orange, & Ginger Rusks, both to be found farther along—and dinner is rounded out nicely.

When flaming drama is in order, reach for Jubilee Cherries, to be flambéed and ladled over ice cream. The Chestnuts in Cointreau Syrup can be served on their own in small stemmed glasses, perhaps with a little whipped cream, or with ice cream either under the chestnuts or spooned over them as a sauce.

SEASON:
Midsummer to early fall

YIELD:
2 quarts

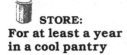

STORE:
For at least a year in a cool pantry

Compote of Plums & Blueberries in Brandied Syrup

Here is an instant dessert, requiring nothing much beyond prying off the lid of the jar: just spoon the fruit and its brandied syrup into pretty dishes and serve it with a pitcher of cream.

If you have a good supply of fruit, you may want to multiply the ingredients to fill as many jars as your water-bath canner will accommodate. However, it's best to poach only enough plums for one quart jar at a time, as described; when all the fruit has been cooked, proceed with the processing instructions.

You can use this recipe for plums alone, if blueberries aren't on hand; use summer plums or, later on toward autumn, use purple (Italian, or prune, or blue) plums.

3 pounds firm-ripe medium-size Santa Rosa or other flavorful plums

1 pint basket (about 3 cups) firm-ripe blueberries

2 cups water

1⅓ cups sugar

¾ cup light corn syrup

6 to 8 tablespoons Armagnac, Cognac, or other good brandy of your choice

1. Rinse and drain the plums; prick the skin of each in 2 or 3 places with a thin skewer or coarse needle. Sort the blueberries, discarding any that are damaged or overripe, then rinse, drain, and roll them in a towel to blot all moisture.

2. Combine the water, sugar, and corn syrup in a preserving pan or a large sauté pan. Bring the mixture to a boil over medium-high heat and boil, uncovered, for 3 minutes.

3. Add half of the plums to the syrup, bring the syrup to a boil again, and poach the plums, shaking the pan often to turn them in the syrup, until they are completely hot through, about 3 minutes.

4. Pack the hot plums in a hot, clean quart-size canning jar or 2 pint jars, layering them with half of the blueberries. Add an inch or two of the syrup and set the jar, using tongs, on a rack in 3 inches of very hot water in the pot you'll use for the boiling-water bath (see the next step).

5. Repeat, cooking and packing the remaining plums and the rest of the blueberries. Add 3 tablespoons of brandy to each quart or 1½ tablespoons to each pint, then fill the jars with boiling hot syrup, leaving ½ inch of headspace. Remove any bubbles (page 324) and add more syrup, if necessary. Seal the jars with new two-piece canning lids according to manufacturer's directions and process the jars for 25 minutes (for quarts) or 20 minutes (for pints) in a boiling-water bath (page 325). Cool, label, and store the jars.

Compote of Peaches and/or Nectarines in Raspberry Syrup

P oach either peaches or nectarines, or some of each, in a rosy raspberry syrup, tuck the result into jars, and you'll have on hand a ready-to-go dessert. It doesn't even need to be chilled—the fruit will be more flavorful at room temperature— and its own syrup serves as sauce; or pass a bowl of soft custard or softened vanilla or peach ice cream to spoon over the fruit.

4 cups (2 to 3 half-pint baskets) red raspberries

3 cups water

2 to 2½ cups sugar, to taste

Lemon juice, as needed

**24 to 30 ripe, unblemished peaches and/or
  nectarines (depending on size)**

6 tablespoons Kirschwasser, optional

1. Sort the raspberries, discarding any that are overripe. Rinse them quickly in a colander under cold water; drain them

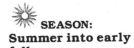
SEASON:
Summer into early fall

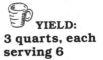
YIELD:
3 quarts, each serving 6

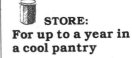
STORE:
For up to a year in a cool pantry

well. Puree the berries in a blender or food processor, in batches if necessary, or work them through a food mill, then press them through a fine-meshed sieve to remove the seeds. Discard the seedy residue, or recycle it to make a version of raspberry vinegar (see the note with Seedless Raspberry Jam, page 125).

2. Combine the raspberry puree, water, and sugar in a preserving pan; bring the mixture to a boil over medium-high heat and boil it for 2 minutes. Taste the syrup; it should be pleasantly acid. If it lacks tartness, add about 2 tablespoons of strained fresh lemon juice. Set the syrup aside.

3. A few at a time, drop the peaches and/or nectarines into a saucepan of boiling water; leave them for a few seconds, then lift them with a slotted spoon into a bowl of cold water set under the running cold tap. When all the fruit has been scalded and cooled, slip off the skins, halve or quarter the fruit, and remove the pits. As you work, drop the skinned pieces into a bowl containing 2 quarts of water acidulated with 2 tablespoons of lemon juice.

4. Bring the syrup to a boil again. Add about a third of the pieces of fruit to the syrup (if you are using mixed fruit, add equal quantities of each to the pot) and poach them carefully over medium heat, turning them from time to time with two wooden spoons, until they are thoroughly hot through (they will be only partially cooked), about 5 minutes. Be careful not to overdo this preliminary cooking of the fruit, which will be completely cooked by the end of step 6.

5. Pack the fruit, hollow sides down, closely into a hot, clean wide-mouthed quart canning jar. Add enough syrup to come halfway up the fruit and set the jar, using a jar-lifter or tongs, on a rack in 3 inches of very hot water in the pot you'll use for the boiling-water bath (see the next step).

6. Repeat steps 4 and 5 until all the fruit has been packed into three jars. If you like, add 2 tablespoons of Kirschwasser to each jar. Fill the jars with boiling-hot syrup, leaving ½ inch of headspace. Remove any bubbles (page 324) and add more syrup, if necessary. Seal the jars with new two-piece canning lids according to manufacturer's directions and process 25 minutes in a boiling-water bath (page 325). Cool, label, and store the jars. To be at its best, the fruit should rest in the syrup for a few weeks before it is served.

Seckel Pears For Dessert— Two Recipes

 SEASON:
October

 YIELD:
3 quarts

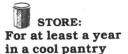 **STORE:**
For at least a year in a cool pantry

Here are two pantry-shelf desserts that are good answers to the question of what to do with Seckel pears, which look unpromising to the uninitiated—they are tiny, tough-skinned, and drab in color. However, they are delicious when poached in either of the two ways described below. Better, they are ready to serve when you are ready for dessert.

Seckel Pears in Red Wine Syrup

Not vinous except in flavor (the alcohol cooks away as the fruit is poached), these pretty little pears are rose-tinted.

About 5½ pounds ripe Seckel pears

Lemon juice, as needed

3 cups tart-flavored, fairly light red wine (Zinfandel is good)

1½ cups water

3 cups sugar, or more if desired

1. Pare the skin from the pears, but leave the stems on; if any stems are overlong, trim them to about a quarter of an inch. As the pears are peeled, drop them into a bowl of cold water acidified with a little lemon juice.

2. Combine the wine, water, and sugar in a preserving pan. Bring the mixture to a boil and simmer it, uncovered, for 3 minutes.

3. Add a third of the pears, well drained, to the syrup and simmer them gently, uncovered, until they are hot through but not soft, about 5 minutes. Pack them carefully, stems up, in a hot, clean wide-mouthed quart canning jar. Add enough of the syrup to come halfway to the top of the jar; set the jar, using a jar-lifter or tongs, on a rack in 3 inches of hot water in the pot you'll use for the boiling-water bath (see the next step).

4. Repeat the last step with the remaining pears, doing them in two more batches. When all have been put into the jars, fill the jars with boiling-hot syrup, leaving ½ inch of headspace. Remove any bubbles (page 324) and add more syrup, if necessary. Seal the jars with new two-piece canning lids according to manufacturer's directions and process for 25 minutes in a boiling water bath (page 325). Cool, label, and store the jars.

Seckel Pears in Vanilla Syrup

Follow the preceding recipe, with these differences: Omit the wine, instead making the syrup with the sugar, 4 cups water, 3 tablespoons strained fresh lemon juice, and 4 teaspoons vanilla extract; or use only 2 teaspoons vanilla and cut a vanilla bean into 3 equal pieces and add them to the syrup. If you use a vanilla bean, be sure to include a section in each jar when canning the fruit.

 SEASON:
**Mid- to late
summer**

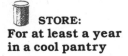 **YIELD:**
3 pints

STORE:
**For at least a year
in a cool pantry**

Dessert Blueberries in Armagnac Syrup

Blueberries in brandied syrup can launch several dessert possibilities. Add spoonfuls of berries and syrup to fresh autumn fruit—diced apples or pears, or both, and sliced blue plums—for an instant compote; ladle berries and syrup over ice cream, or angel cake, or a vanilla-flavored rice pudding or blanc mange; fill meringue shells with the berries and top them with whipped cream; or layer the fruit and syrup with lightly whipped fresh ricotta in parfait glasses.

Armagnac, the *other* great brandy of France, can be replaced here by Cognac, if you wish.

**2 pint baskets (about 6 cups) ripe blueberries,
either wild or cultivated**

6 to 9 tablespoons Armagnac, to taste

3 cups water

2¼ cups sugar

1. Sort the blueberries, discarding any that are damaged or overripe, then rinse and drain them; roll them on a terry towel to remove as much moisture as possible.

2. Divide the berries among 3 hot, clean pint canning jars, shaking them down as you go so they are lightly packed; leave ½ inch of headspace. Pour 2 to 3 tablespoons of Armagnac, according to taste, into each jar.

3. Boil the water and sugar together in a large saucepan, uncovered, for 3 minutes. Fill the jars with the syrup, leaving ½ inch of headspace. Remove any bubbles (page 324), adding more syrup if necessary. Seal the jars according to lid manufacturer's directions and process for 15 minutes in a boiling-water bath (page 325). Cool, label, and store the jars.

Jubilee Cherries

 SEASON:
Mid- to late
summer

 **YIELD:**
3 pints

 STORE:
For a year in a
cool, dark
cupboard

The flambéed dessert called Cherries Jubilee, a great favorite in the Victorian era, remains a pleasure to those who like to climax dinner with flaming tabletop drama. In cherry time, it's the work of moments to seal into jars a supply of the liqueur-spiked fruit, ready to serve over ice cream at short notice. A pint jar is enough for six servings.

The sight of the dark, sweet fruit being flamed in brandy is almost reason enough to give house room to an otherwise seldom-used chafing dish; it's a pity to conduct this ceremony out of view of the diners.

4 pounds dark sweet cherries (about 9 cups after
pitting)

2¼ cups sugar

¾ cup Cointreau or other orange-flavored liqueur
(Grand Marnier, Triple Sec, etc.)

Brandy or Kirschwasser, for flaming at serving time

1. Stem, rinse, and pit the cherries, saving any juice.
2. Combine the cherries and their juice with the sugar in a preserving pan. Heat the mixture over medium heat, stirring it gently or shaking the pan occasionally, until the sugar has dissolved into a smooth syrup and the cherries are hot through; the mixture should not actually boil. Remove the pan from the heat.
3. Divide the liqueur among 3 hot, clean pint canning jars. Lift the cherries from the syrup with a slotted spoon and distribute them among the jars, leaving ½ inch of headspace. Reheat the syrup to boiling and fill the jars with it, leaving ½ inch of headspace. Remove any bubbles (page 324) and add more syrup, if necessary. Seal the jars with new two-piece canning lids according to manufacturer's directions and process for 15 minutes in a boiling-water bath (page 325). Cool, label, and store the jars for at least two weeks before opening.

To serve: Add more liqueur to the sauce, if you like. Then reheat the cherries and syrup, preferably in a chafing dish so that the sight can be enjoyed at the table. Warm ¼ cup of brandy (or Kirschwasser, if you prefer) for a pint of jubilee cherries, pour it over the heated sauce, and set the brandy alight—use a long match, and be careful. Spoon the flaming mixture over vanilla or peach ice cream that has been scooped into individual serving dishes. Crisp sweet wafers are a pleasant accompaniment.

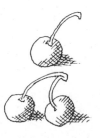

SEASON:
Mid-autumn

YIELD:
About 2½ cups

STORE:
For up to a year in
the refrigerator

Chestnuts in Cointreau Syrup

Quartered chestnuts are poached in a rich syrup to make this chunky delicacy. Tangerines, which are in season together with the new chestnuts, contribute the flavor of their peel while the chestnuts cook, adding a subtle citrus harmony with the orange zest and the Cointreau added at the end.

Spoon this dessert into stemmed glasses and top it with lightly whipped cream, or serve it as topping for the best ice cream you can find.

1½ pounds chestnuts (about 50 nuts)

Peel of 2 large fresh tangerines, all pith scraped from the inside, torn into large chunks

¾ cup sugar

1¼ cups water

⅓ cup light corn syrup

1 tablespoon finely slivered orange zest (outer skin only, no white pith)

⅓ cup Cointreau or other orange-flavored liqueur (Grand Marnier, Triple Sec, etc.)

1. Chop each chestnut in half with a cleaver or heavy knife (lay them flat side down on a cutting board for easy chopping).

2. Place the nuts in a saucepan, add water to cover by 1 inch, and bring them to a boil over high heat. Boil the nuts, uncovered, 3 minutes, then drain them. Pry or pop the halves out of the shells. The skin will usually remain in the shell; scrape off any bits that adhere to the nuts. Halve each piece.

3. Return the nuts to the rinsed-out saucepan; add the skin of one tangerine and enough cold water to cover the nuts. Bring the liquid to a boil, lower the heat, and simmer the nuts gently, partly covered, until they are translucent, about 1 hour. If necessary, add more boiling water to keep the nuts covered.

4. Using a slotted spoon, lift the nuts from the cooking liquid, leaving any scum behind. Discard the liquid and peel.

5. Combine the sugar, the water, and the remaining tangerine peel in the rinsed-out saucepan and bring the mixture to a boil. Simmer the syrup 10 minutes, then add the chestnuts. Bring the syrup to a boil again, then lower the heat and simmer the chestnuts, covered, for 15 minutes. Remove the pieces of tangerine peel. Add the corn syrup and the slivered orange zest; return the sauce to boiling and simmer it for 3 minutes.

6. Ladle the nuts and syrup into a sterilized (page 327) storage jar and add the orange liqueur. Cover the jar, shake it to mix everything, then cool and refrigerate it. The flavor improves for several weeks.

ELEGANCIES FROM YOUR OVEN

For those occasions when a morsel of cake, a sweet biscuit, or a wedge of rich shortbread is just what's needed, here are ways and means of providing your pantry with keepable baked luxuries for dessert, or to serve serenely to drop-ins.

Included in this little section are a wealth of poundcakes, a few rusks, an ingathering of shortbreads (including irresistible double-chocolate and whole-wheat pecan versions), and several other excellent things. Special favorites of mine are the Crisp Sponge Biscuits, so superbly simple that they're addictive. The batter for these bars can also be baked as a cake, as described in the recipe.

When Christmas approaches you may want to stock the holiday larder with a California-style fruitcake—less heavily sweetened than most—and perhaps loaves of fruit-rich Stollen. And don't overlook the unusual Cranberry Keeping Cake.

Almond, Orange, & Ginger Rusks

Crisp and subtly flavored, these twice-baked biscuits go with coffee or tea, or a glass of sweet wine, or a simple dessert of ice cream or fruit compote. They keep beautifully, but if your family is like my family, you will be making them often.

⅔ cup blanched whole almonds

2½ cups sifted all-purpose flour

3 teaspoons baking powder

¾ teaspoon salt

¼ teaspoon ground mace

½ cup (1 stick) butter, at room temperature

¾ cup sugar

½ teaspoon vanilla extract

¼ teaspoon almond extract

2 eggs

3 tablespoons chopped Crystallized Ginger (page 265) or drained Ginger Preserved in Syrup (page 267)

1 tablespoon finely chopped Candied Orange Peel (page 306)

GLAZE:

2 teaspoons milk

Sugar

SEASON:
Any time

YIELD:
About 3 dozen

STORE:
For at least 3 weeks at room temperature

1. Preheat the oven to 350°. Spread the almonds on a baking sheet and bake them, stirring them every 2 or 3 minutes, until they are pale gold, about 10 minutes. Remove the pan of nuts and reset the oven control to 375°. Cool the nuts and chop them coarsely; reserve them. Cover the baking sheet with foil.

2. Sift together the flour, baking powder, salt, and mace; set aside.

3. Cream the butter in a mixing bowl or the large bowl of an electric mixer. Beat in the sugar until fluffy. Beat in the vanilla and almond extracts, then beat in the eggs, one at a time. Stir in the dry ingredients, then the almonds, crystallized ginger, and candied peel. Mix the dough well, or knead it a few strokes on a work surface.

4. Mold the dough into two strips on the foil-covered baking sheet, making each about 12 inches long and 2½ inches wide and placing them 4 inches apart; the centers of the strips should be slightly higher than the sides. Smooth the surface of the strips, then brush them with milk and sprinkle them lightly with sugar.

5. Bake the strips in the center of the oven until they are firm to the touch and pale golden, not browned, about 18 minutes. Remove the pan from the oven; reset the control to 300°.

6. Let the strips cool on the pan for 5 minutes, then carefully remove them from the foil and place them on a wire rack; cool them for 15 minutes longer. Transfer the strips to a cutting surface and, using a sharp serrated knife, cut them crosswise, slightly on the bias, into ½-inch-thick slices.

7. Lay the slices flat on the baking sheet, this time without the foil, and return them to the oven. Bake them for 10 minutes, then turn them and bake them 10 minutes longer. Turn off the heat and let the rusks cool in the oven, with the door open.

8. Store the rusks airtight in a canister.

Poundcakes Plain & Fancy

Like folding money in reserve, these rich little cakes in the freezer promote a serene state of mind. Thawed and sliced, plain poundcake of good character is delicious with a cup of tea, or with coffee, or a glass of Sherry or other wine. Or toast the poundcake, or top it with any of the dessert sauces in these pages, or serve it with a fruit dessert or ice cream that needs a little something alongside.

SEASON:
Any time

YIELD:
4 small (or 2 larger) cakes

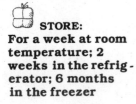

STORE:
For a week at room temperature; 2 weeks in the refrigerator; 6 months in the freezer

Following the main recipe are directions for Miniature Seedcakes, a version flavored with caraway; Macadamia & Lemon Poundcakes, studded with crisp nuts and fragrant with lemon zest; and Ginger Poundcakes, perhaps my favorite, which are enriched with diced candied ginger. Any of these three will make teatime festive.

Miniature Poundcakes

1 cup (2 sticks) butter, unsalted or lightly salted, at room temperature

1¼ cups sugar

4 eggs, at room temperature

1 tablespoon brandy

1 teaspoon vanilla extract

¼ teaspoon ground mace

2 cups sifted cake flour

1 teaspoon baking powder

¼ teaspoon salt

⅓ cup milk, at room temperature

1. Preheat the oven to 325°, with a shelf in the center. Butter 4 small (6 x 3-inch) loaf pans. (Alternatively, use two 8 x 4-inch pans.)

2. Cream the butter well in the large bowl of an electric mixer, beating it on medium-high or high speed until it is fluffy. Add the sugar gradually, continuing to beat, then beat the mixture 2 minutes longer. Add the eggs, one at a time, beating after each addition until the egg is completely incorporated. Add the brandy, vanilla, and mace, then beat the mixture at high speed, scraping down the bowl occasionally, for 5 minutes.

3. Meanwhile, sift together the flour, baking powder, and salt.

4. Add the dry ingredients to the creamed mixture alternately with the milk, beginning and ending with dry ingredients and mixing the batter on low speed after each addition just until it is incorporated. Scrape the bowl down and beat the batter on medium speed for a few additional seconds after the last addition.

5. Divide the batter equally among the prepared pans; smooth the tops. Bake the cakes in the center of the preheated oven until a cake tester emerges clean when inserted into the center, 40 to 45 minutes (for the smaller cakes) or 50 to 60 minutes (for larger cakes).

6. Remove the pans to a wire rack and let the cakes cool in their pans, then unmold them and leave them on the rack for an hour or so to lose any lingering warmth. Wrap them individually in foil and let them mellow for at least 24 hours before serving.

Room-temperature storage is satisfactory for a week or so, but it's preferable to refrigerate the cakes if you plan to store them for up to 2 weeks. For even longer storage, double-wrap the cakes in foil, seal the seams, and freeze the cakes. Frozen cake should be defrosted in its wrapping.

To serve: Add a simple icing if you wish, but it isn't essential; a light dusting of confectioners' sugar is a better choice.

Miniature Seedcakes

For a nostalgic version of this British teatime favorite, add 2 tablespoons of caraway seed to the batter for Miniature Poundcakes. The baking time is the same.

Macadamia & Lemon Poundcakes

Follow the recipe for Miniature Poundcakes, but replace the brandy with 2 teaspoons of very finely grated lemon zest (the colored outer part of lemon rind); reduce the vanilla to ½ teaspoon. At the end of mixing, stir into the batter ½ cup thin-sliced roasted macadamia nuts, preferably unsalted. (If salted nuts are what you have, rub them in a towel before slicing them.) If you like, top the batter in the pans with a sprinkling of more macadamias. The baking time and cooling and storing directions are the same as for Miniature Poundcakes.

Ginger Poundcakes

Follow the directions for Miniature Poundcakes. At the end of mixing the batter, stir in ½ cup very finely diced crystallized ginger, your own (see page 265) or store-bought. The baking, cooling, and storing directions are the same as for Miniature Poundcakes.

Delicate Arrowroot Biscuits

SEASON:
Any time, but especially for tea

YIELD:
About 1¾ pounds

STORE:
For about a month at cool room temperature

If you have ever sneaked a nibble from the baby's box of arrowroot crackers, you know the insidious charm of those mild-mannered bites. This recipe demonstrates that arrowroot cookies aren't for infants only, especially when lemon and anise are added to an eggy, buttery dough.

The ammonium carbonate (also known as "baking ammonia" and "hartshorne") makes very crisp cookies, but it isn't to be found in supermarkets; some druggists will sell it, and it can be mail-ordered (pages 330–331). Very good arrowroot cookies can be made when baking powder is substituted as the recipe suggests, however. Arrowroot (which is, by the way, a versatile kitchen staple—use it to thicken sauces that should be especially bright and clear, and try it for puddings) is best bought by the pound from a supplier of specialty flours, grains, and so on; its price is ridiculously high when it is purchased in jars from spice displays.

1½ cups all-purpose flour

1 cup arrowroot

⅔ cup superfine sugar

¼ teaspoon salt

⅛ teaspoon ammonium carbonate (baking ammonia or hartshorne), or substitute ½ teaspoon baking powder

½ cup (1 stick) sweet cream butter, unsalted or lightly salted

½ teaspoon finely grated lemon zest

¼ teaspoon anise seed, crushed in a mortar or with a rolling pin

2 eggs, well beaten

1 to 2 teaspoons cold milk, if needed

1. Preheat the oven to 325°, with a shelf in the center.
2. Sift together very thoroughly the flour, arrowroot, sugar, salt, and ammonium carbonate or baking powder. Cut in the butter and the lemon zest and anise seed until the mixture is as fine as flour (this is most efficiently done in a food processor). Mix in the beaten eggs to make a firm dough; if using a food processor, run the motor until the dough forms a ball atop the blade. If the dough is crumbly, cautiously add a teaspoonful of the milk and mix it in; add a little more if it is needed, but don't make the dough oversoft.
3. Divide the dough into two portions. Cover a baking sheet with aluminum foil and place one half of the dough on it.

Cover the dough with a sheet of plastic wrap the same size as the foil and roll out the dough ⅛ inch thick, keeping the shape as close to a rectangle as possible. Remove the sheet of plastic and cut the dough into oblongs or diamonds (about 1½ x 2½ inches is a good size; a ruler is a help in making uniform pieces). Lift off the irregular strips at the edges (save them for rerolling) and prick each biscuit in several places with a fork.

4. Bake the biscuits in the center of the oven until they are firm but not at all browned, 10 to 13 minutes. Remove them from the oven, mark over the cutting lines again with the pastry wheel, and remove the biscuits to a wire rack to cool. Shape and bake the remaining dough, including the trimmings; be sure the baking sheet is cool before placing the foil and dough on it.

5. For extra-crisp biscuits, after baking is complete set the wire racks on the shelves of the turned-off oven and leave the biscuits, with the oven door slightly ajar, until they are almost cool. Cool the biscuits completely, then store them airtight for up to a month. Refresh the biscuits in a low (300°) oven for a few minutes before serving them if they have lost any crispness while sojourning in the canister.

Shortbread: Theme & Variations

Bake any of these versions of shortbread—which is perhaps the world's most subtle and delicious cookie or small cake—as a single round, as in the first recipe below, to be divided into wedges; or shape the shortbread as fingers or as round cookies, thus:

Making other shortbread shapes. Instead of pressing the dough into a round baking pan, roll it out ¼ inch thick between sheets of plastic wrap. Peel off the upper sheet of wrap and use a pastry wheel to cut it into "fingers" measuring about 1 x 2½ inches, or oblongs of any size you like; or cut the dough into rounds with a cookie cutter. Transfer the cookies to an ungreased baking sheet, placing them an inch apart; prick them all over, sprinkle them with coarse sugar if you like, and bake them at the temperature specified for each kind of shortbread. The baking time will be 10 to 15 minutes less than for rounds of shortbread; watch the cookies to prevent overbaking; if shortbread actually browns, the flavor is not what it should be.

The Classic Shortbread made by the first recipe is a traditional version except for tiny liberties taken with flavor-

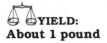

SEASON:
Any time

YIELD:
About 1 pound

STORE:
For up to 2 weeks at room temperature; refrigerate for up to several weeks; or freeze for several months

ings, whereas the variations move farther away from the Scottish sphere; they remain unmistakable members of the shortbread family, however. Other variations are also good: Try adding a handful of chopped candied ginger or chopped black walnuts to the classic version.

Classic Shortbread

½ cup (1 stick) butter, at room temperature
½ cup confectioners' sugar, sifted
½ teaspoon vanilla extract
3 or 4 drops almond extract, optional
1 cup all-purpose flour
2 tablespoons cornstarch
⅛ teaspoon salt

1. Preheat the oven to 325°, with a shelf in the center.
2. Cream the butter, then add the sugar and cream them together until the mixture is fluffy; beat in the vanilla and almond extracts.
3. Sift together the flour, cornstarch, and salt. Work the dry ingredients into the creamed mixture, using the paddle attachment of an electric mixer or, if working by hand, a pastry blender; the mixture will be crumbly. Gather the dough lightly into a ball.
4. Place the dough in an ungreased 10-inch pie pan or a 9- or 10-inch loose-bottomed tart pan. Using the fingers, press the dough into a layer of uniform thickness (this is made easier by covering the dough with a piece of plastic wrap); be sure the dough is well pressed down at the edges as well as the center, and press it firmly into the flutings if you are using a tart pan. If using a pie pan, use a narrow spatula to draw the dough slightly away from the sides of the pan all around, then decorate the edge by pressing it with the tines of a fork. Prick the dough deeply all over with a fork, then mark it into 12 or 16 wedges with a sharp knife, cutting almost through.
5. Bake the shortbread in the center of the preheated oven until it is very pale gold and feels firm when touched lightly, about 40 minutes. Do not let it brown; if while baking it is still soft but beginning to turn golden, reduce the oven temperature to 300°.
6. Cool the shortbread in its pan on a wire rack. While it is still warm, go over the markings again with a sharp knife, separating the wedges completely.
7. Store the shortbread wedges in an airtight container at room temperature, in the refrigerator, or, sealed, in the freezer. Chilled or frozen shortbread benefits from a short but refreshing stay, unwrapped, in a moderate oven. Leave it until it has warmed through, then cool it on a rack before serving it.

Chocolate Chip Shortbread

Make Classic Shortbread (recipe above), omitting the almond flavoring and reducing the vanilla extract to ¼ teaspoon. When the dough has been mixed, work in ⅓ cup miniature chips of real chocolate. Bake the shortbread at 300° instead of 325°; it is done when it is pale golden and firm, about 40 minutes.

Double Chocolate Shortbread

Reduce the flour in the Classic Shortbread recipe to ¾ cup; reduce the cornstarch to 1 tablespoon; sift 3 tablespoons unsweetened Dutch-process cocoa with the other dry ingredients. When the dough has been mixed, work in ⅓ cup miniature chips of real chocolate. Bake as for Chocolate Chip Shortbread.

Whole-Wheat Shortbread

In the recipe for Classic Shortbread, replace the confectioners' sugar with ¼ cup (packed) light brown sugar; sift the sugar before creaming it with the butter. Reduce the vanilla extract to ¼ teaspoon; omit the almond flavoring. Substitute 1 cup whole-wheat pastry flour for the all-purpose flour. Bake the shortbread at 325° for 20 minutes, then reduce oven setting to 300° and bake the shortbread 20 minutes longer, or until it tests done.

Whole-Wheat Pecan Shortbread

Follow the directions for Whole-Wheat Shortbread, stirring ¼ cup of very finely chopped pecans into the creamed mixture before adding the dry ingredients. Bake as for Whole-Wheat Shortbread.

Cranberry Keeping Cake

When the calendar says it's time to make a holiday cake that will keep and improve until Christmas, this spicy, fruity loaf is just the ticket. It can include nuts or not, and either way it is less rich than traditional fruitcakes. It's also quickly made.

The cake can be made with good (meaning dense) commercial cranberry sauce, if you prefer not to use fresh cranberries, or with preserved lingonberries or lingonberry jam.

Swedish food expert Anna Olsson Coombs inspired this cake in her long-out-of-print *Smorgasbord Cookbook,* in which she called it "Norrland's Cake." The method of assembly is hers.

With or without the suggested ornamentation, cranberry cake is a lovely gift.

2½ cups fresh or frozen cranberries, rinsed and drained

⅔ cup granulated sugar

1 teaspoon (packed) finely grated orange zest (outer skin only, no white pith)

½ cup (1 stick) butter

2¼ cups all-purpose flour

2 cups (lightly packed) light brown sugar

2 teaspoons ground cinnamon

½ teaspoon ground coriander

½ teaspoon ground cardamom

¼ teaspoon ground cloves

¾ teaspoon salt

2 eggs

¾ cup dairy sour cream

2 teaspoons baking soda dissolved in 2 teaspoons water

⅔ to 1 cup coarsely chopped pecans (or butternuts, if you're fortunate enough to have them), optional

1. Butter two 6-cup (8½ x 4½ inches) loaf pans, line them with baking parchment, butter the lining, and set them aside.

2. Combine 1½ cups of the cranberries with the granulated sugar and the orange zest in a saucepan. Bring the mixture to a boil over medium heat, stirring it often, and cook it, stirring occasionally, until the berries have popped and the syrup has thickened, about 5 minutes. While the cranberries cook, chop the remaining cranberries coarsely. Add them to the cooked berries and set the mixture aside to cool.

SEASON:
October to late winter

YIELD:
Two 8½-inch loaf cakes, about 1½ pounds each

STORE:
Wrapped airtight, for at least 3 months in a cool pantry or the refrigerator; freeze for longer storage, up to a year

Near our house are sandy bogs where cranberries grow wild, and it's a special pleasure to gather our own crop for this cake as well as for Baked Cranberry Preserves with Cardamom, Sweet & Tart Pickled Cranberries, Cranberry & Currant Relish, Cranberry Ketchup, and Cranberry Cordial. In lean seasons, we gather our cranberries at the supermarket, bringing home a few extra bags for freezing.

3. Melt the butter over very low heat just until creamy, not liquid; set it aside to cool. Preheat the oven to 350°.

4. Sift together the flour, brown sugar, cinnamon, coriander, cardamom, cloves, and salt.

5. Beat the eggs well in a mixing bowl or the large bowl of an electric mixer; beat in the sour cream, then the dissolved baking soda. Beat in the sifted dry ingredients just until mixed, then beat in the melted butter; beat in the cranberry mixture and nuts, if they are used, just until ingredients are blended.

6. Divide the batter between the prepared pans and smooth the tops; lift each pan a few inches from the work surface and drop it to settle the batter. Bake the cakes in the center of the preheated oven until a cake tester emerges dry after probing the center or until the center springs back when pressed lightly, about 1 hour.

7. Set the pans on wire racks and let the cakes cool for 15 minutes, then remove them from the pans and cool them completely on the racks. Remove the paper and wrap the cakes closely in foil or plastic wrap. Store them in a cool cupboard or the refrigerator or wrap them suitably and freeze them. The cakes are ready to serve after a few days, but they continue to improve for weeks. Frozen cranberry cake should be thawed in its wrapper to prevent sogginess.

To decorate a loaf for serving: Brush the top very lightly with light corn syrup and arrange on it a wreath or other design of Candied Cranberries (page 259) or Candied Sour Cherries (page 307) and fresh holly or other evergreen leaves; or use leaf shapes fashioned from candied angelica or green-tinted marzipan. Surround the cake with greenery, or brush the sides with corn syrup and decorate them like the top.

To wrap a decorated loaf as a holiday gift: Set it on cardboard cut to size and covered with foil; enclose the sides in a "fence" of pleated foil or metallic paper slightly higher than the cake, with pinked edges if you have pinking shears. Overwrap the whole pretty thing with cellophane or plastic.

SEASON:
Any time

YIELD:
**4 to 5 dozen
biscuits**

STORE:
**For 3 weeks at
room temperature;
or freeze for 3
months**

Crisp Sponge Biscuits

Golden, eggy sponge cake batter is baked twice to make these delicate bars, perfect as a crisp bite with tea, coffee, or a glass of wine. Their pristine simplicity makes them a good accompaniment for a creamy dessert, too.

The flavor can be varied: use 1 teaspoon vanilla in addition to the almond extract and omit the spices, if you like.

• If you'd like to use this recipe for a sponge cake rather than biscuits, bake the batter in two round or square 8-inch pans. The baking time will be shorter; check the layers after 35 minutes and frequently thereafter until the cake tests done. The layers may be frozen for up to 3 months; thaw them in their wrappers when it's time to serve.

•For a quick but festive cake, sandwich your sponge layers (above) with Chocolate Butter, Nutted or Otherwise (page 241) or Lime or Lemon Curd (page 301) and dust the top of the cake with sieved confectioners' sugar. For a lacy finish, lay a paper doily on the top before the dusting, then lift it off carefully to preserve the pattern.

Butter and confectioners' sugar for the pan(s)

1 cup all-purpose flour

½ teaspoon baking powder

¼ teaspoon salt

¼ teaspoon ground cinnamon

⅛ teaspoon freshly grated nutmeg

⅛ teaspoon ground mace

5 eggs, separated

2 tablespoons cold water

1 cup plus 2 tablespoons granulated sugar

1 tablespoon (packed) grated or very finely chopped lemon zest (outer skin only, no white pith)

¼ teaspoon almond extract

1. Preheat the oven to 325°, with a shelf in the center. Butter the bottom only of a 9 x 13-inch baking pan or two 8-inch square baking pans and dust the buttered surface with confectioners' sugar. Knock out any surplus sugar.

2. Sift together twice the flour, baking powder, salt, cinnamon, nutmeg, and mace. Reserve.

3. Separate the eggs. Reserve the whites in a large mixing bowl. Place the yolks in the large bowl of an electric mixer and beat them on medium-high speed until they are thick. With the mixer running at the same speed, add the water and beat the mixture until it is thick, about 3 minutes. Continuing to beat, gradually add the granulated sugar, scraping the mixture down from the sides of the bowl once or twice. Add the lemon zest and almond extract, beat 1 minute longer.

4. Mixing at the lowest speed of the mixer or folding by hand, add the dry ingredients one-third at a time, mixing after each addition only until no streaks of flour remain.

5. Beat the egg whites until they are stiff but still glossy and not dry. Add the whites to the batter and mix them in on lowest speed of the mixer (or fold them in by hand) just until no streaks of white show.

6. Gently scrape the batter into the prepared pan or pans, smoothing it only enough to fill the corners (it will even out as it bakes).

7. Bake the cake in the center of the preheated oven until it is golden, firm to a touch in the center, and has pulled away slightly from the pan sides, about 60 minutes for one large panful, about 40 minutes for two pans.

8. Invert the pan(s) onto a wire cake rack and let the cake cool upside down. Loosen the cooled cake all around with the tip of a sharp serrated knife and turn it out onto the rack. Using a sawing motion, cut the cake into halves lengthwise, then slice each half crosswise into ½-inch slices.

9. Lay the slices flat on wire cake racks (or you can use baking sheets) and place them in the oven, preheated to just under 200°. Bake the slices, turning them once, until they are a slightly deeper gold in color and crisp throughout, 40 to 60 minutes; if you are using two shelves of the oven, exchange shelf positions of the racks once or twice.

10. Cool the biscuits completely on the racks, then store them in an airtight canister. They can be frozen for longer storage. If they have been frozen, spread them on a baking sheet and refresh them with a few minutes' stay in a 300° oven, then cool them again. Do the same if humid weather causes the biscuits to soften in the canister.

SEASON:
Make a few weeks or months ahead, if you'd like to have this for the winter holidays

YIELD:
2 large cakes, 3½ pounds each, or one 7-pound, 12-inch-long "pullman" loaf

STORE:
For a year or more in a cool pantry or the refrigerator

California Christmas Fruitcake

For someone who grew up in the Golden West, as I did, no fruitcake can be more appealing than one made with as many California fruits as possible, most of them simply dried rather than candied.

My best-of-all-possible cakes shows tawny California colors when it is sliced—gold, peach, apricot, wine-red, brown, and cream—and it's not oversweet. No luridly dyed fruits belong in it, and neither do the pretty but tasteless chunks that are so often sold as candied fruit. So, if at all possible, do candy your own pineapple, orange peel, and sour cherries for this cake; they are vastly better homemade than store-bought. (Directions for candying these fruits begin on page 306.)

The confection that follows is full of nuts. Feel free to swap one kind of nut for another—Brazil nuts, especially if they are oven-toasted first, are good in place of one of the other kinds, but I urge that the hazelnuts be kept. Similarly, substitute pitted prunes for figs if you prefer them. For a touch of bracing tartness, substitute Candied Cranberries (page 259) for part of the candied cherries; rinse off their coating of sugar and pat them dry, or use them in their sugary state.

As dried fruits and nuts are sold in a wild array of package sizes, I've given the weight as well as the measurement for certain items in the ingredients list, to simplify shopping. If you foresee no need for two cakes, the recipe is easily divided in half. On the other hand, you may want to make both cakes and store one for next year; it will keep perfectly in a cool pantry or the refrigerator.

FRUITS AND NUTS:

1 cup (8 ounces) halved or coarsely chopped pitted dates

1 cup golden raisins

1 cup (about 10 ounces) candied cherries (for homemade, see page 307)

1 cup (about 10 ounces) candied pineapple wedges (to candy pineapple, see page 308)

1 cup (8 ounces) dried apricot halves, cut in two

1 cup (8 ounces) dried peaches, cut into ½-inch chunks

⅔ cup (6 ounces) dried pears, cut into ½-inch chunks

⅔ cup (about 6 ounces) diced candied orange peel, preferably homemade (see page 306)

½ cup (4 ounces) light figs, stemmed and cut into thirds (or substitute cut-up pitted prunes)

1 tablespoon (lightly packed) grated lemon zest (outer skin only, no white pith)

¼ cup strained fresh orange juice

½ cup Cointreau or other orange-flavored liqueur (Grand Marnier, Triple Sec, etc.)

2 cups (about 9 ounces) walnut halves

1½ cups (about 8 ounces) unblanched almonds, toasted (see Note)

1½ cups (about 6 ounces) hazelnuts, toasted and skinned (see Note)

THE BATTER:

2 cups all-purpose flour

1½ teaspoons baking powder

¾ teaspoon salt

¼ teaspoon ground mace

6 eggs

1½ teaspoons vanilla extract

Scant ¼ teaspoon almond extract

1 cup sugar

FOR BRUSHING THE CAKE:

½ to ⅔ cup additional orange-flavored liqueur

NOTE:

To toast almonds and to toast and skin hazelnuts: Preheat the oven to 350°. Spread the measured nuts separately on jelly-roll or pizza pans and bake them, stirring and turning them every 2 or 3 minutes, until they smell toasty and a nut, broken open, is pale gold, about 10 minutes; be careful not to let the nuts over-brown. Cool the nuts, then rub the hazelnuts in a towel until as much as possible of the brown skin has flaked off; it isn't important to remove every bit.

1. Butter two 8-cup, 9-inch loaf pans (or a 12-inch, 16-cup "pullman" loaf pan) and line them with baking parchment or brown paper, cutting the paper to extend ½ to 1 inch above the pan rim. Butter the lining paper.

2. Combine in a very large mixing bowl all the candied and dried fruits and the grated lemon zest. Add the orange juice and the ½ cup orange-flavored liqueur and mix everything thoroughly, breaking up any clumps of fruit. Let the mixture stand for at least an hour or for up to 3 hours, mixing it occasionally so the liquid is evenly absorbed.

3. Add the walnuts, almonds, and hazelnuts and mix them well with the fruit.

4. Preheat the oven to 300°.

5. Sift together the flour, baking powder, salt, and mace. Sift the mixture over the fruits and nuts and mix them thoroughly (this is done fastest and best with a pair of clean hands).

6. Beat the eggs until they are well combined, then beat in the vanilla and almond extracts. Continuing to beat, add the sugar gradually and beat until the mixture is pale and thick. Pour the egg batter over the floured fruit and nuts and mix them together gently but thoroughly (again, using your hands is recommended). Be sure the fruit and nuts are not clumped together; each piece should be lightly coated with batter.

7. Divide the batter between the prepared pans, then level the tops in a general way, leaving them slightly bumpy. Lift each pan and drop it a few inches onto the work surface to settle the dough. Bake the cakes in the preheated 300° oven until the tops are golden-brown and a cake tester emerges dry from the center, about 1¾ hours. Midway in baking, exchange the oven positions of the pans for even browning. If the tops seem to be browning too fast or too much, cover each cake loosely with a foil tent only slightly larger than its top. If you are baking the cake in a pullman pan, the baking time will be approximately 10 minutes longer.

8. Let the fruitcakes cool in the pans, set on wire racks, for 20 minutes, then lift them out, remove the paper, and cool them completely on the racks. While they are still warm, I like to pierce the cakes deeply on all sides with a long, sharp, two-pronged fork (or use a thin skewer) and brush them all over with additional liqueur, using ½ to ⅔ cup.

9. If you have made a single large loaf, you may wish to divide it into two or three sections for storage or giving. Wrap the cakes separately in foil and store them in a cool pantry, or refrigerate them. Although the cakes may be served after a week, they continue to mellow and improve for many months and are delicious after more than a year of refrigerated or very cool storage. For long storage, I wrap the cake (or a leftover portion) in cheesecloth, then sprinkle the cloth with brandy before wrapping the whole business in foil.

Overstuffed Christmas Stollen

I f the old gentleman in the red suit ever chooses to linger for breakfast at our house on December 25, he will probably be served a warm slice of this buttery, fruit-filled loaf, with seconds available on the cutting board.

Using a heavy-duty mixer with a dough hook, you can double the recipe to make four loaves; well wrapped or frozen, they keep for weeks, and they also make a welcome gift.* If you have only one oven, divide the kneaded dough and chill half of it while the first two loaves rise; then shape the chilled dough and let it rise for the second round of baking.

FRUITS AND NUTS:

1 cup walnuts

¾ cup golden raisins

½ cup currants

2 tablespoons dark rum

½ cup diced candied pineapple (to candy pineapple, see page 308)

⅓ cup diced candied citron

⅓ cup halved or quartered candied cherries (for homemade, see page 307)

Grated zest of a medium-large lemon

Grated zest of half of a medium-large orange

THE DOUGH:

1 cup milk

¾ cup granulated sugar

1 teaspoon salt

¾ cup (1½ sticks) unsalted butter

⅓ cup lukewarm (115°) water

Pinch of sugar

1 envelope (1 scant tablespoon) active dry yeast

5 to 6 cups all-purpose flour

2 eggs, beaten

1½ teaspoons vanilla extract

¼ teaspoon almond extract

FOR BRUSHING THE DOUGH:

4 tablespoons melted unsalted butter

FOR THE FINISHED STOLLEN:

Confectioners' sugar

SEASON:
This is a Christmastime classic, but good to serve as a coffee cake at any time

YIELD:
2 loaves, about 2 pounds each

STORE:
Wrapped, in cool pantry or cupboard for several weeks; freezer-wrapped and frozen, for up to 6 months

*GIFT NOTE:

To decorate the loaves, sift confectioners' sugar over them and add a decorative pattern of candied fruits and blanched almonds, their undersurfaces brushed lightly with corn syrup to help them stick.

1. Chop the walnuts coarsely; set them aside. Cover the raisins with hot tap water and set them aside. Mix the currants with the rum and set them aside. Prepare the pineapple, citron, cherries, lemon zest, and orange zest and reserve.

2. Heat together the milk, sugar, salt, and butter until the sugar has dissolved and butter melted; cool to 110° to 115°.

3. Meanwhile, add the pinch of sugar to the lukewarm water in a large mixing bowl or the large bowl of a heavy-duty mixer and sprinkle the yeast into it. Let the mixture stand until foamy, about 10 minutes. Stir in the milk mixture, then beat in 2 cups of the flour until the batter is smooth; beat in the eggs. Set the bowl, covered, in a warm spot until the batter has doubled at least, about 45 minutes; it will become very fluffy.

4. Beat in the vanilla and almond extracts. Beat in as much as possible of the remaining flour, then knead in the rest to make an elastic but slightly soft dough. Knead the dough at least 8 to 10 minutes by hand, or about 5 minutes in a mixer.

5. Drain the raisins and pat them dry on a towel; drain any remaining rum from the currants. Combine the raisins, the currants, the nuts, and the remaining fruits and grated zest, mixing them well. Add the mixture to the dough and knead it again until the fruits and nuts are well distributed. Form the dough into a ball and cut it into two equal pieces. Let the dough rest 5 minutes.

6. Pat each portion into an oval about ¾ inch thick, then fold the oval not quite in half lengthwise and pinch the tips to secure the fold. Poke under the surface any protruding nuts or fruit and pinch the dough over them. Transfer each loaf onto a baking sheet covered with buttered baking parchment and adjust its shape. Cover the loaves with towels and let them rise until doubled, about 1 hour.

7. Shortly before the loaves are ready, preheat the oven to 360° (just a hair beyond the 350° mark), with a shelf in the lower third and one in the upper third.

8. Brush the loaves lightly with melted butter. Bake them until they begin to turn pale gold, 20 to 25 minutes, then brush them again with butter and exchange their shelf positions. Reduce the oven setting to 300° and continue to bake the loaves until they are golden brown and just firm, 15 to 20 minutes more; be careful not to overbake them. Remove the loaves from the oven, brush them with any remaining butter, and let them cool on the pans, set on wire racks, for 20 minutes. Slip the parchment, with the loaves, onto the racks and cool the loaves completely.

9. Sift confectioners' sugar over the loaves (or do this at serving time). Wrap the loaves in plastic wrap and/or aluminum foil and store them in a cool cupboard. (For long-term storage, wrap for the freezer, page 328, and freeze.)

10. Frozen stollen should be thawed in its wrappings, then freshened in a moderate (325°) oven for 10 minutes or so. (Warming is good for loaves that have not been frozen, too.)

NOTE:

Sliced stollen makes splendid toast for a festive breakfast, especially if it is spread with a little Quince Marmalade (page 142).

DESSERT SAUCERY

If you have on hand any of the sauces here, all that's needed for a most elegant dessert is a tub of fine ice cream—your own, or the best offering of the best shop in town. Or instead of saucing ice cream, spoon your chosen delectable over a simple pudding made from scratch, or over a slice of sponge, angel, or pound cake.

Some of the ice-cream toppings are for putting by in summertime—Melba Sauce, Three-Fruit Summer Dessert Sauce, Strawberry & Honey Sauce, and others of that ilk should be made while the fruit is fresh and the going is good.

Nesselrode Sauce, one of the most luxurious of sweets, which can be used as the base for a pudding or a special cream pie (directions are given) as well as a sauce, is a temptation to be made in autumn, when the best fresh chestnuts gleam in the market. Cumberland Rum Butter, rich and fragrant, is to have ready for topping a steamed holiday pudding, or even warm gingerbread.

Among the seasonless sauces, particular favorites are Caramel-Mocha Ice Cream Sauce; Chocolate Butter, which can be used as a warm sauce, or as a cake or cookie filling, or in tea sandwiches made of cake or good bread, or as instant "truffles"; and White Chocolate Sauce with Toasted Hazelnuts, *the* world's most wonderful topping for dark chocolate ice cream. There is also a whole set of fudge toppings, each one, as in old fairy tales, "better than the last."

Chocolate Butter, Nutted & Otherwise

Made with dark, very chocolaty Dutch-process cocoa (which is well worth its price), a jarful of this luxurious spread/ sauce/confection has many uses. A lot of it has been consumed at our house while we have tried to decide whether we like it better with or without nuts.

Some of the ways to enjoy it:

•Warm Chocolate Butter slightly by setting the jar in quite warm water; stir it occasionally as it warms, then spoon it over ice cream.

•Add a tablespoonful of amaretto liqueur to a cupful of warmed nutless Chocolate Butter; sauce your favorite flavor of ice cream with the now almond-flavored mixture.

•Let Chocolate Butter soften slightly at room temperature, then spread it as a filling for a gold, white, or chocolate layer cake, or as a glaze for the top of a rich single-layer chocolate cake or a panful of brownies.

 SEASON:
Any time

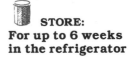 **YIELD:**
About 2½ cups
with nuts, 1¾
cups without nuts

STORE:
For up to 6 weeks
in the refrigerator

•For chocolate cookie sandwiches, spread Chocolate Butter on the bottoms of thin vanilla or chocolate wafers, make sandwiches with more wafers, then wrap and freeze them. Serve these unthawed.

•Spread Chocolate Butter, with or without nuts, on thin slices of pound cake, top the filling with another thin slice, and cut the sandwiches into fingers for sweet teatime nibbles. For less sweet but intriguing sandwiches, use thin-sliced, lightly buttered white bread; trim the edges and cut the sandwiches into strips.

•For instant "truffles," scoop up small spoonfuls of chilled Chocolate Butter, form them into knobby balls, and roll them in sifted cocoa. Return the confections to the refrigerator and serve them within a few hours; or freeze them and serve them without thawing. At serving time, dust the truffles with more cocoa if the original coating has become damp. For a most attractive presentation, arrange the truffles in tiny paper cups.

¾ cup (packed) high-quality Dutch-process cocoa

1 cup sugar

¼ teaspoon salt

½ cup hot water

**¾ cup (1½ sticks) high-quality unsalted butter, at
     room temperature**

½ to 1 teaspoon vanilla extract, to taste

⅛ teaspoon almond extract

FOR NUTTED CHOCOLATE BUTTER:

**1 cup toasted and coarsely chopped walnuts or
     toasted, skinned, and coarsely chopped
     hazelnuts (see Note)**

1. Combine the cocoa, sugar, and salt in the top pan of a double boiler (or use a heatproof bowl that can be placed over a saucepan containing simmering water). Stir the mixture with a whisk until it is thoroughly mixed, then mix in the hot water thoroughly. Set the pan over simmering water and stir the contents until the sugar has completely dissolved and the mixture is hot, about 3 minutes. Remove the top from the base and set it aside; cool the contents to lukewarm.

2. Cream the butter together with the vanilla and the almond extracts in the small bowl of an electric mixer, or use a food processor to beat the butter with the flavorings just until it is light. With the motor of the machine running, gradually add the lukewarm chocolate mixture, continuing to beat just until everything is well combined. Let the chocolate butter cool completely, stirring or whisking it occasionally to lighten its texture. Add the nuts, if you're making the nutted version, then scrape the chocolate butter into a clean, dry storage jar, cover it tightly, and refrigerate it.

NOTE:

To toast walnuts or hazelnuts, spread them on a baking sheet and place them in an oven preheated to 350°. Toast them 8 to 10 minutes, stirring them every two minutes or so; walnuts are done when they are crisp and deliciously nutty-fragrant; hazelnuts are ready when they smell toasty and their skins have loosened. Roll hazelnuts in a towel while they are hot and rub them to remove as much of the skin as possible. Walnuts may be given the same treatment, but it's not essential. Cool the nuts and chop them into coarse chunks. Shake them in a sieve to remove the powdery bits before adding them to the other ingredients.

Cumberland Rum Butter

For those who cherish tradition, it's a pleasure to think of the Old World origins of some of the good things we have long enjoyed in America. Our hard sauce, usually served with steamed holiday puddings, is descended from a delectable substance that seems to have originated in the Cumberland region of England.

At home, Cumberland Rum Butter is not only served as a pudding sauce; it is spread as a filling between cake layers or sweet wafers, and one especially charming tradition prescribes it as the first taste of solid food laid upon the lips of a newborn child.

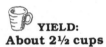 **SEASON:**
Any time

 YIELD:
About 2½ cups

STORE:
**For several weeks
in the refrigerator**

1 cup (2 sticks) lightly salted butter, or unsalted
    butter plus ¼ teaspoon salt, at room
    temperature
1 pound (1 box or 2¼ cups, packed) light brown
    sugar, sifted
⅓ cup dark rum, preferably Jamaican, or more to
    taste
¼ teaspoon freshly grated nutmeg
A pinch or two of ground cinnamon, optional
GARNISH:
Additional freshly grated nutmeg

1. Cream the butter in a mixing bowl with a wooden spoon, or beat it in the large bowl of an electric mixer, creaming it until it is very light. Gradually cream in the brown sugar, then continue to beat the mixture until it is smooth and light. Beat in the rum gradually, then add the nutmeg and, if you include it, the cinnamon.

2. Pack the rum butter firmly into a bowl, smoothing the top. Cover it closely with foil or plastic wrap and refrigerate it for at least overnight before serving it. It will keep, closely covered, for many weeks.

To serve the rum butter: Let it soften at room temperature, then fluff it with a fork and heap it in a serving dish; sprinkle a little freshly grated nutmeg on top. If you like the contrast of cold sauce with hot Christmas pudding (or even warm gingerbread), return it to the refrigerator until serving time.

☀ **SEASON:**
**July through
October**

☕ **YIELD:**
About 4 cups

🥫 **STORE:**
**Sealed, for at least
a year in a cool
cupboard or
pantry; unsealed,
for many months
in the refrigerator**

Melba Sauce

This glowing crimson raspberry sauce shouldn't be reserved only for the classic "Melba" dessert, which is a poached peach half or other fruit bedded on vanilla ice cream; it's also a distinguished topping for the darkest possible chocolate ice cream, or a slice of pound cake (add a tuft of whipped cream), a pristine rice pudding flavored with vanilla rather than cinnamon, or pears poached in vanilla syrup.

The currant jelly blended into the sauce permits it to be cooked only briefly, which preserves the raspberry flavor and aroma and makes unnecessary the starch thickening included in some adaptations of Escoffier's original recipe.

At serving time, you may want to add a nip of spirituous enhancement to the sauce. First choice is framboise, but crème de cassis, cherry brandy, or any of the orange-flavored liqueurs is a companionable addition. A tablespoonful or less to a cupful of sauce is enough.

**6 cups (about 2 pint baskets) raspberries, picked
  over, rinsed, and drained**

1 cup sugar

**1 cup currant jelly, preferably made without added
  pectin**

3 tablespoons strained fresh lemon juice

1. Puree the raspberries in a blender or food processor; pour the puree into a fine-meshed sieve set over a bowl. Press the puree through the sieve with a rubber spatula to remove all possible seeds. Discard the seedy residue.

2. Stir the raspberry puree, sugar, currant jelly, and lemon juice together in a large saucepan over medium heat until the ingredients are completely blended. Raise the heat to high and boil the sauce, stirring it constantly, for 2 minutes. Remove from heat.

3. Skim off any foam from the sauce and ladle it, boiling hot, into hot, clean half-pint canning jars, leaving ¼ inch of headspace. Seal the jars with new two-piece canning lids according to manufacturer's directions and process for 10 minutes in a boiling-water bath (page 325). Cool, label, and store the jars.

4. If you prefer not to seal the sauce, place it in clean, dry jars or other suitable containers, let it cool, cover it, and refrigerate it.

Nesselrode Sauce

 SEASON:
**Autumn and
winter**

 YIELD:
About 6 cups

STORE:
**Indefinitely, in the
refrigerator**

Once the peak of fashion in desserts—the Victorians knew how to enjoy the table!—this delicious compound, based on a combination originated by one M. Mony, the chef for Count Nesselrode, a 19th-century Russian diplomat, seems due for a revival, now that desserts are again respectable. (For some, they have never been anything else!) Over the years, Nesselrode concoctions have been considerably bashed about by shortcuts and commercializations. The sauce recipe that follows isn't limited to the elements of M. Mony's original frozen pudding, but it does preserve the spirit, not to say spirits, of the original.

As making Nesselrode Sauce from scratch involves several simple but time-consuming procedures, it's well worth while to make a good-sized batch. The sauce keeps (and improves) indefinitely, and a jar makes a luxurious gift.

Uses for Nesselrode Sauce: Without prompting, you'll scoop this delectable mixture over ice cream. Or spoon a little into a meringue case. Or have it over pound or angel cake. If people still made genuine cottage pudding (a plain cake served warm, in squares), they would love Nesselrode Sauce as a topping.

Nesselrode Pudding: If you'd like to taste the modern counterpart of the original pudding, drain some of the sauce briefly, not completely (save the syrup) and fold the chestnuts and fruits into a rich Bavarian cream mixture before you add the whipped cream (see a good general cookbook for a Bavarian recipe). Then add the cream and chill the pudding well.

Nesselrode Ice Cream: Fold briefly drained fruits and chestnuts from the sauce (reserve the syrup) into softened vanilla ice cream and refreeze it; serve it with the reserved syrup as topping.

Nesselrode Pie: If it's Nesselrode Pie you crave, erase all memories of the puffy travesties served in restaurants. Instead, follow the example of Craig Claiborne, whose recipe, quoted here with his kind permission, runs along these lines: Add a cupful of fruit and chestnuts drained from Nesselrode Sauce to a stovetop custard (1½ cups milk, 3 egg yolks, ¼ cup sugar, ½ teaspoon vanilla) that has been reinforced, so to speak, by cooking 1 tablespoon plain gelatin with the other ingredients; let the mixture cool, then fold in first 3 egg whites beaten until stiff with ⅓ cup sugar, then ½ cup chilled heavy cream, whipped until stiff. Pile the filling *high* in a baked 10-inch pie shell, chill it well, and there you have it—a perfectly delightful dessert reminiscent of a more opulent age.

1 pound fresh chestnuts

4 cups water

1½ cups sugar

1 tablespoon strained fresh lemon juice

½ vanilla bean

½ cup light corn syrup, or more if needed

¼ cup golden raisins

¼ cup currants

¼ cup seeded muscat raisins (or use dried cherries, page 309, if you have them)

¼ cup dark rum, preferably Jamaican, stirred with ¼ cup sugar

½ cup coarsely diced candied cherries, preferably homemade (page 307), or use part or all drained maraschino cherries, if you don't mind their burden of artificial coloring

¼ cup finely diced candied citron

2 tablespoons finely chopped minced candied orange peel, preferably homemade (page 306)

¼ cup maraschino liqueur

1. Rinse and drain the chestnuts. Using a cleaver or a heavy knife, chop each chestnut in half (lay them flat side down on a cutting board for chopping).

2. Place the nuts in a saucepan, add water to cover by 1 inch, and bring them to a boil over high heat. Boil the nuts, uncovered, 3 minutes, then drain them. Pry or pop the halves out of their shells.* The brown skin will usually remain in the shell; scrape off any bits of skin that adhere. Cut or break the nuts into quarters or sixths, depending on the size of the nuts. Return the nuts to the rinsed-out saucepan, cover them with cold water, bring them to a boil, and simmer them, uncovered, until they begin to be tender, about 30 minutes. Drain the chestnuts, discarding the liquid.

3. Combine the 4 cups water, sugar, and lemon juice in the rinsed-out saucepan; split the piece of vanilla bean lengthwise and add it. Bring the mixture to a boil, boil it, uncovered, 3 minutes, and add the chestnuts. Lower the heat and simmer the chestnuts, uncovered, until they are transparent and very tender and the syrup has thickened, 30 to 45 minutes; stir them occasionally and skim off the foam. (It doesn't matter if some of them break.) Add ½ cup of light corn syrup. Set the chestnuts and syrup aside until the fruits are ready (overnight is fine).

4. Meanwhile, combine the golden raisins, currants, and muscat raisins in a saucepan. Add water to cover and bring them to a boil; boil the fruit for a moment, then remove it from the heat. Let it cool completely, then drain it thoroughly. Return the fruit to a bowl and add the sweetened rum, stirring the mixture well. Let it stand, closely covered, for at least 2

*NOTE:

This shortcut way of getting chestnuts out of their shells is useful whenever whole nuts are not required; it saves time and spares the disposition.

hours and as long as overnight. In another bowl, combine the cherries, citron, and candied orange peel with the maraschino liqueur. Cover the bowl closely and let the fruits stand, covered, for at least 2 hours and as long as overnight.

5. When you're ready to compound the sauce, remove the vanilla bean from the chestnut syrup. (Rinse, dry, and save it for a second use.) Scoop out about a third of the chestnuts, mash them, and return them to the syrup. Stir together the chestnuts and their syrup and the two batches of fruit and their liquid. Check the consistency of the sauce, which should be somewhat dense. If you'd like a more syrupy sauce, add a little more corn syrup plus a little more rum and/or maraschino liqueur.

6. Store the sauce in sterilized (page 327), closely covered jars in the refrigerator. It will be mellow enough for use in 2 weeks or so, but it improves indefinitely. Stir it before use.

Peach & Raspberry Dessert Sauce

Madame Nellie Melba's favorite fruits are combined here in a sauce to be spooned over vanilla ice cream in homage to Peach Melba. Use the sauce also to top any other dessert that could do with a flavorful finishing touch; simple pound or angel cake can be made quite festive with a spoonful.

Nectarines may be used in the sauce instead of peaches; if they are much tarter than peaches (this is not unusual), reduce or omit the lemon juice.

3 cups (2 half-pint baskets) red raspberries

1 cup water

1¾ cups sugar

¼ cup light corn syrup

¼ cup strained fresh lemon juice

4 cups chopped peeled ripe peaches (about 5 or 6 medium peaches)

1. Pick over the raspberries, then rinse and drain them. Puree them in a blender or a food processor, in batches if necessary. Press the puree through a fine-meshed sieve to remove the seeds; discard the seedy residue. You should have at least a cup of juicy pulp; if there is more, that's fine.

2. Combine the raspberry pulp, water, sugar, corn syrup, and lemon juice in a preserving pan. Bring the mixture to a boil over medium-high heat and boil it for 2 minutes, stirring. Add

 SEASON:
Late summer and early fall

 YIELD:
About 3 cups

 **STORE:**
Sealed, for at least a year in a cool cupboard or pantry; unsealed, for many months in the refrigerator

the chopped peaches and continue the cooking, now over medium heat, stirring often to prevent sticking, until the chunks of peach are translucent and the syrup is thickened, 15 to 18 minutes. To test for consistency, remove the sauce from heat and spoon a little onto a chilled saucer. When the sample has cooled, consider it thick enough if it runs only sluggishly when the saucer is tipped sharply. If the sauce seems too thin, cook it further.

3. Ladle the boiling-hot sauce into hot, clean half-pint canning jars, leaving ¼ inch of headspace. Seal the jars with new two-piece canning lids according to manufacturer's directions and process for 10 minutes in a boiling-water bath (page 325). Cool, label, and store the jars. The sauce is ready for immediate use.

4. If you prefer not to seal the sauce for lengthy storage, simply store it, covered but unsealed, in the refrigerator, where it will keep for months.

SEASON:
Midsummer, using fresh fruit; or at any time, with frozen berries and rhubarb

YIELD:
4 cups

STORE:
Sealed, in cool pantry for up to a year; or refrigerate, unsealed, for up to 2 months

Three-Fruit Summer Dessert Sauce

This sauce revives a two-fruit combination (counting rhubarb as a fruit) that was a favorite pie filling back when a day without pie was a day without proper provender. Orange and a touch of cinnamon have been added here. The blueberries dye the rhubarb their own deep purple-red and share their flavor with it, too. The sauce can be made satisfactorily from frozen blueberries and rhubarb, two raw materials that withstand freezing very well. Not incidentally, the presence of the rhubarb is essential (for texture) and almost unguessable.

Some serving suggestions:

•Ladle the sauce, which should be at room temperature, over vanilla, peach, or lemon ice cream; bring out the butter cookies or vanilla wafers.

•Spoon the sauce over slices of sponge, butter, or angel cake, and top the dessert with a tuft of whipped cream. (Our grandmothers would have baked a cottage pudding—an eggless plain cake served warm—for a dessert like this.)

•For a pudding-parfait, make alternate layers of vanilla-flavored soft custard and blueberry-rhubarb sauce, ending with a spoonful of the sauce. Or use ricotta, whipped lightly, in place of the custard.

•For optional oomph, spike the sauce with a little brandy, preferably Armagnac.

**1 pint basket (about 3 cups) blueberries, picked
over, rinsed, and drained**

3 cups diced (½-inch dice) trimmed tender rhubarb

2 cups sugar

½ cup orange juice

**1 stick (about 2 inches) cinnamon, broken into 2 or 3
pieces**

1. Combine all the ingredients in a preserving pan. Heat
the mixture slowly over medium heat, stirring it gently now
and then with a rubber spatula, until it begins to boil. Lower
the heat and simmer the mixture, stirring it occasionally as
gently as possible, until the fruit is tender and the syrup has
thickened slightly, about 30 minutes. Taste; add more sugar if
needed. Remove pieces of cinnamon.

2. Ladle the boiling-hot sauce into hot, clean half-pint
canning jars, leaving ¼-inch of headspace. Seal the jars with
new two-piece canning lids according to manufacturer's directions and process for 15 minutes in a boiling-water bath (page
325). Cool, label, and store the jars.

3. Alternatively, store the sauce, unsealed, in the refrigerator for use within 2 months or so.

Strawberry &
Honey Dessert
Sauce

A light, flowery honey best complements the taste of
strawberries in this topping for ice cream, or pudding, or
yogurt, or plain cake, or even waffles. To make a quick summer
(or anytime) dessert, spoon the sauce over a large sugar
cookie, top it with a blob of sour cream, and serve the
confection while the cookie is still crisp.

2 quart baskets ripe strawberries

2 cups sugar

1½ cups water

¼ cup strained fresh lemon juice

¾ to 1 cup honey, to taste

1. Sort, hull, rinse, and drain the berries, then chop
them; you should have about 5 cups. Set aside.

2. Combine the sugar and water in a preserving pan or a
large sauté pan. Bring the mixture to a boil over high heat and
boil it 2 minutes. Add the berries and lemon juice, return
everything to a boil, and boil the mixture hard over high heat,

 **SEASON:
Early summer, but
possible at any
time, using frozen
berries**

 **YIELD:
About 5 cups**

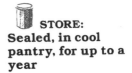 **STORE:
Sealed, in cool
pantry, for up to a
year**

stirring it almost constantly, for 10 minutes. Add the honey and cook the sauce 5 minutes longer, stirring constantly now, until it has thickened sufficiently. To test the consistency, remove the pan from the heat and spoon a little of the sauce onto a cold plate. Let it cool (speed this up by placing it in the refrigerator), then draw a spoon tip or a fingertip through the sauce; if a clear track remains, the sauce is thick enough.

3. Reheat the sauce to boiling, if necessary. Ladle it into clean, hot half-pint canning jars, leaving ¼ inch of headspace. Seal the jars with new two-piece canning lids according to the manufacturer's directions and process for 10 minutes in a boiling-water bath (page 325). Cool, label, and store the jars.

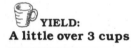

SEASON:
Any time

YIELD:
A little over 3 cups

STORE:
For 3 months or more in the refrigerator; can be frozen for longer storage

Fudge Sauce: Theme & Variations

W hether we're nominal adults or actual kids, most of us love an occasional indulgence like a hot fudge sundae. Twice a year can't hurt?

For such rare occasions, or for an ice-cream party where a choice of toppings is offered (this is a sure-fire entertainment for all ages), here is our family fudge sauce, the product of years of unselfish experimenting. It's properly dense and clingy when spooned over ice cream, and it can be used either at room temperature or after it has been warmed. You can vary this sauce, too—try the amaretto, peppermint, and mocha variations.

Hot Fudge Sauce

1 cup evaporated milk or light cream
2 cups sugar
¼ teaspoon salt
¼ cup light corn syrup
6 tablespoons unsalted butter
4 ounces (4 squares) unsweetened chocolate
2 ounces (2 squares) semisweet chocolate
2 to 3 teaspoons vanilla extract, to taste

1. Measure the evaporated milk, sugar, salt, corn syrup, butter, and chocolates into the upper pan of a double boiler (or use a heatproof bowl that can be set into a saucepan of simmering water).

2. Set the pan over simmering water in the double-boiler base and heat the contents, stirring it occasionally, until the butter and chocolate have melted. Stir the sauce thoroughly and continue to cook it until it is smooth and slightly thickened, about 10 minutes.

3. If any lumps are to be seen, strain the sauce, then cool it for 5 minutes. Stir in the vanilla extract. Scrape the sauce into a storage jar or jars, cool it completely, then cover it and store it in the refrigerator. If you prefer freezer storage for all or part of the sauce, freeze it, covered airtight, in a suitable container (glass is preferable to plastic), allowing ½ inch of headspace.

To serve the sauce: Thaw it unopened if it has been frozen, or let it come to room temperature. To warm the sauce, set the jar in a container of hot water and stir it occasionally until it is warm enough to flow smoothly when it is spooned over ice cream.

Fudge Sauce with Amaretto

Replace the vanilla extract with amaretto liqueur, adding about 2 tablespoons, or the amount that pleases you.

Chocolate Peppermint Fudge Sauce

Replace the vanilla extract with a small amount of peppermint extract. Start with ½ teaspoon, taste, and add more only if it is needed—this flavoring can be overpowering.

Mocha Fudge Sauce

While the basic sauce is still hot, stir in 1 to 1½ tablespoons of freeze-dried coffee crystals, either regular or dark-roast. If you'd like to flavor only part of the sauce, figure on 2 teaspoons of crystals to a cup. If you have coffee powder instead of crystals, reduce the measurement about one-third.

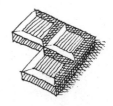

SEASON:
Any time

 **YIELD:**
About 2½ cups

STORE:
**For several months
in the refrigerator**

Caramel-Mocha
Ice Cream Sauce

This starts out to be creamy caramel candy, changes its mind with a little help from the cook, and ends up as an amber-brown, luscious caramel-mocha topping for ice cream. (You can also spoon it over a pudding that needs a lift, or over sponge, angel, or pound cake.) Nuts? Certainly; for a sauce including walnuts and/or Cognac, see the variations that follow

¾ cup light corn syrup

¼ cup water

1 cup sugar

4 tablespoons (½ stick) unsalted butter

1 cup evaporated milk

**¾ cup triple-strength (or stronger) hot brewed
regular or espresso coffee, or ¾ cup boiling
water plus at least a tablespoonful (depending
on the brand) of freeze-dried instant regular or
espresso coffee**

½ to 1 teaspoon vanilla extract, to taste

¼ teaspoon salt

1. Measure the corn syrup, water, and sugar into a large saucepan. Heat the mixture over medium-high heat, stirring it with a straight-ended spatula, until it is boiling vigorously. Dip a pastry brush into cold water and wash down any sugar crystals clinging to the sides of the pan. Add the butter. When boiling resumes, begin adding the evaporated milk very gradually, stirring all the time. Continue to boil the caramel, stirring it constantly to prevent scorching, until it is thick and pale golden-brown, about 10 minutes; if you use a candy/jelly thermometer (recommended), cook it to a reading of about 230°, or until a little of the mixture dropped into ice water forms a soft ball that can be molded in the fingers. Remove the pan from the heat.

2. Stir in the coffee. (Don't be concerned if the whole business looks dreadfully curdled, as it probably will after the milk is added, if not before; the sauce will end up quite satiny.) Stir in ½ teaspoon of the vanilla and the salt.

3. Scrape the mixture into the container of a blender and blend it, starting on low speed and gradually speeding up, until it is smooth. Taste the sauce and add more vanilla, if you like; for more mocha flavor, add more grains of instant coffee.

4. Store the sauce, covered, in the refrigerator. It will thicken somewhat upon chilling, so you may want to let it warm slightly at room temperature before serving it.

Caramel-Mocha Sauce with Walnuts

To 1 cup of Caramel-Mocha Sauce add ¼ to ⅓ cup of chopped, lightly toasted walnut meats. To toast the nuts, spread them in a baking pan and crisp them for about 8 minutes in a 350° oven, stirring them once or twice; bake them just until they are lightly toasted, not actually browned. Cool; chop.

Brandied Caramel-Mocha Sauce

At any point before serving either plain or nutted Caramel-Mocha Sauce, stir in Cognac to taste; start with a tablespoonful of brandy to a cup of sauce, taste, and add more if you wish.

A Touch of Glitter

For any dessert topped with Caramel-Mocha Sauce, add a touch of sparkle by topping the sauce with a little Praline Powder for Desserts, page 303.

White Chocolate Sauce with Toasted Hazelnuts

Because white chocolate isn't dark in color, don't assume it lacks flavor; however, it is more delicate in taste than true (dark) chocolate because its flavor comes from cocoa butter rather than what's called "chocolate liquor," the heart and soul of the cocoa bean.

White chocolate tastes especially marvelous combined with hazelnuts and cream, as in this luxurious sauce to spoon over dark, dark chocolate ice cream. If you can't buy ice cream that's dark and bittersweet, it's worthwhile to make your own.

White chocolate is available in bars, but for the table you may want to order the best quality available from a supplier of bulk ingredients for fine baking and candy making. Bargain chocolate of any kind is no bargain at all.

 **SEASON:**
Any time

 YIELD:
About 2 cups

 STORE:
For 2 months or more in the refrigerator

***TO PREPARE
THE NUTS:**

Toast whole hazelnuts in a shallow pan in a 350° oven until their skins are crisp and the nuts smell rich and toasty, 8 to 10 minutes; shake the pan occasionally. Rub the nuts in a towel to remove as much of the brown skin as possible. When nuts are cool, chop them.

½ pound white chocolate, broken into small chunks

¾ cup heavy cream

½ cup sugar

Pinch of salt, optional

2 tablespoons unsalted butter

½ cup toasted, skinned, and coarsely chopped hazelnuts*

A little hazelnut liqueur (Frangelico), if you like

1. Working in batches, grate the white chocolate in a blender. When all the chocolate has been grated, return all batches to the blender.

2. Combine the cream with the sugar, the optional salt, and the butter in a small heavy saucepan. Set the mixture over low heat and heat it, stirring, until the sugar and butter have melted and the mixture is piping hot.

3. Start the blender motor and pour the hot liquid through the opening in the cover. Blend the sauce until it is thick and smooth, stopping the motor once or twice and scraping down the sides of the beaker. Scrape the sauce into a bowl.

4. Stir in the hazelnuts. If you like (it isn't essential), stir in a tablespoon or two of hazelnut liqueur.

5. Store the sauce, covered, in the refrigerator. To serve, let the sauce return to room temperature, or warm it slightly by setting the container in quite warm water; stir the sauce once or twice as it warms. If it seems too thick, add a little more cream.

THE LAST ACT:
SWEET NIBBLES

A small collection here: The best of sugared and spiced nuts, a nut brittle that rises lightly above the crowd, crystallized ginger and fruits that include a transformation of tomatoes, a sugaring of plums, and a candying of cranberries and kumquats. Any of these confections, set out in tiny paper cups, make after-dinner coffee time a special occasion. All make attractive gifts, too.

Sugared & Spiced Nuts

Crisp-coated frivolities, pecans or walnuts gussied up with a little sugar and a little spice are nibbles for dessert time.

1 egg white

1 tablespoon water

1 pound pecan or walnut halves, or half a pound of each

⅔ cup superfine sugar

1 teaspoon salt

2 teaspoons ground cinnamon

¾ teaspoon ground ginger

¾ teaspoon ground allspice

½ teaspoon ground coriander

1. Preheat the oven to 250°, with a shelf in the lower third and one in the upper third.

2. Whisk the egg white and water together until the mixture is foamy. Stir in the nuts; mix well. Pour into a sieve and drain for 3 minutes.

3. Combine the sugar, salt, cinnamon, ginger, allspice, and coriander in a paper bag; gather the neck of the bag and shake the bag to mix them. Add the drained nuts and shake the bag vigorously to coat them with the sugar and spices. Spread the nuts on two baking sheets, making sure they do not touch.

4. Bake the nuts for 15 minutes, then stir them and spread them out again. Lower the oven temperature to 225° and continue to bake the nuts, stirring them occasionally, until they are well dried and crisp, about 1¼ hours longer; midway, switch the shelf positions of the two pans. Turn off the oven and let the nuts cool with the oven door open.

5. Store the completely cooled nuts airtight.

 SEASON:
Any time

YIELD:
About 1½ pounds

STORE:
For a few days at room temperature; for 3 weeks refrigerated; or for 6 months frozen

SEASON:
Any time

YIELD:
About 1½ pounds

STORE:
Indefinitely at
room temperature

A Brittle of Nuts & Popcorn

T hey may not be *haute* confectionery, but nut brittles are among the most satisfying of sweets: hard-crisp, sweet-salt, and above all *nutty*. When popcorn is added to the nuts, the texture is subtly lightened and the flavor enhanced; for extra-light brittle, you could use 2 cups of popcorn and 1 cup of nuts instead of the quantities given in the recipe.

For this candy the plebeian peanut is not to be despised, but the brittle is not too humble a vehicle for pistachios, almonds, cashews, pecans, or even macadamias, if you can resist devouring them while you work. A variation that is most delicious is to use half black walnuts and half peanuts; a dark and slightly mysterious flavor results.

1½ cups nuts: Use your choice of dry-roasted, unsalted cocktail peanuts, coarsely chopped toasted almonds (see Note), shelled pistachios (lightly salted ones are fine), pecan halves or pieces, black walnut pieces combined half-and-half with peanuts; roasted macadamia or cashew pieces

1 cup coarsely crumbled unsalted fresh popcorn, preferably popped without oil (pop 2 tablespoons corn to make 1 cup)

1½ cups sugar

½ cup light corn syrup or ¼ cup each light and dark corn syrup

⅓ cup water

3 tablespoons unsalted butter

1 teaspoon salt

¼ teaspoon baking soda

1 teaspoon vanilla extract

1. Preheat the oven to 250°, with a shelf in the center; butter a large cookie sheet.

2. Spread the nuts and popcorn on the prepared cookie sheet. Place the pan in the oven and warm the nuts and popcorn for 5 minutes. Turn off the oven and leave the pan in it.

3. Bring the sugar, corn syrup, and water to a boil in a large saucepan over high heat; as the mixture heats, wipe down any sugar crystals on the sides of the pan, using a pastry brush dipped in cold water. When the mixture boils, add the butter and cook the candy, stirring it occasionally, until a candy/jelly thermometer registers 310°. Remove the pan from the heat.

4. Immediately stir in the salt, baking soda, and vanilla.

NOTE:

To toast whole almonds, spread them on a cookie sheet and bake them in a preheated 350° oven, stirring and turning them every 2 or 3 minutes, until they smell toasty and a sample, broken open, is golden inside, about 10 minutes. If natural (unblanched) almonds are used, watch them with special care to prevent overbaking; their brown skin makes it difficult to judge their doneness.

Add the warm nuts and popcorn and stir them in quickly. Spread the candy as thinly and evenly as possible on the cookie sheet, flattening it with a nylon or wooden spatula; don't be concerned if there are gaps or irregular edges. Let the candy cool slightly, just until it can be handled with caution. Protecting your hands with cloths, pull the brittle into sections and stretch them one at a time, beginning with the edge pieces (these harden first). (Alternatively, simply let the brittle cool and harden on the pan, then break it into chunks.) Let the candy cool completely, then store it airtight in a jar or canister.

Tomato Figs—
A Sweetmeat

Tomato figs are mahogany-red in color and remarkably similar to dried figs in texture; they are a bit tarter in flavor, but equally intriguing to the tooth. A delicious nibble as a sweetmeat, they can replace such other fruits as dates or figs in fruitcakes and other baked things. Batches prepared at our house have been quickly raided by interested bystanders, but so far no one tasting them for the first time has been able to identify the raw material.

I hope this recipe will nudge along a modest revival of a homemade confection that was so popular a few generations ago that one enthusiast made an (unsuccessful) effort to patent a formula for them.

4 pounds firm-ripe Italian-type (plum) tomatoes

1¾ cups granulated sugar

1 cup (packed) dark brown sugar

10 whole cloves

2 tablespoons strained fresh lemon juice

Confectioners' sugar

1. Bring a large saucepan full of water to a boil. Plunge in enough tomatoes to cover the surface of the water and leave them for 30 seconds. Lift them out and drop them into cold water. Repeat until all the tomatoes have been scalded. Cut out the stem scar and any hard portion of the underlying core of each tomato; slip off the skin.

2. Arrange the tomatoes in two layers in a preserving pan, sprinkling half of each kind of sugar and half of the cloves over each layer; sprinkle the lemon juice over the top.

3. Heat the tomatoes slowly over *very* low heat, uncovered, occasionally swirling the pan as the juice forms a syrup

SEASON:
Late summer/early fall

 YIELD:
About 1 pound

STORE:
For up to 3 months at room temperature or in a cool cupboard or pantry

with the sugar. Cook the tomatoes very slowly (don't permit them to boil) until they begin to look translucent around the edges, about 30 minutes. Remove the pan from the heat and let the tomatoes cool slightly.

4. Lightly oil wire food-drying racks or several cake racks that have close-set wires. Lift the tomatoes from the syrup one at a time and arrange them on the racks, leaving a little space between them. (Reserve the syrup.) Let the tomatoes drain for a few moments, then flatten each slightly with a rubber spatula (they are quite thick at this point).

5. Set the racks in an oven (either conventional or convection) set at 200°. If using a conventional oven, lower the heat setting to between 140° and 150° after 30 minutes and dry the tomato figs with the oven door slightly ajar; during drying, exchange oven positions of the racks occasionally. If using a convection oven, leave the heat setting at 200° and leave the oven door slightly open; exchange rack positions occasionally. During drying, turn the tomatoes two or three times, flattening them gently each time. After each turning, brush the upper sides with a little of the reserved syrup, which will gradually form a glaze. The figs are done when they are a little leathery but not hard; they will be reddish-brown and glossy. The drying time will depend on the size of the tomatoes, the efficiency of the oven, and the weather (more time will be needed in damp weather); about 8 hours is average. The drying can be done in two or more sessions, if you find that convenient.

7. Cool the tomato figs completely, then roll them in sifted confectioners' sugar and pack them in an airtight canister or jar, with a generous amount of confectioners' sugar between the layers and on top. Store them in a cool, dry spot.

SEASON:
Early fall

YIELD:
About ½ pound

STORE:
At room temperature or in a cool cupboard or pantry for up to 4 months

Sugarplums

Although these glazed fruit halves are certainly a sweetmeat, they are not, alas, the same as those translucent green globes of glacé fruit—whole, firm Elvas plums from Portugal—that are properly entitled to the name "sugarplums." The art of making true sugarplums is beyond the scope of the home kitchen, but these transformed purple, Italian, prune, or blue plums (take your choice of names) are easy to do and delicious to eat. They can also be used in place of other candied fruits in recipes.

2 pounds large firm-ripe purple (Italian, or prune, or blue) plums
¾ cup granulated sugar
Confectioners' sugar, optional

1. Halve the plums and remove the pits. Arrange them close together, cut side up, in a large shallow baking dish. Sprinkle them evenly with the granulated sugar and place them in a turned-on oven with the control set at 300°.

2. Heat the plums until the sugar has formed a syrup with their juice and they are quite hot through, about 30 minutes. Remove the plums from the oven, turn each over (face down, as it were) and let them drink some syrup and cool slightly.

3. Arrange the plums, cut side up again, on wire-mesh drying racks or wire cake racks set over a cookie sheet. Brush the fruit lightly with some of the syrup in the original pan.

4. Place the racks in a conventional or convection oven set at 200° and dry the plums, brushing them with syrup twice more at hourly intervals; before the last brushing, flatten them gently with a rubber spatula. Continue to dry the plums until they are only slightly tacky to the touch and are no longer juicy when pressed; drying will usually take from 5 to 8 hours, depending on the size of the plums. After 5 hours, check them frequently and remove from the oven any that are done. (If left too long, they may become tough.)

5. Cool the sugarplums completely, then store them air-tight in a canister or jar, first dusting them with confectioners' sugar, if you wish.

Imogene Wolcott's Candied Cranberries

Cranberries candied in this fashion will keep perfectly in a glass jar, at room temperature, for many months, not that there is likely to be a need for such longevity. In color they are even brighter than cherries, so they make a pretty holiday garnish for either sweet or savory things. To serve them on their own as a sweetmeat, drop them into tiny bonbon cups, three or four to each. Finally, they are a desirable candied fruit to use in baking in the same way as candied cherries.

There are more complicated ways to candy these tiny native fruits, but the method of Imogene Wolcott, which she says is a Cape Cod recipe, is hard to beat. Here it is, adapted from the 1971 edition of her *Yankee Cook Book*.

1½ cups large firm cranberries, picked over, stems removed

1½ cups sugar, plus additional for coating

1¼ cups water

SEASON:
October to late winter

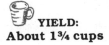
YIELD:
About 1¾ cups

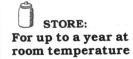
STORE:
For up to a year at room temperature

1. Rinse the cranberries and drain them. Prick each one completely through with a coarse needle, then dry them thoroughly on a towel.

2. Combine the 1½ cups sugar and water in a 10- or 12-inch sauté pan or skillet (the berries should cook in a single layer). Bring the mixture to boil over high heat, stirring until sugar has dissolved. Boil the syrup until it forms a soft ball when a small amount is dropped into ice water (the reading is 234° on a candy/jelly thermometer).

3. Add the cranberries to the syrup and boil them rapidly, shaking the pan often, until the syrup reaches the hard-ball stage (250°), 6 to 10 minutes. The berries will burst their skins during cooking, but this does not affect the final result.

4. Immediately lift the berries from the syrup with a wire skimmer or slotted spoon and scatter them on a nonstick-surfaced or lightly oiled cookie sheet. The cranberries will be lying there in clumps; as soon as they have cooled enough to be touched comfortably, separate them with your fingers or two small forks. Let them cool completely.

5. Place about ½ cup of additional granulated sugar in a bowl. Pick up each cranberry in turn, together with the hardened syrup pooled around it, and reshape it quickly; drop the now globelike berry into the bowl of sugar and roll it around to coat it well, then lift it onto a clean baking sheet to dry for a few hours. Leave the berries until they are no longer sticky.

6. Store the sugared cranberries at room temperature in a tightly closed jar; they will keep almost indefinitely, if the household will let them. If desired, sugar them again at serving time.

SEASON:
Late fall to late winter

YIELD:
About 3 pints of preserves, or 2½ pounds candied fruit

STORE:
Preserves, for at least a year in a cool cupboard or pantry; candied fruit, for up to 3 months at room temperature

Preserved or Candied Kumquats

At Christmastime, candied kumquats are among the most attractive of sweetmeats, especially when nestled in paper bonbon cups in a collection of cookies, candies, and other good things. Use them, too, to garnish the tops of fruit-cakes, and substitute them, cut up, for candied citrus peel in cakes or cookies for an interesting difference.

If you choose to preserve the kumquats in their syrup, present them, with a little of the syrup, as a delicious accompaniment for smoked turkey or chicken, or, especially, for baked or broiled ham. Snipped, they add an intriguing accent to chicken salad. Any leftover syrup is a commendable addition to fruit-salad dressing or fruit punch.

2 pounds bright-skinned, firm kumquats (avoid overripe fruit)

5 cups granulated sugar

3 cups water

Superfine granulated sugar for final coating, optional

1. Rinse the kumquats and remove any stems. If there are any small rusty spots, scrub them with a small stiff brush to remove as much of the discoloration as possible.

2. Place the kumquats in a saucepan and add enough cold water to cover them by 1 inch. Bring them to a boil, partially cover the pan, and simmer the fruit for 10 minutes. Drain the kumquats in a colander.

3. In the same saucepan (no need to rinse it) combine the 5 cups sugar with the 3 cups water and bring to a boil. Boil the syrup 5 minutes, then add the well-drained kumquats. Bring the fruit just to a boil over medium-high heat, then lower the heat and simmer the kumquats, uncovered, for 10 minutes. Pour the fruit and syrup into a shallow bowl and let it stand overnight, covered with a cloth.

4. Return the kumquats and syrup to the saucepan, bring them to a boil, and simmer them for 20 minutes, or until the fruit is translucent and tender when tested with a cake tester or thin skewer. If the syrup should become so thick that it might scorch before the fruit is done, add a little boiling water and continue the cooking.

5. *For preserved kumquats:* When the kumquats are tender, ladle them into hot, clean pint or half-pint canning jars, leaving ¼ inch of headspace, and add boiling hot syrup to the same level. Remove any bubbles (page 324) and add more syrup, if necessary. Seal the jars with new two-piece canning lids according to manufacturer's directions and process for 15 minutes (for either size jar) in a boiling-water bath (page 325). Cool, label, and store the jars.

For candied kumquats: When the kumquats are tender, remove the pan from the heat and cool them in the syrup. Lift the kumquats from the syrup one at a time and arrange them on a wire rack set over a baking sheet. Let them drain and dry at room temperature until they are no longer sticky to the touch; this may take from an hour or two to overnight, depending on the level of humidity. If the weather is damp and the fruit dries slowly, set the racks in an oven set at its "keep-warm" temperature and leave them, with the oven door ajar, until they are no longer sticky. Roll the kumquats in superfine granulated sugar and store them in an airtight container at room temperature. At serving time, roll them in sugar again if necessary.

Fruit Cheeses

Resembling not-too-sweet jam that's firm enough to be sliced, fruit cheeses or fruit pastes are mainly known today as Hispanic or Latin American specialties, although they have a long history in other lands. In Britain, especially, there are old recipes for numberless kinds—cheeses were made (and still can be made) from apricots, gooseberries, cherries, black and red currants, figs, peaches, plums, guavas, raspberries, apples, quinces, and even oranges.

Recipes follow for nectarine or plum cheese and quince paste, which can easily be converted into quince candy. The pastes are delightful sweets to serve with toast for breakfast, or for dessert with good crackers and cream cheese or a mild firm cheese. Whether you make paste or candy from your quinces, there is a bonus—extra quince juice to make into Clear Quince Honey (page 139).

Nectarine or Plum Cheese

This is a recipe pattern that can be followed for peaches or apricots as well as nectarines and plums. The fruit should be firm-ripe, not soft.

Note that there's a bonus of juice from which jelly or syrup can be made. For jelly, follow the directions packed with powdered or liquid pectin; for syrup, add sugar to the juice—about a cup of sugar to each cup of juice—and simmer the mixture for a minute or two. Skim the syrup, then cool and refrigerate it for use in cold drinks or desserts, or over pancakes.

Those who are lucky enough to have a source of damson plums—small, purple-skinned plums that come along at the very end of summer—should use them; their flavor is superb.

4 pounds firm but flavorful nectarines or red- or purple-skinned plums, rinsed and drained

1½ cups water

Spices and/or other flavorings, if desired (see step 3)

Sugar

Tasteless vegetable oil for jars

1. Pit the fruit; if clingstone plums are used, slice them off the pits. Chop the fruit coarsely (your food processor will do it fast) and combine it with the water in a preserving pan. Bring the fruit to a boil and simmer it, covered, until it is very soft, 20 minutes or so for plums, up to 45 for nectarines. If the fruit threatens to stick at any point, add a little more water.

SEASON:
Midsummer to early fall

YIELD:
About 2 cups of fruit cheese; plus about 2 cups of juice

STORE:
For at least a year in a cool cupboard or pantry

2. Pour the fruit and liquid into a food mill fitted with a fine disc and puree it, or puree it in the food processor. Spoon the mixture into a sieve that has been lined with two layers of fine cheesecloth and set over a bowl. Let it drain until the drip of juice slows, then tie the corners of the cloth together and hang it to drip into the bowl overnight, or for at least 6 hours. Reserve the juice for jelly or syrup.

3. Measure the pulp into a preserving pan, taking note of the amount. If you like, add a little spicing: For plums, add a pinch of cinnamon and either the grated zest (outer skin only, no white pith) of an orange or two or three large pieces of dried orange or tangerine peel (see page 213). For nectarines, add a small pinch of ground cloves and a generous pinch each of ground ginger, cinnamon, allspice, and mace.

4. Cook the pulp, uncovered, over medium heat, stirring it often, until it has become very thick (it will mound up in a spoon), up to an hour. Add ⅔ cup of sugar for each cup of pulp you started with; continue to cook the mixture, uncovered, over low heat, stirring it almost constantly now with a straight-ended wooden or nylon spatula, until it is very thick; when it has cooked enough, it will be so stiff that a wide path remains open when the spatula is drawn across the bottom of the pan; this may take from 1 to 2 hours. (If pieces of dried peel have been used, remove them from the mixture after an hour or so.) To verify consistency, remove the pan from the heat and drop a mound of the mixture onto a chilled saucer and put it into the refrigerator. When cold, it should be almost stiff enough to slice (the cheese will stiffen more after it goes into the jars). When you judge the cheese is done, add more spice, if you wish. If the pan has been set aside while you test, reheat the fruit cheese, stirring it constantly, until it is boiling hot.

5. Pack the fruit cheese into hot, clean half-pint canning jars that have been oiled lightly with tasteless vegetable oil; leave ¼ inch of headspace. Seal the jars with new two-piece canning lids according to manufacturer's directions and process for 10 minutes in a boiling-water bath (page 325). Cool, label, and store the jars.

6. To serve, unmold the cheese from the jar and slice it.

Quince Paste or Quince Candy

Quince paste, perhaps the most delicious of all fruit cheeses, is a firm, grainy, dark-red jellied confection to serve as a sweetmeat or as dessert, perhaps with a slice of mild cheese or some cream cheese alongside. It is a delicacy in farflung places, as indicated by its many names in other languages. In Spanish it's *membrillo, dulce de membrillo,* or *membrillate;* in Italian, *cotognato;* in French, *pâte de coings;* and

SEASON:
Late fall

 YIELD:
About 3½ pounds of paste, or 3¼ pounds of candy

STORE:
For many months at cool room temperature

the Portuguese call it *marmelada*—and we haven't even tackled the Middle Eastern versions of this sweet.

Made as a candy as described in step 6 of the recipe, this sweetmeat is pale rosy-pink in color and like firm fudge in texture. It keeps even longer than quince paste.

Notice that the recipe provides a bonus of extra quince juice to use for a batch of Clear Quince Honey (page 139). In the unlikely circumstance that you don't want to make the honey, reduce the cooking water for the quinces by 1 quart.

3 to 3½ pounds ripe quinces (about 6 medium-large)
4½ quarts water
Granulated sugar
Confectioners' sugar

1. Scrub the quinces, removing all the fuzz, and cut out the blossom ends. Cut the fruit into thin slices, cores and all.

2. Combine the sliced fruit and the water in a preserving pan and bring it to a boil. Lower the heat and simmer the fruit, partly covered, until the pieces are very soft, about 1½ hours.

3. Set a large colander or sieve over a bowl and pour in the fruit and juice. Drain the pulp thoroughly, then transfer it to a food mill fitted with the finest disc (or use a sieve) and work it through into another bowl; discard the intractable debris.

4. Measure 4 cups of the juice and reserve it for making Clear Quince Honey (refrigerate the juice until it's wanted, for up to a week). Measure the remaining juice and the pulp into the rinsed-out preserving pan.

5. Bring the quince pulp and juice to a boil, stirring, over medium heat and cook it, stirring it very often with a straight-ended spatula to prevent sticking, until it becomes thick enough to "plop" volcanically. Stir in 1 cup of granulated sugar for each cupful of the pulp and juice you began with and continue to cook the mixture, stirring it almost constantly (constantly toward the end) until it becomes very thick. At this point, decide on your final product and follow the appropriate directions.

6. *If you're making quince paste:* Continue to cook the mixture until it is thick enough to pull away from the sides of the pan as it is stirred; it should hold its mounded shape when a spoonful is scooped up. Remove the pan from the heat and cool the paste for a few minutes, then beat it, preferably using an electric mixer with a paddle attachment, until it is almost cool. Line a jelly-roll pan with plastic wrap and spread the paste in an even layer on it. Let the paste dry overnight, uncovered (if the weather is damp, set it in an oven warmed only by its light, or place it in a convection oven set at between 100° and 130°). When the surface is only faintly tacky, cover the paste with a second sheet of plastic, turn it over, and peel off the plastic now on top. Again let the sheet of paste dry until it is no longer sticky, which could be a day in dry weather or longer under

humid conditions. Cut the paste into rectangles or lozenge shapes. If the pieces seem sticky, let them dry longer on sheets of waxed paper, then dust them with sifted confectioners' sugar and pack them in an airtight container, separating the layers with waxed paper.

For quince candy: Continue cooking the mixture past the point described for quince paste, stirring it absolutely constantly and lowering the heat if necessary to prevent caramelizing the sugar; lower the heat as the candy thickens. When it is evident that the sugar is beginning to melt around the edges (it must not get hot enough to brown even slightly) and the spatula leaves a clear path when it is drawn across the bottom of the pan, remove the quince candy from the heat and let it cool a few minutes. Transfer it to the bowl of an electric mixer and beat it slowly, preferably with a paddle attachment, until it is lukewarm and very thick. Spread the candy about ½ inch thick in two oiled 8- or 9-inch square baking pans and let it cool completely. Cut the candy into lozenges or squares, dust the pieces with confectioners' sugar, and pack them in a canister or other airtight container.

Crystallized Ginger

A favorite confection in Britain and America for centuries, crystallized ginger was formerly always imported, usually from China, at considerable cost. Now that fresh ginger is available almost everywhere in the country, thanks to imports from Hawaii, other Pacific islands, and Central and South America, there is no need to pay many dollars per pound for candied slices. For candying try to get the tender young ginger, called "stem ginger," which comes to Orientally oriented markets around July. It is much juicier and milder than the mature rhizomes; it can be identified by its white, smooth, translucent skin and the pink stubs of leaf sheaths left when the above-ground stems were trimmed away. Mature ginger can be satisfactory when candied, too, but it is much more fibrous and several times as fiery as stem ginger. In shopping for mature ginger, look for silky-skinned, unwithered rhizomes.

The two kinds of ginger require different treatment, as outlined in the following recipe. Older ginger must be repeatedly blanched before it is crystallized, but there's a bonus: save the final blanching water to make a pleasant Ginger Syrup for Cold Drinks (page 284).

Candied ginger is a delicious nibble when you're having a cup of tea or after-dinner coffee. The ginger can also be

SEASON:
Best when made with stem ginger (available from midsummer into fall), but possible at any season

YIELD:
About 1¼ pounds

STORE:
For many months at room temperature

chopped for flavoring ice cream, dessert sauces, cookies, or a special cake.

1 pound fresh stem ginger or smooth-skinned, juicy mature ginger

3 cups sugar, plus additional for coating

3 cups water

2 tablespoons light corn syrup

1. *Preparing stem ginger:* Break the rhizomes apart at the joints and scrape off the thin skin, using a small sharp knife. Trim off the leafy stem bases and any bruised or discolored ends. Slice the sections slightly on the bias into pieces about ¼ inch thick. Place the ginger in a large saucepan, add cold water to cover the pieces by 2 inches, and bring it to a boil over medium heat. Lower the heat, cover the pot, and simmer the ginger for 2½ hours. If the liquid level drops below the ginger at any point, add boiling water. Drain the ginger, add fresh water to cover, and simmer it for another hour, or until the slices are very tender. Drain the ginger.

Preparing mature ginger: Scrape, trim, and slice the rhizomes as described for stem ginger. Place the slices in a bowl, add cold water to cover the pieces by 2 inches, and let them stand overnight. Drain the ginger and place the slices in a large saucepan. Add water to cover the pieces by 1 inch and bring everything to a boil over medium heat. Lower the heat, cover the pan, and simmer the ginger for 10 minutes. Drain the ginger, cover it with fresh water, and repeat the simmering and draining at least three times; after the fourth simmering, taste a scrap of ginger to see whether its hotness suits you. If the flavor is still too strong, change the water and repeat the simmering once or twice more. Continue cooking the ginger in the final water until the pieces are very tender, 2 to 3 hours, adding boiling water as necessary to keep the ginger covered with liquid. (This cooking can be done in several bouts, if that's more convenient.) Drain the ginger.

2. *Candying either stem or mature ginger:* Combine the 3 cups sugar, 3 cups water, and corn syrup in a large saucepan. Bring the mixture to a boil over medium-high heat and boil it 2 minutes. Add the ginger slices. Heat the syrup again to boiling, shaking the pan often, and boil it hard 1 minute. Remove the pan from the heat; let it stand until the ginger and syrup are completely cool, or as long as overnight.

3. Return the pan to the heat and again bring the syrup to a boil. Adjust the heat and simmer the ginger, covered, until the pieces are translucent and very tender, which can take from 1 hour to 3 hours; stir it occasionally. If the syrup becomes too thick before the ginger is translucent, add a little hot water to restore its consistency.

5. Finally, cook the ginger, uncovered, shaking the pan often, until the syrup is reduced to a spoonful or two. Remove the pan from the heat and let it stand a few minutes.

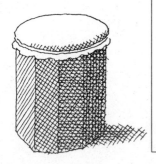

6. Fork the ginger pieces onto a wire rack and leave them to dry at room temperature, a matter of an hour or two. When they are no longer sticky, roll the pieces in granulated sugar to coat them well. Store the ginger in a covered container at room temperature.

Ginger Preserved in Syrup

A little of this ginger, chopped and mixed with some of the syrup, makes a luscious topping for ice cream; or fold chopped ginger and a little of the syrup into whipped cream and fill dessert crêpes with the mixture.

Use either tender young stem ginger or mature ginger, preferably the first. Prepare the ginger as described in steps 1 and 2 of the preceding recipe for Crystallized Ginger. If stem ginger is what you have, you may want to cut it into knobs or joints about the size of a thumbtip instead of slices. Complete step 3 of the recipe.

Ladle the boiling-hot ginger and syrup into a sterilized (page 327) jar, let it cool, and cover it with a sterilized lid. If the syrup should be insufficient to cover the ginger pieces, make a little additional plain syrup in the original proportions and add it while it is hot.

Pantry storage is satisfactory for a few weeks, but refrigeration is recommended for longer storage.

SEASON:
Best when made with stem ginger (available from midsummer into fall), but possible at any season.

YIELD:
About 1 quart

STORE:
For a few weeks in a cool cupboard or pantry; refrigerate for longer storage

NOTE:
The stiffened syrup remaining in the pan can be melted with a little hot water and added to Ginger Syrup for Cold Drinks (page 284).

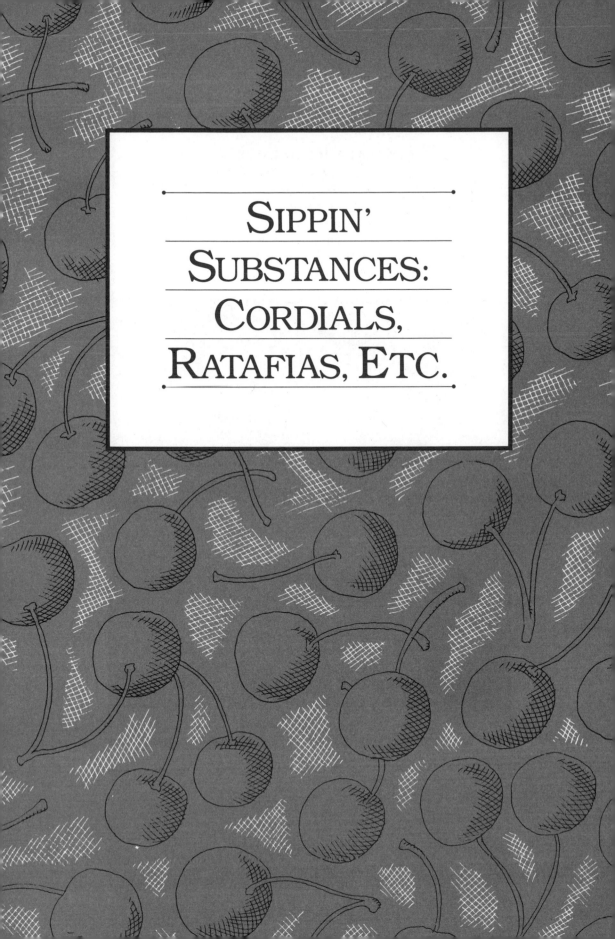

SIPPIN' SUBSTANCES: CORDIALS, RATAFIAS, ETC.

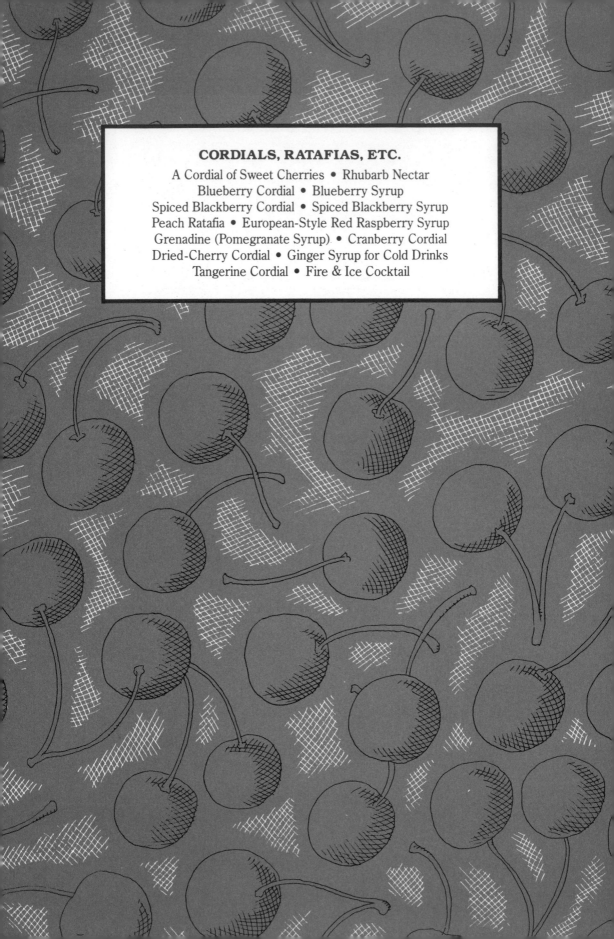

CORDIALS, RATAFIAS, ETC.

A Cordial of Sweet Cherries • Rhubarb Nectar
Blueberry Cordial • Blueberry Syrup
Spiced Blackberry Cordial • Spiced Blackberry Syrup
Peach Ratafia • European-Style Red Raspberry Syrup
Grenadine (Pomegranate Syrup) • Cranberry Cordial
Dried-Cherry Cordial • Ginger Syrup for Cold Drinks
Tangerine Cordial • Fire & Ice Cocktail

Cordial is as cordial does—everyone knows that—but *what* is a ratafia? For all practical purposes it's also a cordial, one whose making is feasible at home; it requires no bales of obscure herbal ingredients, no tangles of copper tubes and other distilling apparatus. In this section we have Peach Ratafia among a selection of sips that includes simple, good cordials made with other summer fruits—cherries, blueberries, blackberries, and raspberries—plus other tipples based on cranberries, dried cherries, and dried tangerine peel.

As the base for nonalcoholic cold drinks, you can choose among syrups made from red raspberries, ginger, blueberries, and blackberries. There is also Rhubarb Nectar as well as Grenadine, which is authentically made here from pomegranate juice, not the nameless substances now used in even the expensive commercial versions.

Finally, for pure deviltry there is a freezer-dwelling bottle of Fire & Ice Cocktail, compounded from vodka and several kinds of hot peppers, to be served icy-cold to those who know *piquant* when they taste it.

A Cordial of Sweet Cherries

After the elements are assembled—the work of 10 minutes—time alone creates this pretty cordial. It requires several months in the jar before it's ready to enjoy; put everything together in midsummer, and well before the winter holidays the fragrant spirits will be ready to sip.

When the cordial has been drained off and bottled, more sugar and brandy can be added to the fruit, now awesomely wrinkled, for a second go-around, as described in the recipe.

2 pounds firm-ripe medium-size sweet cherries, dark or light

2 to 4 cups sugar, depending on sweetness desired

1 quart good-quality brandy

1. Rinse and drain the cherries and roll them on a towel to remove as much moisture as possible. Remove the stems.

2. Divide the cherries between two sterilized (page 327), dry quart jars (or use a half-gallon glass storage jar with a gasket and a clamped lid, if you prefer).

3. Divide the sugar between the two jars, using 2 cups if you are unsure how sweet you want the cordial to be (more can be added later). Add the brandy, which should cover the cherries and sugar generously. Cover the jars airtight and set them in a cool, preferably dark spot where you will remember to check them regularly.

4. Shake the jars every few days or at least once a week; the sugar will gradually dissolve as the cherry juices join the brandy in the syrup. When all the sugar has dissolved, taste the syrup and decide whether you want to add more sugar; if you do, this is the moment. If sugar is added, continue to shake the jars occasionally until it has all dissolved.

5. Leave the cherries in the brandy for a minimum of 3 months; 5 or 6 months is not too long.

6. Strain the cordial from the cherries and funnel it into clean, dry bottles. Cap or cork them (use new corks only) and store them out of the light.

7. If you want to recycle the cherries, add to them half as much sugar and brandy as you used the first time and proceed as before. You may want to leave the cherries in this batch until time to pour the cordial in order to extract all possible flavor.

Rhubarb Nectar

 SEASON:
Late spring
through summer;
or at any time,
using frozen
unsweetened
rhubarb

YIELD:
3 to 4 pints

STORE:
Sealed, in a cool,
dark cupboard or
pantry for up to a
year; unsealed, in
the refrigerator,
for 3 weeks;
frozen, for up to a
year

Although it has been neglected in haute-cuisine circles for too long, rhubarb shows signs of perking into popularity again in such good things as all-American pie fillings, with or without strawberries, and such preserves as Gingery Rhubarb Chutney (page 58). Rhubarb lovers will need no urging to try this drink base.

Ways to use the nectar:

Rhubarb Highball: An inspiration, nonalcoholic, said to date back to early-1900s Hong Kong. For this, combine the nectar with an equal measure of freshly squeezed orange juice; add sweetening, if necessary; pour over finely cracked ice in highball glasses and top up with club soda, with a garnish of fresh mint, if you have it.

Rhubarb-Orange Punch: Make a punch of the nectar and an equal amount of orange juice, plus a little lemon juice and more sweetening if you think the mixture needs it. Pour the mixture over a block of ice to chill; add ginger ale to the punch at serving time.

Rhubarb Cocktail: Shake two parts of Rhubarb Nectar with one part of vodka, rum, or gin and plenty of crushed ice. Strain the mixture into a short-stemmed glass.

3 cups sugar

2 cups water

8 cups red-stalked, tender rhubarb, cut into 1-inch
lengths (about 2 pounds, after trimming)

1. Combine the sugar and water in a preserving pan, bring the mixture to a boil over medium-high heat, and boil it for 1 minute. Add the rhubarb, bring the mixture to a boil again, lower the heat, and simmer it, partly covered, until the rhubarb is very soft, 10 to 15 minutes.

2. Press the hot rhubarb mixture through a food mill fitted with the fine disc, or process it to a puree in batches in a food processor or a blender.

3. Return the nectar to the rinsed-out pan, bring it to a boil, boil it for a moment, and ladle it into hot, clean pint or half-pint canning jars, leaving ¼ inch of headspace. Seal the jars with new two-piece canning lids according to manufacturer's directions and process for 15 minutes (for either size jar) in a boiling-water bath (page 325). Cool, label, and store.

Alternative method: If the nectar will be used within a few weeks, pour it into refrigerator containers, cool it, then cover and refrigerate it. To freeze the nectar, pour it into freezer containers, leaving ½ inch of headspace, cool, cover, and freeze.

SEASON:
Mid- to late
summer

YIELD:
1 to 1½ quarts

STORE:
In a dark cupboard
at room
temperature;
keeps indefinitely

Blueberry Cordial

A clear, brilliant bluish red in color, this sippin' substance is a good destiny for a few of the season's best blueberries. The modus operandi is to produce a syrup first, and you can stop right there, bottling the syrup (see the recipe that follows this one) as a waffle syrup or a base for nonalcoholic coolers. Blended with good vodka (don't skimp on quality here), the syrup becomes an after-dinner cordial with a delicate but true blueberry flavor.

If deciding between recipes is a problem, double or triple the quantities and make a batch of cordial and another of syrup.

1 pint basket (about 3 cups) ripe blueberries
3 cups sugar
1½ cups water
⅓ cup strained fresh lemon juice
Good-quality vodka

1. Sort over the blueberries, removing any stems, and discard any damaged or under- or overripe berries. Rinse the berries and drain them thoroughly.

2. Puree the berries, using a food processor, a blender, or a food mill fitted with a fine disc. Place the puree in a ceramic or stainless-steel bowl; cover the bowl with a thick cloth (such as a terry towel) and let it stand at room temperature for 36 hours. Stir the puree after 2 or 3 hours and several times more during the fermentation period. During this time a "crust" will form at first, and later the puree will become foamy.

3. Line a sieve with one layer of dampened very fine nylon net or two layers of dampened fine cheesecloth and set it over a bowl. Pour in the puree and let it drain. When the flow dwindles, twist the corners of the cloth together and press hard on the pulp to extract all possible juice. (A jelly bag—see page 322—can also be used for draining.) Discard the pulp; measure the juice. You should have about 1⅓ cups.

4. Combine the sugar and water in a saucepan. Bring to boiling over high heat and boil the syrup, uncovered, until it will form a soft ball when a little is dropped into ice water, or until the syrup registers about 235° on a candy/jelly thermometer. Add the blueberry juice and lemon juice, stir the mixture, and let it return to a boil. Simmer it, uncovered, 5 minutes. Remove from heat.

5. Let the syrup cool completely, then stir it thoroughly with vodka in proportions to taste—add ½ to ¾ cup of vodka to each cup of syrup, or mix the syrup and the vodka in equal amounts. Funnel the cordial into clean, dry bottles, cap or cork them (use new corks only), and store them.

Blueberry Syrup

To use this syrup as a beverage base, add about 3 tablespoons to a tumbler containing ice and fill it up with chilled club soda. Try it, too, as a topping for waffles, pancakes, and desserts.

1. Make the syrup as described through step 4 of the Blueberry Cordial recipe above, doubling all ingredients.

2. To can the syrup for pantry storage, ladle it, boiling hot, into hot, clean pint-size canning jars, leaving ¼ inch of headspace. Seal the jars with new two-piece canning lids according to manufacturer's directions and process for 15 minutes in a boiling-water bath (page 325). Cool, label, and store the jars.

3. To store the syrup in the refrigerator, let it cool completely, then funnel it into sterilized (page 327), dry bottles or jars. Cover and refrigerate.

 SEASON:
Mid- to late summer

YIELD:
6 cups

 STORE:
Unsealed, in the refrigerator; sealed, in a cool, dark cupboard or pantry. It keeps for many months either way

Spiced Blackberry Cordial

A tiny glass of this is a warming nip for the cold times; and a little could be spooned over vanilla or raspberry ice cream at any season.

For nonalcoholic Spiced Blackberry Syrup, an equally good benison for pancakes or waffles as well as desserts, see the recipe that follows this one.

6 half-pint baskets (about 8 cups) ripe blackberries

1 cup water

Sugar

½ teaspoon broken cinnamon stick

½ teaspoon whole allspice, slightly bruised

1 whole blade mace

1 whole clove

Small scrap whole nutmeg, or tiny pinch freshly grated nutmeg

2 tablespoons strained fresh lemon juice

Good-quality vodka or brandy

1. Pick over, rinse, and drain the berries. Place them in a food processor and whirl them briefly to a coarse puree, or push them through a food mill fitted with a coarse disc, or place

SEASON:
Mid- through late summer

YIELD:
About 2 quarts

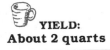 STORE:
In a dark cupboard or pantry at room temperature; keeps indefinitely

them in a preserving pan and crush them with a potato masher or a heavy bottle. Stir in 1 cup water.

2. Bring the mixture to a boil over medium heat. Reduce the heat to low and simmer the berries gently for 10 minutes, stirring them occasionally.

3. Set a sieve lined with one layer of dampened very fine nylon net or two layers of dampened fine cheesecloth over a bowl. Pour the blackberries and juice into the sieve and allow the juice to drip through. When the drip slows to an occasional plunk, gather the cloth and press on the contents with a large spoon, using moderate force, to encourage the flow of juice; repeat the pressing from time to time, being careful to avoid forcing any pulp through the cloth. When the pulp has yielded all possible juice, discard it. (Alternatively, you can use a jelly bag—see page 322—to drain the juice.)

4. Measure the juice into the rinsed-out preserving pan; you should have about 4 cups. For each cup add ½ cup sugar. Stir in the cinnamon, allspice, mace, clove, and nutmeg. Heat the mixture to simmering over medium heat, stirring until the sugar has dissolved. Increase the heat slightly and boil the syrup gently, uncovered, for 3 minutes to extract more flavor from the spices. Remove the syrup from the heat, stir in the lemon juice, and cool to lukewarm.

5. Strain the juice through a very fine-meshed sieve (or a sieve lined with one layer of dampened fine nylon net or two layers of dampened cheesecloth) into a large bowl; discard the spices. Let the juice cool completely.

6. Stir the syrup thoroughly together with an equal quantity of vodka or brandy; or suit your own taste in the matter of proportions, using less or more alcohol per cup of juice. Funnel the cordial into clean, dry bottles, filling them almost to the top. Cap or cork the bottles (use new corks only) and store the cordial in a cupboard or pantry.

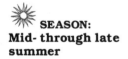
**SEASON:
Mid- through late
summer**

**YIELD:
5 to 6 cups**

**STORE:
Refrigerator or
pantry, keeps
indefinitely**

Spiced Blackberry Syrup

This is Spiced Blackberry Cordial, above, without the alcohol and with additional sweetening. Use it as a dessert sauce, or serve it with waffles or pancakes or dessert crêpes. It also makes a refreshing beverage: Stir about 3 tablespoons into a tumbler of chilled ginger ale and serve while it's fizzy.

1. Make the spiced syrup as directed for Spiced Blackberry Cordial, but in step 4, sweeten it with 1 cup of sugar to each cup of juice; proceed with step 5.

2. If the syrup will be used within a few months, funnel it

into clean, dry bottles or jars and store it, tightly covered (if corking, use new corks only), in the refrigerator.

3. To can the syrup for pantry storage, heat it to boiling and ladle it into clean, hot pint or half-pint canning jars, leaving ¼ inch of headspace. Seal the jars with new two-piece canning lids according to manufacturer's directions and process for 15 minutes in a boiling-water bath (page 325). Cool, label, and store the jars.

Peach Ratafia

**SEASON:
Summer to early
fall**

**YIELD:
About 5 cups**

**STORE:
In a dark cupboard
at room
temperature;
keeps indefinitely**

A peach cordial, rich in flavor and deep amber in color, this easily created ratafia is at its best after at least a few months of quiet mellowing.

After the cordial has been bottled, the slices of brandy-bathed peach can be served as a dessert, with cream. Or you might serve a slice or two in a small brandy snifter of the ratafia. In the latter case, demitasse spoons are a help.

1 cup granulated sugar

½ cup (packed) light brown sugar

½ cup water

**3 cups sliced peeled ripe peaches (start with about
    1½ pounds)**

Peach kernels (see step 2)

⅛ teaspoon ground mace

1 quart good-quality brandy

1. Combine the granulated sugar, the brown sugar, and the water in a saucepan. Bring the mixture to a boil and boil the syrup briskly, uncovered, for 3 minutes. Cool the syrup.

2. Meanwhile, prepare the peaches, cracking the pits and extracting the kernels; add them to the peaches in a clean, dry 2-quart glass jar or a crock that has a snug cover.

3. Stir the cooled syrup, the mace, and the brandy together until they are completely mixed. Pour the mixture over the peaches and stir the whole business. Cover airtight. Set the container aside for at least a month and stir or shake the contents once in a while.

4. Leave the fruit and cordial together until serving time, or strain off the cordial through a fine-meshed sieve and bottle it (if corking, use new corks only). Refrigerate the fruit.

SEASON:
July through
October

SYRUP YIELD:
About 7 cups

STORE:
Unsealed, in the
refrigerator;
sealed, in a cool
cupboard or
pantry. It keeps for
a year or more
either way

European-Style Red Raspberry Syrup

Raspberry jelly is such a delight that I count the preserving season lost if I haven't made some, using store-bought powdered pectin and the directions packed with it. (I use powdered pectin rather than the liquid kind because less sugar is required and the result is therefore fruitier.) After the juice for jellying has been drained from the crushed berries, it seems wasteful to chuck out the remaining pulp, which is full of flavor but too seedy to be used for jam; what else is possible? This raspberry syrup, which can start with either pulp or whole berries, is the answer. It is brilliant in color and rich in flavor and useful for both desserts and beverages.

The method may need a little explanation. It is basically the European way of making syrup by fermenting fruit pulp just long enough to intensify its flavor. However, if one relies on nature to carry out the fermentation, undesirable wild yeasts may find their way into the works and spoil the flavor; adding a little active dry yeast to the pulp is more reliable.

If you live in a part of the country where red raspberries are sold in stingy little trays and priced like jewels, this recipe may be of only academic interest. But if you can obtain raspberries reasonably, do try this waste-not, want-not way to enjoy both jelly and syrup.

Ways to use the syrup: Mix it with chilled club soda or dry white wine, plain or sparkling, for a tall drink; sauce ice cream or a simple pudding with a spoonful; sweeten sliced strawberries or a bowl of mixed fresh or frozen fruit with a dollop; use it as sweetening in any mixed drink where a vivid, fresh raspberry flavor would be welcome.

10 pints (about 5 pounds) red raspberries, if you're making both jelly and syrup; for syrup only, use 5 pints

4 to 6 cups water

1 teaspoon active dry yeast

¾ cup strained fresh lemon juice

4 cups sugar

1. *Making both jelly and syrup:* Use the full quantity of raspberries. Sort, rinse, and drain the berries, discarding any oversoft or moldy ones. Crush the berries thoroughly (processing batches briefly in the food processor is the quickest way), then proceed to step 2 and 3.

To make syrup alone: Use 5 pints of berries, crush them,

omit steps 2 and 3, and proceed to step 4, omitting the 2 cups of water called for there.

2. Set a colander over a bowl and line it with two layers of dampened fine cheesecloth, or a single layer of dampened very fine nylon net; alternatively, arrange a jelly bag (page 322) in its frame over a large bowl. Scrape the crushed raspberries into the draining arrangement and let the juice drain into the bowl. If you are using a lined colander, when the juice flow slows down, tie the corners of the cheesecloth to make a bag and hang it above the bowl to drip. Let the juice drip without pressure for several hours or as long as overnight, then press lightly on the bag to extract as much juice as possible without forcing through any pulp or cloudy juice.

3. Reserve the juice (you should have about 4 cups) for raspberry jelly, made with powdered pectin according to the excellent directions packed with it. (If you wish, the juice may be frozen for future use, or refrigerated for a day or two.)

4. Scrape the pulp from the bag (step 2) or pour the plain crushed berries (step 1) into a large ceramic or stainless-steel bowl. Add 2 cups of the water only if you're using the pulp; add the yeast to either the pulp or the crushed berries. Cover the bowl with a cloth and let it stand at room temperature for a few days (usually about 3 days), stirring the contents twice a day, until the mixture is no longer bubbly when it is stirred. (At this point, it won't look especially appetizing, but press on.)

5. Repeat the draining procedure described in step 2, but this time press and squeeze the contents of the bag to extract all possible liquid, which will be murky.

6. Combine the liquid in a large stainless-steel or enameled pot with the remaining 4 cups of water, the lemon juice, and the sugar. Bring the mixture to a boil over medium-high heat and simmer it briskly, stirring it occasionally, until it has reduced to about 7 cups. Skim the syrup and let it cool, then skim it again.

7. Funnel the syrup into dry, sterilized (page 327) bottles. Cap or cork the bottles (use new corks only) and store them in the refrigerator. Pantry storage is also satisfactory if all air is excluded; either reheat the syrup to almost simmering and seal it in sterilized canning jars with sterilized canning lids (no processing is needed), or dip the corked necks of bottles repeatedly into melted paraffin wax to form a snug seal. Refrigerate after opening.

SEASON:
Autumn

YIELD:
About 2 cups

STORE:
Unsealed, in the refrigerator; sealed, in a cool cupboard or pantry. Keeps either way for at least a year

Grenadine (Pomegranate Syrup)

Delicate in flavor and ruby-red in color, pomegranate syrup is a supporting player rather than a star. As such, it is much used as a flavor-smoother and sweetener in both alcoholic and nonalcoholic drinks; and it's also a pleasant topping for tart pineapple, peach, or nectarine ice cream or sherbet.

Why make your own? Well, you might possess a pomegranate tree (multiply this recipe if you do), or you might like to taste the real thing: a lot of the "grenadine" offered nowadays is compounded of sweetening plus anonymous "fruit" flavors rather than pomegranate juice.

When choosing pomegranates, reject any with a brownish area on the blossom end; such discoloration indicates the beginning of spoilage and off-flavor.

2 medium-large pomegranates
2½ cups sugar
½ cup water

1. Cut the pomegranates open crosswise and pry out the fleshy crimson seeds (the red part is actually the pulpy envelope around a seed), using the tip of a blunt knife. Be careful not to include any fragments of the cottony white pulp in which the seeds are embedded, as it is bitter. You should have about 2 cups of seeds.

2. Using a food processor or a blender, chop the seeds with the sugar and water just long enough to make a rough puree. Don't attempt to make a smooth mixture; it's necessary only to break open the pulpy membranes.

3. Pour the puree into an earthenware or glass bowl and cover it with a cloth. Let it stand at room temperature for 3 days, stirring it daily. If the weather is extremely hot, refrigerate the puree after 24 hours.

4. Line a sieve with dampened, very fine nylon net or two layers of dampened fine cheesecloth and set it over a saucepan of stainless-steel or other nonreactive material. Filter the pomegranate syrup into the pot, allowing it to drip without pressing on the pulp. This will take a few hours; you can speed matters up by tying the cheesecloth lining of the sieve into a bag and suspending it above the pot after the initial flow of juice has slowed down. When all the juice has dripped through, discard the seedy pulp.

5. Bring the syrup to a bare simmer (180°) over medium-low heat, then reduce the heat to very low and scald the syrup,

using a candy/jelly thermometer and watching to be sure you keep the temperature below 200°, for 3 minutes.

6. Skim off any foam, then funnel the syrup into a sterilized (page 327), dry bottle. Let the syrup cool, then cap or cork the bottle (use a new cork only) and store it in the refrigerator.

To seal the syrup for pantry storage: Funnel it into hot, clean half-pint canning jars. Seal with new two-piece canning lids according to manufacturer's directions. Following the method of the boiling-water bath (page 325) but keeping the water at simmering temperature (190°), process the jars for 15 minutes. Cool, label, and store.

Cranberry Cordial

C ranberries, perhaps the best-known native American fruit, are also native to parts of the U.S.S.R., where, quite naturally, the Russians have put them together with their national drink to make a nonsweet, fruit-flavored vodka served as a predinner nip.

The formula below, inspired by Russian example, produces a liqueur-like drink to be served as a cordial after, rather than before, the meal. Put this to steep as soon as the first cranberries bounce onto the market in October and it will be ready in time for Christmas giving or even Thanksgiving sipping.

If gift-giving is in the offing, double or triple the recipe. Lacking one large container for steeping, divide the ingredients among quart-size canning jars.

3½ to 4 cups (a 12-ounce package) fresh cranberries

2 cups sugar, plus more if needed

Several pieces of dried tangerine peel (about 5 square inches in all; see page 213) or substitute 1½ tablespoons grated fresh orange zest (outer skin only, no white pith)

4 whole cloves

4 whole allspice

4 cups good-quality vodka

1. Pick over the cranberries; rinse and drain them. If you are using a food processor, chop them coarsely in two batches, adding half of the sugar and half of the tangerine peel to each batch. (A large-capacity machine will do this in one operation.) Alternatively, chop the cranberries coarsely with a large knife on a cutting board, crumble or chop the dried peel, and stir the

SEASON:
From October through late winter

YIELD:
About 1½ quarts

STORE:
In a dark cupboard at room temperature; keeps indefinitely

cranberries, peel, and sugar together.

2. Place the mixture in a large clean, dry jar or a crock that has a snug lid or, lacking a large container, divide it between two quart canning jars. Bruise the cloves and whole allspice slightly (easiest to do in a mortar) and drop them into the jar(s). Stir in the vodka.

3. Cap the jar tightly (if using a crock, cover it with plastic wrap, then the lid, using enough plastic layers to make a snug fit). Set the container aside at room temperature. Shake or stir the mixture at least once a week and let it stand for a month.

4. At the end of a month, strain out the solids by pouring the mixture into a fine-mesh sieve lined with one layer of dampened fine nylon net or two layers of dampened cheese-cloth and set over a bowl. Gather the cloth, twist it to exert pressure, and squeeze out as much liquid as possible; finally, press on the cloth with a potato masher or other implement to get the last drops. Discard the pulp.

5. Taste the cordial; if you'd like more sweetness and body, boil together ½ cup sugar and ¼ cup water for 2 minutes, cool the syrup, then stir some or all of it into the cordial, according to taste (or use Sugar Syrup for Cordials, page 283).

6. Funnel the cordial into a clean, dry jar or small bottles, leaving behind any sediment (there may be none, if the straining has been carefully done). Cap or cork the container(s) (use new corks only) and store the cordial at room temperature. If any cloudiness (harmless) should form in the bottom of the bottle, either ignore it or decant the cordial carefully into a clean, dry container.

Dried-Cherry Cordial

A sip of this garnet-red cordial is rich with the concentrated fruitiness of dried sour cherries, super-raisins you can make yourself (see page 309) or obtain by mail (see list of sources, pages 330–331).

The cordial is quite different in character from a liqueur made with sweet cherries—witness A Cordial of Sweet Cherries (page 272). Either one is a good thing in a tiny after-dinner glass.

See the note on this page for directions for making a delicious dessert sauce from the cherries used for the cordial.

1 cup (4 ounces) dried sour cherries

2½ cups good-quality vodka

¾ cup, or to taste, Sugar Syrup for Cordials, below

**SEASON:
Any time**

**YIELD:
About 3 cups**

**STORE:
In a cool, dark cupboard; keeps indefinitely**

NOTE:

For waste-not, want-not types, here is how to make a spirited ice cream sauce with the cherries: Com-

1. Combine the dried cherries and the vodka in a jar with a snug nonmetallic lid (an enamel-lined canning lid is fine). Lacking such a lid, cover the jar with a double layer of plastic wrap before putting a metallic lid in place. Cover the jar and set it aside at room temperature for at least 2 weeks or for as long as 2 months, shaking the jar daily or as often as you think of it.

2. Strain the liquid from the cherries, reserving the cherries for another use, if you wish (see Note).

3. Stir the liquid thoroughly with the syrup, then filter the cordial into a sterilized (page 327), dry jar through a coffee filter placed in a funnel. Cover the jar and let the cordial stand for several hours or for a day or two to allow any sediment to settle.

4. Decant the cordial carefully, leaving the sediment behind, into a sterilized, dry bottle. Cap or cork the bottle (use a new cork only) and store the cordial in a cool, dark spot. If more sediment should develop during storage, it is harmless; either decant the cordial again or filter it again, or ignore the deposit.

Sugar Syrup for Cordials

This can be used to sweeten drinks of all sorts, not cordials alone.

1. Stir together 4 cups sugar and 2 cups water in a saucepan. Bring the mixture to a boil, then simmer the syrup 3 minutes, skimming off any scum. Cool, then store in the refrigerator in a clean, dry bottle or jar, tightly closed.

2. To increase the quantity, simply maintain the proportions of twice as much sugar as water.

Ginger Syrup for Cold Drinks

When you make Crystallized Ginger (page 265), this syrup can be a *lagniappe*. To use it for a fizzy ginger drink, pour a few spoonfuls of the syrup over ice in a glass and top it up with club soda; or blend a generous amount of ginger syrup with cold tea and orange juice in a punch bowl, add a chunk of ice, let the punch chill, and finish it with a little club soda.

To enjoy this bonus from candying ginger, reserve the last batch of liquid in which the ginger is cooked before it is candied (see step 1 of the recipe), then boil it in a wide pan until it is reduced by about half. At that point, taste it to see if the flavor

bine the drained cherries with 1½ cups of Sugar Syrup for Cordials (below) and 1½ cups of water. Simmer, partly covered, until the cherries are very tender and the syrup is thick, about 30 minutes. Puree half of the sauce in a blender, return it to the rest, and stir in 2 or 3 drops of almond extract. Cool; refrigerate, covered, for indefinite storage.

YIELD:
About 3½ cups

STORE:
In the refrigerator; keeps indefinitely

SEASON:
Whenever you're making Crystallized Ginger

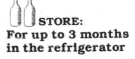
STORE:
For up to 3 months in the refrigerator

suits you; if not, reduce it further.

Measure the liquid and add ¾ cup of sugar for each cup. (Add, too, any leftover syrup remaining from the process of candying the ginger, if you wish.) Boil the syrup, uncovered, 5 minutes; skim off any foam.

Funnel the syrup into a sterilized (page 327), dry bottle or bottles, let it cool, then cap or cork the bottles (use new corks only) and store in the refrigerator.

Alternative method: Simmer about 1 cup of grated, peeled ginger with 3 cups water for 5 minutes. Steep overnight. Strain off and sweeten the liquid as described.

⭐ SEASON:
Any time

☕ YIELD:
1 pint

🍾 STORE:
In a dark cupboard at room temperature; keeps indefinitely

Tangerine Cordial

T his delicious citrus cordial is flavored with dried tangerine peel, prepared as described on page 213. You can use part orange peel, if you like. The cordial is even better, for some, when a little grapefruit peel, dried exactly like tangerine skin, is included at the steeping stage; this contributes a faint bitter edge.

4 ounces (about a cupful) of Dried Tangerine Peel (page 213), including a little dried grapefruit peel, optional

3 cups good-quality vodka

1 cup sugar

½ cup water

1. Crumble the peel well and combine it with the vodka in a clean, dry quart jar (or use a bottle). Cap the container and let it stand where you'll remember to give it a shake or two every day or when you think of it. Let the peel steep in the vodka for 10 days or 2 weeks, until the liquid has taken on a good deal of color and aroma (sniff or taste). For stronger flavor, leave it longer.

2. Strain the flavored vodka through a fine-meshed sieve, pressing lightly on the pieces of peel to obtain the last drops. Discard the peel.

3. Stir the sugar and water together in a small saucepan and bring the mixture to a boil. Simmer the syrup 5 minutes, or until it has thickened a little. Remove any scum. Cool the syrup.

4. Stir the syrup into the vodka, using all of it or as much as your taste directs. Filter the cordial into a clean, dry bottle or bottles through coffee filter paper placed in a funnel. Cap or cork the bottle(s) (use new corks only) and store it at room temperature.

Fire & Ice Cocktail

 SEASON:
Late summer and fall

YIELD:
About 1 pint

 STORE:
In the freezer;
keeps indefinitely

T he spirit—or genie—of this drink comes straight from the "Cajun martinis" credited to the renowned Louisiana chef Paul Prudhomme. He is said to use jalapeño peppers; others say fresh red chili peppers are great; I use what's in the garden, namely Cayenne peppers, as a base and add a touch each of Szechuan and pink peppercorns, plus a little paprika or chili for a more intricately peppery flavor. The resulting fiery compound is to be served ice-cold, and it's for palates that are known to be fireproof; check with guests before offering it. It's most attractive when served from an ice-jacketed bottle; a few red peppers frozen into the ice are a pretty decoration as well as a fair warning of the contents.

2 cups good-quality gin or vodka

2 fresh Cayenne or other small hot red peppers, stemmed and sliced crosswise (keep as many of the seeds as you can)

¼ teaspoon pink peppercorns, drained and patted dry if packed in brine

¼ teaspoon Szechuan peppercorns, slightly crushed

¼ teaspoon imported paprika or a pinch of pure ground chilies (not seasoned chili powder)

1. Combine all the ingredients in a clean, dry jar, cap the jar, and let it stand overnight.

2. Take a cautious taste; if the liquid is piquant enough, strain it through a fine sieve into a measuring pitcher or jar and let it stand, covered, overnight or until the sediment settles.

3. Decant the cocktail into an attractive serving bottle, leaving behind any sediment. Cap or cork the bottle (use a new cork only) and store it in the freezer.

4. *To make an ice jacket for the bottle:* Decant the cocktail into a bottle that will fit loosely inside a quart milk carton with its top removed, or use a round plastic juice container. Freeze half an inch of water in the carton.

5. Set the bottle on the layer of ice, add water to come one-third up the bottle, and freeze this layer. When it is solid, add a frieze of small dried red peppers. Add a little water and freeze the garnish in place. When it is solid, add water up to the shoulder of the bottle and freeze it. Store indefinitely.

6. *To serve:* Dip the outer container into hot water briefly and slip out the ice-jacketed bottle. After serving, return the bottle to the freezer. Note that the ice coating will erode in time if you have a self-defrosting freezer. To prevent this, seal the jacketed bottle into a plastic freezer bag between uses.

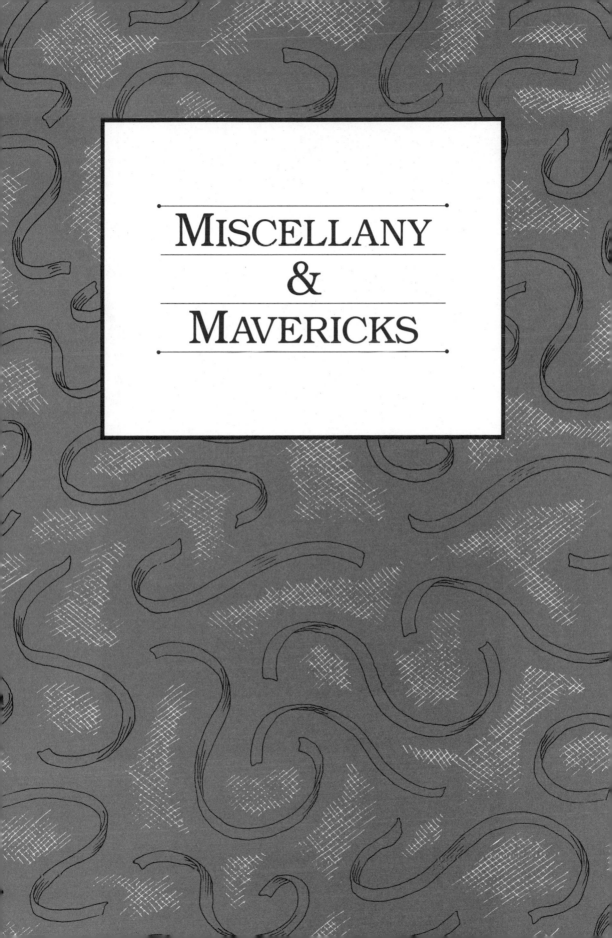

MISCELLANY
&
MAVERICKS

PASTA POINTERS

Semolina Noodles • Porcini Pasta • Peanut Noodles
Hazelnut or Black Walnut Noodles • Spinach Noodles
Herbed Green Noodles • Red-Pepper Pasta, Mild or Hot

DESSERT MAKINGS TO KEEP ON HAND

Lime or Lemon Curd, "Butter," or "Cheese"
Praline Powder for Desserts
Green Tomato, Apple, & Pear Mincemeat
Candied Orange Peel • Candied Sour Cherries
Candied Pineapple • Super-Raisins
Dried Sweet or Sour Cherries
Blueberry or Huckleberry Raisins
Making the Most of Vanilla Beans

A FEW FOR THE FREEZER OR FRIDGE

Pesto for Seasons Without Basil • Frozen Avocado Puree
Clarified Butter • Dried Cheddar Cheese • Crème Fraîche

Somewhere in this book a place had to be found for things that don't fit into the categories of the first seven chapters. So here we have a truly miscellaneous bag of "oats and ants," to quote an ancient jape.

The odds and ends start with some pastas to play with, using such intriguing ingredients as porcini mushrooms, nuts, and red peppers. (Pasta making is especially enjoyable if you have a manual or electric pasta-rolling machine, without which I wouldn't be; not only does it roll out the dough to the degree of thickness or thinness you choose, it does a yeoman job of kneading the dough, a boon unless you feel like doing some invigorating hand-kneading as beneficent exercise.)

Then there are a few offbeat things to freeze or refrigerate for seasons of scarcity, or just for convenience—pesto, avocado puree, clarified butter, dried Cheddar, and crème frâiche.

The small collection of dessert makings goes here because these are ingredients, not finished desserts, and therefore they don't seem to fit into that formal chapter. Here we have Lime or Lemon Curd, a fine fruity garden mincemeat, and Praline Powder. Then there are other good things to keep on hand for use in sweets—candied peels and fruits, dried cherries and berries ("super-raisins"), vanilla in two or three guises, and so on. All too good to be left out.

PASTA POINTERS

The pleasure of creating our own good noodles is no longer a novelty for most enterprising cooks, especially those who own a pasta machine, but interesting flavoring possibilities for basic doughs continue to expand. What follows will include the basic pasta formula I like best—it calls for semolina flour, but all-purpose flour will do—plus a few good variations.

First, though, may we talk about some misbegotten ideas for "fancy" pastas that are still on the loose? Chocolate? All wrong for any savory sauce I can think of, so let's keep this flavoring for desserts. Carrots? The pasta is pretty, but no flavor can be detected; and the same can be said of noodles tinted with beets, tomatoes, artichoke hearts, and any manner of other colorful edibles.

Spinach noodles *are* good, though, as proved long ago by the Italians; and although there is no lack of recipes for these, directions are included below for anyone who needs them. Other flavorings I like for pasta are scallions, certain herbs, mushrooms, nuts (especially hazelnuts and black walnuts), and sweet red peppers or pimientos, which lovers of "hot stuff" can fortify with hot peppers according to conscience.

Pasta is made most quickly by using a food processor and a pasta machine, but all the noodles here are easily makable with nothing more than a board for mixing, kneading, and rolling, a rolling pin, and a sharp knife. How-to's for both machine- and hand-mixed doughs are included with the master recipe for Semolina Noodles.

 SEASON:
Any time

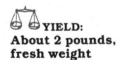 **YIELD:**
About 2 pounds, fresh weight

STORE:
Fresh, for 2 or 3 days in the refrigerator, 1 month in the freezer; partly dried, 2 to 3 weeks in the refrigerator, 1 month in the freezer; completely dried, 3 months in a cool cupboard or the refrigerator, longer in the freezer

Semolina Noodles: Master Recipe & Outline of Methods

The portion of the grain of durum wheat that is called "semolina" makes the best homemade noodles of all because of its high gluten content. Pasta made from semolina flour is pleasantly resistant to the tooth, not mushy, after it has been cooked "al dente," which is why the best imported pastas are made from it. Semolina flour isn't a supermarket item (unless your market is more super than most), but it is widely available as "pasta flour" at health-food stores and specialty food shops. The finer the grind, the better.

Don't be discouraged from tackling semolina noodles by the occasional word (in cookbooks that should know better) that semolina flour is too difficult to use at home. It isn't, actually; although the semolina seems reluctant to combine with the eggs at first, it makes a firm, satiny dough when it is kneaded very thoroughly.

All-purpose flour can be substituted for semolina in this or any of the other noodle recipes; dough made with it usually requires less kneading than semolina dough, and the noodles will be less firm after cooking.

The outline of methods below tells how to make noodles entirely by hand; by hand with a pasta machine used for rolling and cutting the dough; and by using a food processor to make a dough that can be rolled and cut either by hand or by a pasta machine.

**3 cups semolina flour (or substitute all-purpose
   flour for half or all the semolina)**

1½ teaspoons salt, or to taste

3 eggs, slightly beaten

2 tablespoons olive oil

2 to 4 tablespoons water, as required

**Additional flour for dusting dough (all-purpose flour
   will be fine)**

1. Mix and knead the dough by one of the following methods.

To mix and knead pasta dough by hand: Heap the flour in a bowl or on a kneading surface and make a hollow in the center of the heap. Place the salt, eggs, oil, and 2 tablespoons of the water in the hollow. Stirring with your fingers, mix the salt, eggs, oil, and water with a little of the immediately surrounding flour, moving gradually outward as you draw the remaining flour into the dough. When all the flour has been roughly incorporated (you will have a collection of clumps), sprinkle on and work in as much more of the remaining water as needed to make a dough; be careful not to add too much (but if you do, that can be remedied by kneading in additional flour later).

If you're kneading by hand: Gather the dough into a ball, scrape the board clean, dust it with flour, and knead the dough vigorously, using more flour on the board as necessary to prevent sticking, until the dough is smooth and elastic; if in doubt about the kneading, overdo it instead of skimping. Wrap the dough in plastic and let it rest for 30 minutes.

If you're kneading by pasta machine: Mix the dough as described in step 1; gather it into a ball. Set the rollers of your pasta machine at their widest setting. Divide the dough into three or more parts for convenience in handling; cover all but one piece with plastic wrap or foil. Flatten the remaining portion of dough into a rough strip that will pass through the rollers. Pass the dough through the rollers repeatedly to knead it, folding the edges to the center after each rolling. As you roll, dust the strip very lightly with added flour only if necessary to prevent sticking; use a dry pastry brush to remove excess flour. When the strip is satiny it has been kneaded enough and is ready for final rolling and cutting (step 2). Lay it aside for the moment and repeat the kneading process with the remaining dough.

To mix and knead pasta dough in a food processor: Place the flour and salt in the bowl of a food processor fitted with the steel knife and flick the motor on and off briefly to mix them. Break the eggs into a cup, beat them a little with a fork, add the oil and half of the water, start the machine, and add the liquid ingredients gradually through the feed tube. Continue to run the machine for about 30 seconds; if the dough is still crumbly, gradually add as much of the remaining water as you need to create a dough ball that whirls around on top of the blade. Let the dough whirl for 15 seconds or so to knead it thoroughly. Remove the dough, wrap it in plastic, and let it rest for 30 minutes.

2. Proceed to roll and cut the dough:

To roll and cut pasta dough by machine: Pass each strip of dough that has been kneaded with the pasta machine through successively closer settings of the rollers until you have dough of the desired thickness (the #5 setting of most machines is neither too thick nor too thin). Hang each rolled-out dough strip on a pasta rack to dry slightly, or lay it on a lightly floured cloth; roll the remaining strips. Let the strips dry for a short time (how long "a short time" turns out to be will depend on the dampness or dryness of the atmosphere), until they are firm but still pliable to the touch; if overdried, the sheets will be too brittle to permit the cutting of neat noodles. (The only recourse, in extreme cases, is to let the sheets go on to dry completely, then crumble them into bits suitable for soup.) Using the machine's cutters, cut wide or narrow noodles, as preferred; or, for special shapes, use a knife or pastry wheel or cookie cutter. If you will be cooking the pasta within 2 or 3 hours, gather small handfuls of the cut noodles as they emerge from the machine and form them into loose coils on a tray or wire rack and leave them until they are wanted.

To roll and cut pasta dough by hand: Cut the kneaded and rested dough into 4 portions (or more if your rolling surface is small) and wrap all but one piece in plastic or a cloth. On a floured surface, roll the remaining piece of dough out until it is uniformly very thin, stretching it as you roll. Set the piece aside on a floured cloth (or hang it up) to dry until it is firm but still pliable, meanwhile rolling out the remaining pieces. (Experienced pasta makers use a thin, straight rolling pin that is rather like a broomstick and roll the sheet of dough around the pin as they work, frequently stretching the layers out toward the ends of the roller with smoothing motions of the hands. This is fun after the knack is acquired; you must keep the dough dusted with just enough flour to keep the layers from sticking together as the roller does its work of thinning and enlarging the sheet rolled around it.) However you have rolled them, let the sheets of dough dry slightly as described; then carefully fold or roll the partially dried sheet of dough and cut crosswise slices of the desired width, using a very sharp serrated knife. Unroll the noodles, toss them to separate the

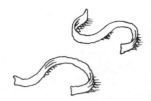

strands, and leave them in loose tangles if they will be cooked within an hour or two; otherwise dry them (step 3). For special shapes, use a sharp knife, a pastry wheel, or a cookie cutter to cut the rolled-out dough.

3. *Drying and storing the noodles:* To dry noodles partly or completely, drape them over a pasta rack, the cloth-covered back of a chair, or other improvised arrangement, or spread them in loose tangles on wire cake racks and turn them occasionally until they have reached the dryness wanted.

For refrigerator or freezer storage, dry the noodles about halfway, so they bend instead of breaking when tested. Gather them into plastic bags, close the bags tightly, expelling as much air as possible, and refrigerate or freeze them.

For cool pantry (or long-term refrigerator) storage, continue drying the noodles until they are brittle, then package them airtight.

To cook semolina noodles: Whether cooked fresh or after partial or complete drying, semolina noodles should be cooked in a large quantity of boiling water, salted if you wish; boil at least 5 quarts to cook a pound of noodles. Add salt to taste after boiling begins, then drop in a few noodles at a time to keep the water boiling at a moderate pace and to keep the strands from sticking together. Fresh noodles are done very soon after they float to the top; this may take only 2 or 3 minutes. Dried noodles take longer, but not as long as store-bought pasta. Test by biting a strand; you don't want to overcook these delicate morsels. Drain the noodles promptly, either by lifting them out with pasta tongs or in a colander, and sauce them promptly, tossing them with two forks.

Porcini Pasta

Dark and earthy in flavor, noodles made with dried porcini as the key ingredient are pure manna for mushroom lovers. Porcini are boletes (boletus mushrooms), often imported in dried form from Italy and France as porcini, funghi secchi porcini, cèpes, and so on. Most dried mushrooms imported from Chile are closely related to European boletes; they may also be used.

Rich in taste, porcini noodles are good enough to be a main dish on their own. Sauce them simply with butter and grated cheese; or have them with a toss of sliced fresh mushrooms sautéed in butter, plus more butter and fresh-ground pepper at serving time; or reduce heavy cream for a sauce and add fresh-snipped chives or a combination of favorite fresh herbs; or just butter the hot noodles lightly and add a spoonful of sauce from the meat or poultry you are serving.

SEASON:
Any time

YIELD:
About 2 pounds, fresh weight

 STORE:
Fresh, 3 days in refrigerator, 1 month in freezer; partly dried, 2 weeks in refrigerator, 1 month in freezer; dried, 3 months in refrigerator, longer in freezer

1 ounce (about ⅔ cup) dried porcini or other high-quality dried boletus mushrooms

1½ cups very hot water

2 eggs, slightly beaten

1½ to 2 teaspoons salt, or to taste

2½ cups semolina flour (or substitute all-purpose flour)

Additional semolina or all-purpose flour for rolling noodles

1. Combine the porcini and the hot water in a small bowl. Cover the bowl and let the mushrooms soak for 30 minutes, stirring them occasionally to loosen any sand.

2. Lift the mushrooms from the liquid into a saucepan, using a slotted spoon. Carefully pour the soaking liquid into the pan, leaving any sand behind (or strain the liquid through a fine sieve lined with cheesecloth).

3. Cook the mushrooms, covered, over low heat until they are soft, about 20 minutes. Lift the pieces into the container of a blender or a food processor with a slotted spoon. Simmer the liquid until it has reduced to 3 to 4 tablespoons and add it to the mushroom pieces, again being careful to leave behind any grit. Puree the mushrooms with the liquid to a smooth paste; you should have about ⅔ cup. Cool the puree.

4. Following the general instructions in the master recipe for pasta (Semolina Noodles, page 290), combine the pureed mushrooms, eggs, salt, and semolina to make a dough; if necessary, add a little more liquid (a few drops of water) or a little more semolina to make a dough that is neither too dry nor too sticky. Knead, rest, roll, and cut the dough as described in the master recipe. Use the mushroom pasta fresh, or store it as described in the master recipe. The cooking procedure is the same.

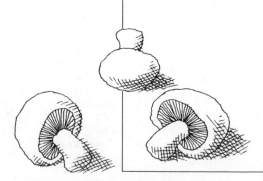

Peanut Noodles

Noodles made with peanuts ground to a slightly grainy paste are especially good as a cold dish sauced with an Oriental-style vinaigrette such as the dressing following the noodle directions. They are also dandy served hot, simply tossed with either melted or slightly browned butter.

For either hot or cold dishes, peanut noodles need only short cooking; directions are in the recipe.

⅔ cup dry-roasted unsalted peanuts (or substitute 6 tablespoons of creamy-style peanut butter)

1½ to 2 teaspoons salt, to taste

2 eggs

Water, as needed

2 cups semolina flour (or substitute all-purpose flour)

Additional flour for kneading and dusting dough (all-purpose flour is satisfactory)

1. Using a food processor or a blender, grind the peanuts to a slightly grainy paste, scraping down the sides of the container once or twice. Measure 6 tablespoons.

2. If you are making the dough in the food processor, return the measured nut paste to it (no need to wash the container). Add the salt, eggs, and 3 tablespoons of water, if you're using semolina flour; use only 2 tablespoons water if you have substituted all-purpose flour. Mix the ingredients with one or two on-off operations of the motor. Add the flour and process the ingredients for about 30 seconds. If the mixture is too dry and quite crumbly, add an additional tablespoonful of water gradually through the feed tube while the motor runs. If the dough still doesn't form a cohesive ball, add more drops of water cautiously, processing the dough until it forms a ball that whirls around on top of the blade. Let the ball of dough whirl for 15 seconds or more to knead it well. Remove the dough, wrap it in plastic wrap, and let it rest for about 30 minutes.

3. If you are making the noodle dough by hand, refer to the general instructions in the master noodle recipe (Semolina Noodles, page 290), and use the mixing method given there, adding the nut paste with the eggs, which should be lightly beaten first.

4. Following the outline of methods in the master pasta recipe (Semolina Noodles), roll out the dough, dry it slightly, and cut it into fine noodles. Spread the noodles on a floured cloth or work surface and let them dry briefly, for up to an hour or two; they should still be pliable when they are cooked or stored. (This pasta isn't suitable for complete drying and shelf storage.)

 SEASON:
Any time

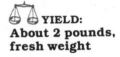 **YIELD:**
About 2 pounds, fresh weight

STORE:
Up to 3 days in the refrigerator; or freeze for up to 1 month

5. If the noodles are not to be used immediately, bag them in plastic and refrigerate or freeze them.

To cook peanut noodles: Drop them by handfuls into at least 5 quarts of boiling, salted water. Stir them, let the water return to a boil, turn off the heat, cover the pot, and let the noodles poach until they are just tender, a matter of 2 or 3 minutes.

Drain them at once and serve them hot; or, for a cold dish, drain the noodles, drop them into a bowlful of cold water and ice, and let them stand until they are thoroughly chilled. They may then be drained and refrigerated for a few hours before they are sauced and served; or drain them and serve them at once with a cold sauce. (An Oriental sauce for cold noodles follows.)

Chilled Peanut Noodles in an Oriental Sauce

For 1 pound of fresh peanut noodles, cooked and chilled as described in preceding recipe

¼ cup imported soy sauce

¼ cup Oriental (roasted) sesame oil

3 tablespoons dark Chinese vinegar (or half balsamic vinegar, half red wine vinegar)

3 tablespoons smooth peanut butter or dry-roasted unsalted peanuts ground to a paste

2 teaspoons sugar

Salt, if needed

About ¼ teaspoon Hot Red Pepper Oil (page 178), or more to taste

½ to ¾ cup crisp fresh scallion rings, including part of the green tops

Whisk everything except the scallions together to make a smooth dressing. Taste; adjust the seasonings, adding more of any ingredient to suit yourself. Toss the dressing and scallions with the cooked, chilled, and drained noodles and serve them at once.

Hazelnut or Black Walnut Noodles

SEASON:
Any time

YIELD:
About 2 pounds,
fresh weight

STORE:
For up to 3 days in
the refrigerator; or
for up to 1 month
in the freezer

More nutted noodles, these are made with either toasted hazelnuts (filberts) or black walnuts. They are especially rich in flavor and therefore highly compatible with game dishes, sauced meats (even pot roast), and poultry.

Follow the directions for making Peanut Noodles, page 295, substituting 5 tablespoons of hazelnut or black walnut paste (see below) for the 6 tablespoons of peanut paste or peanut butter called for. Cook the noodles in exactly the same way and serve them hot, either with melted butter, browned butter, a mushroom sauce, or a spoonful of the sauce of the meat or poultry they are served with.

Preparing the nuts:

For hazelnut noodles: First toast a generous ½ cup of hazelnuts on a baking sheet in a 350° oven until their skins are crisp and the nuts smell rich and toasty, about 8 minutes; shake the pan a few times as the nuts bake. Rub the hazelnuts in a towel to remove as much of the brown skin as possible (it doesn't matter if patches remain), then grind them to a grainy paste in a food processor or blender and measure out the needed 5 tablespoons.

For black walnut noodles: Be sure to use absolutely fresh (and therefore flavorful) nutmeats. The distinctive flavor of these native American nuts, which are rich in oil, is highly perishable once the nuts have been shelled. Taste a sample, if possible, before purchasing, and store your supply in the freezer. To make the paste, use a food processor or a blender to grind a generous ½ cup of the nuts, scraping down the sides of the container once or twice and stopping while the texture is still a little grainy; measure 5 tablespoons of paste.

Any surplus nut paste of either kind is a delicious snack for the cook—spread it on a cracker, add a sprinkle of salt.

SEASON:
Any time

⚖️ YIELD:
**About 2½ pounds,
fresh weight**

📦 STORE:
**Fresh, for 3 days
in the refrigerator,
1 month in the
freezer; partly
dried, 2 weeks in
the refrigerator, 1
month in the
freezer;
completely dried,
3 months in a cool
cupboard or the
refrigerator, longer
in the freezer**

Spinach Noodles

Green noodles are especially attractive to both eye and mouth when they are mingled half-and-half with golden egg noodles, preferably also made with semolina. (See the master noodle recipe, page 290). Cook and drain the two kinds of noodles separately to keep their colors bright, toss them with butter plus freshly grated Parmesan and perhaps a little heated cream, and you have "straw and hay," as the Italians call this fine fresh dish.

I like spinach noodles best when they are made with the freshest possible green leaves. If the greengrocer fails you, substitute a 10-ounce package of frozen spinach; simply thaw, drain, and puree it. (Frozen spinach was blanched, therefore partly cooked, before it went into the freezer.)

**1 pound fresh spinach, picked over, roots trimmed
    off, well washed and drained**

1½ teaspoons salt, or to taste

2 eggs

**4 cups semolina flour (or substitute all-purpose
    flour)**

**Additional flour for dusting dough (all-purpose flour
    is fine)**

1. Bring 2 quarts of water to a boil in a large pot. Drop in the spinach, stir it, and boil it until it is tender, about 3 minutes. Lift the spinach into a colander or sieve, using a slotted spoon. Drain it very well, pressing hard with the back of the spoon to remove as much moisture as possible.

2. Puree the spinach in a blender or food processor, running the motor until the texture is smooth. If the spinach seems at all watery at this point, drain it further in a fine-meshed sieve, or use a sieve lined with cheesecloth to absorb moisture. Measure 1 cup of the pulp and let it cool.

3. Following the general instructions in the master noodle recipe (Semolina Noodles, page 290), combine the pureed spinach, the salt, and the eggs with the semolina flour. Mix, knead, rest, roll, and cut the dough as described. If after kneading the dough seems soft or sticky (this can happen), work in a little additional semolina, and dust the dough generously with semolina or with all-purpose flour as it is rolled.

Herbed Green Noodles

Among the most flavorful of green noodles, these are made with fresh herbs; dried herbs won't do. If you have plenty of fresh herbs, experiment with other kinds or combinations. Chinese or garlic chives are a good bet, and a combination of scallions, thyme, a few leaves of sage, a little fresh rosemary, and a good amount of parsley makes marvelous noodles to go with hearty roasts of pork or veal.

1 cup (packed) fresh basil or sweet marjoram leaves, or a combination of basil, marjoram, thyme, and snipped chives

1 cup (packed) flat-leaf (Italian) parsley, leaves only

2 medium scallions, sliced, including part of the green tops

3 eggs

2 teaspoons salt, or to taste

¼ teaspoon freshly ground white pepper

4 cups semolina or all-purpose flour, or 2 cups each semolina and all-purpose flour

Additional all-purpose flour for dusting dough

1. Puree the herbs, including the parsley and scallions, in a blender or food processor until very smooth. If the puree seems watery, drain it in a fine sieve lined with cheesecloth.

2. Following the general instructions in the master noodle recipe (Semolina Noodles, page 290), combine the puree, eggs, salt, pepper, and flour. Mix, knead, rest, roll, and cut the dough as described. Dry the noodles slightly before you use or store them, for easier handling.

☀ SEASON:
Early summer through fall

⚖ YIELD:
About 2½ pounds, fresh weight

🍎 STORE:
Fresh, for 3 days in the refrigerator, 1 month in the freezer

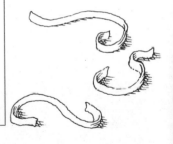

✪ SEASON:
Any, but fresh red
peppers are
abundant in late
summer and early
fall

⚖ YIELD:
About 2½ pounds,
fresh weight

🗃 STORE:
Fresh, for 3 days
in the refrigerator,
up to 1 month in
the freezer; partly
dried, 2 to 3 weeks
in the refrigerator;
dried, 3 months in
the refrigerator or
freezer

NOTE:

To prepare the
pepper puree,
steam 6 very large
or 8 large sweet
red peppers,
stemmed, seeded,
cored, and cut up,
until very soft.
Press the pulp
through a food
mill, or puree the
peppers in a
blender or a food
processor. Or drain
and puree three 4-
ounce jars of
canned pimientos.

Red Pepper Pasta, Mild or Hot

In their mildest version, these noodles take all their flavor from sweet red peppers or canned pimientos. From that baseline you can move toward more hotness, according to taste: Add fresh red chilies or fresh hot peppers to the sweet peppers before they're steamed and pureed; or stir into the sweet-pepper puree some ground, dried red chilies (not the multi-ingredient commercial chili powder), or a little ground hot red (Cayenne) pepper, or hot or medium Hungarian paprika. The ultimate degree of hotness is up to you. Experiment, unless you already know the sky's the limit for piquancy as far as your palate is concerned.

Serve any version of these salmon-pink noodles with chicken simmered in sour cream, or with a mild veal stew, or with any fish, fowl, or meat dish that can use a zippy accompaniment. And try ladling some good chili (the real thing, with no beans) over a nest of red pepper noodles and topping the composition with grated "store" cheese.

1 cup pureed steamed sweet red peppers (see Note) or canned pimientos, plus (optional) any of the following, or a combination, for "hot" noodles:

From a pinch to ½ teaspoon ground hot red (Cayenne) pepper

Up to 4 tablespoons hot or medium Hungarian paprika

Up to 4 tablespoons pure chili powder (ground dried chilies)

Or include 1 or 2 fresh red chili peppers or a few small fresh hot peppers when preparing the sweet pepper puree

3 egg yolks

2 teaspoons salt, or to taste

4 cups all-purpose flour

Additional all-purpose flour for dusting dough

1. Place the pepper puree in a fine-meshed sieve lined with two layers of *dry* cheesecloth and set over a bowl. Let the puree drain for as long as convenient, an hour or longer. You should have 1 cup, give or take, of firm puree.

2. Add to the puree any of the hot-pepper enhancements, if you wish. Following the instructions in the master noodle recipe (Semolina Noodles, page 290), combine the puree, egg yolks, salt, and flour. Mix, knead, rest, roll, and cut the dough as described. Dry the pepper pasta partly or completely, or use it at once or store it fresh.

DESSERT MAKINGS TO KEEP ON HAND

Together with the dozens of desserts in a preceding chapter, the pretty provisions that follow will give you a running start on the last course, whether it be for a planned or an impromptu occasion.

There are many delicious uses for Lime or Lemon Curd (also called "butter" or "cheese") beyond those detailed with the recipe, but one of the best combinations is either kind of curd served over or under fresh or thawed frozen blueberries; you don't have to reserve this rich harmony of flavors for a tart shell in the way suggested in the mini-recipe on page 302.

The Praline Powder is scarcely less versatile; and the three-fruit meatless mincemeat that follows it is a fine fallback for filling purchased tiny tart shells when there is a dessert emergency and no time to make homemade pastry.

The recipes that round out the section—for candied fruits, dried berries and cherries, and brandy-based vanilla extract and Vanilla Sugar—are especially valuable when fine baking deserves the best of ingredients.

Lime or Lemon Curd, "Butter," or "Cheese"

No matter how many times one version or another of this limy (or lemony), buttery-sweet, keepable delicacy has been described in print, there is always someone who wants to know how to make it, once it has been tasted. So here is how to add to your store of pantry luxuries an endlessly useful, delicious mixture. Serve it for breakfast, in place of fruit preserves, to spread on toast, toasted brioche, or Portuguese sweet bread; use it as filling between layers of crisp puff pastry; or spoon it into individual tart shells; or make Lime and Blueberry Tart, page 302; or spread the curd between sponge-cake layers for a formal dessert, or between pairs of thin cookies for an impromptu hit.

Made with fresh summer limes, this custardy delight is especially good, reminiscent of nothing so much as a superb Key lime pie; but lemon curd has its votes for first place, too. Either version, made as directed here, is delicate and fluffy, not overfirm.

Lime or lemon curd keeps like a charm in the fridge for as long as 3 months; experimental jars have remained in perfect condition much longer.

 SEASON:
Any time, but limes are most plentiful in summer

 YIELD:
3 cups

 **STORE:**
In the refrigerator for 3 months

Enough ripe, fragrant, bright-skinned limes or lemons (about 3) to yield 1 tablespoon of grated zest and ½ cup of strained juice

½ cup (1 stick) plus 2 tablespoons unsalted butter, cut up

Pinch of salt

4 egg yolks

1 whole egg

1¼ cups sugar

1. Run 2 inches of water into the base pan of a double boiler and set it over medium heat to come to a brisk simmer.

2. Grate or shred enough zest—the thin outer colored layer of the peel only, no white pith—from washed and dried limes or lemons to make 1 tablespoon (packed) of lime zest, 1½ tablespoons (packed) lemon zest. Place the zest in the top pan of the double boiler. From whichever fruit you're using, extract and strain enough juice to make ½ cup; add the juice to the zest. Drop the cut-up butter and the pinch of salt into the pan. Set aside.

3. Beat the egg yolks and whole egg together at high speed in the large bowl of an electric mixer until they are foamy; gradually add the sugar, continuing to beat the mixture until it is pale, fluffy, and very thick, about 5 minutes.

4. Scrape the egg mixture into the double-boiler top and set the top into the base containing simmering water. At once begin whisking the mixture; cook it, whisking it constantly, until it has thickened smoothly and is steaming hot, about 10 minutes. Be careful not to overcook the curd; it is done when it will coat a metal or wooden spoon heavily. Remove the upper pan from the hot water.

5. Pour the curd into a fine-meshed sieve set over a bowl and press it through with a rubber spatula, leaving the shreds of zest behind (discard these). Scrape the curd into sterilized (page 327), dry jars, let it cool uncovered, then cap the jars with sterilized lids. Refrigerate the curd.

Lime & Blueberry Tart

Please try the lime curd as the basis of what is probably the best fresh blueberry tart ever tasted: Spread half an inch of the curd in a fully baked and cooled tart shell and top it with a closely packed layer of fully ripe (and therefore flavorful) blueberries. Chill the tart until serving time, preferably for no more than 2 or 3 hours. Just before serving the tart, dust Vanilla Sugar (page 312) or superfine granulated sugar over the berries. A little lightly whipped but unsweetened cream might be served with the tart.

Praline Powder For Desserts

Ajar of this stardust powder, made by pulverizing what is basically a brittle confection of toasted nuts, is culinary money in the bank. It keeps for months at room temperature, even longer in the freezer, always ready to enhance desserts and pastries; I have a test jar that is well into its second year, with no change in quality. Use your favorite kind of nuts; chefs tend to concentrate on hazelnuts (filberts) and almonds, but pecans and pistachios make excellent praline, too.

Ways to use praline:

• As a quick fix for store-bought (or your own homemade) ice cream: Soften a quart of vanilla, chocolate, or eggnog ice cream and fold in ⅓ cup of Praline Powder; refreeze the ice cream and serve it with optional whipped cream and a sprinkling of more Praline Powder.

• Spoon chocolate or fudge sauce over coffee or vanilla ice cream, top with praline.

• For a crunchy topping on a fruit tart that will be served warm, sprinkle the tart with Praline Powder a few minutes before the end of baking. (The topping will tend to melt if the tart stands very long.)

• *Nut-Crusted Crème Brûlée:* Make custard for crème brûlée according to your best recipe and chill it in a shallow serving dish that can tolerate the heat of the broiler. Shortly before serving time, strew the custard with Praline Powder and broil the top about 4 inches from the preheated broiler element until it is crisp, watching it constantly to prevent burning—forming the crust takes only moments. Refrigerate the dish for up to half an hour; if the topping is broiled too far ahead of time it will lose its crunch.

• Fold Praline Powder into stiffly whipped cream and fill a chocolate cake that has been sliced horizontally into several extra-thin layers; spread plain whipped cream on the top and border it with a band of densely sprinkled praline.

• Top servings of fruit compote with Praline Powder just before serving.

• Sprinkle Praline Powder over buttered waffles or French toast.

1 cup whole blanched almonds or unblanched hazelnuts, lightly toasted (see Note)

¾ cup sugar

3 tablespoons light corn syrup

3 tablespoons water

¼ teaspoon salt, optional

SEASON:
Any time

YIELD:
About 2 cups

STORE:
For months at cool room temperature; indefinitely in freezer

NOTE:

To toast the nuts, spread them on a jelly-roll pan or cookie sheet and bake them in a preheated 350° oven for 7 or 8 minutes, stirring them every minute or two; be careful not to let them become more than slightly gold inside (break a sample to check). Cool the nuts completely. It isn't necessary to remove the skins of the hazelnuts after they are toasted, but rub off any loose bits if you wish.

1. Preheat the oven to 250°.

2. Butter a cookie sheet lightly. Spread the nuts on it and place them in the oven to warm through. Leave them for 10 minutes, shaking the pan once or twice. Turn off the oven, open the oven door, and leave the pan in it.

3. Combine the sugar, corn syrup, and water in a small heavy saucepan. Bring the mixture to a boil over high heat; after boiling starts, wipe down with a wet pastry brush any sugar crystals on the sides of the pan. Boil the syrup until it begins to turn a light caramel color—if you use a candy/jelly thermometer, the reading will be between 320° and 340°. Quickly add the salt, if you are using it, and the warmed nuts. Stir the mixture quickly, then pour it onto the buttered cookie sheet that held the nuts; spread it out with a wooden spoon or spatula.

4. Cool the brittle completely, then break it into small pieces. Working in batches, grind it to a fairly fine powder in a food processor or a blender. Store the Praline Powder airtight.

SEASON:
Fall, before frost

YIELD:
About 8 pints

STORE:
Sealed, for at least a year in a cool cupboard or pantry; unsealed, for up to a year in the refrigerator

Green Tomato, Apple, & Pear Mincemeat

The only meat in this fruity compound is in its name. Delicious as old-fashioned mincemeat-with-meat can be, it is a heavy mixture, often a bit too much for today's appetites; and because of its meat and/or suet content, meaty mincemeat also requires canning under steam pressure if it is to be safely preserved for shelf storage. This formula produces a mincemeat that is safely canned in a boiling-water bath; it can also be refrigerated unsealed.

If you don't have a tomato patch to raid for green fruit, check farm stands in the fall, before frost is due. Use completely green tomatoes; they should not show white, yellow, or pinkish cheeks. If some tomatoes show color, set them aside in a warm but not sunny spot to ripen for the table.

Using the mincemeat:

•Straight from the jar, a pint will fill an 8-inch pie adequately. With the addition (which I recommend) of diced fresh apple, some nuts, perhaps a few snipped dried apricots (an especially happy touch), and an added tot of rum or brandy, a pint will fill a 9-inch pie.

•Use the mincemeat in any cookie recipe calling for the store-bought kind as an ingredient or filling.

3 quarts coarsely chopped completely green
    tomatoes, scrubbed and trimmed of stem scars

1 tablespoon non-iodized salt

1½ quarts diced, peeled, and cored firm, tart
    apples, the firmer the better

1 quart diced, peeled, and cored firm, slightly
    underripe pears

2½ cups dark seedless raisins

Grated zest (outer skin only, no white pith) and
    chopped pulp of 1 large or 2 medium oranges

Grated zest of 1½ large lemons

½ cup cider vinegar

½ cup undiluted frozen apple concentrate, thawed

3½ cups (packed) light brown sugar

2 teaspoons ground cinnamon

½ teaspoon ground allspice

½ teaspoon ground cloves

½ teaspoon ground ginger

½ cup dark rum, preferably Jamaican

1. Stir the chopped green tomatoes and salt together, then scrape them into a colander and let them drain for 2 hours.

2. Combine the drained tomatoes with the apples, pears, raisins, orange zest and pulp, lemon zest, vinegar, apple concentrate, sugar, cinnamon, allspice, cloves, and ginger in a preserving pan. Bring the mixture to a boil over medium-high heat. Lower the heat and cook the mincemeat, uncovered, stirring it often, until it is thick enough to mound in a spoon when a sample is dipped up, about 1 hour. Be careful to stir often enough to prevent sticking toward the end of cooking.

3. Stir in the rum and ladle the boiling-hot mincemeat into hot, clean pint canning jars, leaving ½ inch of headspace; remove any air bubbles (page 324). Seal the jars with new two-piece canning lids, according to manufacturer's directions, and process them in a boiling-water bath (page 325) for 25 minutes. Cool, label, and store the jars. Let the mincemeat mellow for a month before using it.

Alternatively: Store the mincemeat, covered but unsealed, in the refrigerator.

SEASON:
Any time

YIELD:
About ½ pound

STORE:
For many weeks at room temperature, in the refrigerator, or in a cool cupboard or pantry

Candied Orange Peel

Perfectly delicious just to munch, full of flavor for cakes and other baking, and remarkably simple to prepare, home-candied peel leaves only the slenderest excuse for purchasing the commercial product. Double this recipe if you like—the timings are about the same.

These directions apply equally well to grapefruit and lemon peel. Just don't mix various kinds of citrus in a batch—to keep the flavors pristine, it's better to candy them separately.

3 medium-large, bright-skinned oranges

1½ cups water

1¼ cups sugar

3 tablespoons light corn syrup

1. To remove the peel from the oranges, score it into quarters, if necessary cutting a slice from the top and the base of the orange in order to free the sections. Using a blunt knife or the bowl of a spoon, pry the quarters of peel off the fruit. Save the oranges for another use.

2. Scrape as much as possible of the white pith from the inside of each peel section; a serrated grapefruit spoon does this fast, but the edge of a teaspoon also serves.

3. Combine the peel with enough water to float it generously in a saucepan. Bring to a boil and simmer for 10 minutes. Drain the peel, add fresh water, and repeat. Drain the peel again, add fresh water, and cook the peel until it is tender when poked with a knife tip, 15 to 25 minutes. Drain the peel in a sieve.

4. When the peel has cooled, snip it into ¼-inch strips (kitchen scissors do this fast).

5. In the same saucepan (no need to rinse it), combine 1½ cups of water with the sugar and corn syrup. Bring to a boil and boil for 3 minutes. Add the drained peel and cook at a simmer, covered, until the peel begins to look translucent; remove the cover and continue to cook the peel until the syrup has reduced to a spoonful or two, watching carefully toward the end to prevent burning.

6. Fork the peel onto wire racks to cool and dry. If you'd like it to be crisp, set the racks in a barely warm oven (heated by a pilot light, a viewing light, or by being turned on briefly at "warm"); or just leave the peel at room temperature until its texture suits you. For a sugary finish for peel to be served as a sweetmeat, roll the strips in granulated sugar while they are warm, then dry them thoroughly.

Candied Sour Cherries

Because they actually taste like what they are, I like to candy a batch of canned sour cherries when I'm gathering the ingredients for holiday baking. Although they are not as shapely or as improbably red as commercially prepared cherries—they are unimposing in size and dark in color—they are rich in cherry flavor, which is just what's needed in, for example, California Christmas Fruitcake (page 236).

2 cans (16 ounces each) sour cherries packed in water*

3 cups sugar

¼ cup light corn syrup

1. Drain the cherries, reserving the juice. Measure 1⅓ cups of the juice into a large, shallow pan (a skillet or a sauté pan is ideal); if there isn't enough juice, add water.

2. Add the sugar and corn syrup to the juice and boil the mixture, uncovered, over medium-high heat until the syrup spins a short thread when drops are poured from a spoon, 4 to 5 minutes.

3. Add the cherries and cook them, uncovered, over medium heat until they begin to be translucent, shaking the pan often, 20 to 25 minutes. (If the syrup gets quite thick and threatens to caramelize, add a tablespoonful of water when this happens, and watch the cooking carefully.) Remove the pan from the heat. Pour the cherries and syrup into a bowl and let them stand for several hours or overnight.

4. Return the cherries and syrup to the pan and bring them to a boil over medium heat; simmer until the syrup is thick but not caramelized, 3 to 5 minutes. Remove from the heat.

5. Lift the cherries onto wire racks set over a baking sheet, using a two-tined fork or (if you're adept) a pair of chopsticks. Let them drain until dripping stops, then transfer the racks to a clean pan or pans and dry the cherries in an oven set at 200°, watching them to be sure they don't become too desiccated; remove and cool them when they are still slightly tacky, after about 20 to 30 minutes. When they have cooled, they should be only slightly sticky. If they seem damp, return them to the oven for as long as needed, keeping an eye on them. Cool the cherries.

6. Store the cherries in a closed plastic bag or container, or a glass jar with a snug lid.

SEASON:
Any time

YIELD:
About 1 pound

STORE
At room temperature, in the refrigerator, or in a cool cupboard or pantry for up to 6 months; freeze for longer storage

*NOTE:

If fresh cherries are available (they are scarce), pit them and simmer them until just tender in water to cover. then proceed with the recipe.

SEASON:
Any time

YIELD:
About 1 pound

STORE:
For several months at room temperature, in a cool cupboard or pantry, or in the refrigerator

Candied Pineapple

Unless you can purchase commercially candied pineapple that tastes like fruit, not Kleenex, it's well worth while to convert canned slices or wedges into a flavorful confection or baking ingredient.

2 cans (20 ounces each) unsweetened sliced pineapple or pineapple chunks canned in pineapple juice

2⅔ cups sugar

¼ cup light corn syrup

1. Drain the pineapple, reserving the juice. Measure 1½ cups of the juice into a large, shallow pan (a skillet or sauté pan is ideal); if there is insufficient juice, add water.

2. Combine the sugar and corn syrup with the juice and boil the mixture, uncovered, over medium-high heat until the syrup spins a short thread when drops are poured from a spoon, about 4 minutes.

3. Add the pineapple, which should fit into the pan in a single layer; if you are using slices and they won't all fit, cut some into halves or quarters. Cook the pineapple, uncovered, over medium-low heat, shaking the pan and basting the pieces often until they are translucent, about 45 minutes. If the syrup thickens too much and threatens to caramelize at any point, add about a tablespoonful of water and lower the heat a little. In any case, watch the pineapple carefully after it has cooked awhile. Remove the pan from the heat.

4. Lift the slices onto wire racks and let them drain over a jelly-roll pan until dripping stops. (Save the syrup; use it to candy lemon or grapefruit peel, or serve it over waffles or ice cream.) Set the racks on a clean pan and dry the pineapple in a 200° oven until the surface is no longer sticky, about 30 minutes. Cool the pineapple again, pack it between sheets of plastic wrap in an airtight container, and store it at room temperature or refrigerate it.

Super-Raisins

Raisins" prepared by drying fruits other than grapes are interesting to eat, well worth preparing for themselves in spite of their one-time status as a substitute. In earlier times the dried grapes we call "raisins" and "currants" (when fresh these, too, are grapes) were imported luxuries, seldom seen at all in remote places. Cooks who couldn't obtain them found that home-dried berries and cherries were a more than satisfactory replacement. Given the recent rediscovery of America's culinary roots, it is not surprising that dried sour cherries are being sold by at least one chic purveyor of mail-order foods, with who knows what other small fruits to follow?

As the directions in the recipes indicate, preparing dried cherries, blueberries, or huckleberries is quite simple; you don't need a dehydrator, although of course you can speed up the proceedings if you have one and follow the manufacturer's directions.

If you would like to add some other fruits to your repertory, follow the cherry directions for such berries as raspberries, blackberries, black raspberries, youngberries, boysenberries, loganberries, and olallieberries. Strawberries aren't recommended for drying, as they tend to lose much of their flavor. If you should have plants of fruit properly called currants, whether red, black, or white, or can otherwise obtain them—they are now hard to find—use the blueberry directions, which should also be followed for cranberries.

•Use super-raisins, soaked as described, in place of store-bought raisins in puddings, pies, fruit or spice cakes, Irish soda bread, muffins, scones, or cookies; include them in your homemade mincemeat; or eat them as is and enjoy a nibble of concentrated fruitiness.

Dried Sweet or Sour Cherries

These drying directions produce fine results with sweet cherries, which are the only kind available to most of us. However, if you can find sour (pie) cherries, they are even more flavorful after drying; they are the starting point for Dried-Cherry Cordial (page 282).

2 pounds firm-ripe sweet or sour cherries
Sugar, if desired

1. Stem, rinse, drain, and pit the cherries, losing as little juice as possible. If sweet cherries are very large, halve them. If you are using sour cherries and wish to leave in the pits for the almond-like flavor they contribute, place the cherries in a

SEASON:
Summer

YIELD:
About 2 cups,
loosely packed, of
pitted cherries;
more if unpitted

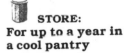
STORE:
For up to a year in
a cool pantry

sieve and plunge them into boiling water for 30 seconds, then cool them in ice-cold water and drain them well.

2. Fasten cheesecloth smoothly over two large oblong cake racks or an oven shelf, using paper clips or staples; or, if you have them, use three round cake racks with close-set spiral wires; these require no cheesecloth.

3. Arrange the cherries, cut sides up if they have been halved, close together on the racks. If desired, sprinkle them very sparingly with sugar, using no more than a tablespoonful in all. (This helps to start the emergence of juice, the first step in the drying process.)

Oven-drying method: Heat the oven to 200°. Set the racks on baking sheets (to catch any drips) and place the sheets in the oven. Leave the cherries for 20 minutes. Turn off the heat and let the oven cool with the door closed. Reset the control to between 120° and 140°, turn on the oven, and dry the cherries for 2 to 4 hours more (for halves) or for as much as 5 or 6 hours for whole cherries. The fruit is sufficiently dried when it is leathery but pliable, like raisins from a freshly opened box; don't leave the cherries until they become hard. During drying, once no more juice is being exuded, the drying process can be speeded up by removing the baking sheets under the racks. If you have a convection oven, the whole job will take less time than required by a conventional oven; consult the oven manufacturer's instructions. Lacking instructions, set the oven temperature somewhere between 120° and 140°.

Sun-drying method: Proceed through step 3. Set the racks in full sun, protecting the cherries from insects with cheese-cloth stretched over props so it does not touch the fruit. Leave the cherries in the sunlight as long as it lasts, turning them when the upper sides begin to become leathery. Store the trays indoors overnight and resume the drying the next day. Turn the cherries twice a day for the 2 to 4 days (depending on Old Sol) the drying will take. If dark or damp weather comes along, switch to the oven, set at 120° to 140°.

4. Cool the cherries completely, then store them airtight in a sterilized (page 327), dry jar. Leave the capped jar on the counter out of sunlight for 2 or 3 days and inspect it daily; if any fogging appears inside, oven-dry the cherries further, then re-store them and repeat the check for moisture.

To use the cherries: Soak them until they are soft in warm or hot water to cover; this will take an hour or more. Drain them well and pat them dry before using them in any way raisins would be used; they are especially good in fruitcakes and other baking.

Blueberry or Huckleberry Raisins

The Native Americans knew a thing or two about preserving wild foods for winter use, and the early settlers from Europe were quick to learn from them. Lacking such luxuries as genuine raisins, the colonists adopted dried blueberries with enthusiasm.

Sun drying works well for these as well as for huckleberries, which are quite flavorful though seedy; an oven method is also given below.

2 pint baskets (about 6 cups) firm-ripe blueberries or huckleberries

1. Pick over the blueberries or huckleberries, then place half of them in a sieve or colander and plunge it into a potful of boiling water to blanch for 20 to 30 seconds; remove the berries and drop them into a bowl of water and ice cubes. Repeat with the rest of the berries. Drain the berries thoroughly.

2. Cover two very large cake racks or oven shelves with tightly stretched cheesecloth and pin or staple it in place; or use several round wire cake racks with closely set spiral wires (these require no cheesecloth). Spread the berries in a single layer on the racks for the drying process.

Sun-drying method: Set the racks outdoors in full sun, covering them with propped-up cheesecloth as a defense against insects. Leave the berries in the sun all day, then bring them indoors out of the dew at night. Repeat the sunbathing the next day and for as many days as necessary, turning the berries at least once a day. The total time required will depend on the size and juiciness of the fruit as well as the heat of the sun; count on at least 2 days. The berries are dry enough when they are very firm, almost hard, yielding no moisture when squeezed. If the sunlight fails you, switch to the oven as described below. When the berries are dry, go to step 4.

Oven-drying method: Proceed through step 2. Heat the oven to 200°. Set the racks in the oven and set the timer for 20 minutes. At the end of that time, turn off the heat and leave the berries until the oven has cooled. Turn it on again at a setting between 120° and 140° and dry the berries until they are very firm. If you use a convection oven, follow by the manufacturer's directions, or set the heat between 120° and 140°.

4. Transfer the dried berries to a sterilized (page 327), dry jar or jars and cover them airtight. Set the jar where you can observe it, but keep it out of the sunlight; if any sign of moisture develops on the inside of the glass within 2 or 3 days, oven-dry the berries further and re-store them. You may want to check them again for moisture to be sure they will keep.

 SEASON:
Mid- to late summer

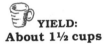 **YIELD:**
About 1½ cups

STORE:
For up to a year in a cool cupboard or pantry

TO USE DRIED BLUEBERRIES OR HUCKLEBERRIES:

Cover them with hot water and soak them until they have plumped up and softened, which usually takes a few hours. Drain them and use them exactly like raisins or currants.

SEASON: Any time

Making the Most Of Vanilla Beans

Vanilla, one more time: If you can obtain good, glossy, flexible, and highly aromatic vanilla beans, buy some and enjoy the best of vanilla flavoring in several ways besides the basic trick of adding a whole bean or a section to custards or fruits as they cook.

Brandy-Based Vanilla Extract

Pour ½ cup of Cognac or other good brandy into a clean, dry bottle that will hold it with room to spare. Cut 3 or 4 vanilla beans into inch-long pieces. Split each piece lengthwise, dropping the halves into the brandy as you go and being careful not to lose the tiny seeds, which hold much of the flavor. Cork or cap the bottle and set it aside for a few weeks. Give it a shake occasionally and check the progress of the steeping; the vanilla can be used whenever its flavor suits you. Add more brandy to top up the bottleful as the level drops with use, but give the extract a chance to stand a while after you do so. Topping-up can be repeated as long as the flavor of the extract is good.

Vanilla Sugar

A baker's secret that is easy to adopt, vanilla-flavored confectioners' sugar is the loveliest of toppings for simple cakes—poundcakes, for example—that are traditionally not iced. Granulated sugar so flavored is exquisite with fruits, and can also be used in baking.

To do: Bury whole or split vanilla beans in a container holding a pound or so of confectioners' sugar or extra-fine granulated sugar. Cover the container tightly. The sugar will be sufficiently scented with vanilla to be used in a week or so. Add more sugar to the jar when you use some of its contents; the beans will be effective for many months.

A FEW FOR THE FREEZER OR FRIDGE

Here is a purely personal selection of things to have on hand for longer or shorter storage; it could be added to without end if books were elastic.

Such a volume would include many other things that are good to store away when they are at their best—chestnuts in the fall, when they first come to market and are heavy and fine (I shell and bag a supply for the freezer); many other kinds of nuts, to be refrigerated or, better, frozen, to maintain high quality for months; choice and hard-to-get fruits and berries, which can be "put by" in the freezer for future desserts by anyone who has the help of a good general cookbook; and fruits for later preserving, either frozen as is or partially prepared, give you a running start toward unusual preserves. And more—but that's another book.

Pesto for Seasons Without Basil

For pesto lovers who may not have come across instructions for preparing a freezer supply of this wonderful basil sauce, here is the best formula I know, based on the method of Italian food expert and cookbook author Marcella Hazan.

I make this when I get my hands on a spanking-fresh bunch of *excellent* basil, from my garden or a fine farmstand. (I say "excellent" because, like a lot of other things, basil can be good, better, or best, depending.)

Fresh, unblemished basil, the bunches rinsed, leaves stripped off and blotted dry, and gently packed down to measure 3 to 3½ cups

¾ cup to 1 cup fine olive oil, to taste

3 large cloves garlic, or more to taste, peeled and chopped

3 tablespoons pine nuts (pignolias) or coarse-chopped toasted walnuts (see Note)

½ to 1 teaspoon salt, or to taste

At time of use: Parmesan and Romano cheese

1. Combine everything except the cheese in the container of a food processor, or divide the ingredients into batches and use a blender. Turn the motor on and off rapidly, scraping down the sides of the container once or twice, to process the pesto to the texture you like—some prefer a smooth pesto, others like a fine-chopped mixture. Mix the blender batches.

2. Pack the pesto into small freezer containers such as

 **SEASON:
Midsummer to fall**

 **YIELD:
About 2 cups**

**STORE:
For at least 6 months in the freezer**

NOTE:

Toast coarsely chopped walnuts on a baking pan 8 to 10 minutes in a 350° oven, stirring them once or twice. Rub them in a towel to remove any loose skin; cool them before adding them to the other ingredients.

straight-sided half-pint canning jars, leaving ½ inch of head-space to permit expansion. Seal the containers and freeze the pesto at 0° or less.

To use the pesto: Thaw the amount you'll need (in the refrigerator, if time permits. A cupful is enough for 4 to 6 servings of pasta.) While the pasta boils, blend your chosen cheese into the thawed pesto, adding 3 or 4 tablespoons of freshly grated cheese to each cup of sauce. You can use the classic combination of cheeses—three or four parts imported Parmesan (preferably Parmigiano Reggiano) plus one part of Pecorino Romano, a sharper Italian cheese, or all Parmesan if that's your preference. Check the seasoning of the mixture—you may want more salt, depending on the saltiness of the cheese. If the pesto is too stiff to mix easily with the hot pasta, thin it with a big spoonful of the hot cooking water before tossing pasta and pesto together with a chunk or two of soft butter. Serve the sauced pasta at once, offering more grated cheese at the table.

Frozen Avocado Puree

A vocados always seem to be plentiful when you don't happen to need them, but only available in a rock-hard stage when you feel like guacamole or avocado ice cream.

Given a little freezer space, this situation can be reme-died. Watch for the butteriest avocados of the year—see description at left (I'm prejudiced—I'm from California)—and allow them to ripen to perfection at room temperature. Then mash the flesh (or sieve it quickly, to prevent darkening) and blend it with lemon juice—about 2 teaspoons per large avocado—or a very little ascorbic acid powder (vitamin C), a tiny pinch per avocado, dissolved in a few drops of water and stirred into the pulp.

Pack the puree firmly into freezer containers, being care-ful to leave ½ to 1 inch of headspace. Seal the puree airtight and freeze it at once at 0° or below. It will keep well for up to a year in the freezer. Thaw it in the refrigerator before turning it into guacamole, a dip, a cold soup, or ice cream.

SEASON:
All year, but to my mind the best of all avocados are the California-grown Hass variety, which has warty, purple-black skin; its main season is April to November

STORE:
For up to a year in the freezer

Clarified Butter

Butter that has been clarified is excellent for sautéing foods (unlike whole butter, it won't scorch readily), and it is also indispensable for sealing pots of meat or fish paste. If you clarify a pound or so of butter at a time, you will have a supply always at hand in the refrigerator.

1. Place 4 sticks (1 pound) of good butter (preferably sweet cream butter, unsalted) in a heavy saucepan and set the pan over low heat. Heat the butter, taking a look at it from time to time to make sure that it is not overheating, for 15 minutes; it will bubble and look foamy, evidence that its moisture is being cooked away. Continue to simmer the butter for 20 to 25 minutes in all, without disturbing it. It has been sufficiently clarified when the boiling action (caused by the evaporation of moisture) lessens and the foamy top crust begins to look dry. Do not let the butter get hot enough to even *think* about getting brown during the clarification.

2. Remove the butter from the heat and let it stand for 5 to 10 minutes to settle. Carefully skim off the top crust, reserving it, if you like, to season vegetables (it has abundant flavor). Carefully pour off the clear golden liquid into a completely dry jar or crock; stop pouring before the sediment in the bottom of the pot is disturbed. (These good dregs, like the foam, can season vegetables, if you are of the waste-not persuasion.)

3. Cool the clarified butter until it begins to congeal, cover it airtight, and refrigerate it.

Dried Cheddar Cheese

For baking such savory things as Ultimately Cheesy Cheddar Bread (page 160), or Beaten Cheese Biscuits (page 170), or for cooking any dish requiring the zing of sharp Cheddar, a supply of high-quality cheese that has been partly dehydrated to concentrate its flavor is good to have on hand. This is a do-it-yourself project—I know of no source of store-bought dried cheese other than sawdusty ready-grated Parmesan, of which the less said the better.

If you need only enough dried cheese for a batch of bread, or if your drying space is limited, use 1 pound of cheese.

1. Grate or shred fine 1½ pounds of high-quality, natural,

extra-sharp Cheddar or Cheddar-type American cheese (processed cheese won't do).

2. Pick up the cheese by handfuls and strew it evenly on two or three baking sheets or, even better, on fine-meshed wire drying racks. Place the pans in a convection oven set at 130° to 140°, or in an electric oven that has been heated for 2 or 3 minutes at its "keep warm" setting. Turn on the light in the electric oven to maintain gentle heat, or leave the convection oven turned on.

3. Dry the cheese, turning it with a spatula every few hours, until it is quite crumbly (it will be slightly oily), 6 to 12 hours, depending on the moisture content of the cheese and the method of drying. (The drying can be done intermittently, if the oven is needed for other purposes.)

4. Cool the cheese (it won't be very warm) at room temperature, then crumble it fine and store it, in a completely airtight container, in the refrigerator or freezer.

SEASON:
Any time

YIELD:
A little over 1 pint

STORE:
For at least 2 weeks in the refrigerator

Crème Fraîche

This is a reprise, for anyone who needs it, of the best way to keep a supply of heavy cream on hand for cooking or for serving with desserts. Fresh, pasteurized heavy cream has a short life; "ultrapasteurized" cream keeps well, but it tastes so awful that there is little temptation to use it. That leaves the field open to this mildly tart French-style cream, which is nothing more than heavy cream that has been ripened by letting it stand after adding dairy sour cream. Use crème fraîche in place of heavy cream in cooking. It can also be whipped.

1 pint (2 cups) heavy (whipping) cream, not ultrapasteurized

¼ cup cultured (dairy) sour cream from a fresh batch

1. Warm the heavy cream in a thick-bottomed saucepan, stirring, until it is just blood-warm (a drop on the inside of your wrist will feel neither warm nor cold), 85° to 90° on an instant-reading thermometer.

2. Whisk in the sour cream thoroughly. Pour the mixture into a bowl that has been scalded with boiling water and dried. Cover the bowl and let it stand until the cream has thickened slightly, 8 to 12 hours at moderate room temperature, longer in cold weather or in a cold house.

3. Stir the cream and refrigerate it, covered, for 8 hours or more before using it. It will thicken further as it chills.

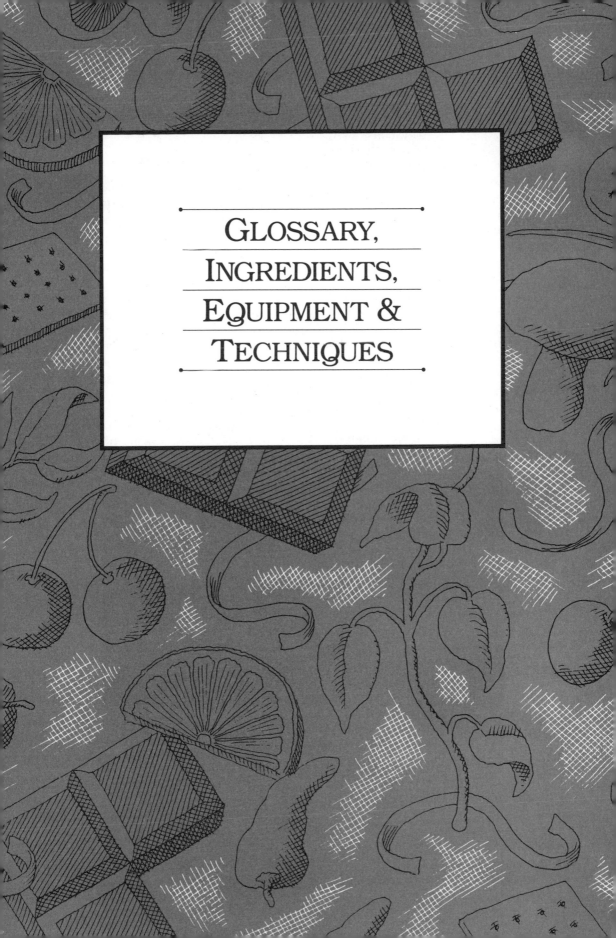

GLOSSARY, INGREDIENTS, EQUIPMENT & TECHNIQUES

AIR BUBBLES, REMOVING: See **PRE-PARING, FILLING, AND SEALING JARS.**

ALTITUDE: Altitude affects certain pre-serving operations. At elevations above 1,000 feet there is a change in the ther-mometer reading indicating when a jelly or other preserve will pass the **JELLY TEST** (see) and in the time required for process-ing jars of food in a boiling-water bath (see **PROCESSING JARS IN A BOILING-WATER BATH**).

Rule of thumb for jelly test: At an elevation of 1,000 feet or less, jelly will be done at the thermometer reading—220°—indicated in recipes. At a higher elevation, you need to determine the temperature at which water boils and then, from that tem-perature, arrive at the "done" tempera-ture for jelly. To check the temperature at which water reaches a vigorous boil, hold an instant-reading or candy/jelly thermom-eter upright in the water, its tip or bulb well immersed. To the reading, add 8 de-grees to determine the jellying point for preserves. Example: At sea level and slightly above, water boils at 212°, so jelly jells at 220°.

The processing time in a boiling-water bath: If a recipe directs processing for 20 minutes or less, this timing is correct for elevations up to 1,000 feet. At 1,000 feet, add 1 minute of processing time; for each additional 1,000 feet or fraction, add 1 minute more. If the basic processing time in the recipe is more than 20 minutes, add 2 minutes at 1,000 feet; add 2 minutes more for each additional 1,000 feet or fraction.

AMMONIUM CARBONATE, BAKING AM-MONIA, or **HARTSHORN:** Names for an old-fashioned but useful predecessor of baking powder that makes certain baked goods, especially cookies, exceptionally crisp.

BAKING AMMONIA: See **AMMONIUM CARBONATE.**

BAKING POWDER: Use what is available; the recipes are written for current types.

BAKING SODA, BICARBONATE OF SODA, or **SODIUM BICARBONATE:** This substance interacts with acidic ingredients in dough to form a leavening gas. It is a component of some baking powders.

BICARBONATE OF SODA: See **BAKING SODA.**

BOILING-WATER BATH or **WATER-BATH CANNER:** See **PROCESSING JARS IN A BOILING-WATER BATH.**

BOTTLES: Almost any attractive bottle made of sturdy glass (it must be strong enough to be boiled) can be recycled to hold a cordial, syrup, fruit or herbal vine-gar, seasoned oil, pepper sauce, or what-ever. Old or new, bottles must be sparkling clean; wash, rinse, and boil them for 15 minutes, starting with cold water. Leave the boiled bottles on their sides in a low oven ("keep-warm" temperature, or around 150°) until there is no sign of moisture inside. For sealing bottles, use their screw caps (boil to sterilize); or see **CORKS.**

BRAN: Unprocessed bran, not breakfast cereal, is meant; most supermarkets stock unprocessed wheat bran and oat bran, as do health-food stores.

BUBBLE-FREER: One name for a flat plastic rod used to remove air bubbles from filled jars of food before sealing (see **PRE-PARING, FILLING, AND SEALING JARS**). To use, run it down between food and glass in several places. You can substi-tute the handle of a long wooden spoon, or a bamboo cooking chopstick.

CALCIUM HYDROXIDE: See **PICKLING LIME.**

CANDY/JELLY THERMOMETER: See **JELLY TEST** and **THERMOMETERS.**

CANISTERS: For airtight storage, a canis-ter with a loose cover can be snugged up by placing a sheet of foil or a doubled sheet of plastic on top before fitting on the cover.

CANNING JARS: These are jars made of

sturdy, tempered glass that can withstand the heat processing of foods put up at home. They come in both regular and wide-mouthed designs, with a capacity of ½ pint, 1 pint, 1½ pints, and 1 quart. (Formerly 2-quart jars were made in the U.S., but these are not now recommended for home canning—they are too large to allow complete heat penetration during processing.) New jars now are mainly of the Mason type, named for their 19th-century inventor. Current models are made by Kerr, Ball, and some other manufacturers. They are packed with a supply of two-piece vacuum lids. Still found in many homes are the older type of Mason jars, which are sealed with porcelain-lined zinc caps and rubber rings. These closures are described in **CANNING LIDS,** below.

Also still rattling around and still usable, if in good condition, are clamp-closed **IDEAL JARS** (see that entry for how to use them), which are sometimes still reproduced.

The European type of clamp-closed jars (Le Parfait is a well-known brand) are often available in housewares departments. Parfait-type canning jars, which have wire-encircled glass covers that can't get lost because they're hinged to the jar, come in many sizes. They're convenient for storing certain pickles that should be closely covered but don't require processing. The largest, holding 2 liters or more, are also great for storing flour and other bulky ingredients. Aside from such uses, most experts don't recommend these jars, as their closures don't allow the requisite exhausting of air during processing in a boiling-water bath. If you want to try sealing and processing foods in them, follow the manufacturer's instructions, as these jars are handled differently from the superficially similar American clamp-closed (Ideal) kind.

CANNING LADLE: Useful for soups, too, this ladle has a "wing" on either side of the bowl, making it possible to get every drop out of the crease between the side and bottom of the preserving pan.

CANNING LIDS: Most often used today are *two-piece vacuum lids,* sometimes called "dome lids." They are the type packaged with modern Mason jars, and they are what is meant when "two-piece canning lids" are referred to in the recipes. The screw bands of these lids can be reused; the inserts—flat or slightly domed disks with a band of sealing compound around the edge of the underside—should be used only once. Instructions for using jars and lids are packed with jars and with replacement lids and lid inserts. Directions may differ slightly from brand to brand; if you don't have the manufacturer's recommendations, here is a reliable procedure:

Using two-piece vacuum lids: Wash the two parts of each lid (the inserts must be new), rinse them, and drop them into scalding-hot water and leave them, off the heat, until they're needed. (If the recipe directs you to use sterilized lids, use boiling water.) To use, lift an insert out of the water with small tongs and lay it in place on the filled jar (see **PREPARING, FILLING, AND SEALING JARS**), whose rim has been wiped clean of any spills. Set the screw band over the insert and screw the band only moderately tight, using a dry cloth to protect your hand. Don't tighten the band desperately hard, and don't proceed by putting the insert into the band and applying the set to the jar together; this can prevent proper sealing. Proceed to processing the jars (see **PROCESSING JARS IN A BOILING-WATER BATH**) and subsequent steps. Do *not* tighten the bands after processing, even if they seem loose; to do so may break the seal. After the jars have cooled 12 to 24 hours, test for seal: The center of the lid (the "dome") will be slightly depressed if the seal is complete. If the center is elevated, press it down with a finger; if it stays down, all is well. Or use the "ping" test: Tap each lid with the tip of a teaspoon. If the sound is clear, you have a seal; a dull thunk indicates an unsealed jar. Recap and reprocess an unsealed jar (the processing time is the same as before), or refrigerate the food and use it within its normal refrigerator life. Wipe sealed jars with a damp cloth, label them, and store them. If you wish, the screw bands may be removed before storage. To open, pry up the flat cap with a knife blade or the blunt end of a beer opener.

Using porcelain-lined zinc caps: These old-time caps are still usable, if in good condition, for sealing the old-fashioned Mason-type jars for which they were designed. Be sure the jars and the porcelain linings of the caps are undamaged. Wash the lids in soapy water, rinse them, then sterilize them by boiling them 15 minutes, even though the sealed jars will undergo processing later; leave the lids in the hot water until you're ready to use them. Meanwhile, wash and rinse the number of new rubber rings you'll need (never reuse rubber rings); pour hot water over them and leave them to keep warm. To apply the caps to hot, filled jars (see **PREPARING, FILLING, AND SEALING JARS**), fit a warm, wet rubber jar ring down onto the shoulder of the jar, being careful not to overstretch the ring. Screw the sterilized lid down tightly, then loosen it with a turn of about ¼ inch. After processing the jars (see **PROCESSING JARS IN A BOILING-WATER BATH**), follow the steps in those directions to complete the seal, cool the jars, test the seals, and store the jars. To open a jar, tug on the ring tab with pliers. If the ring is stubborn, soak the jar upside down in enough hot water to cover the ring, then try again.

CHOPPING or **CRUSHING:** Recipes indicate the desirable method for crushing or chopping ingredients if it makes a difference. I often use my food processor, which gives quicker results than the nonmechanical alternatives. When there's a big chopping job to do, it may be worthwhile to unlimber a food grinder. If you use your food processor or blender, be careful not to turn the material into a mush or puree by overprocessing.

COCOA: For the best flavor, Dutch-process unsweetened cocoa powder is worth its price. However, standard unsweetened cocoa can be used.

CORKS: For stoppering bottled vinegars, oils, cordials, or syrups in either decora-tive or workaday bottles, corks are practical and attractive. Use only new ones—recycled corks can cause spoilage. It's a good idea to boil new corks in a covered saucepan for 15 minutes. After corking a bottle, you can add a decorative touch (and a tight seal) by dipping the cork and upper part of the neck repeatedly into melted wax, letting each coat dry before dipping again. (You can also attach ribbons or other ornaments this way.) Plain paraffin wax is fine; for a colorful seal, chop up a bright-colored candle or candle stub (preferably unscented) and melt it with the paraffin, in a metal container (such as a clean can) set in simmering water; melting wax directly over heat asks for flare-ups and trouble.

CORN SYRUP: There are two kinds, light (or white) and dark, which has a faintly molasses-like flavor. Use the kind specified, unless the recipe indicates that either type will do.

DOME LIDS: See **CANNING LIDS.**

FILTERING: For sparkling-clear fruit vinegars, syrups, and cordials, filtering is a boon. Use a cone-type coffee filter (free of any film of oil from its normal use), lined with a dampened filter-paper cone; or use a funnel, with a lining improvised from folded filter paper. Pour the liquid into the filter gradually and don't rush the process.

FLOURS: Use the kind specified, or the suggested substitution; not all flours are interchangeable. Among those called for in *Fancy Pantry* are all-purpose, bread, cake, whole-wheat, whole-wheat pastry, and semolina flours.

To measure: Stir the flour and heap it lightly in a dry-measure cup; level the top by sweeping off the excess. Don't sift flour before measuring it unless the recipe so directs.

FREEZER WRAP: See **WRAPPING FOOD FOR THE FREEZER.**

FULL, ROLLING BOIL: For preserves, just what it says: a boil so vigorous it can't be stirred down. This rate of boiling is important when making preserves with pectin; these require precise timing of a full boil for correct consistency.

FUNNELS: For filling jars fast and neatly, an inexpensive plastic or metal canning funnel, wide enough at the bottom to allow large chunks to pass easily, keeps spills off the rim and the outside of the jar. For bottling liquids, you'll need a narrow-necked plastic or metal funnel.

GIFT WRAPPING: For bottled items, dip tops in colored wax (see **CORKS**), perhaps attaching ribbons or other ornaments by means of the wax coating. Tie rounds of pretty cloth in place over the tops of jars, using ribbons or bulky yarn; if screw bands of lids have been removed for storage, first replace them for the convenience of the recipient. You can also overwrap a jar in bright cellophane, gather the cellophane at the top, and secure it with a colorful cord. Choose attractive crocks, canisters, apothecary jars, baskets, or boxes and repack things ordinarily stored in utilitarian containers. To any package, add an attractive label or hang tag with the name of the contents, the donor, serving suggestions, and so on. Especially if the food has been transferred to an ornamental container for presentation, the label should include how-to-store information.

GINGER, FRESH: Two kinds are used—mature ginger, which is what most markets have; and stem ginger, pink-sprouted and tender-skinned, usually obtainable only for a while in midsummer, and then most often in places where an Oriental clientele exists. Dried ginger has its uses, but neither that form nor ground ginger is a substitute for the fresh rhizomes.

HARTSHORN: See **AMMONIUM CARBONATE.**

HEADSPACE: The space between the rim of a container and the top of its contents; it may be as little as $\frac{1}{8}$ inch or as much as an inch; it's important to leave the correct amount when filling preserving jars or freezer containers.

HOT PEPPERS: A caution: When you're preparing any kind of fresh hot peppers, work at arms' length, or at least not close to your face, preferably wearing rubber gloves; never, never touch your face (most especially your eyes) after handling peppers until your hands have been most thoroughly washed and dried. Soap and rinse rubber gloves, too, as well as any utensils that have come in contact with these fiery vegetables.

IDEAL JARS: Still in use but no longer manufactured except as novelties, these old-fashioned canning jars with two metal clamps or bails have separate glass lids that are sealed to the jar by means of a rubber ring (a new ring is used each time). If you have old jars of this type (or decorative reproductions) in good condition, they can be used. Don't use jars or lids with cracks or nicks, or with wire bails that don't work properly (check them out with an old ring, with the lid in place).

To use: Prepare jars and rings and fill jars as described in **PREPARING, FILLING, AND SEALING JARS** and in **CANNING LIDS.** To seal the filled jar, fit a warm, wet rubber ring over the mouth, seating it on the ledge without overstretching it. Wipe the rim of the jar and set the glass lid in place. Raise the longer (upper) bail, fitting it into the notch in the lid; leave the lower bail in "up" position. The upper bail holds the lid in place during processing; the lower loop is pressed down to complete the seal when processing is finished. For completing and testing the seal and storing jars, see **PROCESSING JARS IN A BOILING-WATER BATH.**

To open a sealed Ideal jar, lift both bails, then use the tip of a blunt knife to pry up the rubber ring enough to let in a little air to release the seal.

JAR LIFTER: An ingenious pair of tongs, designed to grip hot jars securely from above. The jaws of the usual type are plastic-covered and the handles are wooden, so the tongs don't transfer heat to your hand. You can use long-handled barbecue tongs as jar lifters, too, but their hold is less secure.

JAR RINGS: These red rubber gaskets function as seals for certain types of jars; see **CANNING JARS** and **CANNING LIDS.**

JELLY BAG: An arrangement for draining the juice from fruit in order to make jellies, fruit honeys, and syrups. A metal ring is set on detachable legs that perch on the rim of a bowl, which catches the juice; from the ring is suspended a detachable cloth pouch to hold the food to be drained. A jelly bag is convenient but not essential. You can improvise: Line a colander or a large sieve, set over a bowl, with one or two layers of closely woven cheesecloth or (even better) very finely woven nylon curtain material, which is easy to rinse out and infinitely reusable. When draining is partially accomplished, tie the corners of the cloth to make a bag and suspend it from a knob or hook, with the bowl beneath. Don't squeeze the contents of the jelly bag if you want brilliant jelly; a little gentle encouragement is okay (push lightly on the sides of the bag with the back of a spoon), but squeezing may cause bits of pulp to emerge, causing cloudiness in the jelly.

JELLY GLASSES: Glasses of heat-resistant tempered glass, sometimes with ornamental pressed designs, for storing jelly; they usually come with covers of plastic or metal to protect the paraffin seal over the jelly. If covers are missing, fold aluminum foil over the tops of cooled glasses and add a rubber band.

JELLY TEST: There are several ways to test the doneness of jelly, jam, or other preserves that are "jellied." If no method is specified in a recipe, use the cold-spoon test, or test the mixture with a candy/jelly thermometer.

The cold-spoon test: Dip up a small amount of the boiling mixture in a large, cold metal spoon and immediately pour it back from the side of the spoon, held far enough above the surface to avoid steam. If the jelly, jam, or other preserve isn't sufficiently cooked, the syrup or mixture will fall in a stream or in separate drops. When it's ready, the last few drops in the

spoon will join together and fall or shear off cleanly in a small sheet. (The test is sometimes referred to as the "sheet test.") When repeating the test, first rinse and dry the spoon; coagulated remnants of the first test can distort results.

The cold-saucer test: For some preserves that should not set firmly, this is the handiest test of doneness; recipes will indicate when it is suitable. A small amount of the hot preserve is spooned onto a chilled saucer and placed in the refrigerator to cool completely (remove the pot from the heat while this goes on). The recipe will indicate how the sample will look when it is done; sometimes the sample is checked by drawing a finger through it, sometimes by tilting the saucer to see whether and how much the surface wrinkles. If the preserve doesn't pass the test, resume cooking and test again.

Using a candy/jelly thermometer: This is the most precise of the tests. The thermometer, a special type that records readings as high as 400°, should stand upright in the pot with its bulb well covered by the mixture but not touching the bottom of the pot. Read the thermometer at eye level, or as close as you can come to eye level. A preserve has reached the jellying point when the reading is 8° above the boiling point of water at that elevation; standard recipes assume that the preserving is being done at 1,000 feet or below, where water boils at 212°, so jelly is done at 220°. To calculate the reading at an elevation higher than 1,000 feet, see **ALTITUDE.**

Timing the cooking: This method is used in place of a test for doneness *only* for preserves made with added pectin. Follow the timing in the recipe exactly.

KNEADING: See Breadmaking Basics, page 150.

LABELS, LABELING: Form the habit of always labeling your pantry items, wherever or however you're going to store them. Freezer tape is tenacious for labeling frozen things. For most other items, pressure-sensitive office labels are more convenient to use than labels that must be moistened, and they stay in place better. Use a waterproof marker or pen to be sure of lasting legibility, and include the date you made the item and, where appropriate, the date by which it should be used. If you decide to give something as a gift, an ornamental label can be stuck right over the storage label.

LOX: Pacific salmon that has been salt-cured but not smoked (although smoked salmon is occasionally mislabeled as lox); a delicatessen staple, especially in the Northeast. The cut called belly lox is most succulent, but any lox is fine for making marinated (pickled) salmon at home; see page 30.

MASON JARS: See **CANNING JARS; CANNING LIDS.**

MUSHROOMS, DRIED: Imported dried boletus mushrooms are a valuable staple, for special dishes as well as certain *Fancy Pantry* recipes. These mushrooms may be labeled boletus, boletes, cèpes, ceps, porcini, funghi secchi porcini, Steinpilze, and so on. Or they may be labeled just "dried mushrooms." Most come from Europe; less expensive grades are imported from Chile. If the mushrooms are true boletes, they show small pores, not gills, on the original undersurface of the pieces. Sniff to make sure there is a rich aroma, and store them in a closed canister, where they will keep well for a long time.

MUSTARD: For information on mustard seed and mustard powders, see Making Your Own Mustards, page 179.

NUTS: All nuts, shelled or not, keep best stored airtight in the freezer or refrigerator. When buying, taste shelled nuts to be sure they haven't deteriorated. Instructions for blanching, skinning, and toasting nuts are found with the recipes requiring these procedures.

OLD PRESERVING RECIPES: A caution: Many beguiling old canning and preserving recipes are still in circulation, many of them calling for outmoded or actually un-safe methods. One such old method is open-kettle preserving, which is sealing and storing food without a final heat processing in the jar. A corresponding procedure is now used *only* for certainly heavily sweetened preserves, especially jellies, and some brined and/or well-vinegared foods (sugar, salt, and vinegar, in sufficient amounts, are effective preservatives). Other old wrinkles to be avoided are oven-processing filled jars; steamer canning, an unreliable processing method not to be confused with steam pressure canning in a pressure cooker, which is a standard method; and adding offbeat ingredients (aspirin is one example) that are supposed to "preserve" foods without adequate processing. Be cautious about using *any* old preserving instructions, "old" meaning directions that go back more than ten years or so; at the least check them against current knowledge, which you can do by telephoning the Cooperative Extension Service in your area, often called the "county agent." (An excellent reference is *The Ball Blue Book,* published by the Ball Corporation, Muncie, Indiana 47302, long-time makers of canning jars.)

Be aware that ingredients, too, can change over time in ways that make once-acceptable procedures unsafe. For example, modern strains of tomatoes are so low in acid that it's no longer safe to can them by methods or according to timings developed for the high-acid tomatoes that were once the norm.

PECTIN: This substance occurs naturally in fruits, in lesser or greater concentrations; in the presence of sufficient acid and sugar, it brings about the "jelling" of preserves. In some recipes here, commercial pectin is called for because the ingredients lack natural pectin. Use the type called for, either powdered pectin, which comes in 1¾-ounce packages, or liquid pectin (Certo is the best-known brand), which is packed in 3-ounce pouches and 6-ounce bottles. These types of pectin aren't interchangeable; and don't substitute for either one the special type used for making low-sugar preserves. It can be used successfully only with recipes worked out for it.

PEPPERCORNS: If the recipe doesn't specify white or black, suit yourself.

PICKLING CROCKS: For preparing pickles and other acidic or strongly salty foods, use ceramic, stoneware, or glass crocks or jars; food-grade plastic is also satisfactory. Never use copper, brass, iron, aluminum, or galvanized zinc containers, all of which react undesirably with salt and acid. Stainless steel is acceptable.

PICKLING LIME, CALCIUM HYDROX-IDE, or **SLAKED LIME:** These all refer to a substance that lends crackling crispness to certain pickles. (It can be omitted, as the recipes indicate.) Pickling lime is packed in bags and can usually be found with canning supplies. Another form of this product is calcium hydroxide USP, available in small bottles at pharmacies (it has certain medicinal uses). This form is also used, in much smaller amounts, in pickling.

PORCELAIN-LINED ZINC JAR CAPS: See **CANNING LIDS.**

PREPARING, FILLING, AND SEALING JARS: Most of the *Fancy Pantry* foods sealed in jars also undergo processing (sterilizing) in the jar in a boiling-water bath, although there are a few exceptions; some recipes direct you to seal the food into sterilized jars, with sterilized lids, without subsequent processing in the jars. This is standard and safe practice for jellies and certain other foods that are highly sweetened, salt cured, and/or acidic.

Preparing containers: Before using any jar or jelly glass, inspect it for cracks, scratches, or nicks. If there is damage, particularly to the sealing rim, don't use the jar; a small crack or even a bad scratch can cause it to crack when it is filled. However, a jelly glass to be sealed with paraffin (see **SEALING WITH PARAFFIN**) with a slightly nicked rim can be used, as the rim isn't involved in sealing.

If the recipe directs you to process the filled jars in a boiling-water bath, prepare the jars by washing them in soapy water, rinsing them, and plunging them into scalding-hot water. Leave them until you're ready to fill them; they should be hot when they are filled. The jars will be sterilized, with their contents, when they are processed. Lids, too, should be washed, rinsed, and held in scalding-hot water until they're used. If your jar closures employ rubber jar rings (gaskets), wash, rinse, and hold new rings (never reuse them) in hot, not boiling, water.

If the recipe calls for using sterilized jars or glasses, boil the washed and rinsed containers 15 minutes in water to cover. Just before filling them, invert them on a clean, folded towel to drain briefly; fill them while hot. To prepare sterilized lids for sterilized jars (two-piece vacuum lids only are recommended), wash and rinse the screw bands and the inserts (which must be new), then cover them with boiling water and leave them until they are needed.

Filling jars or jelly glasses: Use a canning funnel to prevent spills onto the rim or outside of the containers. Ladle the food into the jar, leaving the headspace (distance between food and rim) specified in the recipe.

Remove air bubbles, if the recipe directs this step, by inserting a flat plastic "bubble-freer" rod between the glass and the food in several places; or use a long bamboo cooking chopstick, or the handle of a long wooden spoon (avoid a metal implement). If the headspace increases after air bubbles are removed, add food or liquid to reach the correct level. With a fresh cloth dipped into hot water, wipe the rims of jars or glasses and the threads of jars to remove any food spills, which can interfere with sealing if the spill is on the rim or, if it's on the threads, permit mold growth which can infiltrate and break the seal during storage.

Sealing jars: Seal each jar as it is filled, following the directions of the jar and/or lid manufacturer, if you have them; or see the directions above for **CANNING LIDS** and for **IDEAL JARS.** Exotic jars, including some European types such as Le Parfait, have their own special directions, which should be followed.

If processing is called for, proceed to that step (see **PROCESSING JARS IN A BOILING-WATER BATH**) and the subsequent steps—completing the seal (when required), cooling the jars, testing the seal, and storing the food.

To seal jelly with paraffin: See **SEALING WITH PARAFFIN.**

PRESERVING PAN: Using just the right pot makes a great contribution to the pleasures of preserving. A big, heavy, wide stainless-steel pot (a large surface speeds cooking) holding at least 6 quarts (even bigger is better, except for very small batches) is the most versatile, as stainless steel is nonreactive and easy to clean. However, anodized (dark or light gray) heavy aluminum works well, as does a heavy enameled iron pot (thin enamelware is to be avoided). Avoid iron pans; a plain aluminum pot can be used, if there is no objection to this metal's reactivity with acids and salt. For making sweet preserves I enjoy using a handsome French preserving pan of unlined copper; it transfers heat efficiently and its wide surface also shortens cooking time. However, a copper preserving pan can't be used for pickling or general cooking, as the metal reacts undesirably with too many foods, and the pan must be polished penny-bright with vinegar and salt immediately before each use.

PRESSURE COOKER: See **STEAM PRESSURE CANNER.**

PROCESSING JARS IN A BOILING-WATER BATH: This is a type of heat processing (as is canning in a steam pressure canner). One method or the other must be used to ensure the safety and keeping ity of foods "put up" in jars. The boiling-water bath has its limitations—it can't be used for meats and other low-acid foods, for instance—but it is highly satisfactory for all the put-up jobs in this book. If you use an old recipe, check it first; see **OLD PRESERVING RECIPES.**

How to process jars: As each jar is filled and capped (see **PREPARING, FILL-ING, AND SEALING JARS**), set it on a rack or a folded cloth in a water-bath canner or other sufficiently deep pot, half filled with simmering water. (Inexpensive enamelware canners are available in various sizes; they come with basketlike racks that keep the jars from touching and also serve for lifting the jars en masse from the pot. A canner or any other pot must be large and deep enough to permit the jars, standing on the rack, to be covered by at least 1 inch—better 2 or 3 inches—of vigorously boiling water; allow an additional couple of inches of depth for boiling room.) Space the jars at least an inch apart to allow heat circulation, and don't allow them to touch the sides of the pot. When all jars are in place, add boiling water to cover lids by at least 1 inch; 2 or 3 inches is better. Bring the potful to a full boil over high heat and start timing; maintain a vigorous boil for the processing time given in the recipe. (See **ALTITUDE** for instructions on adjusting processing times for elevations above 1,000 feet.) Cover the pot or not, as you prefer, during processing. When processing is complete, remove the jars from the water and set them well apart to cool on wire racks, or a wood surface, or a counter padded with towels or newspaper. Avoid a chilly surface—hot jars in contact with marble, tile, or metal are likely to crack.

Completing the seal, when needed: At this point, the seal is completed for two kinds of closures: the covers of Ideal jars, on which you now press down the shorter bail, which was left in "up" position during processing, and the porcelain-lined zinc caps of old-type Mason jars, which are now tightened firmly (protect your hand with a cloth). *Do not* tighten the band of a two-piece lid, even if it is loose; doing so may break the seal. Leave the jars to cool completely.

Testing the seal: After 12 to 24 hours, test the seal as appropriate for the type of lid:

Two-piece vacuum lids: The center of the lid (the "dome") will be slightly depressed if the seal is complete. If the center is elevated, press it with a finger; if it stays down, all is well. Or use the "ping" test: tap each lid with the tip of a teaspoon. If the sound is clear, you have a seal; a dull thunk indicates an unsealed jar. Recap and reprocess an unsealed jar (the processing time is the same as before), or refrigerate the food and use it within its normal life expectancy.

Porcelain-lined zinc lids: Hold the jar at a sharp angle, almost upside down; if any bubbles rise through the contents, the jar isn't sealed. Reseal it with a fresh ring and reprocess it (same time as before), or refrigerate the jar and use the food within an appropriate period.

Ideal-type clamp lids: Test the seal of Ideal jars by tilting the jar downward at a sharp angle; if air bubbles rise, the jar isn't sealed. Reseal it with a fresh ring and reprocess it for the same time as before, or refrigerate it and use the food within its normal refrigerator life.

European-style clamp lids: Follow the manufacturer's directions for jars of the Parfait type, if you have experimented with processing them. In the absence of instructions, unlock the clamp of the jar gently, then lift the jar a few inches, holding it by the rim of the glass cover. If the seal holds, re-clamp the cover and store the jar. If it doesn't hold, decide whether to reprocess it (use a new ring) or refrigerate it and use the contents soon.

Storing the jars: Wipe each jar clean with a damp cloth (a little food can boil out of the jars in the course of normal processing and film the jars), label them, and store them. Screw bands of two-piece lids may be removed or left in place, as you prefer.

PUNCHING DOWN, IN BREADMAKING: See Breadmaking Basics, page 150.

REFRIGERATION: Recipes indicate when refrigeration is recommended for basic storage. Refrigerate pantry-shelf items in jars (preserves, relishes, etc.) after the jar has been opened.

REMOVING AIR BUBBLES: Many (but not all) foods sealed in jars need to be de-bubbled before the jar is sealed; follow the recipe indication on this point. For how-to's, see **PREPARING, FILLING, AND SEALING JARS**, above.

RUBBER RINGS: See **JAR RINGS.**

SALT: Recipes specify certain kinds for certain uses. Non-iodized pure salt, such as dairy salt or canning (pickling) salt, should always be used when it's called for. Table salt is okay when no type is specified, as in baking. If you substitute coarse (kosher) salt for fine salt, increase the measurement by about one-third; and vice versa.

SEALING WITH PARAFFIN: Wax sealing is satisfactory for jelly, especially if it's in glasses, and a very few other preserves; don't use this method unless the recipe says so. Cut new paraffin wax (never reuse wax) into small chunks and melt it in a clean, dry metal container set in a pan of simmering water. (A well-cleaned and dried food can is a satisfactory wax container; you can bend the edge into a lip for pouring.) While the wax melts, wipe any splashes of jelly from the headspace of the glass with a fresh cloth and hot water. Pour a thin (1/8 inch or less) layer of wax onto the hot jelly, making sure it touches the glass all around. If any bubbles appear in the wax, prick them. Let the wax set, then remelt the remaining wax and add a second, very thin layer; tilt the glass to seal the second coat all around. Cover the cooled jelly with the plastic or metal lids that came with the glasses, or fold aluminum foil over each glass and fasten it with a rubber band. Store the container of cooled wax in a plastic bag until next time.

SHEET TEST: See **JELLY TEST.**

SKIMMER, SKIMMING: To skim preserves most easily, use a skimmer, a long-handled spoon with a mesh bowl; stainless steel is the best material. Use the skimmer to urge scum or clumps of foam to one side of the pan, then lift the gathered material quickly and discard it; repeat skimming until the surface is clear. You'll use this utensil for soups and broths, too.

SLAKED LIME: See **PICKLING LIME.**

SLOW-COOKER: Experiment with using a

slow-cooker, if you have one, for projects, such as making ketchups, that involve lengthy cooking; it reduces pot-watching delightfully.

SODIUM BICARBONATE: See **BAKING SODA.**

SPICE MILL or **GRINDER:** Not for pantry projects only, one of these inexpensive electric mills is indispensable if you appreciate fresh-ground seasonings. You can use a coffee mill of the type with a horizontal "windmill" blade in its cup; these are virtually identical with most spice mills. Wipe out the bowl and wipe the blade with paper towels after use; don't attempt to wash the mill. Once in a while, grind a little rice to remove lingering spice oils. If you use the same mill for coffee and spices, you'll want to do this often, or whenever you switch uses. You can use a blender for grinding only if there is a large enough quantity of material to engage the high-set blade.

STEAM PRESSURE CANNER: This utensil—which is a large pressure cooker—is not required for any of the recipes in *Fancy Pantry*. Instead, **PROCESSING JARS IN A BOILING-WATER BATH** (above) is employed for heat sterilization.

STERILIZATION: *Fancy Pantry* foods sealed in jars are sterilized by **PROCESSING JARS IN A BOILING-WATER BATH** (see). To sterilize empty jars, bottles, jelly glasses, lids, corks (new ones only), or utensils when the recipe directs use of sterilized items, boil them for 15 minutes in water to cover.

STORAGE, STORAGE TIMES: Each recipe indicates suitable storage environment(s). After pantry-shelf jars have been opened, refrigerate them. The storage times accompanying the recipes are on the conservative side; many foods, stored as suggested, will keep much longer than the time given.

SUGAR: When granulated sugar is called for, it makes absolutely no difference whether cane or beet sugar is used. Other sugars—light or dark brown, confectioners', and so on—should be the type specified by the recipe.

THERMOMETERS: Indispensable if your kitchen is often in action. An *oven thermometer* is a check on whether your oven control is working correctly; the control can be off by as much as 50° before the problem is noticed otherwise. *An instant-reading thermometer* is placed in the liquid or the food just long enough to take a reading. *A candy/jelly thermometer,* used in preserving, gives the most accurate information on stage of doneness a preserve has reached; see **JELLY TEST.**

TIMERS, TIMING: A timer is a necessity unless clock-watching is a hobby. Having more than one is a help when more than one culinary project is going at once.

TWO-PIECE VACUUM LIDS: See **CANNING LIDS.**

VACUUM LIDS: See **CANNING LIDS.**

VINEGAR: Various kinds are used in the recipes here; substitutions are suggested where appropriate. For pickling, vinegar should have between 4 and 6 percent acidity, so don't pickle with home-made vinegars, which can vary widely in acidity. Distilled white vinegar won't darken light-colored ingredients, so it is preferred for much but not all pickling. Also used in *Fancy Pantry* recipes are balsamic, cider, white wine, red wine, and Oriental rice vinegars. As vinegars to be flavored with herbs, spices, or fruits, choose high-quality products only; cheaper grades aren't worth even their lower price. You can make your own wine vinegars; see the index.

VODKA: This is used as the base for several cordials. Quality counts; don't be beguiled into using cheap vodka. It can be both harsh and nasty.

WATER-BATH CANNER: See **PROCESSING JARS IN A BOILING-WATER BATH.**

WATER FOR PICKLING: Anyone who lives in a hard-water area knows about bathtub rings and other woes. Here's another: hard water has a poor effect on the quality of brined and/or fermented pickles such as Grapeleaf Dills. If your water makes suds only reluctantly or otherwise shows it's hard, use distilled water for pickles. You can also try softening your hard water this way: Boil the water for 15 minutes and let it stand for 24 hours. Remove any surface scum, then ladle the water into another container, leaving behind the sediment. Add 1 tablespoon of distilled white vinegar to each gallon of boiled water.

WRAPPING FOOD FOR THE FREEZER: Use freezer-weight foil or plastic, plastic bags, or plastic or screwtop glass containers intended for freezer use. Lids of plastic containers are seldom airtight; tape the closure to prevent deterioration of the contents. Double-bagging is perhaps the best protection against both freezer burn and the infiltration of foreign odors or flavors. Press out or otherwise get rid of all possible air inside bags; you can use a drinking straw to "drink" the surplus air inside the almost-closed bag, thus drawing the bag tightly around its contents; pinch the opening closed as you withdraw the straw, then complete the seal.

Breads, other baked goods: Double-bag; or wrap large items in foil individually, smaller things in batches, folding the wrap snugly or taping it; overwrap or bag in plastic and seal. Thaw baked goods in their wrappings to prevent sogginess.

Potted meats and other items in unsealed jars or crocks, if recipe says freezing is okay: Wrap the container tightly in foil and tape it; overwrap or bag in plastic and seal again.

Label packages with freezer tape, using a waterproof marking pen; or make a label on a slip of paper and put it under the transparent outer wrap. Date the labels, and include a "use-by" date unless your freezer inventory system is infallible (mine isn't).

See also **GIFT WRAPPING.**

YEAST: Recipes specify active dry yeast (the regular kind, not the fast-rising type), measured either by the envelope or by spoon measurements. It's far less costly to buy yeast in jars or bulk than in individual packets; refrigerated in a capped jar, it keeps a long time.

ZEST: The outer, colored layer of the peel of citrus fruits. Shave off zest with a swivel-bladed peeler, or use a small tool called a zester, which removes the zest in tiny shreds. Be careful not to include any of the underlying white pith; it is bitter.

MAIL–ORDER SOURCES, RECIPES BY SEASON, & INDEX

MAIL-ORDER SOURCES

*A*s we go to press, these concerns accept mail orders. Some issue catalogues, some don't; as this may change, write or call for a catalogue or ordering information.

AMERICAN SPOON FOODS
411 East Lake St., Petoskey, MI 49770. (616) 347-9030. Dried mushrooms, including morels; Michigan maple products, dried sour cherries, and native nuts are also among the offerings.

ARROWHEAD MILLS
Box 2059, Hereford, TX 79045. (806) 364-0730. Grains, flours.

BALDUCCI'S
424 Ave. of the Americas, New York, NY 10011. (212) 673-2600. This famous Greenwich Village store has fine oils, cheeses, Provençal olives, dried boletus mushrooms, even truffles, plus fresh and prepared foods.

BROOKSTONE
5 Vose Farm Road, Peterborough, NH 03458. (603) 924-7181. "Homewares" are now also offered by this firm, long known for high-quality tools.

CASA MONEO
210 West 14th St., New York, NY 10011. (212) 929-1644. Full of beans, chilies and other peppers, coffee, chocolate, spices, flours (including manioc, masa, rice, plantain), tropical fruits, oils, and whatever else Latin American or Hispanic cuisines might require.

CHEESES OF ALL NATIONS
153 Chambers St., New York, NY 10007. (212) 964-0024. Hundreds of cheeses from around the world.

CHEF'S CATALOG
3915 Commercial Ave., Northbrook, IL 60062. (312) 480-9400. Choice equipment, much of it professional; some foods.

COMMUNITY KITCHENS
P.O. Box 3778, Baton Rouge, LA 70821-3778. (504) 381-3900. Famous for coffees, this firm offers some food specialties and ingredients, plus some kitchenwares.

CRATE AND BARREL
P.O. Box 3057, Northbrook, IL 60065. (312) 272-2888. Kitchenwares and housewares, among other temptations.

EL MOLINO FOODS
1078 Santa Fe Dr., Denver, CO 80204. (303) 623-7870. Latin American foods.

GARDENER'S SUPPLY COMPANY
133 Elm St., Winooski, VT 05404. (802) 655-9006. Products for cooking, pickling, and preserving; canning kits and books.

GREAT VALLEY MILLS
687 Mill Road, Telford, PA 18969. (215) 256-6648. Grains, flours.

GWALTNEY OF SMITHFIELD, LTD.
P.O. Box 489, Smithfield, VA 23430. (804) 357-3131. Virginia hams, bacon.

HERB GATHERING, INC.—TASTEFULLY CREATIVE SEEDS (formerly J.A. DEMONCHAUX SEEDS)
5742 Kenwood, Kansas City, MO 64110. (816) 523-2653. Imported vegetable and herb seeds, books on gardening, herbs, and food, seeds for crafts (dried flower arrangements).

HILLTOP HERB FARM
P.O. Box 1734, Cleveland, TX 77327. (713) 592-5859. Well-established herb growers/purveyors.

KAM MAN
200 Canal St., New York, NY 10013. (212) 571-0330. A supermarket crammed with Oriental products in unbelievable variety.

KATAGIRI COMPANY
224 East 59th St., New York, NY 10022. (212) 755-3566. Mostly Japanese, but also many other Oriental items.

KITCHEN BAZAAR
4455 Connecticut Ave. NW, Washington, D.C. 20008. (202) 363-4600. A dandy pot and pannery, with equipment from simple to super.

MAID OF SCANDINAVIA
3244 Raleigh Ave., Minneapolis, MN 55416. (612) 927-7996. If you can't find it elsewhere, look here; better yet, start here. Baking and confectionery supplies are a specialty, but there's also a large selection of cookware and ingredients.

MEXICAN CONNECTION
142 Lincoln Ave., Santa Fe, NM 87501, (505) 988-2940. Tex-Mex, Cal-Mex, New Mexico-Mex ingredients; you can get pure, whole or ground chilies of several kinds here.

MISSOURI DANDY PANTRY
212 Hammons Dr. East, Stockton, MO 65785. (417) 276-5121. Black walnuts, pecans, almonds, cashews, pistachios, macadamias are among the impeccably fresh nuts.

NEW ENGLAND CHEESEMAKING SUPPLY CO.
PO Box 85, Ashfield, MA 01330. (413) 628-3808. Fine cheesecloth for any purpose, plus everything else needed for making cheeses, yogurt, ice cream.

NICHOLS GARDEN NURSERY
1190 North Pacific Highway, Albany, OR 97321. (503) 928-9280. Herbs of all kinds, plus temptations for gardeners in many modes.

PAPRIKAS WEISS
1546 Second Ave., New York, NY 10028. (212) 288-6117. European items, especially; also good for spices, flours, hard-to-find utensils.

THE SAUSAGE MAKER
177 Military Road, Buffalo, NY 14207. (716) 876-5521. Everything needed for brining, curing, seasoning, or smoking meats, poultry, and fish, at home or professionally.

SELECT ORIGINS, INC.
Box N, Southampton, NY 11968. (516) 288-1382. Herb specialist.

SUNNYLAND FARMS
P.O. Box 549, Albany, GA 31703. (912) 883-3085. Super nuts, from garden-variety to rare; dried fruits, too.

VERMONT COUNTRY STORE
P.O. Box 3000, Rt. 7, Manchester Center, VT. 05255-3000. (802) 362-2400. Flours and grains, but also maple specialties, Seville orange marmalade base, and a wonderful collection of old-tiny personal and household items whose time has come around again.

WALNUT ACRES
Penns Creek, PA 17862. (717) 837-0601. Not for purists only, this specialist in high-quality, organically grown foods.

WILLIAMS-SONOMA
P.O. Box 7456, San Francisco, CA 94120-7456. (415) 652-1515. The mail-order address to which all cooks want to go when they die. Fine source for culinary and table-top items, some unusual edible specialties.

THE WOODEN SPOON, INC.
Route 6, Mahopac, NY 10541. (914) 628-3747. "Cooking tools and gourmet gadgets" is their catalogue motto.

ZABAR'S
2245 Broadway, New York, NY 10024. (212) 787-2000. One of the big city's wonders, with an eye-boggling array of ingredients and prepared foods (including lox). There's also a huge cookware shop known for its good prices.

SEASON-BY-SEASON RECIPE GUIDE

Recipes not listed here are suitable for year-round use.

SPRING INTO EARLY SUMMER

Apricot Preserves, 114
Chervil Vinegar, 197
Gingery Rhubarb Chutney, 58
Herbed Green Noodles, 299
Herbs, frozen, dried, & preserved: *See*
    Herbs: Stretching the Summer, 204
Mango & Tamarind Chutney, 56
Marinated Salmon or Herring, 28
Rhubarb Nectar, 273
Salt-Cured Salmon, 29
Smoked Fish Paste, 26
Smoked Mackerel, Bluefish, Bonito,
    Tuna, or Swordfish, 24
Spinach Noodles, 299
Strawberry & Honey Dessert Sauce, 249
Strawberry Preserves, 112
Strawberry Vinegar, 192
Tarragon Jelly: *See* Fresh Herb Jellies, 78

SUMMER

Basil Jelly: *See* Fresh Herb Jellies, 78
Bing Cherries in a Sweet Nine-Day
    Pickle, 89
Black Cherry Preserves, 117
Blackberry Vinegar, 195
Blueberry & Orange Preserves, 118
Blueberry Cordial, 274
Blueberry or Huckleberry Raisins, 311
Blueberry Relish, 76
Blueberry Syrup, 275
Blueberry Vinegar, 194
Cherry Vinegar, 193
Chervil Vinegar, 197
Chive Mustard, 181
Coarse-Ground Mustard with Honey &
    Tarragon, 183
Cold-Pickled Cornichons, 96
Compote of Peaches and/or Nectarines in
    Raspberry Syrup, 219
Compote of Plums & Blueberries in
    Brandied Syrup, 218
Cordial of Sweet Cherries, 272

Crystallized Ginger, 265
Dessert Blueberries in Armagnac Syrup,
    222
Dried Sweet or Sour Cherries, 309
Dried Tomatoes Italian-Style, 41
Escoffier's Condiment of Sweet Peppers,
    70
European-Style Red Raspberry Syrup,
    278
Extra-Crisp Bread & Butter Pickle
    Slices, 99
Four-Fruit Chutney, 59
Four-Fruit Vinegar, 190
Fresh Herb Jellies (Basil, Tarragon, or
    Mint), 78
Ginger Marmalade, 145
Ginger Preserved in Syrup, 267
Grapeleaf Dills, 97
Green-Fire Pepper Sauce, 177
Herbed Green Noodles, 299
Herbs, frozen, dried, & preserved: *See*
    Herbs: Stretching the Summer, 204
Hot & Sweet Red Pepper Jam, 71
Huckleberry Spread, 119
Jubilee Cherries, 223
Mango & Tamarind Chutney, 56
Marinated Salmon or Herring, 28
Melba Sauce, 244
Melon Marmalade, 140
Melon Moons, 86
Mint Jelly: *See* Fresh Herb Jellies, 78
Nectarine or Plum Cheese, 262
Olive Oil Flavored with Fresh Herbs, 201
Peach & Raspberry Dessert Sauce, 247
Peach or Nectarine Jam with Brown
    Sugar & Rum, 121
Peach Ratafia, 277
Peerless Red Raspberry Preserves, 124
Pickled Hot, Hot Green Peppers, 103
Purple Basil & Orange Jelly, 80
Red-Pepper Pasta, Mild or Hot, 300
Red Raspberry Vinegar, 196
Roasted Antipasto Peppers, 33
Salt-Cured Salmon, 29
Seedless Blackberry Jam, 120
Seedless Raspberry Jam, 125

LATE SUMMER

INDEX